SPECIAL STUDIES

Aerial Interdiction

Air Power and the Land Battle in Three American Wars

Eduard Mark

**Center for
Air Force
History** 1994

Washington, D.C.

Library of Congress Cataloging-in-Publication Data

Mark, Eduard Maximilian.
    Aerial interdiction: air power and the land battle in three
American wars: a historical analysis / Eduard Mark.
       p. cm.—(Special studies)
    Includes bibliographical references (p.   ) and index.
    ISBN 0-912799-74-9 (case).—ISBN 0-912799-73-0 (paper)
    1. United States—History, Military—20th century. 2. World
War, 1939-1945—Aerial operations, American. 3. Kore-
an War, 1950-1953—Aerial operations, American. 4. Vietnam-
ese War, 1961-1975—Aerial operations, American. 5. United
States. Air Force—History—20th century. I. Title. II. Series:
Special studies (United States. Air Force. Office of Air Force
History)
E745.M36 1992
358.4'00973—dc20   92-13489
                                                           CIP

For sale by the Superintendent of Documents, U.S. Government Printing Office,
Washington, D.C. 20402

Foreword

This analytical work by Dr. Eduard Mark of the Center for Air Force History examines the practice of air interdiction in three wars: World War II, the Korean war, and the war in Southeast Asia. It considers eleven important interdiction campaigns, all of them American or Anglo-American, for only the United States and Great Britain had the resources to conduct interdiction campaigns on a large scale in World War II. Dr. Mark proposes what he considers to be a realistic objective for interdiction: preventing men, equipment, and supplies from reaching the combat area when the enemy needs them and in the quantity he requires. As Mark notes, there has been little intensive scholarship on the subject of interdiction especially when contrasted with the work done on strategic bombardment.

In the wake of the Persian Gulf war, the reader will no doubt be impressed by the comparatively low performance of weapons in these pre–Gulf war campaigns. DESERT STORM showed that recent advances in technology had enabled interdiction to reach new levels of effectiveness, especially in night operations. Yet, as the reader soon discovers, interdiction in the pre-Gulf campaigns sometimes profoundly influenced military operations. As is often the case in military history, the effects were often serendipitous—not as planned or anticipated, but present nevertheless. By the middle of the Second World War, aircraft were already demonstrating that they could have a devastating impact upon a military force's ability to wage war. Field Marshal Erwin Rommel, for example, complained bitterly during the North African and Normandy campaigns about air power that, in his memorable words, "pinned my army to the ground" and otherwise denied his forces both supplies and the ability to freely maneuver.

The aircraft and weapons that caused the German commander such problems were, by today's standards, primitive. The accuracy of bombing was calculated in terms of circles with radii of hundreds or even thousands of feet. Bridges took dozens, sometimes hundreds, of sorties to destroy, meaning that a simultaneous taking-down of an enemy's transportation network was impossible. A single target also required strike packages of hundreds of airplanes. Target "revisiting" because of poor bombing accuracy meant that aircraft loss rates were often alarmingly high. Yet, even with all of these limitations, air attack still had the ability to hinder, limit, and eventually help defeat a robust, well-trained, and well-equipped opponent. It is important that this be recognized, just as it is important that we recognize that modern air war, as shown in the Gulf conflict, is very different and more effective, not only from that of 1941–1945, but from the more recent Vietnam era as well.

The challenges posed by aerial interdiction from the dust of the Western Desert to the triple canopy of Southeast Asia gave but a hint of how devastating an attacker the airplane would prove in the Gulf War of 1991. There, advanced strike aircraft—some of them stealthy as well—dropped precision munitions with shattering effect against the Iraqi military machine. As shocking as it might seem, revolutionary advances in precision navigation and weapons technology had largely reduced the previous experiences of interdiction to historical anecdote, not historical prediction. Today, in the era of Global Reach—Global Power, the lessons of aerial interdiction through Vietnam are instructive, for no other reason than this: they reveal how far modern airpower has come.

Looking back after the Gulf war, it is important to understand what air attack—and particularly air interdiction—did or did not accomplish during what might be termed "the formative era" of modern air power—the period from World War I through the decade of the Vietnam war. Within that period are the doctrinal roots and historical experience that formed the underpinnings for the utilization of air power in the Persian Gulf war, and for its future employment as well. This book, by tracing air interdiction from the Western Front through Vietnam, and by examining both its failures and successes, fills an important gap in the history of air power and enables us to appreciate to an even greater degree the profound significance that air power possesses now and for the future.

RICHARD P. HALLION
Air Force Historian

Preface

Interdiction, which the Air Force Manual 1–1, *Basic Aerospace Doctrine of the U.S. Air Force*, defines as actions "to delay, divert, or destroy an enemy's military potential before it can be brought to bear effectively against friendly forces," is one of the oldest forms of aerial warfare. All the major belligerents in World War I resorted to attacks upon their adversaries' lines of communication almost immediately after the outbreak of hostilities in August 1914. During World War II interdiction contributed importantly to Anglo-American victories in North Africa, Italy, and France. It was markedly less successful in Korea and Southeast Asia, but remains an important mission of the U.S. Air Force.

The present work examines eleven representative interdiction campaigns waged by the U.S. Air Force and its predecessor, the U.S. Army Air Forces, during the Second World War, the Korean conflict, and the war in Southeast Asia. One aim has been to provide an accurate, accessible, and reasonably complete account of these campaigns. Another has been to analyze them with a view to determining what tactics and conditions have fostered successful interdiction.

I wish to express my gratitude to the members of the final panel that reviewed this manuscript in 1989: Dr. B. Franklin Cooling, Office of Air Force History; Dr. Richard G. Davis, Office of Air Force History; Professor I.B. Holley, Jr., Duke University; Dr. Richard H. Kohn, Chief of the Office of Air Force History; General William W. Momyer, U.S. Air Force (retired); Colonel John A. Warden III, U.S. Air Force; Colonel John Schlight, U.S. Air Force (retired); Colonel John F. Shiner, Deputy Chief of the Office of Air Force History; Dr. Wayne Thompson, Office of Air Force History; and Mr. Herman S. Wolk, Office of Air Force History. I am also indebted to Dr. Richard P. Hallion, then of the U.S. Air Force Systems Command, now U.S. Air Force Historian, for his comments. I am no less obliged to mention the help given by the staff of the Military Reference Branch of the National Archives. Particularly deserving of mention is Mr. George Wagner, now retired, whose unrivaled knowledge of the German military records was of the greatest assistance. Recognition is also due Mr. Charles von Lüttichau, formerly of the U.S. Army's Center for Military History, for patiently answering my many questions about German logistics.

I should be particularly derelict if I failed to acknowledge the assistance of my colleagues in the Center for Air Force History who have patiently answered many questions and generously shared the results of their research with me. All errors of fact and interpretation are of course my own. I owe a special debt of thanks to my editor, Barbara Wittig, for her tireless efforts. I also acknowledge the unique contributions of Susan Linders and Kathy Jones, graphic artists of the 1100th Resource Management Group, Air Force District of Washington. The visualizations that they provided for this book add immeasureably to its substance and appearance.

EDUARD MARK

Contents

Section I: World War II

Section II: The Korean War

Section III: The War in Southeast Asia

Maps

Photographs

Tables

Charts

Introduction

The present work is one in a series of volumes of case studies produced by the Center for Air Force History to explore various dimensions of aerial warfare. Its subject is interdiction—the practice of attacking the unengaged potential of enemy armies—as the U.S. Air Force has employed it in three wars: World War II, the Korean conflict, and the war in Southeast Asia. The purpose of interdiction is to prevent men, equipment, and supplies from reaching a place of combat when the enemy needs them and in the quantities he requires. When an interdictor's attacks upon lines of communication render a hostile army weaker than it would otherwise have been, interdiction has to that degree been successful. When the enemy's offensive or defensive powers remain unimpaired, interdiction has failed. The measure of success for an interdiction campaign, in short, must be its effect on the ground battle. This is the criterion that informs the chapters of this study.

Interdiction campaigns have succeeded through some combination of three methods. The first of these is attrition—the destruction of men and matériel. The second is blockage—the damming up, as it were, of the enemy's lines of communications. The third method is to induce systemic inefficiencies in the enemy's logistical system by forcing him to rely upon circuitous routes or means of transport slower or less capacious than would otherwise have been available to him.

Interdiction was an important mission of the American air arm in each of the three conflicts discussed in this book. Both its success and its failures were at times of considerable importance. Yet the historical literature on the subject is by no means rich. Scholars have often dealt with interdiction as an incidental part of battles or campaigns, but have rarely subjected it to close scrutiny. The relative neglect of interdiction contrasts markedly with the attention that historians have paid to strategic bombardment and other aspects of aerial warfare. One consequence of this state of affairs is that a good deal of misinformation appears in both historical works and in the considerable body of quasi-scholarly research that the U.S. government has sponsored to consider the value of interdiction.

Whatever the reason for the relative neglect of interdiction per se as a subject of scholarly investigation, military planners have had cause to regret it. War-gaming has achieved much sophistication in our time, but the record of past wars remains the strategist's best laboratory. The past may not teach "lessons," but a knowledge of it can suggest useful ways of looking at present problems. One purpose of the present study, accordingly, has been to provide an accurate and reasonably complete account of eleven important and representative interdiction campaigns. All the examples are American or Anglo-American. Apart from the natural interest of the U.S. Air Force in its own experience, there are several reasons for this emphasis. Only the United States and Great Britain had the resources to wage interdiction intensively and on a large scale in World War II. And except for Israel no nation has since had the opportunity to practice it as often as the United States. That the United States and its British ally have been the greatest practitioners of interdiction was fortunate for this inquiry. The relevant British and American records for World War II are available in their entireties. Also accessible, by virtue of Germany's defeat, are the records of the *Wehrmacht*. It was therefore possible to base seven of the chapters of this book on the records of both the interdictors and the interdicted. This would not have been possible for the Eastern Front in World War II, or for any of Israel's wars. The last four chapters, which deal with Korea and the war in Southeast Asia, were written without access to Chinese and Vietnamese records. They are therefore somewhat more conjectural than the first seven.

While an accurate recounting of the past was the book's first priority, it was not its only objective. The work also seeks to identify those conditions and practices that have tended to promote the success of interdiction campaigns—or their failure. Both the descriptions of individual campaigns and the theoretical essay that concludes the work invoke a fundamental distinction between tactical and strategic interdiction. There are several reasons why the present study uses these terms in preference to those now current—"battlefield interdiction" and "deep interdiction." The first consideration is simply historical. Through World War II and into the Korean conflict, American airmen classified aerial operations as either "tactical" or "strategic," and even assigned them to "tactical" and "strategic" air forces. The primary distinction between battlefield interdiction and deep interdiction is distance from the battleline. The essential difference drawn between "strategic" and "tactical" interdiction, on the other hand, was not spatial; it was rather relative immediacy of effect. One bombardment manual of the 1920s, for example, defined tactical missions as "those whose successful execution is intended to have an immediate effect on the outcome of the operations of the ground forces." It offered as an example the harassing or destruction of reserves "within supporting distance of hostile combat elements." Strategic operations, on the other hand, were "missions in furtherance of the national aim, whose successful execution is intended to have a more or less removed effect on the operations of the ground forces." The manual cited the example of ammunition destroyed before it had been "moved forward to be used in a particular phase of operations."[1]

Because the concepts of tactical and strategic operations inform not only many of the documents upon which this book is based but even the organization of some of the air forces whose actions it recounts, it has been convenient to adopt them. The terms "tactical" and "strategic" interdiction, moreover, possess a clarity and conceptual strength that "battlefield" interdiction and "deep" interdiction do not. The latter expressions imply that distance from the front constitutes the primary distinction to be drawn between different forms of interdiction. What is actually of crucial importance in the planning of interdiction operations is *time*. It has, to be sure, usually been the case that interdiction closer to the front was designed to affect the battle over a shorter term than were actions deeper in the enemy's territory. But in the age of air power there is no necessary correlation between distance and relative immediacy of effects. A commander might, for example, order an attack on an airfield hundreds of miles behind the front because he had intelligence that an airborne assault was to be staged from it in a matter of hours. The hypothetical attack is clearly not on the "battlefield," yet its purpose is to counter a potential tactical emergency. To carry the illustration further: The same commander might also be engaged in systematically attacking motor transport and supply points immediately behind the front in order to affect the enemy's logistical capacity over the longer term—a strategic objective, but not one sought by strikes deep within the enemy's rear areas.[2]

Some additional notes about terminology are in order. This study identifies eight conditions that have affected the outcomes of interdiction operations. The conclusion discusses their relative importance, but it will be useful to introduce and explain them here. Three of these conditions have characterized the situation of interdictors; and five, the targets they attacked.

---

1. 1st Lt C. McK. Robinson, Air Service Tactical School, "Bombardment," 1924–1925, Air Force Historical Research Agency, Maxwell Air Force Base, Ala., 248.101.9. (Hereafter documents from the Historical Research Agency are identified only by number.)

2. For a comparatively recent defense of the concepts of tactical and strategic interdiction, see Edmund Dews, *A Note on Tactical vs. Strategic Air Interdiction* (The Rand Corp., RM–6239–PR, Santa Monica, 1970).

Conditions Characteristic of Successful Interdiction Campaigns

Successful interdictors have had sufficient *intelligence* about their enemies' lines of communication and tactical dispositions to identify targets the destruction of which would promote interdiction. Good intelligence has also enabled interdictors to select the appropriate weapons for engaging targets and to keep abreast of their enemies' efforts to foil interdiction. Interdiction campaigns have tended to be dynamic affairs in which the attackers have had to change their methods constantly to cope with repairs and efforts at evasion.

Without exception, successful interdiction campaigns, whether tactical or strategic, have been characterized by *air superiority*, here conceived as a largely unimpeded access to the enemy's airspace. There is no example of successful interdiction in which the interdictor had to fight for air superiority in the course of his interdiction campaign, as the U.S. Air Force attempted to do during the Rail Interdiction Plan in Korea and LINEBACKER I in Vietnam. It is important to note that antiaircraft weaponry has occasionally been almost as effective as fighters in denying air space to would-be interdictors. Even the rudimentary antiaircraft weapons with which the Germans defended the Strait of Messina in 1943 sufficed to protect the evacuation from Sicily. Chinese antiaircraft weapons contributed to the defeat of the Korean STRANGLE in 1951, and the North Vietnamese were on the verge of driving the fixed-wing gunships from Laos when COMMANDO HUNT VII ended prematurely because of the Easter Offensive of 1972.

Successful interdiction campaigns have also been generally characterized by *sustained pressure* on enemy communications throughout the period of operations. The targets of interdiction are either replaceable (vehicles) or repairable (engineering features). It is therefore imperative that the pressure on the enemy be sufficiently great to prevent him from replacing or repairing what has been destroyed. This requirement applies particularly to strategic campaigns because their longer duration allows the enemy greater opportunity to make good his losses. During the Italian STRANGLE, for example, the Allies destroyed bridges and other engineering features faster than they could be repaired, thereby forcing the Germans' railheads back far enough to place an insupportable burden on their motor transport. Conversely, the Rail Interdiction Plan in Korea failed because the Chinese Air Force and antiaircraft defenses held the destruction of North Korea's railroads to a rate with which the repair crews could keep pace.

Characteristics of Interdiction Targets Successfully Attacked

The targets of interdiction campaigns must be sufficiently detectable to make their destruction feasible. The attribute of *identifiability* may be regarded as a function of (1) the inherent nature of the target, (2) the conditions under which the target is engaged, and (3) the technology of the attacker. The importance of identifiability is underscored by the problems that a lack of identifiability has posed to the U.S. Air Force in the past. Easily the most serious of these has been darkness. Before the advent of the fixed-wing gunship with its formidable array of sensors, it was impossible to attack motor vehicles traveling at night with any reasonable expectation of success. During World War II and again in Korea the effectiveness of interdiction campaigns was repeatedly limited by the inability of the Air Force to operate effectively at night. Conversely, the success of other interdiction campaigns owed much to highly visible targets—ships during the North African campaign, railroads in France and Italy.

The fewer the conveyances, routes, and depots of a transportation system, that is, the greater the degree of *concentration*, the more subject is the system to interdiction because of the enemy's larger investment in each potential target. A chief reason for the vulnerability of the Axis' supply lines to Africa was its dependence on convoys, in which large quantities of supplies were apportioned among a small number of ships. Conversely, the failures of interdiction in Korea and Vietnam were partially attributable to the dispersal of the enemy's supplies among thousands of trucks.

The concept of *channelization* subsumes that of "choke point." The fewer the routes to handle the enemy's supplies and reinforcements, the greater the loss or delay caused by the severance of any one of them. Railroads have been comparatively easy to interdict precisely because they are highly channelized. The Allies exploited this characteristic repeatedly during the Second World War. The vulnerability of railroads, upon which the Germans depended heavily, was a fundamental reason for the successes of interdiction in France and Italy. Truck-based logistical systems, on the other hand, have been difficult to interdict because road systems tend to be elaborately redundant and resistant to damage. The failures of interdiction in Korea and Laos testify to this.

When the enemy has a *high rate of consumption*, whether due to heavy combat or extensive movement, interdiction operations are more likely to affect his capacity to fight. This is so for two general reasons: First, when the enemy is subject to constant need, he will be less able to build up stockpiles and therefore more likely to suffer critical shortages if his lines of communications should be either severed or constricted.

The second reason why high consumption aids interdiction is that the enemy will be less able to afford the luxury of using indirect routes or less efficient methods of supply, the advantage of which is a relative invulnerability to aerial attack; for example, the substitution of trucks for railroads. The importance of a high rate of consumption to the success of interdiction is shown by the markedly more successful results achieved by American interdiction operations in World War II than in Korea and Vietnam. In Europe the United States fought the army of a modern industrialized state which needed a large quantity of supplies to sustain its fronts. In Korea and Vietnam the United States fought the armies of poor, unindustrialized countries; their low rate of consumption contributed in a major way to the failures of interdiction. The unconventional nature of the war in Southeast Asia, moreover, often allowed the enemy to decline battle before he had prepared himself.

The more subject an enemy's logistical system to demands depriving it of surplus capacity, or the less its inherent capacity relative to the demands placed upon it, the harder it will be to compensate for damage inflicted upon it. It is important to note that *logistical constriction* differs from a high rate of consumption, although the two conditions are often discussed as one. For while a high rate of consumption is perhaps the most common cause of logistical constriction, inadequate logistical arrangements may create it even when fronts are stable and quiescent. In such cases interdiction may be possible even when the enemy's rate of consumption is relatively low. This was the case, for example, during the Italian STRANGLE.

A final note about terminology: This study only infrequently observes the distinction commonly made between "logistical" and "counter-mobility interdiction." This distinction is real enough, but often hard to make. It is, moreover, rarely useful. Most interdiction campaigns have been both "logistical" and "counter-mobility." A successful logistical campaign, moreover, is likely to affect tactical mobility through the destruction of roads and engineering features (bridges, tunnels, and viaducts, to name the most common kinds) and is almost certain to do so through a reduction of the enemy's supply of fuel, spare parts, and vehicles. Similarly, counter-mobility interdiction sufficiently effective to impair an enemy's mobility will probably also interfere with his supply.

Section I

World War II

Origins of Aerial Interdiction

Soon after the Wright brothers demonstrated the feasibility of powered flight in 1903, soldiers began to consider the military potential of the airplane. Reconnaissance was the first military use envisioned for the new invention, but the idea of bombardment closely followed. An enterprising Italian officer inaugurated the new mode of warfare by dropping several small bombs on a Turkish camp in North Africa on November 1, 1911, during his country's brief war with Turkey for possession of Libya. Two years later the Spanish bombarded tribesmen in Morocco. The year 1913 also saw construction of the first aircraft designed specifically as bombers—the Italian Caproni Ca 30 and the British Bristol TB-8.[1] When war came to Europe in August 1914, most of the combatants' war planes were still unarmed reconnaissance aircraft. Bombing began haphazardly; pilots dropped hand grenades, artillery shells, and even darts. But within months Britain, France, and Germany had all fitted aircraft with sights and bomb racks.

Technology had transformed the battlefield in the century between the end of the Napoleonic Wars and the beginning of World War I. The industrial revolution had made it possible to equip and supply armies of unprecedented size. In the field, these swollen forces depended utterly upon railroads, for only by rail could the masses of supplies they required be moved. The dependence of armies upon a fragile and inconcealable web of rails soon attracted the attention of airmen. As early as 1911 the Italian theorist Giulio Douhet foresaw the use of aircraft to attack railroads.[2] In 1914 the fledgling air forces of the warring states moved quickly to turn theory into practice.

The powers of the Entente took the lead. The French attacked a railroad used by the Germans on August 14, 1914, when the war was but a few days old. On September 30 aircraft of the Royal Navy Flying Corps, a small but adventuresome service, attacked a rail junction at Cambrai in

---

1. Robin Cross, *The Bombers: The Illustrated Story of Offensive Strategy and Tactics in the Twentieth Century* (New York, 1987), 7–8.
2. *Ibid.*, 7.

order to disrupt German troop movements. The French, who began the
war with the largest and best-prepared air force of any belligerent,
quickly developed an ambitious bombing campaign. A directive of the
French General Headquarters, issued on October 8, 1914, called for far-
ranging attacks on German communications. In December 1914 the
French extended their campaign to Germany itself when they bombed a
railroad station in Freiburg. For much of 1915 they attempted to disrupt
German war industries by bombing factories. This first attempt at strategic bombing ended after heavy losses in the summer of 1915. Lines of
communication and supply depots close behind the German front were
thereafter the chief targets of French bombs.[3] The British, too, became
ambitious practitioners of interdiction. Whether they were more active
than the French is a question not easily answered, for France never produced a counterpart to the lengthy and detailed British official history,
The War in the Air by Walter Raleigh and H.A. Jones. But together the
British and the French certainly practiced interdiction more than the Germans. Fighting at steep odds throughout the war, the Germans were generally on the defensive in the air battles over the front. The account of
the air war by the commander of the German air forces, General Ernst
von Höppner, mentions interdiction scarcely at all.[4]

Whether or not the British devoted more effort to interdiction than
the French, they were certainly more daring. The appearance of pursuit
aircraft in 1915 led to prodigious losses among the bombers of all the
combatants. The French responded by abandoning strategic bombardment altogether and attacking German communications only at night.[5]
But the British, as an interwar American study noted, "continued their
daylight operations and suffered uncomplainingly the losses incurred."[6]
The plans for the British spring offensives of 1915 called for the Royal
Flying Corps to hinder the movement of German reinforcements through
systematic attacks on rail lines and rail centers. During the British attacks
on Neuve Chapelle (March 1915), British aircraft attacked the railway
station at Courtrai on March 10. They returned to the same target on
April 26 during the Battle of Ypres.[7] These early attacks were quite hap-

---

3. *Ibid*, 12, 15; Charles Christienne and Pierre Lissarrgue, *A History of French Military Aviation*, translated by Francis Kianka (Washington, 1986), 57, 80–90, 102–3, 110, 116.

4. Ernst Wilhelm von Höppner, *Germany's War in the Air*, translated by J. Hawley Larned (Leipzig, 1921; typescript in the Army War College Library), 42, 46.

5. Air Corps Tactical School (ACTS), "Genesis of Bombardment Aviation: Preface to Bombardment Text," Jan 1, 1938, 248.101.9; Cross, *Bombers*, 34; Christienne and Lissarrgue, *French Military Aviation*, 89–90.

6. ACTS, "Genesis of Bombardment Aviation."

7. Cross, *Bombers*, 16.

hazard. Some were the work of a single aircraft, and the reconnaissance machines drafted for bombing were still poorly suited for the mission.

The British soon developed a more systematic approach to interdiction, and the resulting operations soon bore a considerable conceptual resemblance to those of later wars. Maj. Gen. Hugh Trenchard, commander of the Royal Flying Corps in France, who became a preeminent theorist of strategic bombardment during the interwar period, played a pivotal role in this process. In the summer of 1915 Trenchard prevailed upon the British General Headquarters to order that there should no longer be "spasmodic efforts against unsuitable or unimportant targets" to influence purely local situations. There should rather be "sustained attacks with a view to interrupting the enemy's railway communications . . . in conjunction with the main operations of the Allied Armies."[8] Two wings specially trained for this purpose went into action during the Battle of Loos with newly developed and reasonably effective bombsights. Between September 23 and October 13 British aircraft dropped nearly five and a half tons of bombs on German railroads. These attacks cut railroad lines in sixteen places and destroyed or damaged at least five trains. German records examined after the war revealed that traffic had been halted for several days, although this did not prevent the Germans from moving needed reserves into the Loos sector.[9]

Railroads remained the principal target of Allied interdiction, but marching troops and motor transport also came under attack. During the Battle of the Somme (July 1916), British fighters, having won a temporary air superiority, strafed German trenches and columns while bombers struck at rail centers. Reconnaissance aircraft kept roads and rails under surveillance to detect major troop movements and to keep intelligence officers abreast of efforts at repair. German airmen, led by the great ace Oswald Boelcke, soon forced the Royal Flying Corps to curtail its operations. The British responded by targeting German airfields. Despite their lack of success during the Somme offensive, attempts at interdiction, usually accompanied by strikes on German airfields, were a feature of British plans for the rest of the war.[10] During the final German offensive—the so-called Ludendorff Offensive of March 1918—fighters and bombers attacked German trains. During the Allied counteroffensive near Amiens the following summer the British tried to cut off the Ger-

---

8. Air Marshal Sir Robert Saundby, *Air Bombardment: The Story of Its Development* (New York, 1961), 12.

9. Cross, *Bombers*, 17–18.

10. *Ibid.*, 32; Walter Raleigh and H.A. Jones, *The War in the Air*, 6 vols (Oxford, 1922–37), 2:206–35, 327–34, 4:124, 144–45, 165–66, 180–81, 187–88.

man retreat by bombing all the bridges across the Somme. They failed, but did inflict insupportable losses on the German fighters that rose to defend the bridges.[11]

The Germans, impressed by the effects of British strafing during the Battle of the Somme, introduced specially designed ground attack aircraft in 1917. They were at first employed against Allied positions on the front; only in 1918, it appears, did the Germans undertake interdiction operations on anything like the Allied scale. During the Ludendorff Offensive German aircraft strafed and bombed Allied convoys and columns. The following summer they attacked many bridges in an attempt to slow the Allied advance.[12]

The last year of the war also saw the first American attempt at interdiction. Influenced by long talks with Trenchard, Brig. Gen. Billy Mitchell, who directed the combat operations of the Air Service of the American Expeditionary Forces, planned for interdiction to accompany the American offensive against the Saint-Mihiel Salient in September 1918. Commanding a mixed force of 1,500 French and American aircraft, Mitchell won local air superiority for several days. He divided his force into two brigades which struck alternately at the flanks of the German salient and at its communications with the rear. According to some accounts, the incessant strafing of roads leading from the salient contributed to the taking of many prisoners when the Germans retreated.[13]

Postwar investigation revealed that on the whole, interdiction had only rarely had an effect on the fighting. In no case had the effect been decisive. One reason for this was the ease with which railroads could be repaired. Even seemingly spectacular successes had often yielded only marginal results. On July 16, 1918, for example, British aircraft exploded a German ammunition train at Thionville. So great was the blast that ten locomotives parked nearby were destroyed. But efficient German *Eisenbahntruppen* (railroad troops) restored the line to full operation within two days. Bridges had proved to be particularly difficult targets. Near the end of the war, the Chief of the Air Staff, Maj. Gen. F.H. Sykes, wrote that "experience has shown that a bridge offers so small a target

---

11. Raleigh and Jones, *War in the Air*, 6:440–42, 454–62; Cross, *Bombers*, 56–57.

12. Von Höppner, *Germany's War in the Air*, 57; Air Historical Branch of the British Air Ministry (AHB/BAM), "Development of the German Ground Attack Arm and Principles Governing Its Operations Up to the End of 1944," Dec 1, 1944 [prepared by the Air Historical Branch of the *Luftwaffe*], Translation VII/14, 1947, 512.621, 1–2.

13. Robert T. Finney, "The Development of Tactical Air Doctrine in the U.S. Air Service, 1917–1951 (1952)," K110.7017–1, 7–11; Alfred F. Hurley, *Billy Mitchell: Crusader for Air Power* (New York, 1964), 35–36.

that even from low altitude it is exceedingly difficult to hit; even direct hits will not as a rule cause any prolonged interruption of traffic." Attacks at the requisite low altitude, moreover, "must inevitably be costly as all important bridges are very strongly defended against aircraft attack."[14]

As one British airman who flew in the Great War later wrote, "the war ended without providing any convincing proof of the offensive power of aircraft."[15] Interdiction nonetheless continued to be recognized as a fundamental mission of air power. Theorists of air power generally agreed that the primary task was to gain air superiority through the destruction of the opposing air force. They further concurred that when air superiority had been won, the victorious air force should turn its attention to helping the ground forces by direct attacks on enemy formations and the disruption of the lines of communication.[16] The manuals of the U.S. Army Air Corps Tactical School, for example, devoted considerable space to ways in which air power could "harass or interdict, delay or disperse" hostile formations.[17]

While there was general agreement that air power should aid armies, opinion diverged considerably about how air forces should be controlled. The basic question was how much independence airmen should have from the ground forces. In Germany the answer was—very little. When the German air force was resurrected during the 1930s most of its staff officers were drawn directly from the army. These officers showed little inclination to challenge the priorities of the senior service. The subordination of the Soviet Air Force was even more complete: It was constructed primarily for close air support. Soviet aerial squadrons were assigned to support particular divisions. The French Air Force gained its independence in 1933, but the strict construction the French put upon unity of command and the traditional predominance of the army left little room for flexibility in tactical operations and excluded altogether the possibility of independent air strategy.[18]

American airmen were part of the Army and were therefore organizationally as well as doctrinally subordinate to the ground forces. The

14. Cross, *Bombers*, 65.
15. Saundby, *Air Bombardment*, 21.
16. R.J. Overy, *The Air War 1939–1945* (New York, 1981), 10–11.
17. Quote by 1st Lt C. McK. Robinson, Air Service Tactical School, "Bombardment," 1924–1925, 248.101.9, 3; ACTS, *Bombardment Aviation* (February 1931), 40–42, 54–55; Air Service Tactical School, *Attack* (1924–25), 168.69–3, 1–5, 36–43; ACTS, *Attack Aviation* (1935–36), 1–5. As bombers grew in size and capacity and became more suitable for long-distance strategic operations against the enemy's homeland, interdiction came to be viewed as a preserve of the lighter attack bombers. ACTS, *Light Bombardment Aviation* (1940), 248.101–11, 1–2.
18. Overy, *Air War*, 12–13.

War Department Training Regulation 440-15 of 1926 left little doubt of the airmen's status, stipulating baldly that the mission of the air service was "to aid the ground forces to gain decisive success."[19] The airmen chafed at what they saw as their bondage, for with many European colleagues they believed that an independent air arm could most efficiently exploit the flexibility of air power—its ability to strike disparate targets or quickly to concentrate on a few, as the strategic situation might require. The Americans, moreover, had developed a theory that strategic bombardment of the enemy's homeland would contribute more to victory than the prosaic tactical missions favored by ground commanders forever worrying about the taking of a certain hill or the defense of a town.[20] Doctrinal revisions of the 1930s and early 1940s attached ever greater weight to strategic bombardment. In theory, at least, the airmen had greater leeway, for their heavy bombers would ordinarily range beyond the ground forces' sphere of influence. But tactical aviation remained at the beck and call of the land forces—even after the War Department stipulated in its Field Manual 31-35 of 1942 that all air forces in a theater be controlled by an airman.

Only in Britain had the airmen's vision of independence been realized. The Royal Air Force (RAF) became a service coordinate with the Army and Navy in 1918. Not surprisingly, it construed its responsibility to support the army differently from the dependent air services of other nations. British airmen argued that the successful exploitation of air power was incompatible with the parceling of air power to army units— the scheme explicitly embraced by the Soviets and at least implicit in the arrangement of all the other major powers. They stressed that the target of priority should be the enemy's air force, which was to be attacked systematically and comprehensively—in the air, on its airdromes, and in the factories of its homeland. Only when hostile air power had been destroyed would the RAF devote itself extensively to close air support.[21]

In the early opening stages of World War II, most of the major combatants tried interdiction to one degree or another. During the German invasion of Poland, the *Luftwaffe* systematically interfered with the efforts of the Polish Army to concentrate against the invaders by attacking roads and railroads. When the Poles did concentrate, their counteroffensive was thwarted by the destruction of bridges across the river Bzura. The destruction of railroads and the strafing of Polish columns disorganized the retreat of the Polish Army on the Vistula River. Attempts to

---

19. War Department, Training Regulation 440-15, *Fundamental Principles for the Employment of the Air Service*, Jan 26, 1926, sec I, paras 3, 4a.
20. Overy, *Air War*, 13.
21. *Ibid.*, 13-14.

cut off the Polish retreat by destroying the bridges across the Vistula failed—only one bridge fell. But the constant attacks on the crossings further slowed and disorganized the Polish retreat, factoring in the Germans' later envelopment and destruction of the larger part of the Polish Army.[22] The Germans used similar tactics during their invasion of France in 1940. While some German bombers hammered points of resistance or broke up Allied offensives, others nearly paralyzed the French rail system. Bombing and strafing greatly hindered the road movement of the Allied forces.[23]

The British attempted to respond in kind. The Advanced Air Striking Force (AASF)—ten squadrons of Blenheim medium bombers and Fairey Battle light bombers with two squadrons of fighters for escort—attempted to stop the advancing German columns by attacking natural bottlenecks such as bridges and road junctions. Two squadrons of Whitley heavy bombers based in England were to aid the AASF by bombing road and rail communications immediately east of the Rhine. The effort was foredoomed. Fighters were too few to escort the bombers, and the Battles, slow and underarmed, suffered extraordinary losses: one aircraft for every two sorties. Time and again, entire formations were lost trying to stem the German advance. The Blenheims, for the same reason, fared little better. At great cost, the RAF slowed the Germans in places, but the sacrifices were in vain, for the reeling Allied infantry could not take advantage of the respites.[24]

Interdiction figured in German air operations in Russia. After surprise attacks on airfields had destroyed much of the Soviet Air Force, bombers not needed for close air support directed their attacks against roads and rail lines in the rear of the Red Army. The principal purpose of these missions was to hinder the retreat of Soviet armies as the Germans sought to envelop them. The *Luftwaffe* developed special units to destroy railroad bridges after the Soviets proved they could rapidly repair stations and trackage.[25]

With the fall of France, North Africa became the principal theater of the Anglo-German war. Both sides depended on sea transport for sup-

---

22. Paul Deichmann, *German Air Force Operations in Support of the Army*, edited by Littleton B. Atkinson, Noel F. Parrish, and Albert F. Simpson (USAF Hist Monograph 163, Maxwell AFB, Ala, 1962), 154; Cross, *Bombers*, 96; AHB/BAM, "The *Luftwaffe* in Poland—September 1939," Jul 11, 1944 [prepared by the Air Historical Branch of the *Luftwaffe*], Translation VII/33, 1947, 512.621.
23. Alistair Horne, *To Lose a Battle: France*, 1940 (Boston, 1969), 210, 239, 371, 472.
24. Denis Richards and Hilary St. George Saunders, *Royal Air Force: 1939-1945*, 3 vols (London, 1953-54), vol 1: *The Fight at Odds*, 109-21.
25. AHB/BAM, "Air Operations on the Russian Front in 1941," Mar 25, 44 [lecture by *Hauptmann* Baltrusch], Translation VII/34, 1947, 512.621, 6-7.

plies. British aircraft based on Malta attacked Italian and German convoys in concert with the Royal Navy, while German and Italian aircraft based in Sicily tried to prevent the resupply of Malta and succeeded in forcing the British to direct most of their convoys for Egypt all the way around southern Africa. In North Africa the British hammered out much of the doctrine they and their American allies would use for the rest of the war. Air Marshal Sir Arthur W. Tedder, Air Officer Commanding in Chief, Middle East, and Air Marshal Sir Arthur Coningham, commander of the Desert Air Force, bore chief responsibility for the doctrinal transformations thrashed out in the deserts of North Africa.[26]

The first transformation was the development of a system of command that reconciled the RAF's traditional insistence on independence of action with the demands of the army for support. Under the system that evolved in North Africa, the commanders of the air and ground forces were coequals with equal access to the theater commander, their headquarters physically proximate but organizationally separate. From the perspective of military efficiency, the strength of this system was that the air commander, who controlled separate tactical and strategic air forces, could evaluate requests from the ground commander and integrate them into an effective air strategy designed to support the designs of the theater commander.[27] The political strengths of the new system were also notable. The independence of the air commander from the ground commander obviated the fears of airmen that their aircraft would be divided into ineffectual "penny packets" (a favorite phrase of Coningham's) subordinated to disparate elements of the ground forces. "Air warfare," Tedder afterwards wrote, "cannot be separated into little packets; it knows no boundaries on land or sea other than those imposed by the radius of action of the aircraft; it is a unity and demands unity of command."[28] But the subordination of the air commander to the theater commander, who was invariably an army man, reassured the soldiers that their interests would not be neglected by airmen bent on proving untested theories at their expense.

Coningham's other major contribution was to translate the RAF's by-then traditional air superiority doctrine into a practical and effective strategy for gaining and maintaining control of the skies. He argued that "penny packets" of aircraft, tied to the ground forces, could never win

---

26. It has, however, been too little noted that Coningham and Tedder built on the work of other officers, particularly Army Brig John Woodall. Shelford Bidwell and Dominick Graham, *Firepower: British Army Weapons and Theories of War, 1904–1945* (London, 1982), 264–65.
27. Overy, *Air War* 86–88.
28. Sir Arthur Tedder, *Air Power in War* (London, 1948), 91.

air superiority, which he saw as an absolute sine qua non for success in the land battle. This was quite conventional, as was his view that the battle for air superiority had to be waged comprehensively. Coningham's contribution was to show the value of continuous action and to demonstrate more effectively than any commander had done in the past the flexibility of air power—its ability to concentrate and shift quickly from one target to another. He gathered his fighters in large formations, in order to gain numerical superiority wherever the *Luftwaffe* could be brought to battle. He employed these arrays in continuous sweeps to wear the enemy down. Air-to-air combat was but one dimension of the battle. The fighters regularly strafed the *Luftwaffe*'s airfields and the motor transport upon which it depended for its supply of fuel, spare parts, and ammunition. Light and medium bombers attacked airdromes and supply depots around the clock, while heavier bombers attacked ports and logistical centers deeper within the enemy's territory. As the German fighter force grew weaker, the RAF's interdiction operations became progressively more intensive, but never at the expense of attacks on the *Luftwaffe* whenever it showed signs of resurgence. When all went according to plan, as it did at the second battle of El Alamein (October 1942), the German army was not only stripped of its air cover but starved of supplies. Coningham's insistence on continuous operations contrasts with the initially successful counterair operations of the Germans in the Soviet Union. They devastated the Soviet Air Force during the first days of their invasion of the USSR through well-conceived attacks on Soviet airfields. But then the *Luftwaffe* slackened its counterair operations on the assumption air superiority had been "won."[29]

The remaining doctrinal innovation of the North African air war, a three-phase model for the employment of air forces in combined-arms offensives, was implicit in Coningham's method of winning air superiority. The phases—which marked not discrete stages but shifting operational emphases—were air superiority, interdiction, and close air support. The success of this design, first at El Alamein and soon after in Tunisia, established it as the paradigm for all succeeding Anglo-American operations.

---

29. Overy, *Air War*, 86; Tedder, *Air Power*, 38–39.

Chapter 1

---◆◆◆---

Northwest Africa
November 1942–May 1943

The battle for Tunisia was the first interdiction campaign of the Second World War in which American airmen participated. The severing of the Axis' convoy routes to Northwest Africa represented a triumphant application of the aerial doctrine developed by the British in the Egyptian desert and served as a model for later interdiction campaigns. It was a major reason for the revision of American aerial doctrine that resulted in the publication of the famous FM 100–20, *Command and Employment of Air Power*, in July 1943. The Allied triumph vividly illustrates the importance of intelligence and air superiority to successful interdiction. The catastrophe that befell the Axis is an equally graphic demonstration of the hazards of relying upon a means of conveyance as identifiable and concentrated as ships where there is danger of aerial attack.

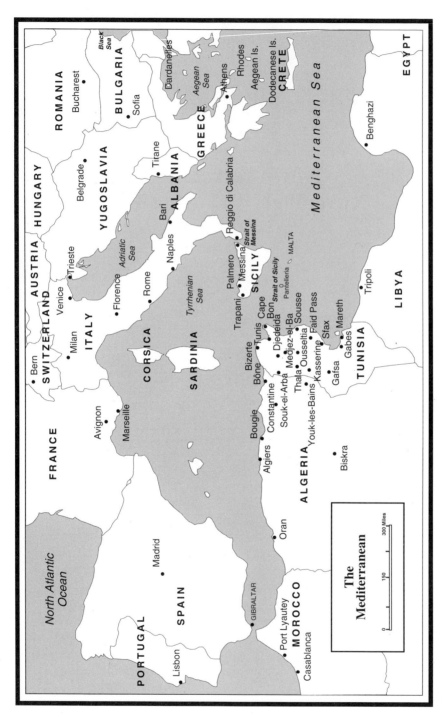

The
Mediterranean

300 Miles

Map 1.

The Second World War spread to Africa on June 10, 1940, when the Italian dictator Benito Mussolini led his ill-prepared nation into the conflict. The British rapidly conquered the Italian colonies of Somaliland, Eritrea, and Ethiopia. In early 1941 they routed an Italian army in Cyrenaica and seemed about to conquer Italy's last African stronghold, Libya. But in reality the North African campaign had just begun, for in February 1941 there came to the aid of the Italians two German divisions under the command of Lt. Gen. Erwin Rommel. Problems of supply plagued Rommel's *Afrika Korps* from the first. British ships and aircraft from Egypt and Malta ravaged the convoys that plied the Mediterranean between Italy and the Libyan ports of Tripoli and Benghazi. Rommel nonetheless prevailed for a year and a half. In mid-1942 he seemed on the verge of conquering Egypt until the British Eighth Army under General Sir Claude Auchinleck stopped him in July at the first battle of El Alamein. A renewed bid for Egypt failed the next month at Alam Halfa. Both sides then began to prepare for a decisive contest in the fall.

As the antagonists faced each other uneasily in the Egyptian desert, an Allied expeditionary force assembled in British and American ports. Its destination was the French colonies of Morocco and Algeria, far to Rommel's rear. The decision to invade Northwest Africa was the result of a long and somewhat acrimonious debate between the British and their American allies. At the ARCADIA Conference, which had convened in Washington on December 22, 1941, Prime Minister Winston S. Churchill and President Franklin D. Roosevelt had approved two strategic plans. The first, BOLERO, had called for a marshaling of forces in Great Britain for an invasion of the Continent. The second, SUPER-GYMNAST, had envisioned Anglo-American landings in Northwest Africa to destroy Rommel and block a much-feared German move into Spain.[1]

Washington had soon questioned the feasibility of SUPER-GYMNAST. The Americans argued that the shortage of shipping would so limit the size of the landing force that there was little prospect of success without the support of the French colonial authorities. And it was doubtful, they stressed, that officials of the German-dominated government of Marshal Henri Pétain would aid the Allied enterprise. Equally questionable, in the American view, was the assumption that the Spanish would, or could, forestall a German effort to cut the supply lines of the invading force by seizing Gibraltar. That would leave the Allies perilously dependent upon a single railroad line from the distant Atlantic port of Casablanca.

These considerations led the Americans to propose in April 1942 that SUPER-GYMNAST be canceled in favor of a maximum effort to invade France in order to relieve German pressure on the Soviet Union. Their plan called for a small invasion in the fall of 1942. This operation, SLEDGEHAMMER, was designed only to seize a beachhead. An invasion in overwhelming force, ROUNDUP, was to follow in April 1943. The British agreed to this plan only with serious reservations. In June, Churchill urged that a revised and enlarged SUPER-GYMNAST be substituted for SLEDGEHAMMER. He based his plea upon an undeniable fact: The construction of landing craft had lagged so badly that the Allies could land no more than six divisions in France in 1942. Even if so small a force managed to survive, Churchill argued, too few Germans would be drawn from the Eastern Front to help the beleaguered Soviets. Roosevelt, strongly supported by the American Joint Chiefs of Staff, resisted a change of plans. But in July Churchill flatly refused to invade the continent in 1942. From this refusal there could be no appeal, for most of the men for SLEDGEHAMMER would have had to be British. The Americans, anxious to get their army into action and to do something to aid the Soviets, agreed to a rehabilitated SUPER-GYMNAST in 1942, with ROUNDUP to follow in 1943.

TORCH, the invasion of French North Africa, was the Allies' first major amphibious invasion of the war. It was conceived and executed in very short order. Planning began with Roosevelt's final approval on July 25, 1942; D-day was November 8. The ultimate objective was Tunisia, the anvil upon which the Eighth Army was to break Rommel. But a prudent regard for German air power dictated that the invaders should not

---

1. For the evolution of Allied strategic plans relating to North Africa, see Maurice Matloff and Edwin M. Snell, *Strategic Planning for Coalition Warfare: 1941–1942* [U.S. Army in World War II: The War Department] (Washington, 1953).

hazard their fleet by landing in Tunisia itself. Fighters from Gibraltar and Malta, the closest Allied bases, could not reach Tunisia; German bombers from Italy, Sicily, and Sardinia could do so easily. Allied planners therefore decided to descend first upon Morocco and Algeria.[2]

On D-day, an entirely American force of 34,000 landed on the Atlantic coast of Morocco and captured Casablanca to guard against a German attack through Spain. A second American force of 31,000 came ashore in western Algeria to take the port of Oran. The easternmost landing was made near Algiers in central Algeria by an Anglo-American force of 31,000 under a British commander, Lt. Gen. K.A.N. Anderson. (*Map 1*) A few of the approximately 1,700 British and American aircraft committed to TORCH were flown onto improvised fields from Gibraltar and from an American aircraft carrier to protect the landing and to provide cover for the thrust into Tunisia.[3] Efforts to arrange a friendly reception from local French officials loyal to Pétain failed. But French resistance was generally half-hearted, and the Allies secured their objectives within a few days. On November 11, 1942, the French colonial authorities signed an armistice agreement with the Allied commander, General Dwight D. Eisenhower, and changed sides.[4]

The movement of convoys toward Africa from England and America had not escaped the attention of the Axis. Mussolini and the German Commander in Chief, South, Field Marshal Albert Kesselring, had correctly concluded that the Allies would land in French North Africa. They were unable, however, to effect strong countermeasures. Hitler had tried to conciliate the French since the armistice of 1940. He had left southern France unoccupied and had not sought to introduce German forces into France's African colonies. He was loathe to depart from this policy on the strength of Mussolini's speculations. He and *Reichsmarschall* Her-

---

2. Dwight Eisenhower, *Crusade in Europe* (Garden City, 1948), 80.
3. The round figure of 1,700 represents the reported strength of the American Twelfth Air Force (1,244 aircraft) and the British Eastern Air Command (454 aircraft). These figures are misleading, however. Because of difficulties of transporting the aircraft from Britain to North Africa, and the great problems of basing them once they arrived, the buildup of Allied air power was gradual, although the inadequate records from this period make precise estimates of Allied strength difficult. In December, for example, the Allies had only about 600 aircraft in all of Northwest Africa. David Syrett, "Northwest Africa, 1942-1943," in Benjamin Franklin Cooling, ed., *Case Studies in the Achievement of Air Superiority* (Washington, 1992); Wesley Frank Craven and James Lea Cate, eds, *The Army Air Forces in World War II*, 7 vols (Chicago, 1948–57; Washington, 1983), vol 2: *Europe: TORCH to POINTBLANK, August 1942 to December 1943*, 116.
4. Save when otherwise specified, all accounts of Tunisian combat derive from George F. Howe, *Northwest Africa: Seizing the Initiative in the West* [U.S. Army in World War II: The Mediterranean Theater of Operations] (Washington, 1957).

mann Göring, in any case, were of the opinion that the Allies would probably land in southern France. The *Oberkommando der Wehrmacht (OKW)*,[5] on the other hand, first expected the blow at Dakar in French West Africa and then in Libya. In this last error the *OKW* was seconded by its Italian counterpart, the *Commando Supremo*.[6] Although Kesselring was unable to move a German division to Sicily for possible use in North Africa, he did succeed in raising the strength of the *Luftwaffe* there and on Sardinia to about 400 fighters and bombers. The distance to Algiers was such, however, that the German bombers were unable to operate effectively against the Allied fleet.[7]

Although TORCH achieved strategic surprise, the Germans were quick to respond. On November 9, the day after the invasion, German troops began to arrive in Tunisia from Italy. By the end of the month, aerial convoys of Junkers Ju 52 transport aircraft had ferried in more than 15,000 men. Heavy equipment and an additional 2,000 men arrived by convoy at the principal Tunisian ports of Tunis and Bizerte. On November 14, General Walter Nehring arrived to take command of the rapidly forming German force, the *Fifth Panzerarmee*.[8] The transfer of 155 aircraft to Tunisia raised German strength in North Africa, Sicily, and Sardinia to nearly 700 combat aircraft by the end of December.[9]

Lt. Gen. Sir Bernard Law Montgomery, since August the commander of the Eighth Army, had driven the Germans into headlong retreat at the second battle of El Alamein in October. Rommel soon after concluded that it would be impossible for the Axis to hold North Africa. German submarines had lost the Battle of the Atlantic, he argued, and the Anglo-Americans would in time muster in Africa a force too large to be resisted. He urged that his army consolidate with Nehring's and launch an offensive to beat back the Allies long enough to permit the

---

5. The *OKW* was the high command of the German armed forces (the *Wehrmacht*). As the attention of the high command of the army (the *Oberkommando des Heeres*) was progressively absorbed by the war against the Soviet Union, the *OKW* assumed responsibility for the war in the west. This division of labor obtained for the duration of the war.

6. General Hellmuth Felmy, "The German Air Force in the Mediterranean Theater of War" (unpublished manuscript, 1955), K113.107-61, 534-50; Albert Kesselring, *Kesselring: A Soldier's Record* (New York, 1954), 161-65.

7. Kesselring, *Soldier's Record*, 163; Howe, *Northwest Africa*, 187-88; British Air Ministry (BAM), *The Rise and Fall of the German Air Force (1933-1945)* (London, 1948), 145. Italy had at this time about 515 aircraft of all types. They were so situated, however, that they played no significant role in the Tunisian campaign. This seems not to have bothered the Germans, who had no confidence in the Italian air force. BAM, *Rise and Fall of the German Air Force*, 145.

8. Howe, *Northwest Africa*, 257-58; Craven and Cate, TORCH to POINTBLANK, 2:6.

9. BAM, *Rise and Fall of the German Air Force*, 152.

evacuation of the German forces from Africa for the defense of Europe.[10] But Hitler was adamant that an invasion of southern Europe should be staved off as long as possible by a stand in North Africa—even, as he seems eventually to have concluded, at the cost of the forces sent there.[11] Kesselring, ever inclined to optimism, believed that indefinite resistance would be possible in mountainous Tunisia where the Allies would have to operate at the end of a long overland line of supply. He shared Rommel's opinion that logistics would be decisive, stating on November 24 that "in the last analysis everything depends upon supply." But he differed from the general in his conclusion that the "air and sea situations" were "not unfavorable," as the convoy routes from Italy to Tunisia were shorter and easier to protect than those to Libya.[12]

Having secured Algiers, General Anderson set out for Tunis on November 11. Nearly 400 miles of mountainous terrain separated Algiers from Tunis. An advance wholly overland would therefore have been too slow, as the campaign had become a race against the German airlift from Italy. On November 11 TORCH's reserve force landed at Bougie, 100 miles east of Algiers. The loss of three of the four transports involved in this operation to German aircraft after they had disembarked their troops confirmed the wisdom of the decision to make the initial landings farther west. Bône fell to British paratroopers on November 12. An American airborne force took Gafsa three days later, as the larger part of Anderson's task force struggled overland by road and rail. By November 16, advance parties reached the Tunisian frontier. Only small skirmishes had so far occurred between the Anglo-Americans and small German and Italian patrols.

---

10. Erwin Rommel, *The Rommel Papers*, edited by B.H. Liddell Hart and translated by Paul Findlay (New York, 1953), 360–62, 365–66, 419.

11. Even in March 1943, as he ordered an eventual tripling of the supplies sent to Tunisia, Hitler declared himself of the opinion that the consolidation of both his armies there within a narrow bridgehead meant "the beginning of the end" ("*Die Zurückführung beider Armeen in einem engen Brückenkopf um Tunis und Bizerte ist der Anfang der Ende*"). A German historical study of 1944 justified this course upon two grounds: The stand in Tunisia delayed the Allied invasion of Italy, and it prevented the Allies from using the shortest route to the Far East—through the Mediterranean and the Suez Canal. The consequent drain upon Allied shipping, the Germans seem to have calculated, would defer the opening of a second front in France. Msg, *OKW* to General Jürgen von Arnim, Mar 21, 1943, Roll 416, T–313, Record Group (RG) 1027, National Archives and Records Administration (NARA); Air Historical Branch of the British Air Ministry (AHB/BAM), "The Battle for Tunis, November 1942–May 1943," Jul 17, 1944 [prepared by the Air Historical Branch of the *Luftwaffe*], Translation VII/25, 1947, 512.621, 20.

12. *Rommel Papers*, 365–66; Howe, *Northwest Africa*, 262; Kesselring, *Soldier's Record*, 153–54, 165–66; Felmy, "German Air Force in the Mediterranean Theater," 578–79.

Anderson began his general offensive on November 24. In the face of intensifying German resistance, the Allied forces captured Djedeida on November 28. A mere twelve miles from Tunis, Djedeida marked the farthest Allied advance of the winter campaign, for Nehring recaptured it on December 1. Stymied by German resistance and rains that made roads and airfields unusable, Eisenhower halted the advance. He consolidated his forces along a line that ran from Medjez-el-Bab in the north through Ousseltia and Faid south to Gafsa.

The Allies had lost the race for Tunis. Part of the price they would pay was the presence of Rommel and his *First Italian Army* (the former *Afrika Korps*) in Tunisia. Rommel's plan for a concentration of forces in Tunisia had not been initially well received by his superiors, who insisted that he make a stand in western Libya. This decision, however, was reversed in December. The Germans had earlier decided upon a series of local offensives to enlarge their constricted Tunisian bridgehead. For this reason, Nehring was replaced on December 9 by an experienced commander of armor withdrawn from Russia, Maj. Gen. Jürgen von Arnim. But when the reserves to support the offensive strategy were diverted to meet a developing crisis on the Russian front, reinforcement of von Arnim's force by Rommel's became necessary if there was to be an active defense of Tunisia.[13] When the *First Italian Army* reached Tunisia it joined with the *Fifth Panzerarmee* to form *Heeresgruppe Afrika* which Rommel commanded.

When the Germans later reflected upon their defeat in Tunisia, it seemed to them that the Allies had come only "gradually" to realize that "supplies were the weak link of the Axis position in Tunisia."[14] This perception may seem strange, given the success with which the Royal Navy had for so long attacked convoys bound for Libya. But the progressive consolidation of the Axis' forces in Tunisia spelled a respite for the Axis' convoys by reducing the scope of Allied naval action. The Italians had heavily mined the Strait of Sicily. Convoys for Tunis, which staged from Sicily, were relatively safe from naval attack as long as they remained within the channels left within the minefields. (*Map 2*)

The manifold problems of the Allied air forces also delayed effective attacks on the convoy routes from Sicily. Not until February 1943 were they ready to begin antishipping operations on a large scale. The Desert Air Force of the British Eighth Army was for much of January and February beyond range of the Strait of Sicily. The Germans, moreover, had

---

13. Howe, *Northwest Africa*, 326, 363–64.
14. AHB/BAM, "A Tactical Appreciation of the Air War in Tunisia," Oct 31, 1944 [prepared by the Air Historical Branch of the *Luftwaffe*], Translation VII/6, 1946, 512.621, 10.

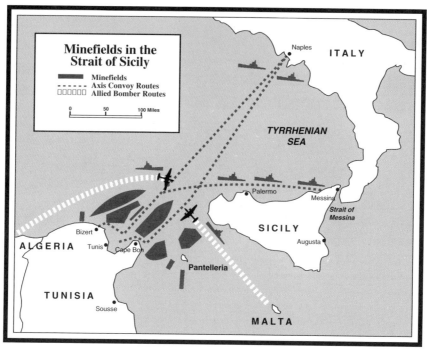

Map 2.

so methodically plowed and mined the airfields of western Libya that the Desert Air Force was slow to start operations even when it was within range of the convoy routes. It became fully operational in Tunisia only around March 1.[15] The situation of the Allied air forces already in Tunisia and eastern Algeria—the American Twelfth Air Force and the Royal Air Force's (RAF's) Eastern Air Command—was more serious still. Throughout December and January they had to contend with a potent *Luftwaffe* and intractable problems with basing, training, supply, and organization. The Germans began 1943 with slightly more aircraft in Tunisia than the Allies. January 1 saw 690 German combat aircraft in Tunisia or within range of it; the Allies had 480.[16] While the Allied air forces had larger establishments of aircraft in the theater, they were unable to bring their full strength to bear because of the poor quality of their advanced airfields and the logistical disruptions caused by their rapid ad-

---

15. AHB/BAM, "R.A.F. Narrative (First Draft): The Middle East Campaigns," vol 4: "Operations in Libya, the Western Desert and Tunisia, July 1942–May 1943," 00895278, 484.

16. Williamson Murray, *Strategy for Defeat: The* Luftwaffe, *1933–1945* (Maxwell AFB, 1983), 182–92.

An Axis ship is shown within 200 feet of an attacking Mitchell bomber from the Northwest African Strategic Air Force. Moments later, the ship blew up. *National Archives.*

vance. In early December, the Allies had only three forward fields for their fighters: Bône, Youks-les-Bains, and Souk-el-Arba. These were, respectively, 120, 150, and 70 miles from the front. The latter two were nearly unusable during the heavy rains of the North African winter. This defect was not easily remedied—the American engineers responsible for the fields had not received their heavy equipment, and the portion of Tunisia held by the Allies was hilly and afforded few alternative sites.[17]

Bases were also a problem for the Allies' bombers. Not until late December did the opening of airfields near Constantine, Algeria, put the Strait of Sicily within range of medium bombers. Logistical difficulties impeded the functioning of these bases once established, and only in February were operations at all efficient, although medium bombers had begun antishipping operations on a small scale in early January.[18] B-17s had begun to attack the ports of Tunis, Bizerte, Sousse, and Gabes early in December. But distance was a limiting factor even for these long-range aircraft: They had to operate from an inadequate field near Oran, 630 miles from Tunis—farther than London was from Berlin. A move to a better field at Biskra in western Algeria in late December increased the

---

17. Craven and Cate, *TORCH to POINTBLANK*, 89.
18. *Ibid.*, 118, 126; Lect, Col Howard E. Engler, Informational Intelligence Series, Office of the Chief of Air Intelligence, AAF, No. 43–113, Jul 5, 1943, 142.0343.

sortie rate of the heavy bombers somewhat.[19] But maintenance and repair remained so inadequate for all components of the Allied air forces that in his report of December 4 Eisenhower quoted his airmen to the effect that "near or complete breakdown" would ensue within two to seven days unless operations were curtailed.[20] The inexperience of the Twelfth Air Force exacerbated all these problems. On December 21 the Twelfth's commander, Maj. Gen. James Doolittle, estimated that fully 75 percent of his men were untrained or only partially trained. At this time the Allies could on any day operate only about a third of the aircraft they had in Northwest Africa.[21]

The position of the Germans with respect to bases was much more fortunate. Besides their airdromes in Sicily and Sardinia, they had at Sidi Ahmed, El Aouina, Sfax, Sousse, and Gabes well-constructed fields, which, in contrast to the muddy tracts of the Allies, were usable throughout the rainy North African winter. These bases were the chief reason for the *Luftwaffe*'s air superiority: It could station more fighters within range of the Tunisian battlefield than the Allies. The Axis also controlled the well-drained coastal plains, large portions of which were usable without preparation as landing fields. This was a particular advantage for close air support as long as the *Luftwaffe* had air superiority. Because the Germans could station dive bombers close to the front lines, their ground commanders could quickly receive support from these aircraft, which had little to fear from the distantly based fighters of the Allies.[22] Eisenhower reported on December 4 that air support for his forces had been "insufficient to keep down the hostile strafing and dive-bombing" that had been "largely responsible for breaking up all attempted advances by ground forces."[23]

Organization problems compounded the Allies' material disadvantages. American air doctrine had been evolving in the same direction as that of the British. Field Manual FM 31–35, *Aviation in Support of Ground Forces* (April 9, 1942), provided that in each theater of war there should be an air support command to assist the ground forces. Each air support command was to be led by an airman, but this officer had mark-

19. Craven and Cate, *TORCH to POINTBLANK*, 108, 118–19. As though it was not bad enough that Tunis was farther from Oran than London was from Berlin, the B-17s in North Africa were far fewer than those in Britain, and had nothing like the same logistical support.
20. Msg, Eisenhower to the Combined Chiefs of Staff, Dec 3, 1942, in Howe, *Northwest Africa*, 320.
21. Twelfth Air Force, Minutes of Staff Meeting, Dec 21, 1942, 650.03-2; Craven and Cate, *TORCH to POINTBLANK*, 116.
22. Craven and Cate, *TORCH to POINTBLANK*, 89; BAM, *Rise and Fall of the German Air Force*, 148–49.
23. See note 20 above.

edly less independence than his British counterpart. There was no indication that he was to be equal in rank to the ground commander. More important, FM 31–35 stipulated that "the most important target at a particular time will usually be that target which constitutes the most serious threat to operations of the supported ground force. The final decision as to priority of target rests with the commander of the supported unit." This disturbed airmen because FM 31–35 also provided that "aviation units may be *attached* to subordinate ground units." The flyers were not mollified by the injunction that such attachments should be "exceptional and . . . resorted to only when circumstances are such that the air support commander cannot effectively control the combat aviation assigned to the air support command." They feared that in practice the army would seize upon this provision to parcel out air power among units of the ground forces. Their apprehensions were soon realized. Not long before the landing in Northwest Africa, Eisenhower—who had not created a joint command for the British and American air units assigned to TORCH—ruled that the commanders of the major task forces should have control of the aircraft assigned to support them.[24]

Eisenhower's decision had seemed reasonable since many Allied components would be operating at a considerable distance from the general headquarters. General Anderson, dismayed by the effect of German dive bombers on his untried troops, availed himself of the prerogative it afforded him during his drive on Tunis. He demanded and received a group of fighters from the RAF for employment as a constant "air umbrella" over his army. The airmen, led by Air Chief Marshal Sir Arthur W. Tedder, the senior officer of the RAF in the theater, argued that this dispersion of aircraft was the worst of choices in the face of a superior *Luftwaffe*. Rather, they argued, the Allies should group their airplanes under a single commander so that at least local air superiority could be achieved for critical tasks. The Allies were further plagued by problems of coordination between the ground and the air forces. The much-respected Allied naval commander in the Mediterranean, Admiral Sir Andrew B. Cunningham, signaled in despair to London that the organization of the air forces in Tunisia was completely chaotic.[25]

---

24. Howe, *Northwest Africa*, 86, 107–8; Field Manual (FM) 31–35, *Aviation in Support of Ground Forces*, Apr 9, 1942, ch 2, sec 1, paras 6, 10 (emphasis added); Allied Forces Headquarters, Ops Memo No. 17, subj: Combat Aviation in Direct Support of Ground Units, Oct 13, 1942, 103.2808; Ltr, Brig Gen James H. Doolittle to Maj Gen George S. Patton, subj: TORCH Air Support, Sep 13, 1942, 650.03–2.

25. AHB/BAM, "R.A.F. Narrative (First Draft): The North African Campaign, November 1942–May 1943," 00895747, 143, 203.

Air Chief Marshal Sir Arthur Tedder *(right)* **meets with his Deputy Commander in Chief for Air, Maj. Gen. Carl A. Spaatz** *(center)*. **Also present is Air Marshal Sir Keith Park** *(left)*, **the air officer commanding Royal Air Force Malta at the time.**

Tedder, who tirelessly urged Eisenhower to create a unified command for the air forces, at length prevailed upon the supreme commander to appoint one of the most experienced of American airmen, Maj. Gen. Carl A. Spaatz, as his Deputy Commander in Chief for Air. Although Spaatz's position, which he assumed on December 5, 1942, was essentially advisory, he soon managed to impose on the Tunisian air forces a division of labor loosely patterned after the organization the British had employed so well in the Egyptian desert. Spaatz made the British Eastern Air Command primarily responsible for support of the ground forces, and he employed the medium and heavy bombers of the American Twelfth Air Force chiefly against airfields and ports.[26]

Spaatz's appointment was the first in a series of steps that led to a total restructuring of the Allied air forces in Northwest Africa. On De-

---

26. Craven and Cate, *TORCH to POINTBLANK*, 106–8; AHB/BAM, "North African Campaign," 80–81, 129–48.

cember 31 Eisenhower proposed that all the air forces in Northwest Africa be grouped under a new organization called the Allied Air Force, with Spaatz in command. The British not surprisingly assented to what was essentially their own proposal. They did, however, recommend that Eisenhower go one step further and group units by function regardless of nationality. Eisenhower stated his general agreement with this recommendation, but for the present thought it wise to preserve the separate identities of the Twelfth Air Force and the Eastern Air Command within the newly formed command structure.[27]

The Allied Air Force was activated on January 5, 1943. Several days later (January 14–24, 1943), Roosevelt and Churchill, each with his military staff, met at Casablanca. The conference was on several scores a triumph for the British. It was agreed, as they had proposed, that North Africa should be used as the staging area for offensive action against Sicily. Casablanca also marked the final acceptance of British organizational principles, for the conferees prescribed a general structure of command for the Mediterranean theater that replicated the tried-and-tested British system. General Sir Harold Alexander was to become Eisenhower's Deputy Commander in Chief with responsibility for the ground forces. Tedder, as chief of the Mediterranean Air Command, was to become air commander for the entire Mediterranean theater, while Spaatz, working closely with Alexander, would command in Northwest Africa an air force thoroughly integrated along the functional lines suggested by the British in December. When this unified force, the Northwest African Air Forces, became operational on February 23, 1943, it comprised three major commands: the Strategic Air Force, the Tactical Air Force, and the Coastal Air Force.[28] The principal missions of the Strategic Air Force were destruction of the Axis' ports and airfields. The Tactical Air Force was to be led by Tedder's coarchitect of aerial victory in the eastern desert, Air Vice Marshal Sir Arthur Coningham. Coningham's responsibilities were air superiority and close air support. The tasks of the Coastal Air Force were to protect Allied shipping and destroy that of the Axis. The Coastal Air Force, drawn almost entirely from units of the Royal Air Force, had few aircraft suitable for the latter purpose. Two squadrons of American B–26 Marauders were therefore attached to it from the Strategic Air

---

27. Craven and Cate, TORCH to POINTBLANK, 106–10; AHB/BAM, "North African Campaign," 143–46.

28. These commands existed for operational purposes only. The American Twelfth Air Force continued for purposes of administration; that is, it paid and supplied the American units in the Northwest African Air Forces.

Participating at the Casablanca Conference in January 1943 in the decision to forego an attack on France for one on Sicily are, in the front row, *(left to right)*, **General Henry H. Arnold, Admiral Ernest J. King, Prime Minister Winston S. Churchill, President Franklin D. Roosevelt, General Sir Alan Brooke, Admiral Sir Dudley Pound, and General George C. Marshall. In the back row, same order, are Lt. Gen. Sir Hastings L. Ismay, Vice Admiral Lord Louis Mountbatten, Brig. Gen. J. R. Deane, Field Marshal Sir John Dill, Air Chief Marshal Sir Charles Portal, and Mr. Harry Hopkins.** *Library of Congress.*

Force for the antishipping mission. The Strategic Air Force also provided P–38 Lightning fighters to escort the B–26s.[29] (*Table 1*)

The Allies' troubles of December and January, while serious, were nothing that could not be overcome with better weather and an intelligent application of the lessons of experience. The Axis faced only a single major problem, but it proved intractable and in time led to disaster: Its position in Tunisia was logistically untenable. The Germans, the primary instigators of the fatal commitment in Northwest Africa, had made too many optimistic assumptions about the availability of shipping in the Mediterranean. They had, in particular, counted too much on vessels they planned to seize from France.[30] The burden of transporting supplies

29. Craven and Cate, *Torch to Pointblank*, 113–15, 161–65. On February 23, 1943, the Coastal Air Force had only twenty-six Beaufighters and six Swordfish. Hist, Twelfth Air Force, "The Twelfth Air Force in the Tunisian Campaign," 2 vols, n.d., 650.01–2, 27. For the attachment of the B–26s and P–38s, see Memo, Maj Philip P. Hennin, subj: Counter-Shipping Force, Mar 25, 1943, 652.547.

30. In his appreciation of mid-March 1943, Hitler referred to hopes current at the end of 1942 that it would be possible to supply the forces in Africa with the Italian ships on hand and those expected from France, whose merchant Ma-

Table 1. Principal Units of Northwest African Air Forces, June 1, 1943

Unit*	Aircraft Assigned
Strategic Air Force	
U.S. Bombardment Groups	
2d, 97th, 99th, 301st	B–17
310th, 321st	B–25
17th, 319th, 320th	B–26
U.S. Fighter Groups	
1st, 14th, 82d	P–38
325th	P–40
RAF† Wings (4)	Wellington
Tactical Air Force	
Tactical Bomber Force	
U.S. Bombardment Groups	
47th	A–20
12th,‡ 340th‡	B–25
RAF† Wings (2)	
SAAF§ Wing (1)	
Tactical Reconnaissance Squadrons (2)	
XII Air Support Command	
U.S. Fighter Groups	
33d, 324th‡	P–40
31st	Spitfire
U.S. Fighter-Bomber Groups	
27th, 86th	A–36
U.S. 111th Observation Squadron	
Western Desert Air Force	P–40
RAF†	
SAAF§	
U.S. Fighter Groups	
57th,‡ 79th‡	
Coastal Air Force	
U.S. Fighter Groups	
81st, 350th	P–39
52d	Spitfire
RAF† Wings (3)	
Air Defense Commands (2)	
U.S. Antisubmarine Squadrons	
1st, 2d	
Miscellaneous Units	
Troop Carrier Command	
U.S. 51st Wing	
60th, 62d, 64th Groups	C–47
U.S. 52d Wing	
61st, 313th, 114th, 316th‡ Groups	C–47
RAF† 38 Wing	

Unit*	Aircraft Assigned
Training Command	
Replacement Battalions (3)	
U.S. 68th Observation Group	
Miscellaneous Training Units	
Photographic Reconnaissance Wing	
U.S. 3d Photographic Reconnaissance and Mapping Group	
RAF† Squadrons (2)	
FAF** Squadron (1)	

*The assigned strength of the U.S. Army Air Forces groups was as follows: **heavy bombers**—48 planes (4 squadrons, 12 planes each); **medium bombers, light bombers**, and **dive bombers**—57 planes each (4 squadrons, 13 planes each, plus 5 headquarters planes); **fighters**—75 planes (3 squadrons, 25 planes each); and **troop carrier**—52 planes (4 squadrons, 13 planes each). In each instance, the strength was normal, except in the case of the heavy bombers, where normal unit equipment was thirty-five aircraft.

†Royal Air Force.

‡Ninth Air Force.

§South African Air Force.

**French Air Force.

SOURCE: Craven and Cate, *TORCH to POINTBLANK*, 417.

to Tunisia therefore fell upon Italy, for Germany's merchant fleet was blockaded in the North Sea.

When Italy surrendered in September 1943 there remained to her 272 merchantmen with a burden of 500 tons or more—in all, 748,578 tons of shipping.[31] A fleet of this size would have sufficed to supply Tunisia had it not been for the Axis' strategic overextension and a shortage of vessels suitable for the dangerous run to Tunisia. Only speedy ships were suit-

rine was seized when the Germans occupied the area of that country theretofore controlled by the Vichy regime. He acknowledged that the expectations had been ill-founded. *OKW* to von Arnim, Mar 31, 1943, Roll 416, T–313, NARA. The Germans obtained 450,000 tons of shipping from the French in January 1943. Of this amount, less than 100,000 tons was suitable for the supply of Africa. An urgent program to construct small boats began in January 1943 but appears to have accomplished little. Brig Gen Conrad Seibt, "Railroad, Sea and Air Transport Situation for Supply of Africa Through Italy (January–May 1943)," MS D–093, RG 338, NARA, 2–6.

31. Commander Marc' Antonio Bragadin, *The Italian Navy in World War II*, translated by Gale Hoffman (Annapolis, 1957), 365 table 9. This total reflects some 400,000 tons of shipping taken late in 1942 from France. According to another estimate, the Italians may have had a grand total of as much as 1,362,682 tons at the time of their surrender. Martin Van Creveld, *Supplying War: Logistics from Wallenstein to Patton* (London, 1977), 198.

able, and by 1943 they were scarce. Too many had been lost on the Libyan route. The ships also had to be small—to make them difficult targets for aircraft and to minimize the effect of losses.[32] But small vessels, too, were lacking by 1943. In February 1943 the Axis had, even with recent seizures from France, only about 300,000 tons of shipping suitable for the run to Tunisia, and by no means all of it was available for that purpose. About half of the remaining ships were damaged, and the Allies systematically bombed Italian shipyards to slow repairs.[33] The Axis, moreover, also had to sustain the garrisons and considerable populations of Sicily, Corsica, Sardinia, and the Dodecanese Islands. Sicily alone required 200,000 tons of coal each month. Of this amount, the inadequate railroads of southern Italy could move but a fifth to the Strait of Messina for transshipment by ferry or lighter.[34] The combined effect of all the foregoing was that at no time between January and May 1943 were more than 30,000 to 50,000 tons of shipping available to supply North Africa.[35] There was yet another problem in the Italian Navy's shortage of destroyers. Convoys laden with critical supplies were often delayed because there were no unengaged warships to escort them.[36]

The German commanders in Tunisia were on the horns of a dilemma that admitted of no solution: Their logistical support was inadequate, yet the only appropriate strategy required a prodigal expenditure of supplies. Von Arnim, who had been predicting disaster since January, outlined the predicament in an appreciation of February 26, 1943, which Rommel seconded shortly thereafter. Von Arnim estimated that *Heeresgruppe Afrika* was responsible for the maintenance of 120,000 soldiers and 230,000 civilians. The quartermaster of the *Heeresgruppe* put its average monthly consumption of supplies at 69,000 tons. The chief transportation officer of the *Commando Supremo* had estimated early in Feb-

---

32. Michael Salewski, *Die deutsche Seekriegsleitung, 1935–1945*, 2 vols (Munich, 1975), 2:253, 265. The importance of this was demonstrated when two large ships carrying 15,000 tons of ammunition—perhaps two weeks' supply for *Heeresgruppe Afrika*—were sunk in April by aircraft within sight of Bizerte after their escorts had successfully repelled several attacks during the crossing. Vice Adm Friedrich Ruge, *Der Seekrieg: The German Navy's Story, 1939–1945*, translated by Cmdr M.G. Saunders, R.N. (Annapolis, 1957), 332.

33. In December 1942 fully 53 percent of all of Italian shipping was laid up for repair. AHB/BAM, "Battle for Tunis," 9.

34. Ruge, *Der Seekrieg*, 331. The supply of coal to Sicily was necessary for the operation of the supply route to Tunisia. When the island's coal reserves fell dangerously low in late February, it was necessary to divert shipping that would otherwise have been used to supply Tunisia. AHB/BAM, "Battle for Tunis," 16.

35. Seibt, "Railroad, Sea and Air Transport."

36. At one apparently representative point during the Tunisian Campaign, only eleven of Italy's thirty-three destroyers were operational. AHB/BAM, "Battle for Tunis," 14.

ruary that he could send only 70,000 to 82,000 tons of supplies monthly to Tunisia. Since the convoys would be subject to an anticipated loss rate of 25 percent, meeting even minimum requirements of the *Heeresgruppe* was highly improbable.[37] Matters were even worse than these figures implied. Superior Allied armies were converging on Tunisia. Little prospect existed that the forces of the Axis, hemmed in on the shore of northeastern Tunisia, could long withstand the Allies' concerted assault. Defeat of the Allied armies in detail before they could mass was therefore imperative. At least one enemy army, von Arnim argued, had to be put "out of action for six months. . . . All other victories would change nothing, but only postpone the inevitable." But an active defense, with a heavy employment of armored forces, would entail a much greater than normal expenditure of supplies. To implement this strategy, and to allow for inevitable disruptions of supply by enemy action and weather, the *Heeresgruppe* would have to *receive* not less than 140,000 tons monthly. Only then, von Arnim concluded, would a successful defense against the impending general offensive of the Allies be possible. As yet, Tunis was "*a fortress . . . without reserves of ammunition or food.*" Were he in Eisenhower's place, he observed, "I would not attack, but with every means attack convoys and harbors while battering the *Luftwaffe.*" With a complete disruption of supply, Tunis must fall by July 1.[38]

The Germans and Italians launched a series of limited offensives in January and February to bloody Eisenhower's forces before the formidable Eighth Army arrived from the east. In January, von Arnim's *Fifth Panzerarmee* faced Anderson's First Army in western Tunisia, while in the south the *First Italian Army* awaited the pursuing Montgomery. The heart of the *First Italian Army*'s position was the Mareth Line, a heavily fortified position, constructed by the French before the war against an Italian attack from Libya. It ran from the inland mountains through the town of Mareth to the sea, athwart the coastal plain that was the only route of advance for a large force. In late January, the *Fifth Panzerarmee* inflicted stinging setbacks on the British and French in a series of limited attacks near the towns of Ousseltia and Faid. The next month, von Arnim attacked the British through the Faid Pass toward Kasserine while Rommel, with the *First Italian Army*, struck at Gafsa through the Kasserine Pass. The inexperienced American II Corps retreated in disar-

---

37. Memos, von Arnim to Rommel, subj: *Beurteiling der Lage im Tunesischen Raum*, Feb 26, 1943, and Rommel to Kesselring, Mar 1, 1943, both in T-313, Roll 416, NARA; Howe, *Northwest Africa*, 512–13. On January 12, 1943, Kesselring had put the capacity of the system at 60,000 tons a month. Felmy, "German Air Force in the Mediterranean," 612.

38. Von Arnim to Rommel, Feb 26, 1943 (emphasis in the original).

AERIAL INTERDICTION

ray until it managed to make a stand at Thala. Rommel then withdrew back through the Kasserine Pass to resume his position on the Mareth Line. Von Arnim's offensive also petered out, and by March 1 the Allies had recovered their original positions.

Even as they repulsed the Axis' desperate thrusts, the Allies began to implement the strategy that in barely more than two months would result in their conquest of Tunisia. Not surprisingly, given the presence of both Coningham and Tedder, it was closely based on the three-stage model for a combined arms offensive developed in the Egyptian desert.[39] The first task the Allies set for themselves was to wrest air superiority from the Axis. While still fighting for command of the air, the Anglo-Americans planned to turn their attention to the vulnerable convoys that plied the Strait of Sicily. An all-out offensive was planned for early May to destroy *Heeresgruppe Afrika* once it had been weakened logistically and denuded of air support.

Coningham set forth his plans for winning air superiority in an operations directive of February 10, 1943. He called for "a continued offensive against the enemy in the air" and "sustained attacks on enemy main airfields." The attacks on the airdromes fell by day to strafing fighters and large formations of light and medium bombers, occasionally helped by heavy bombers from the Strategic Air Force. Light bombers, acting singly or in small formations, pressed the attack by night.[40] The Germans noted with some surprise that in February and March the Allies began to place so much emphasis on counterair operations that they stinted on close air support for their ground forces.[41]

---

39. There was not, it appears, a single document in which the Allied plans were laid out. The strategy must be deduced from the decisions of the Casablanca Conference and a number of specific orders issued in February 1943. It will be recalled that at Casablanca the Coastal Air Force was given the mission of attacking the enemy's convoys, while the Tactical Air Force was to attain air superiority with the help of the Strategic Air Force, which was to bomb German airfields. On February 10 Coningham outlined his plan for aerial superiority, which is described later in this chapter. It should be recalled the British approach to combined-arms warfare, so evident in the organization of the Mediterranean Allied Air Forces, was by this time fully worked out and had found expression in General Montgomery's "Notes on High Command in War." The three-stage strategy was incorporated in the American War Department FM 100–20, *Command and Employment of Air Power*, issued July 21, 1943. At the time, American airmen cited the Northwest African campaign as the foremost example of the three-stage approach.

40. Northwest African Tactical Air Force, Gen Op Directive, Feb 10, 1943, attached to Memo, Brig Gen Laurence S. Kuter to General H.H. Arnold, subj: Organization of American Air Forces, May 12, 1943, 614.201–2, annex 3.

41. AHB/BAM, "The Course of the War in the Mediterranean Theatre of Operations, January 1–May 13, 1943," Jul 29, 1944 [prepared by the Air Historical Branch of the *Luftwaffe*], Translation VII/72, 1948, 512.621, 10. At one

38

German airfields in Sicily were inherently vulnerable: No radar protected them from surprise attack, and their coastal locations precluded antiaircraft defense in depth. Towns and olive groves, moreover, hemmed in the fields so that parked aircraft could not be dispersed properly. German airfields in Tunisia did permit adequate dispersion, and radar and observers protected them against surprise attacks. But incessant Allied air attacks forced the Germans to divide their aircraft among many small fields, which led to a considerable loss of efficiency.[42]

The counterair campaign forced the *Luftwaffe* to devote a considerable portion of its strength to defending its bases: "Even the taking-off at the air bases," a German study noted, "could often only be done with fighter protection. The forces set aside for safety measures had to be proportionally strong."[43] The *Luftwaffe* could ill afford this diversion of aircraft, for Allied air strength was growing rapidly while the Germans, short of industrial capacity and beset from other quarters, could barely replace their losses. While they had begun 1943 with more aircraft (690 combat aircraft) in and around Tunisia than the Allies (480 combat aircraft), their position deteriorated as the Anglo-Americans began to overcome their problems with basing and supply. The improvements permitted the Allies to fly into the combat zone not only aircraft that they had had to leave at Gibraltar or in Algeria but many new ones from Britain and the United States. By March 21 the two principal components of the Northwest African Air Forces—the Tactical and the Strategic Air Forces—disposed 1,501 combat aircraft, while German strength had risen not at all. At the end of the Tunisian Campaign (May 13), it was about what it had been in January—695 combat aircraft.[44]

An interesting feature of the Tunisian Campaign is that the Allies were able to begin telling attacks on the Axis' lines of communication before they had won general air superiority. Allied and German sources concur that the period of Allied air superiority over Tunisia began about

---

point in late March during the opening phase of the Allied spring offensive, Lt Gen George S. Patton, commander of the American II Corps, complained that his forward units were being continually bombed: "Total lack of air cover for units has allowed the German Air Force to operate almost at will." Coningham, however, refused to be diverted from his counterair operations. AHB/BAM, "North African Campaign," 175–76.

42. Craven and Cate, *TORCH to POINTBLANK*, 175, 184; AHB/BAM, "Tactical Appreciation of the Air War in Tunisia," 5–7; Hist, Twelfth Air Force, "Counter Air: Counter Air Force Operations in the Mediterranean Theater," n.d., 650.03-2.

43. AHB/BAM, "Course of the War in the Mediterranean Theatre of Operations," 10, 18–19.

44. Murray, *Strategy for Defeat*, 182–92; BAM, *Rise and Fall of the German Air Force*, 250, 258; Hist, Twelfth Air Force, "Twelfth Air Force in the Tunisian Campaign," 11, 34, 36.

April 1,[45] while Allied aircraft had been regularly attacking the Axis' convoys and ports since late February. This the Allies had been able to do because the *Luftwaffe* had to fight under a serious strategic disadvantage: Once the Allied air forces were established in Tunisia, the Axis' lines of communication were wholly vulnerable, while those of the Allies remained largely exempt from retaliation. German aircraft based in Sicily and Sardinia tried to attack the Allied ports in Algeria and Morocco—Port Lyautey, Bône, Oran, and Algiers—that sustained Eisenhower's command, but their lack of range and ordnance-carrying capacity restricted them. No German fighters had the range to accompany the bombers, and when the Allies emplaced strong air defenses, the raiders' losses quickly became insupportable.[46] The same problems hobbled German efforts to attack Allied convoys.[47] Even before the Allies had a numerical preponderance, the strategic asymmetry seriously disadvantaged the *Luftwaffe*, for the Allies, having comparatively safe supply lines, could mass their aircraft to win local air superiority.[48] Lacking aircraft in numbers sufficient to contend for air superiority *and* to defend their convoys, the Germans had to concentrate upon protecting their vital supply lines. By conceding air superiority in this way, they facilitated the attacks on their air bases that progressively reduced their ability to provide air cover for the convoys.[49]

On February 19, 1943, Eisenhower observed that the enemy was receiving about 75 percent of his requirements. "The termination of the Tunisian campaign," he observed, "depends on the extent to which we can disrupt enemy lines of communications."[50] Tedder specified the pri-

---

45. AHB/BAM, "Course of the War in the Mediterranean Theatre of Operations," 19; Hist, Twelfth Air Force, "Counter Air Force Operations in the Mediterranean Theater."

46. The only German bombers in the Mediterranean at this juncture were Junkers Ju 88s. At the range at which they were required to operate against the Allied ports, the Ju 88 carried only about 1,650 pounds of bombs. AHB/BAM, "Tactical Appreciation of the Air War in Tunisia," 4–5. For the growth and effectiveness of Allied air defenses, see AHB/BAM, "North African Campaign," 95–97.

47. BAM, *Rise and Fall of the German Air Force*, 149–52; AHB/BAM, "Tactical Appreciation of the Air War in Tunisia," 2–5.

48. A German study put the matter thusly: "With the advance of their bases, the enemy fighter bombers were in a position to attack our supply vessels, necessitating the use of still larger forces of fighters for convoy escort duties. Having the advantage of the initiative, the Anglo-Americans were always able to gain air supremacy by temporarily concentrating their forces in a definite area, even after our fighter strength had been increased." AHB/BAM, "Tactical Appreciation of the Air War in Tunisia," 6.

49. *Ibid.*, 5–7.

50. *Ibid.*, 10; F.H. Hinsley *et al.*, *British Intelligence in the Second World War*, 5 vols (London, 1979–), 2:573.

orities of the antishipping campaign in an operational directive of March 7, 1943, ordering that the "normal mission" of even the "strategic striking forces" was "the air attack of Axis sea, land and air lines of communications and supply to and from Tunisia." Ships were the target of first priority. Tedder assigned the greatest importance to tankers traveling between Sicily and Tunisia. He ranked tankers sailing between Italy and Sicily next, and then freighters bearing military supplies. Ports followed ships in importance. The greatest priority went to Tunis and Bizerte, then came the other Axis-held ports in North Africa; the Sicilian ports of Palermo, Messina, and Trapani; and the Italian port of Naples.[51]

The bombing of ports in Italy, Sicily, and North Africa fell to American heavy bombers—B-17s of the Twelfth Air Force and B-24s of the Libya-based Ninth Air Force. These attacks destroyed ships and supplies outright. Their chief effects, however, were to make an already marginal logistical system still less efficient and to expose the convoys to greater perils at sea. At Tunis and Bizerte the heavy bombers periodically destroyed or damaged the cranes used to unload the ships; they so demoralized the native laborers who manned the ports that eventually the importation of stevedores from Germany became necessary. A ship of 1,500 tons required a full day to unload, and a vessel of 5,000 tons required three days. This slowed down the turnaround time of convoys, thereby reducing the capacity of the system as a whole.[52]

Kesselring's optimism about supplying Tunisia had been based largely on the fact that the sea route from Italy to Tunisia was only about a third as long as that between Italy and Libya. Ships sailing to Tunisia would therefore be less exposed to air attack. They could also be protected from the Royal Navy by the very extensive minefields of the Strait of Sicily, the last of which was laid in the winter of 1942–1943.[53] The original plan for supplying Tunisia had sought to take advantage of this protection by transporting supplies the length of Italy by rail and then ferrying them across the narrow and easily defended Strait of Messina to Sicily. At Palermo and other Sicilian ports supplies were to be transferred to ships for the short and protected run across the Strait of Sicily. But the advantages of this route were denied the Axis by the efforts of American bombers which, operating at short range, were much more effective against the Sicilian ports than they were against Naples. On March 22 American bombs ignited an explosion in the harbor of Palermo that devastated nearly thirty acres of docks and sank four mer-

---

51. AHB/BAM, "North African Campaign," 161–62.
52. Howe, *Northwest Africa*, 365–66; Felmy, "German Air Force in the Mediterranean," 601.
53. Bragadin, *Italian Navy in World War II*, 241.

Awaiting a briefing by their squadron commander in front of a Consolidated B–24 Liberator, this bomber crew of the Ninth Air Force *(above)* prepares to fly a mission against Axis shipping in the Mediterranean. Lt. Gen. Henry H. Arnold *(right)*, Commanding General, Army Air Forces, meets with men of the Ninth Air Force during a visit to the western desert. He has just returned from the Casablanca Conference. *Top photo, courtesy of the Library of Congress.*

chant ships. In February, the bombers succeeded in forcing convoys to stage from Naples rather than from Sicily, tripling the distance they had to sail for Tunisia and thereby canceling the advantage of the Tunisian route over that of the Libyan. North of Sicily, moreover, convoys, unprotected by minefields, became liable to attack by British ships and submarines from Gibraltar.[54]

Even the minefields of the Strait of Sicily ultimately redounded to the disadvantage of their creators. Their success in protecting shipping from surface attack was bought at the price of severe channelization of the convoy routes. The success of the British in laying minefields within those of the Axis worsened the channelization and resulted in a truly nightmarish problem of navigation for Italian seamen. Along the route of less than ninety miles from the western end of Sicily to Cape Bon the passage for convoys was nowhere more than three miles wide; for forty miles it was no more than one mile in width, and at some points less than half a mile wide.[55] Within this narrow corridor the ability of vessels to manuever was constrained, and their vulnerability to aerial attack correspondingly increased.

The marginally adequate and severely channelized logistical system of the Axis gravely jeoparidized the supply of *Heeresgruppe Afrika*. But the final seal of doom for the enterprise was an Allied advantage that came to light only after the passage of more than three decades. The British, with some initial help from the Poles and the French, had succeeded in breaking many of the Germans' most important ciphers. The information from this source, known as ULTRA, gave the Allies information about the Axis' convoys that the official history of British intelligence in the Second World War describes as "virtually complete." Daily digests disseminated to Allied air planners and naval commanders made known all points of origin, destinations, and schedules, and ships known to be carrying supplies of particular importance for *Heeresgruppe Afrika* could even be targeted specifically.[56] The greatest secrecy shrouded the whole operation; targets, however tempting, were never attacked unless some other source duplicated the information, lest ULTRA be compromised.[57] Despite such precautions, the Germans at length realized the Al-

---

54. Maj Richard Feige, "The Relationship Between Operations and Supply in Africa," MS D-125, RG 338, NARA, 8; Felmy, "German Air Force in the Mediterranean," 716.

55. Bragadin, *Italian Navy in World War II*, 241-43.

56. When *Heeresgruppe Afrika* surrendered in May 1943, the Allies found themselves with 50,000 more prisoners than they had anticipated. Provisioning of the prisoners, however, proved no problem. Thanks to the selective targeting of ships bearing fuel and ammunition, the prisoners were well fed. Hinsely *et al.*, *British Intelligence in the Second World War*, 2:614.

57. National Security Agency, SRH-037, "Reports Received by the U.S. War Department on the Use of ULTRA in the European Theater, World War II"; Grp Capt R.H. Humphreys, "The Use of 'U' in the Mediterranean and Northwest African Theaters of War," 2, 11-14; Hinsely *et al.*, *British Intelligence in the Second World War*, 2:575. One of the biggest drawbacks the Allies faced in their antishipping campaign was that they for a long time lacked sufficient reconnaissance aircraft to provide the necessary cover for ULTRA. See, for example,

lies had very precise information about convoy movements, but drew the wrong conclusion about its source. Far from thinking their codes broken, they attributed the Allied information to disaffection in the ranks of their Italian allies.[58]

In the early days of the Tunisian Campaign Allied air commanders had tried to attack enemy merchantmen in port. They soon found that the turnaround time of the B-17s was too slow. Poor though the facilities of the Tunisian ports were, many convoys unloaded and put to sea before a strike could be mounted. Occasionally, B-17s attacked shipping at sea, but their slow turnarounds and inaccurate bombing thwarted attempts to catch convoys in midpassage. B-26 medium bombers attached to the Coastal Air Force therefore became the chief weapon of the aerial antishipping campaign. The airfields to support their operations were ready by February 1, 1943, but three weeks of bad weather over the Strait of Sicily delayed operations. The Marauders almost always attacked ships at sea because they had suffered heavy losses earlier when they braved the heavy antiaircraft defenses of Tunis and Bizerte. At first they employed a skip-bombing technique developed in the Pacific: The flyers approached their prey abeam and at low altitude, releasing their bombs so that they caromed from the surface of the sea into the sides of the targeted vessels. The tactic was at first highly effective, but was defeated when heavier antiaircraft armament on the merchantmen forced the bombers to attack from about 10,000 feet. From this altitude bombing accuracy was abysmal. The aviators then resorted to attacking in staggered flights at low and medium altitudes in an attempt to divide and confuse the antiaircraft gunners. These attacks, one pilot recalled, were "never entirely successful." Toward the close of the campaign a weakening of antiaircraft fire permitted a return to skip bombing; at this stage, the weakness of the *Luftwaffe* permitted employing as dive bombers the P-38s originally detailed to escort the B-26s.[59] The B-26s were aided by British aircraft from Malta, which now used against Tunisia-bound convoys the deadly skills they had honed attacking the Libyan convoys. Royal Air Force Malta, which had been placed under Tedder's opera-

---

Memo, Brig Gen Lowell W. Rooks to Maj Gen W. Bedell Smith, subj: Review of Situation Regarding Enemy Supplies to Tunisia, Mar 5, 1943, 0403/10/267, Box 9, Numeric File, 1943-45, RG 331, Records of Allied Force Headquarters, Headquarters Mediterranean Allied Air Forces, Directorate of Operations and Intelligence, Air Plans Section, NARA.

58. AHB/BAM, "Battle for Tunis," 16.

59. Engler lecture; Hist, Twelfth Air Force, "Twelfth Air Force in the Tunisian Campaign," 2:19; *ibid.*, annex 2; Twelfth Air Force, "Operations Bulletin No. 2," May 31, 1943, 1-12.

tional control, used two kinds of aircraft for antishipping operations: the Albacore torpedo-bomber and the versatile Beaufighter.[60]

Despite the difficulties posed by antiaircraft fire and a late start, the antishipping campaign was eminently successful in reducing the flow of supplies to *Heeresgruppe Afrika*. The Allies learned from ULTRA that of all the merchantmen that set sail for Tunisia in March, nearly half had been sunk—but a fifth had been lost in February. Because of the shortage of ships and general derangement of its logistical system, during the critical months of March and April the Axis was able to load only 140,572 tons of supplies for Tunisia. This equates to a barely adequate average monthly shipment of 70,286 tons, which was then subjected to a frightful loss rate.[61] In April, 41.5 percent of all cargos were lost. This was slightly less than the percentage lost in March, but in April only 29,233 tons of supplies reached Tunisia—March's figure had been 43,125. Of the vessels lost in these months, aircraft claimed about two-thirds.[62] By the end of April, Admiral Friedrich Ruge, sent to Rome to expedite the flow of supplies to Africa, had come to agree with the conclusion reached some time before by the Italian Navy—that the losses on the run to Tunisia had become so great that they could no longer be justified by *Heeresgruppe Afrika*'s slim chance for survival. Berlin, however, continued to insist on throwing good money after bad.[63]

The effect of the curtailed flow of supplies on the German and Italian forces in Tunisia was great. Even before the interdiction campaign became effective, their logistical position was weak. On February 13, Rommel's quartermaster reported that he had not received enough supplies to cover consumption; the shortage of ammunition was critical when the attack through the Kasserine Pass began the next day.[64] With the beginning of serious interdiction in late February, the logistical position of the Axis' armies grew steadily worse. In early March, Rommel was still able to mount the Axis' last offensive of the campaign. He struck at the advancing Eighth Army near Medenine, only to be repelled with heavy losses in tanks. Thereafter, the fortunes of *Heeresgruppe Afrika* declined rapidly. By the end of March, Montgomery had outflanked

---

60. AHB/BAM, "North African Campaign," 162-63.

61. Bragadin, *Italian Navy in World War II*, 357 table 2.

62. Ruge, *Der Seekrieg*, 330; Hinsely *et al.*, *British Intelligence in the Second World War*, 2:607-8.

63. *Oberquartiermeister, Deutche-italienische Panzerarmee Afrika*, to *Oberkommando des Heeres*, Feb 13, 1943, and *Oberquartiermeister, Panzerarmee Afrika,* to *Oberkommando des Heeres*, Apr 1, 1943, both in Roll 344, T-78, RG 242, NARA; Salewski, *Die deutsche Seekriegsleitung*, 2:263-64.

64. *Oberquartiermeister, Deutche-italienische Panzerarmee Afrika*, to *Oberkommando des Heeres*, Feb 13, 1943.

the Mareth Line, forcing the Germans to retreat north up the coast and to yield the ports of Sousse and Sfax. At this point the ailing Rommel left Africa, never to return. Von Arnim succeeded him as commander of *Heeresgruppe Afrika*. On the western front the First Army began a sustained offensive that by March 17 succeeded in capturing Gafsa. Not far from there, the two Allied armies linked up on April 7; four days later the *First Italian Army* joined the *Fifth Panzerarmee*. As the Tunisian Campaign entered its last month the forces of the Axis were completely hemmed in a small bridgehead defined by a front that stretched 100 miles from Cape Serrat just west of Bizerte to Enfidaville southeast of Tunis.

Heeresgruppe Afrika lacked the fuel and ammunition to counter the final Allied offensive. It reported on March 28 that it had entirely depleted its reserves of both commodities. On April 1 the quartermaster described the logistical situation as "very bad." On April 10 the Allies intercepted a message that told of an armored division that for want of fuel had abandoned its equipment and retreated on foot.[65]

From the earliest days of the Tunisian Campaign, the Germans had attempted to compensate for their inadequate supply of shipping by the extensive use of air transport. Nine groups of Ju 52 transports—468 aircraft—carried urgently needed supplies, particularly fuel and ammunition. They were aided by thirty large six-engine Me 323 transports. On some days as many as 585 tons were ferried across the Strait of Sicily, although the average appears to have been close to 172 tons a day.[66] The Allies knew the details of the airlift from ULTRA, but the same problems that delayed antishipping operations stayed action against the German airlift. Strategic considerations dictated further delay. The assault upon the aerial convoys, Operation FLAX, was planned in early February but not implemented until April. FLAX was a card that could not be played more than a few times, as shown by the relative impunity with which the surviving Axis transports operated at night after the trap had been sprung. The flight time across the Strait of Sicily was so short that interception could be made only with precise intelligence. The Germans, understanding this but not knowing that their codes had been compromised, operated by day. Since their enemy had the option of flying by night, the Allies delayed implementation of FLAX until the most German transport aircraft were in operation so that the blow would be as decisive

---

65. Hinsley *et al.*, *British Intelligence in the Second World War*, 2:607.

66. Maj Gen Ulrich Buchholz, "Supply by Air of the Enlarged Bridgehead of Tunis from 1 December 1942 to 11 May 1943," MS D–071, RG 338, NARA, 2, 7, 13. During the 172 days of the airlift (November 9, 1942–May 11, 1943), a total of 31,386 tons of supplies were carried to Tunis. See *ibid.*, table 3. The Ju 52 had a maximum capacity of 1.8 metric tons; the Me 323, about 10 metric tons. AHB/BAM, "Operations in Libya, the Western Desert and Tunisia," 522.

The German Defeat in Tunisia *(clockwise, from the top)*: **German POWs stack captured arms, no longer a threat to Allied forces. An allied soldier inspects a 6-barrel rocket projector known as a** *Nebelwerfer.* **Amid mounds of German tires, some British soldiers search for salvageable matériel. A disabled multibarrel 37-mm antiaircraft gun, camouflage still clinging to its sides, will no longer harry Allied pilots.**

as possible. They also wanted to destroy the transports when they were most needed, and therefore timed FLAX to coincide with both a high point of the antishipping campaign and the final assault on Tunis.[67]

The transport aircraft were mostly based at fields near Naples and Palermo; a few staged from Bari and Reggio di Calabria. Flights usually began at Naples and proceeded after stops in Sicily to the main Tunisian terminals, Sidi Ahmed and El Aouina. Occasional flights went directly to Tunisia, picking up their escorting fighters over Sicily.[68] FLAX called for fighters to intercept the aerial convoys over the strait. There were also bombing attacks on the overcrowded staging fields in Sicily and unusually ambitious antishipping sweeps. On April 6 P–38s intercepted a large formation of Ju 52s a few miles from the Tunisian coast while bombers attacked airfields in Sicily and Tunisia. Further attacks on aerial convoys followed on April 10, 11, 18, and 19. These resulted in the destruction of about 123 Ju 52s and 4 Italian SM 82s. On April 22 an entire convoy of twenty-one Me 323s was destroyed; two of these giants had been destroyed earlier for a total loss of twenty-three. Thereafter reduced numbers of Ju 52s flew at night.[69] FLAX dealt the German air transport fleet a blow from which it never recovered—and ended *Heeresgruppe Afrika*'s last chance for any significant resupply of its rapidly dwindling supply of fuel.

Having been prevented by logistical problems from employing the strategy that might have permitted a prolonged stand in Africa, *Heeresgruppe Afrika* was in its last days hard put to defend itself at all because of crippling shortages of ammunition and, especially, of fuel.[70] Near the end, von Arnim had been able to move his headquarters only because of the providential discovery of a drum of aviation gasoline on a beach— flotsam, presumably, from one of FLAX's victims. He surrendered him-

---

67. Craven and Cate, *TORCH to POINTBLANK*, 191; Memo, Kuter to Arnold, May 12, 1943; Northwest African Tactical Air Force, "T.A.F. Operation Plan for Final Assault on Tunis," April 6, 1943, 614.201–2. Just how precise was the intelligence derived from ULTRA may be seen from what the authors of FLAX considered "the necessary information required to formulate" their plan: "(1) Size of enemy air transport formation; (2) Airports of departure; (3) Intermediate stopping points; (4) Airports of arrival; (5) Time of departure; (6) Time of arrival; (7) Route followed; (8) Fighter escort; (9) Fighter cover from Tunisia; (10) Antiaircraft defenses at terminal airdromes." Office of the Assistant Chief of Air Staff, Intelligence, "Tactics Employed by the Northwest African Air Force Against Enemy Aerial Transport," Jul 1, 1943, Command Informational Intelligence Series 43–112, 142.034–3.

68. Buchholz, "Supply by Air of the Enlarged Bridgehead of Tunis," 2–10.

69. *Ibid.*, 10–12.

70. Gustav von Värst, "*Kämpfe der 5. Panzerarmee in Tunesien von Anfang März 1943 bis zur Waffenstreckung*," MS D–001, RG 338, NARA, 11–12.

self and his army on May 12, having with his own hands set fire to his headquarters caravan.[71]

The Tunisian Campaign affords a clear example of the decisive importance of logistics in modern warfare. In Tunisia, and North Africa generally, the Axis had usually prevailed when it met its foes on anything like equal terms. *Heeresgruppe Afrika* was neither outfought nor outgeneraled; starved of supplies, it yielded at length to the superior numbers of a lavishly equipped enemy. "The final decision was fought out on the ground," a German study concluded, "but the effect of the air war on supplies and morale had already determined the outcome of the battle."[72] As Kesselring had foreseen, supply had indeed been "everything."

The great success of the Allies in Tunisia had several consequences. It represented a triumph for the three-stage concept of aerial operations that the British had developed in the eastern desert. For the rest of the war, the basic pattern for Allied combined arms offensives remained air superiority, interdiction, and close air support for the ground forces. Tunisia also saw final acceptance of the idea that the control of air power in a theater of operations should reside in a single commander, equal in authority to the ground commander with whom he worked closely in executing the plans of the theater commander. This organizational conception, together with the three-stage concept of aerial operations, was in the summer of 1943 written into FM 100–20, *Command and Employment of Air Power*, which many airmen regarded as a virtual charter of independence from the ground forces.[73]

So powerful an argument was the victory in Tunisia for the centralization of air power and the coequal status of air commanders with those of the ground forces, that some American airmen came perilously close to attributing the Allied victory in Northwest Africa entirely to the triumph of their views in the reorganizations of December 1942 through February 1943.[74] But however fruitful the organizational changes of February 1943 might have been, the primary reasons for the success of Allied interdiction are to be found elsewhere. The material advantage of the Allied air forces was ultimately so crushing that it is difficult to see how the Anglo-Americans could have failed once they dealt with their problems of inadequate supply and improved their airfields. The Axis' logisti-

71. Howe, *Northwest Africa*, 664–67.
72. AHB/BAM, "Tactical Appreciation of the Air War in Tunisia," 1.
73. War Department FM 100–20, *Command and Employment of Air Power*, Jul 21, 1943, 1–2, 10–12.
74. See, for example, Memo, Kuter to Arnold, May 12, 1943.

cal system was inherently inadequate. Too few suitable ships remained to Italy by 1943 to support Tunisia adequately; the loss of a comparatively small number of vessels therefore quickly pitched *Heeresgruppe Afrika* into logistical crisis. There was, moreover, a strategic asymmetry between belligerents that greatly favored the Allied side: The Axis' supply lines were open to attack while those of the Allies were virtually exempt because of Germany's lack of strategic bombers. The Anglo-Americans were therefore able to go on the offensive even before they had general air superiority over Tunisia. The *Luftwaffe* was forced to divide and redivide its aircraft in an ultimately futile attempt to protect convoys, ports, and airfields from a foe who could usually concentrate his aircraft to win local air superiority. From ULTRA, finally, Tedder and his colleagues had essentially complete information about the movements of the enemy's convoys through the constricted channels in the minefields of the Strait of Sicily.

Chapter 2

The Sicilian Campaign
July–August 1943

Having driven the Axis from Tunisia, the Allies invaded Sicily on July 10, 1943. There ensued five weeks of heavy fighting. Throughout, Allied airmen dominated the skies but failed in their attempts to block the reinforcement and supply of the island's garrison. In August, all the German defenders of Sicily and many of the Italian withdrew safely across the Strait of Messina with most of their equipment despite efforts of the Allied air forces to stop the retreat. Apart from the resourcefulness of the Germans, there were many reasons for the success of Operation *LEHRGANG*, as the evacuation was called. The Allies' bad luck and faulty evaluation of intelligence were not the least of these. But the fundamental reason for the embarrassing finale of the invasion of Sicily was the failure of the Allied commanders to view the interdiction of a German retreat from the island as a fundamental strategic requirement that had to be integrated into the plans of all three services. The failure to do so placed entire responsibility for stopping the retreat on the air forces. For this reason, a mistaken decision made on August 11 by Air Vice Marshal Coningham of the Northwest African Tactical Air Force—to release the B–17s of the Strategic Air Force from their commitment to help with the mission of interdiction—had irretrievable consequences.

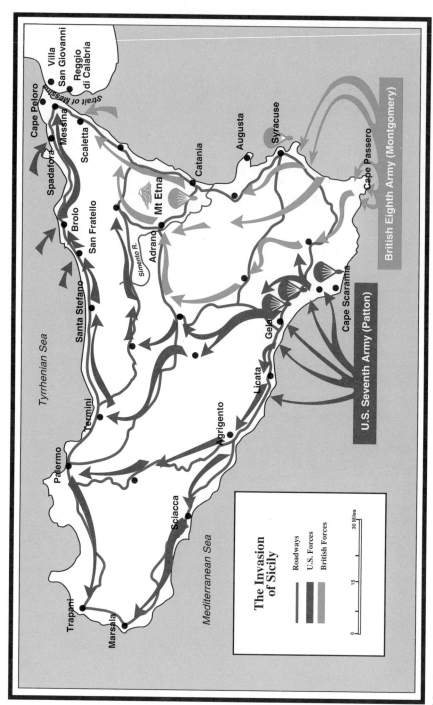

The Invasion
of Sicily

Roadways
U.S. Forces
British Forces

0   15   30 Miles

British Eighth Army (Montgomery)

U.S. Seventh Army (Patton)

Villa
San Giovanni

Reggio
di Calabria

Cape Peloro

Messina

Scaletta

Spadafora

Strait of Messina

Catania

Augusta

Syracuse

Mt Etna

Cape Passero

Brolo

San Fratello

Adrano

Simeto R.

Santa Stefano

Cape Scarama

Termini

Gela

Licata

Tyrrhenian Sea

Palermo

Agrigento

Sciacca

Mediterranean Sea

Trapani

Marsala

Map 3.

T̲he decision to invade Sicily was made
when Prime Minister Winston S. Churchill and President Franklin D.
Roosevelt met with the Anglo-American Combined Chiefs of Staff at Casablanca in January 1943. Though in accord with the British preference
for peripheral attrition of the Axis, the Sicilian operation, code named
HUSKY, was no more the product of a long-term strategy than TORCH,
which had resulted from the American failure to persuade the British
that an early invasion of France was feasible. For HUSKY, the controlling
circumstance was the unanticipated rigor of TORCH. The Allies had
hoped for what Churchill called "the peaceful occupation" of French
Africa; they had planned for a campaign of no more than several weeks.
But the Axis' prodigal investment in Tunisia so belied these expectations
that at Casablanca the conferees learned that the final offensive could
not start before March and would require no less than 500,000 men.[1]

TORCH had thus ensured that there could be no invasion of France
before mid-1944. How then to maintain pressure on the Axis and to employ the great force assembled in Africa? The invasion of Sicily commended itself to the Americans because it promised ultimately to free
shipping for their cherished objective, the invasion of France. Sicily's position athwart the Mediterranean—ninety miles from Africa and but two
from Italy—had required that Allied convoys to Egypt and the Far East
sail south around the Cape of Good Hope. The long detour around Africa represented an effective loss of shipping that the opening of the
Mediterranean promised to relieve.[2]

---

1. Albert N. Garland and Howard McGaw Smyth, with Martin Blumenson,
Sicily and the Surrender of Italy [U.S. Army in World War II: The Mediterranean Theater of Operations] (Washington, 1965), 1–2.
    2. *Ibid.*

The British needed no convincing. The proposed invasion of Sicily accorded with their desire to weaken the Axis through attritional struggles in areas of secondary importance before the coup de grâce of cross-channel invasion. They anticipated that the fall of Sicily would draw German divisions from France and perhaps Russia to guard against Allied moves against Sardinia, the Balkans, or the Italian mainland. They thought it possible that the conquest of Sicily might even occasion the fall of the Italian dictator Benito Mussolini and the diversion of still more German divisions to occupy Italy. These hopes the Americans shared, though with them they counted for less than the anticipated increased availability of shipping.[3]

The decision to invade Sicily marked the limit of Allied understanding at Casablanca regarding operations in the Mediterranean. The Americans, restive at the delay in invading France, were anxious that HUSKY should mark a halt in that theater. The British, more opportunistic in their approach to strategy and less anxious for a final decision upon the fields of France, intimated an invasion of Italy if the Sicilian enterprise prospered greatly.[4]

Planning for HUSKY began in February and continued throughout the spring. Some knowledge of Sicily's geography is necessary for an understanding of how the operation evolved. The island has roughly the shape of a triangle, the base of which, the eastern coast, is about 120 miles in length. The two sides, the northern and southern coasts, are each about 175 miles long. In the northeastern angle stands the city of Messina, separated from the mainland by the Strait of Messina, which at its narrowest point is about two miles in width. Allied supremacy on the sea and in the air made the strait the corridor through which the forces of the Axis on Sicily had to be supplied—and their only route of escape in defeat. (*Map 3*)

A landing around Messina to cut off the Axis garrison was considered and rejected by the Allied planners. The strait lay beyond the range of their tactical aircraft, and the Royal Navy, remembering the disastrous Dardanelles campaign of 1915, declined to hazard its ships against shores believed heavily fortified. Nor would a landing at Messina address at an early moment the threat of Axis air power. For the Axis' airdromes on Sicily were largely clustered around Palermo and Catania, neither of which was close to Messina. Remembering how aircraft based in Sicily had dominated the Mediterranean for much of the war, the officers who controlled the first stages of planning for HUSKY resolved that Palermo

---

3. *Ibid.*
4. *Ibid.*

and Catania should, with their airfields, be captured within several days of the initial landing. Their determination to capture these port cities was reinforced by the great uncertainty that surrounded the technique, yet in its infancy, of supplying armies over the beach. The plan that finally resulted from these considerations called for widely separated landings, one set clustered near Palermo on the northern coast, the other around Syracuse on the eastern shore.[5]

Here matters stood until April when General Sir Bernard Law Montgomery, theretofore closely occupied with the closing stages of the Tunisian Campaign, had a chance to study the plans for HUSKY. He objected strenuously to the plan for widely separated landings. The Italian garrison on Sicily was large, but the planners had tended to discount it because of the poor showing of the Italians in Africa. "Never was there a greater error," wrote Montgomery. He observed that some Italians had fought well in Tunisia, and ventured that more would do so as the war approached their home shores. If the Italians did resist strenuously, he continued, the invasion might be defeated in detail because the two landing forces could not reinforce each other.[6]

As a result of Montgomery's objections, the plan for HUSKY was entirely recast. The whole force was now to come ashore around Cape Passero, Sicily's southernmost point. The Western Task Force, the American Seventh Army under the command of Lt. Gen. George S. Patton, was to land along a stretch of the southern coast between the small port of Licata and Cape Scaramia. The Eastern Task Force, the British Eighth Army under Montgomery, would land on the eastern side of the island, the left edge of its sector falling on Cape Passero. Each force's sector was about forty miles long, while twenty miles separated the right flank of the Western Task Force from the left flank of the Eastern. Eight divisions, or nearly 150,000 men, were to land in the first three days of the invasion; the invading force would number 478,000 before the end of the campaign. D-day was set for July 10—a compromise between the desire of the naval commanders for a dark night and the need of paratroopers leading the invasion for some moonlight.[7]

Eisenhower's deputy, General Sir Harold Alexander, commanded the Fifteenth Army Group, which comprised the Anglo-American forces poised to invade Sicily. The plan of attack reflected Alexander's judgment that the American infantry were too inexperienced to be entrusted with demanding tasks. It directed that the British Eighth Army should

---

5. *Ibid.*, 58–59; S.W.C. Pack, *Operation "Husky": The Allied Invasion of Sicily* (New York, 1977), 27–32.
6. Garland *et al., Sicily and the Surrender of Italy,* 58–61.
7. *Ibid.*, 62–63; Pack, *Operation "Husky,"* 33–41.

advance along the eastern coast toward Messina, capturing en route the major ports of Syracuse, Augusta, and Catania, while the American Seventh Army protected its flank. As the American sector had only two small ports, Licata and Gela, logistical difficulties threatened a further diminishment of the Seventh Army's role. The Americans deeply resented the prospect of playing a humble role while the British, like the Romans before them, went on to glory as conquerors of the ancient city of Syracuse.[8]

Both Air Chief Marshal Sir Arthur W. Tedder, commander of HUSKY's air forces, and Admiral Sir Andrew B. Cunningham, the naval leader, had reservations of a more substantial nature. They both regretted the decision to forego the airfields at Catania and Palermo as early objectives. Order-of-battle intelligence from ULTRA indicated that the enemy was concentrating his air force on Sardinia, Sicily, and Pantelleria, and that as many as 795 aircraft, 545 of them German, might attack the invasion fleet.[9] To meet this danger, the Allies resolved to capture Pantelleria before invading Sicily. Only from this island, halfway between Tunisia and Sicily, could fighters cover the invasion. Further to diminish the aerial danger to the invasion, the attacks upon Sicilian airdromes begun during the Tunisian Campaign were to be continued and intensified. There were also to be raids against German air bases as far afield as Sardinia, Italy, and the Aegean Islands to disguise Allied intentions and to destroy aircraft that might be transferred to oppose HUSKY. The Allied air forces, finally, laid plans for the early occupation of captured Sicilian airfields by Allied squadrons.[10]

In May, the incessant raids on their airfields in Sicily and Sardinia drove the Germans to remove their bombers to the Italian mainland. On June 12, Allied bombers began a focused effort to drive German fighters from their bases in western Sicily. Fragmentation bombs soon took a heavy toll of the pursuit planes, as the island's rough terrain made for cramped airdromes on which it was difficult to disperse aircraft properly. The Allies later found the island's airfields littered with the wreckage of about 1,000 airplanes, many of them the victims of bombers. When German pilots did manage to loft from their cratered fields to attack the American B-17s, they found their numbers too few and their aircraft too lightly armed.[11] Neither the German nor the Italian air force was able to

---

8. Garland *et al., Sicily and the Surrender of Italy*, 88–91.

9. F.H. Hinsely *et al., British Intelligence in the Second World War*, 5 vols (London, 1979–), vol 3, pt 1, 71.

10. *Ibid.*, 63, 69–70.

11. Air Historical Branch of the British Air Ministry (AHB/BAM), "The Campaign in Italy," pt 1, chap 3 in "High Level *Luftwaffe* Policy in the Mediterranean, May–June 1943," and "Air Defense Against the Allied Landing in

intervene when the Allies subjected Pantelleria to severe aerial bombardment in late May and early June. The island's demoralized garrison surrendered on June 11, even before it detected the approach of British assault craft.[12]

The Allies learned from signals intelligence that as early as February the Germans had concluded that an invasion of Sicily was likely to follow the fall of Tunisia; they had all but ruled out an invasion of the Balkans. To shake this certitude, the British began an ambitious program of strategic deception, Operation MINCEMEAT. Documents purporting to detail an invasion of Greece and hinting at one of Sardinia were planted on a body made to seem that of a staff officer killed in a plane crash at sea. Carefully placed in a current that bore it to Spain, the corpse was recovered and the contents of the bogus documents duly communicated to the Germans. Commandos not long after attacked radar stations in Crete to lend verisimilitude to the deception. Sardinia and Greece were well chosen for their roles in MINCEMEAT, as both were plausible objectives. Sardinia would have been an excellent base from which to invade either Italy or southern France; from there, moreover, Allied aircraft could range over Italy and southern Germany. For these reasons the German Commander in Chief, South, Field Marshal Albert Kesselring, had for a while thought Sardinia the probable Allied objective. Hitler expected an attack on the Balkans for reasons equally plausible: The area was vital to the German economy and its peoples disposed to the Allied cause.[13]

The Germans were never wholly taken in by MINCEMEAT, and by May, Kesselring and several Italian officers were quite certain that Sicily was the next Allied target. But some uncertainty prevailed in both the Italian and German high commands until D-day, July 9. The resulting dispersal of forces was most helpful to the Allies. One German division went to Sardinia and another went to Greece together with several shiploads of Italy's best troops. There was a similar diffusion of air power: Between May 14 and July 3 Germany increased the number of its aircraft in the Mediterranean theater from 820 to 1,280. But the strength of the

---

Sicily," ca. 1947–1948 [prepared by General Paul Deichmann and Colonel (no first name given) Christ, respectively], Translation VII/94, 1950, K512.621, pp 1–2 in both documents.

12. Garland *et al.*, *Sicily and the Surrender of Italy*, 70–72; AHB/BAM, "R.A.F. Narrative (First Draft): The Sicilian Campaign, June–August 1943," 00895773, 38–39, 43–44. For a graphic description of the enfeebled state of the *Luftwaffe* during the Sicilian Campaign, see Johannes Steinhoff's memoir, *The Straits of Messina: Diary of a Fighter Commander*, translated by Peter and Betty Ross (London, 1971).

13. Hinsley *et al.*, *British Intelligence in the Second World War*, vol 3, pt 1, 78–79; Garland *et al.*, *Sicily and the Surrender of Italy*, 44–46, 64–65; Hugh Pond, *Sicily* (London, 1962), 19–20.

squadrons based in Sicily and southern Italy only rose from 615 to 635, most reinforcements having gone to Sardinia, Greece, and northern Italy.[14] The Northwest African Air Forces on July 5, by contrast, controlled 4,920 aircraft (excluding gliders). About 2,900 of these were fighters and bombers.[15]

The neglect of Sicily's defenses, however, was not total. The Italians had begun to improve the island's fortifications in March, although seemingly little was accomplished. As most of the Italian units on Sicily were poorly equipped and dispirited, Mussolini, having originally rejected an offer of five German divisions for the defense of Italy, agreed on May 22 to accept four. By early June two of these—the *Hermann Göring Panzer Parachute Division* and the *15th Panzer Grenadier Division*—had reached the island. The defense of Sicily was entrusted to General Alfredo Guzzoni. The Italian *Sixth Army* comprised six coastal divisions, two coastal brigades, one coastal regiment, and four mobile divisions. The German infantry numbered 32,000; the Italian, 200,000. As the Italian coastal units were of particularly low quality, Guzzoni's plan of defense called for an early counterattack by his six mobile divisions, four Italian and two German. The coastal units, unfit for maneuver, were to hold in place long enough to allow the mobile divisions, waiting inland in reserve, to counterattack before the invaders could establish a firm foothold.[16]

A rapid buildup of the German forces was crucial, for it was clear that the two German divisions, with their better equipment and greater fighting spirit, were of disproportionate importance. Although the *Luftwaffe* and the *Kriegsmarine* had long been active in Sicily, the first units of the army did not arrive until June. Because of the damage done to Italy's railroads by Allied bombing, the Germans had to move men and supplies into southern Italy primarily by truck. The Allies also bombed the two major highways of southern Italy, but without much effect.[17]

---

14. British Air Ministry, *The Rise and Fall of the German Air Force (1933-1945)* (London, 1948), 258–59; Vice Adm Friedrich Ruge, "The Evacuation of Sicily," MS X-111, Record Group (RG) 338, National Archives and Records Administration (NARA), 5. The Italian Air Force had about 300 fighters and 150 bombers in Sicily, Sardinia, and southern Italy. But they suffered from a very low rate of serviceability and played no significant role in the campaign. AHB/BAM, "Sicilian Campaign," 63.

15. Daily Status Report, Northwest African Allied Air Forces, Jul 5, 1943, 612.245-1.

16. Garland *et al., Sicily and the Surrender of Italy*, 73–83.

17. Ruge, "Evacuation of Sicily," 17–18. Ruge states, and an Allied study confirms, that the railroad lines on the mainland leading into Calabria were often cut and service was interrupted. British Air Ministry to General Spaatz, Dec 29, 1943, enclosing Rpt, by Professor Solly Zuckerman, "Air Attacks on Rail and Road Communications," 519.425-1, 9–16.

In the Strait of Messina the Germans maintained a system of marine transport separate from that of the Italians. Sicily had been served in peace by six large train ferries, each capable of carrying about thirty rail cars, passenger or freight. They had, however, proved vulnerable to Allied bombing, as had the docks and rail sidings they required in Messina and the mainland ports of Reggio di Calabria and Villa San Giovanni. Nor were the ferries sufficiently flexible in their operation to cope with a highly variable flow of convoys. Each of the German services, accordingly, had organized its own transport across the strait. The craft most employed was the Siebel ferry, a motorized raft constructed by linking two bridging pontoons with a deck. Also present were assault boats—large motorboats—and several varieties of landing ships similar to the LCIs (landing craft, infantry) and LCTs (landing craft, tanks) of the Allies. The Italians organized a transport system of their own using the surviving train ferries, several small steamers, motorized rafts, and motor torpedo boats.[18]

The separate transport systems of the German services did not function well. Early in the reinforcement of Sicily, the commander of the German naval forces in Italy, Vice Admiral Friedrich Ruge, arranged for a single officer to be responsible for the coordination of all German shipments across the strait. Chosen was Captain Baron Gustav von Liebenstein, a man of exceptional energy and ability. Before he became Sea Transport Leader, Messina Strait, the several German supply systems had been hard put to ship 100 tons a day. Von Liebenstein set a target of 1,000 tons for his unified system and exceeded it. His principal innovation was to direct that trucks from the mainland be ferried over with their cargos. Previously, the cargos had been unloaded for transshipment, then loaded on other trucks when they arrived in Sicily. The new arrangement saved time and best used the Germans' limited supply of motor vehicles.[19]

The Allies attempted to impede the reinforcement of Sicily by bombing heavily the ports of Messina, Reggio di Calabria, and Villa San Giovanni. The bombing began in May and peaked between June 18 and 30, when the Northwest African Air Forces' heavy bombers (B-17s) flew 317 sorties against these targets, and its medium bombers (B-25s and B-26s) flew 566. Heavy bombers (B-24s) of the Ninth Air Force flew 107 sorties. The effect of these raids on the German buildup was, as Vice Admiral Ruge later wrote, "insignificant."[20] By the end of May, the Germans

---

18. Ruge, "Evacuation of Sicily," 14–17, 31–32.
19. *Ibid.*, 32–33, 40–41.
20. Wesley Frank Craven and James Lea Cate, eds, *The Army Air Forces in World War II*, 7 vols (Chicago, 1948–57; Washington, 1983), vol 2: *Europe*:

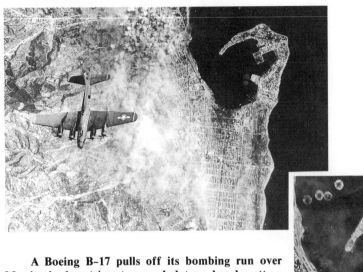

A Boeing B–17 pulls off its bombing run over Messina harbor *(above)*; seconds later a bomb pattern from the raider speckles the shoreline and harbor area *(right)*.

had ceased to use the ports, and the Italians had largely done so too. The traffic across the strait employed fourteen improvised facilities on the beaches of the mainland and twelve on the Sicilian strand. At these places there were portable jetties for the Siebel ferries which, unlike the landing craft and assault boats, were not designed for beaching. Allied intelligence was slow to note the transfer of operations from the ports to the beaches.[21]

The antiaircraft defenses of the Strait of Messina were formidable. By the closing phase of the Sicilian Campaign, they may well have been the strongest in Europe. But there was one great weakness. None of the guns defending the strait could engage aircraft flying at more than 20,000 feet. The Axis' transport system was therefore defenseless against the American B–17s, which in the cloudless skies of the Italian summer could bomb from nearly 30,000 feet. The Germans had designed and built a gun effective against the B–17 at its maximum bombing altitude, the 88-mm *Flak 41*. But at Hitler's orders, the entire first run of production had been sent to Tunisia and there lost.[22]

TORCH to POINTBLANK, *August 1942 to December 1943*, 434–47; Ruge, "Evacuation of Sicily," 42–43.

21. Ruge, "Evacuation of Sicily," 35–37; Gustav von Liebenstein, "German Ferrying Traffic in Messina Straits," app B to *ibid.*, 4.

22. Ruge, "Evacuation of Sicily," 23; Deichmann, "Campaign in Italy,"

The dispersion of the landing sites was designed to address this weakness. As Ruge later wrote, "The danger from heavy bombing was countered to a sufficient degree by leaving the ports and loosening up the targets. It was next to impossible, even with exceptionally heavy attacks, to knock out enough ferries and to block the traffic effectively."[23] The wide dispersion of the landing sites presented a problem of its own, though not one the Allies could exploit before they had seized landing fields in Sicily: The sites were so widely scattered that the antiaircraft guns, many as they were, could not protect them all adequately. The sites insufficiently covered would therefore have been vulnerable to low-altitude attack by fighter bombers, had any been based within range of the strait. But by the time the Allies had bases in Sicily, the Germans had largely obviated this danger by equipping their ferrying craft with antiaircraft armament and barrage balloons.

The failure of the Allies to stop the traffic from the mainland condemned them to bloody battle. Between early June and early August, the Germans shipped nearly 60,000 men, 13,700 vehicles, and 40,000 tons of supplies to Sicily from Italy.[24]

On the afternoon of July 9, 1943, the largest armada in the history of war assembled in the waters off Malta: 160,000 men, 14,000 vehicles, 600 tanks, 2,500 transports and 750 warships, plus landing craft. That night, as the fleet moved toward Sicily, American paratroopers and British glider units landed on the island. Although widely scattered by high winds and poor navigation, the airborne forces disrupted Axis communications and spread panic among the Italians. The landings from the sea began before dawn and met little resistance. As General Alexander subsequently wrote, the Italian coastal divisions "disintegrated almost without firing a shot and the field divisions, when they were met, were also driven like chaff before the wind." Thus the first day of battle saw responsibility for the defense of Sicily fall upon two German divisions, neither battle-tested.[25]

Elements of the *Hermann Göring Panzer Parachute Division*, striking on July 11 at American troops who had landed near Gela, delivered

---

3–4. Garland is incorrect to state that the two batteries of 170-mm guns that the Germans had in Calabria for shore defense could be used against aircraft. Garland *et al., Sicily and the Surrender of Italy*, 376.

23. Ruge, "Evacuation of Sicily," 37.

24. Carlo D'Este, *Bitter Victory: The Battle for Sicily, 1943* (New York, 1988), 547.

25. Pond, *Sicily*, 43. For a brief account of the ground fighting in Sicily, see B.H. Liddell Hart, *History of the Second World War* (New York, 1971), 433–46. For a detailed account, consult Garland *et al., Sicily and the Surrender of Italy*, 147ff.

the only dangerous counterattack on the landing beaches. Tanks leading the assault were within several hundred yards of the sea when naval gunfire drove them back. The British landing was unopposed save for the fainthearted resistance of the Italian coastal units. The *Luftwaffe* flew 275 to 300 sorties daily against the Allied fleet from July 10 through July 12, and sank several vessels. The Allies captured some airfields on July 10, and from these the Northwest African Tactical Air Force soon flew as many as 1,200 sorties a day in support of the ground forces. During the first four days of the invasion, the *Luftwaffe* lost about 150 aircraft, its sortie rate declining to fewer than 150 daily.[26]

Within several days Montgomery had cleared the southeastern corner of Sicily and struck out for Catania. His advance was stopped at the Simeto River several miles from the city. British glider troops and commandos had seized two essential bridges, but were driven back by a brigade of the German *1st Parachute Division* that had fortuitously jumped into Sicily at just the right place to blunt Montgomery's thrust. The bridges were recaptured several days later, but in the meantime the Germans had assembled a force sufficient to block the direct route to Messina.

Frustrated in this fashion, Montgomery attempted a circuitous advance through the hills around Mount Etna, but the Germans stopped him at Adrano. This check gave Patton the opportunity to graduate from the role of flank guard. Opposed by few Germans, he was able to drive north to Palermo, which fell on July 22. From there the Seventh Army advanced along the northern coast, steadily pursuing the retreating Germans until it also ran into stiffening resistance around Mount Etna which, with associated terrain, dominates the eastern portion of Sicily. The arrival from the mainland of elements of the *29th Panzer Grenadier Division* had made it possible for the Germans to construct a more or less continuous line of resistance across Sicily.

In the middle of the battle, General Hans Hube arrived to command the German forces, which had been organized into the *XIV Panzer Corps*. General Guzzoni continued in nominal command of the Axis forces, but Hube politely ignored the Italian in practice. His mission was to lead an orderly withdrawal from Sicily, and the Germans thought it wise to keep this intention to themselves because they believed Italian security lax. The proximate cause for the decision to withdraw was the deposition of Mussolini by the Fascist Grand Council on July 25. Hitler, fearing treachery, ordered an immediate retreat from Sicily on the day of Mussolini's fall. Assurances of loyalty from the new government of Mar-

---

26. AHB/BAM, "Sicilian Campaign," 51–52, 61–62.

shal Pietro Bagdolio soon led him to change his mind somewhat: The evacuation of Sicily was now to be delayed as long as possible.[27]

The *Oberkommando der Wehrmacht* (*OKW*) had committed German divisions to the defense of Sicily primarily to gain time for the improvement of Italy's defenses. Hube, as noted, had arrived in Sicily with instructions to anticipate an eventual withdrawal from the island. The *OKW* reserved for itself to order the evacuation. Hube, however, feared that instructions from Berlin would arrive too late, and that again, as in Tunis, men would be uselessly sacrificed. He took it upon himself in July to return to Italy every support unit that could be spared from Sicily; support elements of the *1st Parachute Division* and the *29th Panzer Grenadier Division* had never been sent to the island.[28] Kesselring apparently shared Hube's fears. Concerned by signs that Italy would forsake her alliance with Germany, he declared at a commanders' conference on July 27 that the forces in Sicily should prepare for withdrawal. On August 2, he approved an evacuation plan, *LEHRGANG*, devised by Hube's chief of staff, Col. Gogislaw von Bonin. On August 7 the British finally took Adrano with the support of the Seventh Army, imperiling the German retreat to Messina. And on the night of the same day the Americans had staged a small landing at San Fratello behind the lines of the *29th Panzer Grenadier Division* in an attempt to cut off the German retreat to Messina along the northern coast. Although contained, the assault quickened the pulses of the German commanders, whose worst fear was an amphibious "end run" in force. The next day, Kesselring gave the order for *LEHRGANG*.[29] Once the Germans had decided on an early withdrawal, they notified the Italians, who had laid plans for their own escape.

On August 10 General Hube notified his commanders of Kesselring's decision to begin *LEHRGANG*. The chief concern of the Germans was Allied air power. The army feared that movement by day would be impossible. The Navy was somewhat more optimistic, believing, as Ruge recorded sarcastically, that it would be possible to cross in the early morning, "immediately after lunch and late in the afternoon, taking Anglo-Saxon habits into account." The army prevailed, and it was de-

27. Garland *et al., Sicily and the Surrender of Italy*, 306–7.
28. Gogislaw von Bonin, "Critique of the Italian Campaign, 1943–1944," MS T–2, RG 338, NARA, 149–51; Ruge, "Evacuation of Sicily," 43–46.
29. Garland *et al., Sicily and the Surrender of Italy*, 374–75. The German commanders later asserted that a landing in force behind their lines could certainly have cut off their retreat to Messina. See, for example, Walter Fries, "The Battle of Sicily," MR T–2, RG 338, 39–40.

cided to withdraw under cover of darkness. The Germans were resigned to abandoning much of their heavy equipment.[30]

LEHRGANG was scheduled to begin on the night of August 11, the first of five nights on which crossings were planned. The retreat was to employ the ferry routes that von Liebenstein had developed during the campaign. The plan took every advantage of Sicily's geography. By withdrawing into the northeastern corner of the Sicilian triangle, the Germans would have a progressively narrower front to defend. Thus could they maintain a resistance with ever-diminishing forces and, it was hoped, delay the Allies' discovery of the exodus. Hube planned to withdraw his forces to five successive lines of resistance. After each displacement, the divisions were to release up to two-thirds of their troops for movement toward the points of embarkation, where the ferries were to be prepared to move 8,000 men across the strait each night.[31] The successful implementation of this plan probably would not have been possible but for the rugged Sicilian topography which in many places allowed handfuls of determined men to hold a position against a numerous foe.

The number of vessels available to the Germans varied somewhat throughout *LEHRGANG*. The maximum was eighty-six on August 16. All were small craft—the same types used by the German transport system throughout the battle for Sicily. The narrowness of the Strait of Messina offset their lack of capacity. The Italians, who coordinated their plans with those of the Germans, were less well provided with vessels. They used the one surviving train ferry—a large vessel that could carry 3,000 men—together with two small steamers, four motor rafts, and some motor torpedo boats. No Italian vessel could carry vehicles, as could the German landing craft and Siebel ferries.[32]

Crucial to *LEHRGANG'S* success were the defenses against attack by sea and air. (*Map 4*) In late July, Colonel Ernst Baade had become Commandant, Messina Strait, and assumed responsibility for all German units assigned to defend the passage. For protection against large warships, he had two batteries of 170-mm guns with ranges of ten miles. He also had four Italian batteries of 280-mm mortars and two of 150-mm guns. These last, however, the Germans believed useless because of obsolete fire-direction apparatus.[33] The number of antiaircraft guns guarding

---

30. Ruge, "Evacuation of Sicily," 47–48.
31. Garland *et al., Sicily and the Surrender of Italy*, 377–78; von Bonin, "Critique of the Italian Campaign," 155; Fries, "Battle of Sicily," 36.
32. Gustav von Liebenstein, "Final Report as Supplement to the War Diary of Sea Transport Leader Messina Straits," Enclosure A to Ruge, "Evacuation of Sicily," 27; Samuel Eliot Morison, *History of United States Naval Operations in World War II*, 15 vols (Boston, 1952–62), vol. 9: *Sicily-Salerno-Anzio*, 212.
33. Ruge, "Evacuation of Sicily," 39–40.

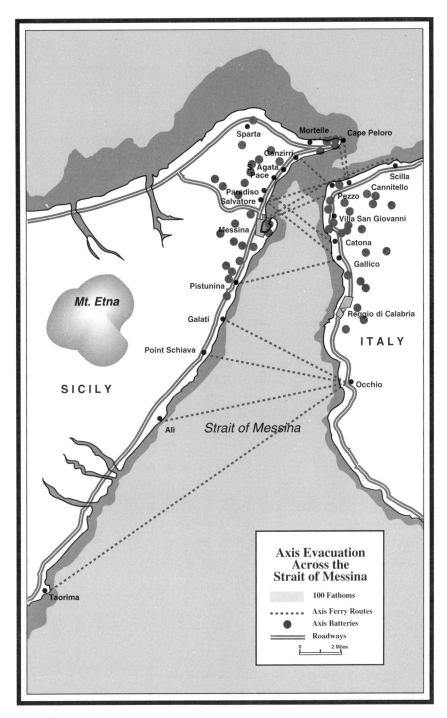

Sparta · Mortelle · Cape Peloro

Ganzirri

Agata
Pace

Scilla

Paradiso · Cannitello
Salvatore

Pezzo

Villa San Giovanni

Messina

Catona

Gallico

Pistunina

Galati

Reggio di Calabria

Point Schiava

ITALY

Occhio

Ali

Strait of Messina

Mt. Etna

SICILY

Taorima

**Axis Evacuation
Across the
Strait of Messina**

100 Fathoms

Axis Ferry Routes

Axis Batteries

Roadways

0   2 Miles

Map 4.

the strait is uncertain, but it was large. Rear Admiral Pietro Barone, who directed the Italian evacuation, reported that there were 150 German 88-mm and Italian 90-mm guns, all capable of engaging surface as well as aerial targets. Augmenting these dual-purpose weapons were many smaller caliber antiaircraft weapons such as the four-barreled 20-mm *Flakvierling 28*. This weapon, frequently mounted on ferry craft, was particularly deadly against low-flying aircraft because of its high rate of fire and its traversability. An authoritative German document of August 14 reports the number of German antiaircraft guns as 333. As this figure excludes the Italian guns, it is possible that the commonly cited figure of 500 weapons approximates the true strength of the strait's antiaircraft defenses.[34] Allied flyers believed that this was "the greatest AA [antiaircraft artillery] concentration in the world."[35] To the last, however, there were no guns capable of engaging high-flying bombers.

The first sign of an impending withdrawal from Sicily came from documents found on the body of a German officer killed by the Eighth Army on or slightly before July 31. While the documents gave no date for a retreat, they showed that one was being planned.[36] ULTRA furnished more evidence the next day. A decrypt of August 1 revealed that each German division in Sicily had a ferry point assigned to it and that ferrying for "practice and experimental purposes" had occurred the previous night. This message was followed on August 5 by another from von Liebenstein in which he requested more barrage balloons and improved lighting for the ferrying points.[37] On August 4, the G–2 Section of Allied Force Headquarters (AFHQ) found "no adequate indications that the enemy intends an immediate evacuation of the Messina bridgehead." But the information from ULTRA had already persuaded Alexander that a German retreat was imminent.[38] On August 3, he signaled Tedder and Admiral Cunningham that "indications suggest that the Germans are making preparations for withdrawal to the mainland when this becomes necessary. . . . We must be in a position to take immediate ad-

---

34. Capt S.W. Roskill, *The War at Sea, 1939–1945*, 3 vols (London, 1954–), vol 3: *The Offensive, 1st June–31st May 1944*, 145–46; Garland *et al., Sicily and the Surrender of Italy*, 375n; AHB/BAM, "State of Flak and Ammunition on 14 August, 1943," in "Extracts from War Diary of Fortress Commandant, Messina Strait (Colonel Baade), 14 July to 2nd August, 1943," Translation VII/161, 1956, K512.612, 17.

35. Hist, 79th Fighter Grp, August 1943, 13. See also Hist, 57th Fighter Grp, 1943, 9; Hist, 340th Bombardment Group, 1943, n.p.

36. D'Este, *Bitter Victory*, 527.

37. Hinsley *et al., British Intelligence in the Second World War*, vol 3, pt 1, 96.

38. AFHQ Weekly Intel Summary, No. 50 (Aug 10, 1943), 621.607, AF/HO.

vantage of such a situation by using full weight of the Naval and Air Power. You have no doubt co-ordinated plans to meet this contingency . . . ."[39]

Cunningham and Tedder had in fact laid no plans for dealing with a German evacuation, even though there was no prospect of the Germans' being overrun on the ground. As late as August 8 the Seventh and Eighth Armies were, respectively, seventy-five and fifty miles from Messina. Determined resistance and the skillful use of mines and demolitions had slowed the Allied advance to a snail's pace. There remained the possibility of landings by air or sea behind the Axis' lines. Montgomery adamantly opposed the former course, apparently because of the failures of several small British airborne raids against German communications. In his characteristically methodical way, he insisted upon adhering to his original plan of advancing around Mount Etna. Patton, anxious to beat the British to Messina, attempted a series of small amphibious landings behind enemy lines to block the German retreat along the northern coast. The first, as related above, was made at San Fratello on August 8; the second came at Brolo on August 11; and the third, at Spadafora on August 16. All failed to trap the Germans. The first landing was made on the wrong beach; the force for the second was too small and was easily contained by the enemy, while the third came at a place Patton had already passed on his march to Messina. A British landing on the southern coast that the long-reluctant Montgomery had mounted on August 16 also came ashore west of the retreating Germans.

On receiving Alexander's request for action to prevent an evacuation, Cunningham signaled to both Tedder and Alexander that he would increase the activity of his motor torpedo boats, but the admiral insisted that action by larger vessels had to await the silencing of coastal batteries by aerial attack. "As the coastal batteries are mopped up it will be possible for surface forces to operate further into the Straits." His position was, and the American naval commander agreed, that Allied ships lacked the spotting and ranging devices needed to engage the batteries.[40] Cunningham, like so many British naval officers of his generation, remembered the Dardanelles. He did not fail to note that the Strait of Messina resembled the entrance to the Black Sea, and feared to bring his ships within range of the Italo-German shore batteries.[41] Tedder agreed that

---

39. AHB/BAM, "Sicilian Campaign," 80.
40. AHB/BAM, "The R.A.F. in Maritime War," vol 7: "Mediterranean Reconquest and the Submarine War, May 1943 to May 1944," pt 1, 203; Morison, *Sicily-Salerno-Anzio*, 216, 216n.
41. It is difficult to say at this remove how justified Cunningham's fears were. Colonel von Bonin thought the coastal defenses inadequate. Perhaps with greater authority, Vice Admiral Ruge and the Axis high command generally were

the suppression of the batteries was imperative and declared that it would be undertaken "at once." But nothing in the sources, Allied or Axis, shows that the batteries were attacked, and they certainly remained undamaged.[42] Remarks that Cunningham made both at the time and subsequently suggest that the admiral thought LEHRGANG unstoppable. The way in which he dispersed the fleet on a variety of tasks also indicates that he had decided early that using the fleet to halt the evacuation would be pointless.[43] British torpedo boats made the sole effort at naval interdiction. Venturing into the strait at night, they were quickly repulsed by searchlight-equipped batteries.[44]

Because of the inability of the ground forces to impede the German withdrawal and the reluctance of the naval forces to attempt to do so, the burden of stopping LEHRGANG fell upon Air Vice Marshal Arthur Coningham, commander of the Tactical Air Force. At least several airmen urged early consideration of measures to prevent a German exodus. The commander of the Desert Air Force, Air Vice Marshal Harry Broadhurst, advised Coningham on August 3 that an evacuation might be imminent, noting that "the quite exceptional flak on both sides of the Strait of Messina will need, I think, the use of [B–17 Flying] Fortresses."[45] Coningham replied pessimistically on August 4:

> But the night is our problem, and though the increasing moon will help, only a positive physical barrier, such as the navy can provide, would be effective. The difficulties of operating naval forces in the narrow part of the Strait is obvious and I do not see how we can hope for the same proportion of success as at Cap Bon.[46]

---

not greatly worried by the prospect of naval interference with a retreat across the Strait. Bonin, "Critique of the Italian Campaign," 148–49; Ruge, "Evacuation of Sicily," 39–40.

42. AHB/BAM, "Mediterranean Reconquest and the Submarine War," vol 7, pt 1, 204. Tedder's memoirs, which gloss over the embarrassing finale of the Sicilian Campaign, are silent about his promise to attack the batteries. *With Prejudice: The War Memoirs of Marshal of the Royal Air Force Tedder* (Boston, 1966), 453. It is possible that the experience of the bombing of Pantelleria discouraged Tedder. That island was heavily attacked for many days in most favorable circumstances shortly before HUSKY. A careful study concluded that while heavy bombardment might be expected "to destroy communications, command installations and fire control apparatus of CD [coastal defense] and AA [antiaircraft] batteries . . . [it] should not be relied upon to damage so badly a majority of the guns that they cannot be fired by direct laying sooner after bombing ceases." Staff Study, Allied Forces HQ, subj: Lessons Learned from Operations Against Pantelleria, Jul 12, 1943, Air 23/3305, 123978, Public Records Office. (Courtesy of Richard G. Davis.)

43. Morison, *Sicily-Salerno-Anzio*, 216–17.

44. *Ibid.*, 213.

45. AHB/BAM, "Sicilian Campaign," 80.

46. *Ibid.*, 81.

The same day, Tedder cabled Coningham to tell him that representatives of the Strategic Air Force (which controlled the B–17s) would be at his headquarters the following day, August 5, to discuss coordinated action against the seemingly now imminent evacuation. This represented a reversal of policy on Tedder's part, for he had ruled on August 2 that the Strategic Air Force should not help the Tactical Air Force in operations against Messina but rather concentrate on attacking Rome and Naples to drive Italy from the war.[47] Having secured the cooperation of the Strategic Air Force, Coningham issued an operating instruction on August 6 to provide for the enemy's evacuation. The order stated that the operation was imminent and predicted it would be staged under cover of darkness at the narrowest part of the Strait of Messina where antiaircraft defenses were thickest. The directive called for constant aerial surveillance of the strait to detect the operation at the earliest possible moment. British Wellington bombers of the Strategic Air Force, which specialized in night operations, were to begin bombing the probable points of embarkation north of Messina every night. (They had already begun to do so on the night of August 5.) Upon certain indications that the Germans had begun to retreat by night, formations of light and medium bombers would join the Wellingtons. Coningham also allowed for the possibility that the enemy might evacuate by day. In that event, the B–17s would swing into action: One wave of seventy-two Flying Fortresses would at 0900 attack the beaches of departure. There would follow a massive attack by fighter bombers; at 1100, a second wave of B–17s would bomb again, whereupon the fighter-bombers would return. If needed, the medium bombers of the Strategic Air Force would attack in the afternoon.[48]

On the night of August 5–6 the Wellingtons bombed beaches in the immediate vicinity of Messina.[49] On the night of August 6–7 they extended their attacks to the beaches running north along the Sicilian coast from Messina to Cape Peloro. The raids continued through the night of August 12–13, save for the night of August 7–8 when the beaches south of Messina were bombed as far as Scaletta. The attacks were all on target—the beaches were easily identifiable, even at night, and of substan-

47. AHB/BAM, "Mediterranean Reconquest and the Submarine War," vol 7, pt 1, 204, 209C. It appears that General Doolittle's concern that his crews were nearing exhaustion played a part in Tedder's decision. Craven and Cate, TORCH to POINTBLANK, 473–74.
48. Craven and Cate, TORCH to POINTBLANK, 81–82.
49. The Wellingtons operated at night because their crews had been trained to do so. British doctrines favored night bombing operations because of the heavy losses the RAF had incurred earlier in the war trying to bomb Germany by day. The British partiality for night operations in any event nicely complemented the American preference for operating by day.

tial size. In all, the Wellingtons flew 633 sorties and dropped 1,183.6 tons of bombs through the night of August 13.[50]

The Germans began their evacuation on the night of August 11–12. All went according to schedule until about 2100 hours when the operation, already slowed by the tardiness of troops in reaching the beaches, was stopped altogether when eighty-four Wellingtons loosed 159 tons of bombs, both high explosive and fragmentation. There were no casualties, but even the disciplined Germans could not continue their evacuation with bombs falling all about. The operation resumed in the early hours of August 12, but was *again* halted on the night of August 12–13 by ninety-two Wellingtons that dropped 180.25 tons of bombs between 2107 and 0445 hours. When the attacks had ceased, von Liebenstein, dangerously behind schedule, ordered the evacuation to continue throughout the day of August 13. The Germans thereafter crossed mostly by day, chiefly for fear of the Wellingtons.[51]

Even as the Wellingtons interrupted the Germans' retreat, the Allies debated among themselves whether an evacuation was occurring. Somewhat prematurely, intelligence officers of the Eighth Army concluded as early as August 8 that the retreat across the strait had begun. They based their conclusion on photographic reconnaissance showing Siebel ferries sailing empty to Sicily but returning full. Allied Force Headquarters' G–2 remained skeptical. An appreciation it published on August 10 for the week ending August 7 found the pattern of German shipping consonant with continued operations in Sicily. Notwithstanding additional decrypts of August 10 and 11 apparently related to an evacuation, the G–2 may have remained unconvinced until August 13 when there could be no further doubt.[52]

A little past 1500 on August 13, the log of the Tactical Air Force's command post stated that because of the increased shipping visible in the strait

> the evacuation is held to have begun. All fighter and fighter/bomber missions are to be stepped up and directed against ships, barges, and

---

50. Intel and Ops Summaries, Northwest African Strategic Air Force, Aug 1 through Aug 13, 1943, 615.307–1.

51. *Ibid.*, Aug 12, 13, 1943; Garland *et al., Sicily and the Surrender of Italy*, 409–10; von Liebenstein, "Final Report as Supplement to the War Diary," 26. Von Liebenstein also thought that daylight crossing was more efficient, but it took the bombing of the nights of August 11–12 and 12–13 to persuade the army to go along with his preference. AHB/BAM, "War Diary of Naval Officer-in-Charge, Sea Transport, Messina Strait," 1943, Translation VII/156, 1956, 512.621, 14.

52. Hinsley *et al., British Intelligence in the Second World War*, vol 3, pt 1, 97–98.

beaches. T.B.F. [Tactical Bomber Force] are to be taken off land targets and put on to evacuation vessels and targets. Effort is to be maximum and a greater percentage of casualties are to be expected. All informed.[53]

The Tactical Air Force was to attack alone, for in a signal to Tedder of August 11 Coningham had released the Strategic Air Force from its commitment to attack the evacuation beaches with B–17s:

It now appears clear Hun has decided to evacuate. At same time there is as yet no large scale movement of shipping by day and there seems little doubt they are [taking] and will continue to take full advantage of darkness. Even if withdrawal should develop on big scale now feel we can handle it with our own resources and naval assistance. Therefore suggest Strategic be released from possible day commitment in Messina area in order that they may be freely employed against Strategic [objectives] and exploit situation in Italy proper. Recommend continuation maximum Wellington effort.[54]

Coningham assumed reasonably—and accurately—that the Germans intended to withdraw by night. His conclusion that the Wellingtons could deal with the evacuation was also correct. That very night, and again the next, the British bombers disrupted *LEHRGANG*, putting von Liebenstein dangerously behind schedule. It is likely that Coningham's statement that "even if withdrawal should develop on a big scale [we] now feel we can handle it with our own resources" refers *not* to a reevaluation of the threat that flak in and around the strait posed to tactical aircraft, but rather to his confidence in the Wellingtons, which ever since the night of August 5 had been demonstrating their ability to strike the beaches by night.[55]

Why then did Coningham release the B–17s? He had had them on hold for nearly a week—their only operations had been to bomb various communications targets in and around Messina on August 5, 6, and 9.[56] A backlog of missions had begun to accumulate. Tedder had been pushing for one in particular—a strike on Rome in maximum strength which

---

53. AHB/BAM, "Mediterranean Reconquest and the Submarine War," vol 7, pt 1, 206.

54. *Ibid.*, 208.

55. The intelligence operational summaries of the Strategic Air Force for August 5 through 11 record that all of the Wellingtons' strikes were on target. They also state that secondary explosions and fires were observed every night. Intel and Ops Summaries, Northwest African Strategic Air Force, Aug 6 through 11, 1943, 615.3071–1.

56. AHB/BAM, "Mediterranean Reconquest and the Submarine War," vol 7, pt 1, 205A.

he believed might drive Italy from the war.[57] An urgent military reason also existed for attacking Rome: The plan to paralyze Italy's railroads in preparation for the invasion of the mainland, which was then less than a month distant, called for a major attack on the marshaling yards of the Italian capital. Coningham seems to have gambled that the Germans would not evacuate Sicily until after the raid on Rome. Given his confidence that the Germans would evacuate by night, such a bet would not have appeared unduly hazardous because the Wellingtons remained to him.

As the fortunes of war had it, *LEHRGANG* became a daylight operation on August 13 and was discovered only hours *after* the entire force of B-17s struck at Rome's marshaling yards that afternoon.[58] The bombers then had to stand down and were out of action until August 17, by which date *LEHRGANG* had ended. It is likely that several circumstances contributed to the unusually long stand-down. At this time five groups of B-24s were on loan to the Twelfth Air Force from the Eighth Air Force in England. They too mounted a major raid on August 13—to Wiener Neustadt in Austria. Thus, just as *LEHRGANG* began, the Allied strategic bombing force suffered a tremendous albeit temporary diminishment of its striking power—crews were exhausted, supplies depleted, and aircraft in need of maintenance and rearming. The Strategic Air Force's notoriously inadequate bases also had to prepare for the arrival on August 17 of the B-17s from the famous Schweinfurt-Regensburg mission. They staged from Britain, but were scheduled to go on to North Africa as part of an early effort to coordinate operations between the northern and southern theaters.[59] While no document or memoir so states explicitly—the reticence in Allied memoirs and records on these points is very

---

57. It should be noted that for all the enthusiasm of the Americans for strategic bombardment no reason exists to believe that either Spaatz or Doolittle opposed the use of the B-17s in the tactical role envisioned in Coningham's anti-evacuation plan of August 6. Spaatz, indeed, was most critical of Tedder for the latter's reluctance to use the heavy bombers tactically: "Too much insistence exists in the mind of Tedder that there be a differentiation between Tactical and Strategic Air Forces. Under certain battle conditions they should be considered as one Air Force and should be applied as was done in the case of Pantelleria." Diary of Carl A. Spaatz, Box 11, Papers of Carl A. Spaatz, Library of Congress (LC).

58. The force that raided Rome included 125 B-17s. At midnight of August 13, the Northwest African Air Forces had 187 operational B-17s (none was lost in the raid on Rome). Intel and Ops Summary, Northwest African Air Forces, Aug 13, 1943; "Status of USAAF Aircraft of Northwest African Air Forces as of 0001 Hours, 14 August 1943," 650.245.

59. Intel and Ops Summaries, Northwest African Air Forces, Aug 13 through 17, 1943, 615.3071-1; Craven and Cate, *TORCH to POINTBLANK*, 483, 682-83.

striking—it is probable that the intensive employment of the heavy bombers on August 13 and the need to prepare for the arrival of the aircraft from the United Kingdom on August 17 removed the B–17s from the battle against the German evacuation.[60] Coningham, in short, may have made—and lost—two wagers with fate: First, that the Germans would not evacuate until after the daytime strategic bombing force had recovered, and second, that the evacuation would in any event probably proceed under cover of darkness.

The error of releasing the B–17s was compounded by another miscalculation: Once the Germans had begun to retreat by day, the Wellingtons were diverted from the Sicilian beaches to those of the mainland. There they bombed with little effect points along the coast running from Villa San Giovanni as far north as Palmi and Scalea, most of which were in no way related to the evacuation.[61] (Even though the crossings were now chiefly by day, Vice Admiral Ruge records that a continuation of the earlier attacks would have still disrupted *LEHRGANG* somewhat.[62]) Photographic reconnaissance had shown craft of the kind used in the evacuation at several beaches in and just north of the Gulf of Gioia— chiefly at Palmi, Tropea, and Pizzo. Allied intelligence therefore concluded that the forces from Sicily were proceeding to these places, where the Germans were known to use the beaches as stations for coastal traffic. *LEHRGANG* was in fact chiefly confined to the Strait of Messina. The truth was not quickly learned: An intelligence report of the Tactical Air Force for August 15 declared, "Enemy continued orderly evacuation across the Straits, dispersing to points as far north as Gioia."[63] The at-

---

60. The observation of Admiral Samuel Eliot Morison is perhaps pertinent: "The final episode of this campaign has never received proper attention; partly for want of information, partly because nobody on the Allied side has cared to dwell on it." Morison, *Sicily-Salerno-Anzio*, 209.

61. Northwest African Strategic Air Force, Intel and Ops Summaries, Aug 14 through 18, 1943, 615.3071-1.

62. Ruge, "Evacuation of Sicily," 50.

63. Intel and Ops Summaries, Northwest African Air Forces, Aug 13 through 18, 1943; Intel and Ops Summary, Northwest African Tactical Air Force, Aug 15, 1943, 614.307-1. In an intelligence appreciation of August 7, the Tactical Air Force had expressed the opinion that the Germans would for two reasons probably land troops evacuated from Sicily on the beaches between Scilla and Pizzo: (1) The beaches had already been developed as logistical storage sites for the coastal traffic from Naples, so forces landed there could immediately be fed and reequipped before they moved to the concentration point; (2) as some of the forces withdrawn from Sicily would be taking up defensive positions on the eastern side of the Strait of Messina, there would be congestion unless units following were sent elsewhere. Intel Appreciation, Northwest African Tactical Air Force, subj: Enemy Evacuation of Sicily Across Messina Straits, No. 8 (Aug 7, 1943), 626.6314-1. The role of these northern sites in *LEHRGANG* was in fact peripheral. Some of the craft used in the operation were refueled at the northern

tacks on the northern beaches reportedly produced secondary explosions, which probably encouraged intelligence analysts to believe that they correctly discerned additional and longer evacuation routes of some importance in use at night.[64]

The entire responsibility of stopping LEHRGANG thus fell on the Northwest African Tactical Air Force. Between August 13 and 16, the last full day of the evacuation, Coningham's organization flew 1,173 sorties against Axis shipping in the Strait of Messina. Of these, 946 were flown by fighter-bombers (P–40s) and dive bombers (A–36s, a variant of the P–51 Mustang) of the Western Desert Air Force, and 227 by the medium bombers (B–25s) and light bombers (A–20s) of the Tactical Bomber Force.[65]

Though they variously judged the accuracy of the flak, the attackers always found it "heavy" or "intense."[66] The strength of the Italo-German defenses will be seriously underestimated if gauged solely by downed aircraft, for the guns claimed no more than five, and possibly as few as three.[67] More indicative are the damage statistics: Of the bombers that flew 96 sorties on August 15, 28 were holed by flak as were 30 of the fighter-bombers. The next day 44 bombers were hit on 96 sorties.[68] "The immense concentration of flak on both sides of the Narrows," wrote a staff officer of the Tactical Air Force on August 15, "makes it impossible to go down and really search for targets with fighter bombers. It also greatly restricts the use of light bombers."[69]

The German accounts of Operation LEHRGANG show that the daylight attacks of the Tactical Bomber Force neither inflicted significant damage nor, in contrast to the night attacks of the Strategic Air Force, slowed the pace of the evacuation. From the number of aircraft damaged

---

sites; some wounded were also unloaded there. See AHB/BAM, "Mediterranean Reconquest and the Submarine War," vol 7, pt 1, 188.

64. See, for example, Intel and Ops Summaries, Northwest African Strategic Air Force, Aug 12, 13, 14, 1943.

65. Intel and Ops Summaries, Northwest African Air Forces, Aug 13 through 16, 1943. LEHRGANG ended about 0600 on Aug 17, 1943; no missions were flown that day.

66. Intel and Ops Summaries, Northwest African Air Forces, Aug 13 through 16, 1943; Intel and Ops Summaries, Northwest African Tactical Air Force, Aug 13 through 16, 1943; Sortie Rpts, 340th Bombardment Grp, Aug 15, 16, 1943.

67. In the general vicinity of the straits the following aircraft were lost between Aug 13 and 16: two P–40s, two B–25s, and one A–36. It is possible that the A–36 and one of the P–40s were lost on operations not against LEHRGANG. Intel and Ops Summaries, Northwest African Air Forces, Aug 13 through 16, 1943.

68. Ibid.

69. Claude Pelly [rank not stated] to Grp Capt E.C. Huddleston, Aug 15, 1943, Folder 0407/490, Box 28, RG 331, MATAF HQ, NARA.

B-25s of the Northwest African Air Forces head through the flak above the Italian mainland. Unable to slow the German passage across the Strait of Messina, these medium bombers flew constantly against lines of communication leading to the area.

it may be plausibly argued that evasive maneuvers and psychological pressures affected the calculations of the bombardiers. Possibly also contributory to the ineffectiveness of the daylight attacks was the comparatively low tonnage of the bombs dropped. On the nights of August 11–12 and 12–13 the Wellingtons had released 339.5 tons of bombs; on August 15 and 16 the medium and light bombers dropped 153.6 tons.[70]

Less uncertainty surrounds the failure of the fighter-bombers to impede *LEHRGANG*. For most of the operation, flak deterred and baffled the Allied pilots. On August 13, von Liebenstein noted in his war diary that "only in the Messina Strait . . . the enemy displays caution and avoids actual low-level attacks, as there he is brought under fire from all sides." Toward evening on August 14 he wrote that ferrying proceeded "smoothly throughout the day, with hardly any interference from the usual fighter-bomber raids." On August 15 he recorded his astonishment that "the enemy has not made stronger attacks in the past days. There has frequently been a pause of 1–2 hours between individual fighter-bomber raids, while high-level attacks have been practically non-existent. It is only during the night that raids are frequently incessant." Only on the last full day of *LEHRGANG*, August 17, did von Liebenstein describe the attacks as "intense."[71] Theretofore the Allies had attacked in flights

---

70. Intel and Ops Summaries, Northwest African Air Forces, Aug 12 through 16, 1943.

71. AHB/BAM, "War Diary of Naval Officer-in-Charge," 21, 22, 25, 28; von Liebenstein, "German Ferrying Traffic," 7–8. Von Liebenstein was of the opinion that even the small measure of success that the Allies had in their attacks

of about a dozen aircraft and made no headway against the fires from both banks of the strait and the armed ferrying craft. But on August 16, at 30- to 45-minute intervals, fighter-bombers came by twos and threes down the ravines that break the bluffs of the rugged Sicilian shore. Appearing suddenly over the beaches, they swooped down on the evacuation craft that dotted the waters. But German defenses held. The flak and barrage balloons forced the pilots to dodge too nervously during their few seconds over the strait for accurate aiming.

The Allies' attempt to stop *LEHRGANG* was further handicapped by their failure to attack what was perhaps the single weakest link in the enemy's transportation system. The Germans in their retreat through eastern Sicily's mountainous terrain, no less than the Anglo-Americans in their advance, were prisoners of roads. But whereas the Germans slowed their enemy through the clever and extensive use of demolitions, the Allies made no persistent effort to return the injury with their bombing force. This constituted a serious mistake, for only a single road served each shore of the strait. These arteries suffered attacks, but at a tempo that did not overstrain the capacities of the engineering units assigned to clear them. The Germans held the opinion that persistent attacks on these roads, together with around-the-clock heavy bombardment of the beaches, would have jeopardized the evacuation. "On the whole," Vice Admiral Ruge afterwards wrote, "night bombing was the greater nuisance of the two forms of air attack. The greatest would have been a concentration of annihilation bombing by night and day, and of dive bombing on selected points of the main roads on either bank." It was, he added, "a great relief that Allied bomber command never pursued this [latter] idea as tenaciously as some others."[72]

According to Kesselring's report to Berlin, 38,846 soldiers, 10,356 vehicles, and 14,949 tons of supplies were evacuated during the seven days of Operation *LEHRGANG* which ended at dawn, August 17, when General Hube sailed with his staff from Messina, a mere two hours before the arrival of Patton's advance guard. The Italian evacuation had ended at noon of the preceding day, when the last of 62,000 soldiers left for the mainland. The Italians also saved 227 vehicles and 41 artillery pieces and would have saved more had not the Germans helped themselves liberally to the equipment of their allies.[73] Considerable uncertainty surrounds the cost of *LEHRGANG* to the Axis. Admiral Ruge wrote

---

would have been denied them had there been more ammunition for the antiaircraft weapons and more of the 20-mm automatic weapons. Von Liebenstein, "Final Report as Supplement to the War Diary," 20.

72. Ruge, "Evacuation of Sicily," 37.

73. Morison, *Sicily-Salerno-Anzio*, 215n, 216, 216n.

after the war that the Italians had lost one small vessel and the Germans about six, while perhaps another seven or eight craft were damaged. But the logs of just two of the five units performing the evacuation—the *2d* and the *4th Landing Flotillas*—record the loss of eleven boats.[74] Von Liebenstein's war diary mentions loss of but a single life, but the logs of the same two landing flotillas record ten deaths.[75] Nonetheless, the claims that Coningham presented in his report on the evacuation—23 boats sunk, direct hits on 43 more, and 201 "near misses"—were probably excessive.[76] The Tactical Air Force's own intelligence reports spoke of the enemy's "orderly evacuation."[77]

The cautious, even plodding, strategy pursued by the Allies in their conquest of Sicily made the success of *LEHRGANG* possible, if not certain. There has been criticism of the decision to land initially so far to the west of Messina. Given, however, the uncertainties that surrounded the *Luftwaffe* and the state of the Italian morale, it can only be called prudent. The subsequent conduct of the campaign is less defensible. Once the Allies were ashore, had established air bases, and determined the caliber of the Italian resistance, there was no insuperable obstacle to an end run in force. Given the Allies' overwhelming numerical superiority, the thousands of ships at their disposal, and the lack of any German reserves, the only deterrent to such an operation was the failure to think of it in time. The landings at Brolo and elsewhere were too hastily contrived to be of the requisite size. "We were puzzled," recalled a German general, "that no major landing had been carried out behind German lines. . . . Such landings could have been disastrous to the German troops."[78]

Allied naval forces were curiously inactive. Years later, Admiral Cunningham brought himself to admit that "much more consideration should have been given" to using the naval forces to stop the evac-

74. Ruge, "Evacuation of Sicily," 52; AHB/BAM, "Mediterranean Reconquest and the Submarine War," vol 7, pt 1, 224. *LEHRGANG* was executed by the *2d, 4th,* and *10th Landing Flotillas* and the *Pioneer Landing Battalion 771.* The British found the logs of the first two units after the war.

75. AHB/BAM, "War Diary of the Naval Officer-in-Charge," 25; AHB/BAM, "Mediterranean Reconquest and the Submarine War," vol 7, pt 1, 224.

76. Air Vice Marshal Arthur Coningham to General Carl A. Spaatz, Aug 19, 1944, Folder 0407/490, Box 28, RG 331.

77. Intel and Ops Summary, Northwest African Tactical Air Force, Aug 15, 1943.

78. Walter Fries, "The Operations of the *29th Panzer Grenadier Division* in Sicily," MS T-2, RG 338, 132.

uation.[79] Despite the admiral's protestations about the problems of spotting and ranging, British and American official naval histories of the
campaign hold that shore batteries could perhaps have been attacked
from the sea with little danger to ships. The batteries could perhaps have
been engaged by firing overland from the waters north and west of Cape
Peloro or from the southern entrance of the strait from positions west of
Reggio.[80] Once they had been silenced, smaller warships could have entered partway into the strait and disrupted the flotilla of ferries while
larger vessels shelled the beaches from which the withdrawal was being
staged. In Cunningham's defense, however, it must be said that it is difficult to see how the spotting for the vessels attacking the batteries overland could have been arranged without the use of aircraft, the survival of
which in the heavily defended air space over the strait can only be called
problematic. There also remains the unanswered question of why Tedder
never ordered the attacks on the shore batteries that he promised. Protected as they were by the dense flak, they could probably not have been
taken out by the Tactical Air Force. But Tedder also controlled the
B–17s of the Strategic Air Force, which, pursuant to Coningham's directive published August 6, bombed various communications targets in and
around Messina on August 5, 6, and 9.[81] They would perhaps have been
better directed against the batteries.

Even with the caution of the army and the inactivity of the fleet,
those in the best position to know—the German managers of *LEHR-
GANG*—affirm that air power alone could at the very least have disrupted
the operation and inflicted heavy loss. The question is why it so signally
failed to do anything of the kind. Studies of the Sicilian Campaign have
favored two explanations—the strength of the antiaircraft defenses and
the faulty interpretation of intelligence. The density of antiaircraft defenses was not an insuperable obstacle to hindering *LEHRGANG*. That the
antiaircraft guns sufficed to fend off the medium bombers and fighters is
a matter of record. But these same defenses, now almost legendary in
their formidability, were perfectly defenseless before the high-flying
heavy bombers that the Allies had in abundance. The beaches were not
difficult targets; the Wellingtons, bombing at night and unequipped with
the advanced American Norden bombsight, had hit them repeatedly from
10,000 feet. High-flying B–17s could have plastered the beaches by day,
while some of the fighter-bombers attacked the vital access roads to the

---

79. Oliver Warner, *Admiral of the Fleet: Cunningham of Hyndehope*
(Athens, Ohio, 1967), 211.
80. Morison, *Sicily-Salerno-Anzio*, 216–17; Roskill, *War at Sea*, 3:149–51.
81. AHB/BAM, "Mediterranean Reconquest and the Submarine War," vol
7, pt 1, 205A.

evacuation beaches—probably with greater success than they achieved in their sorties against the small, agile, and well-armed craft within the heavily defended straits. Had the Allies pursued by day the bombing of the beaches that had been so successful on the nights of August 11–12 and 12–13, some considerable portion of the Italo-German force would have probably been caught by the Seventh and Eighth Armies.

The impression has prevailed that the crucial failing of Allied intelligence was its failure to detect the evacuation in time. That the Allies were two days late in establishing that the retreat was under way was actually of little practical importance. For while the evacuation began at night on August 11 and went undetected until early daylight on August 13, the night-bombing Wellingtons had so disrupted it that by August 13 only 15,000 German soldiers had been ferried to Italy.[82] The Allies could scarcely have done more if they had had *LEHRGANG*'s exact schedule. More serious, however, were the failures to understand that *LEHRGANG* totally depended on two vulnerable roads and that nearly all troops removed from Sicily passed directly across the strait and did not disperse to points along Italy's southwestern coast—the faulty perception that put the Wellingtons off-target on August 13.

Most important to the failed air effort against *LEHRGANG* was Coningham's release of the B–17s on August 11. On August 11, he weighed a possibility—that the Germans might cross by day—against a certainty—that attacks on Italy's rail system were necessary for the impending invasion of the mainland—and released the heavy bombers. His decision was not unreasonable. That *LEHRGANG* became a daytime operation just as the B–17s were bombing Rome—and therefore about to begin a lengthy stand-down—was more bad luck than the dereliction at which some writers have hinted.

For their failure to stop the exodus from Sicily the Allies were to pay a great price, both in blood and time. By August 1943 Germany's resources were stretched so thin, and her lines of communication with Italy so frayed, that it was only slowly and with difficulty that her Italian garrison was strengthened with divisions additional to those sent to Sicily. For just this reason, observed General Heinrich von Vietinghoff, subsequently German commander in Italy, *LEHRGANG* was of truly "decisive importance," for without the men rescued from Sicily "it would not have been possible to offer effective resistance on the Italian mainland south of Rome."[83]

---

82. Magna Bauer, "Axis Tactical Operations in Sicily, July–August 1943," MA R–145, RG 338, 42.
83. AHB/BAM, "The Campaign in Italy," 1947, Translation VII/97, 1950 [from the original by Heinrich von Vietinghoff], 512.621, ch 6, 2.

Chapter 3

―――▸◂――

Salerno: The Invasion of Italy
September 1943

On September 9, 1943, the Allies began their reconquest of western Europe by landing in Italy at the Gulf of Salerno. The purpose of Allied interdiction during this operation was, as it was later at Anzio and in Normandy, to prevent the Germans from building up their forces faster by land than the invaders could by sea. The distance of Salerno from the Allied air bases in Sicily severely limited the number of fighters available to support the landing; most with the range to do so had to be dedicated to providing air cover for the invasion fleet against the *Luftwaffe*'s spirited attacks. Interdiction therefore fell almost entirely to heavy and medium bombers which tried through the bombing of bridges, road junctions, towns, and other presumed choke points to impede the movement of German divisions to the beachhead. Their failure to slow the German concentration at Salerno—which had nearly disastrous consequences for the Allies—illustrates with unusual clarity the difficulty that interdictors have always faced in trying to slow the movement of motor vehicles when unable to employ fighters for low-level attacks. Conversely, when the Allies did employ their fighters for strafing at the height of the fighting around Salerno, they succeeded for the first time in nearly paralyzing German tactical mobility—albeit with much help from naval gunfire. The Allies and the Germans both took this demonstration to heart.

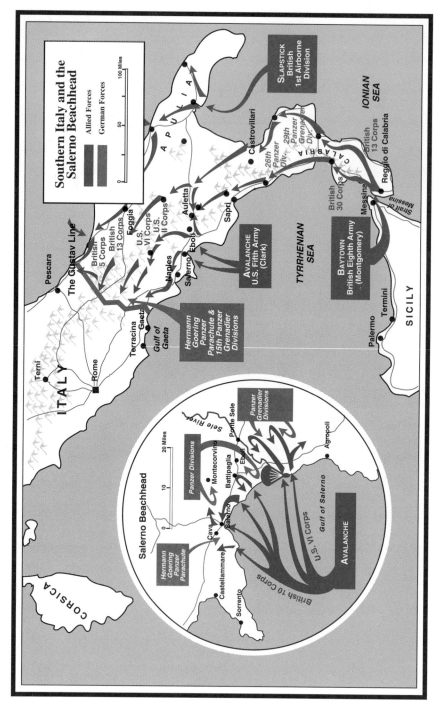

Southern Italy and the Salerno Beachhead

Allied Forces
German Forces

0   50   100 Miles

ITALY

Terni
Rome
Pescara

The Gustav Line

Terracina
Gaeta
Gulf of Gaeta

Hermann Goering Panzer Parachute & 15th Panzer Grenadier Divisions

Naples
British 5 Corps
British 13 Corps
Foggia
U.S. VI Corps
U.S. II Corps
Salerno
Eboli
Auletta
Sapri

APULIA

Castrovillari

AVALANCHE
U.S. Fifth Army (Clark)

26th Panzer Div.
29th Panzer Grenadier Div.

CALABRIA

TYRRHENIAN SEA

BAYTOWN
British Eighth Army (Montgomery)

British 13 Corps
Reggio di Calabria
Messina
Strait of Messina

British 30 Corps

SLAPSTICK
British 1st Airborne Division

IONIAN SEA

Palermo
Termini

SICILY

CORSICA

Salerno Beachhead

0   10   20 Miles

Sele River
Ponte Sele

Panzer Divisions

Montecorvino
Battipaglia
Eboli

Cava
Salerno

Panzer Grenadier Divisions

Hermann Goering Panzer Parachute

Castellammare
Sorrento

Agropoli

Gulf of Salerno

U.S. VI Corps

British 10 Corps

AVALANCHE

Map 5.

Even as they prepared for the invasion of Sicily, the Anglo-American leadership debated the course to be followed thereafter. Further initiatives in the Mediterranean theater seemed advisable because the unexpected length of the North African campaign had pushed OVERLORD, the attack across the English Channel, back to the spring of 1944. Only in the Mediterranean was it possible to maintain pressure on the Axis to help the hard-pressed Soviets. Discussions of how to proceed reflected well-established strategic preferences. The Americans, insisting that future operations in the Mediterranean should not detract from the preparations for the invasion of France, favored taking Corsica and Sardinia. The islands were well suited to serve as staging areas for operations against southern France, and so small an operation threatened no drain on the resources of the greater venture. The British, in keeping with their partiality for peripheral attrition, gave serious consideration to an invasion of the Balkans, with the conquest of southern Italy to be undertaken as a preliminary step.

When President Franklin D. Roosevelt and Prime Minister Winston S. Churchill met with the Combined Chiefs of Staff at the TRIDENT Conference in Washington (May 12–15, 1943), they agreed that Italy should be driven from the war at the earliest possible moment. So signal a success would placate the impatient publics of England and America, and no other action, short of a landing in France, could better aid the Soviets, for no less than thirty Italian divisions on occupation duty in France and in the Balkans would require replacing by German units. But how was this to be done? The United States would countenance no invasion of the Balkans through Italy. The British, however, advanced an argument against invasions of Corsica and Sardinia to which Americans had no reply: If the conquest of these islands failed to drive Italy from the war, then an invasion of the Italian mainland would be necessary. But a

AERIAL INTERDICTION

second amphibious invasion would be impossible before the spring of
1944, and in the interim nothing would have been done to help the Soviets. Did it not make sense, therefore, to invade Italy once Sicily had
fallen?

Some American planners were swayed by this argument; others were
moved by the consideration that from central Italy bombers could reach
Germany unhindered by the powerful antiaircraft defenses that the Germans had built in France and western Germany. But enough resistance
remained to another major commitment of resources in the Mediterranean that Washington's assent to an invasion of Italy, when it came
some weeks after TRIDENT, was conditional. The Combined Chiefs of
Staff directed the Allied Supreme Commander, General Dwight D. Eisenhower, to prepare plans for both the invasion of Italy and a Sardinian-
Corsican operation. If Sicily was easily won, an invasion of Italy would
follow. The quick collapse of Italian resistance in Sicily convinced even
General George C. Marshall, OVERLORD's staunchest advocate, that Italy
could be invaded without prejudice to the cross-channel attack. On July
18 Eisenhower successfully petitioned the Combined Chiefs of Staff to
proceed with the invasion of Italy, for which his staff had been preparing
since June.

The first version of the plan called for the British to cross the Strait
of Messina and seize the ports of Reggio di Calabria and San Giovanni.
The capture of Sardinia, if ordered, was to be an American operation,
while the so-called Free French were to take Corsica. By July many Allied officers were committed to a second landing near Naples. Some
Americans, fearing for OVERLORD, opposed it at first, but there were
powerful arguments for striking at central Italy. The early capture of a
major city could not fail to cripple Italian morale. Naples, moreover,
was a large and modern port north of territory well suited for defense
against invaders from the south. At Marshall's suggestion, the Joint
Chiefs commended the capture of Naples to Eisenhower. The British enthusiastically embraced the idea and expanded it to include an early advance on Rome to entrap the German forces in southern Italy. This ambitious plan they called AVALANCHE. The Americans assented after the
fall of Mussolini on July 25, 1943, vanquished their last qualms about a
major effort in Italy. Both the British and Americans too readily accepted that the fall of the Fascist regime would cause the Germans to
withdraw their forces from Italy after major Allied landings. The Italian
campaign, then, was conceived as a brief prelude to OVERLORD.[1]

---

1. Martin Blumenson, *Salerno to Cassino* [U.S. Army in World War II: The
Mediterranean Theater of Operations] (Washington, 1969), 3–19.

With the decision to land near Naples, the choice of the Gulf of Salerno as the site of the invasion was all but inevitable. The Bay of Naples was heavily fortified and beyond the range of tactical aircraft based in Sicily. The Gulf of Gaeta was closer to Naples than the Gulf of Salerno was, but its beaches were unsuitable for amphibious operations. Salerno was itself beyond the range of most single-engine aircraft, but a landing farther to the south offered no decisive tactical advantages over the one already slated for Calabria. Salerno, moreover, was a port city (albeit a minor one), and there was at Montecorvino, three miles inland, an excellent military airfield. With the decision to land at Salerno, the Calabrian effort, which was to be undertaken by Field Marshal Sir Bernard Law Montgomery's Eighth Army, became subsidiary. BAYTOWN, as it was called, was to precede AVALANCHE and, it was hoped, divert German forces that might otherwise be sent to Salerno. Airfields were to be established near Reggio and San Giovanni, themselves of value as ports, to support the major thrust to the north. (*Map 5*)

The planning for BAYTOWN and AVALANCHE was completed by August 19. The former was scheduled for September 3, the latter for September 9. Lt. Gen. Mark W. Clark of the American Fifth Army would command AVALANCHE. Assigned to make the landing were the British 10 Corps, comprising the 1st and 7th Armoured and the 46th and 56th Infantry Divisions, and the American VI Corps, composed of the 82d Airborne and the 1st, 3d, 34th, and 36th Infantry Divisions. Also attached to Clark's force were several units of British commandos and three battalions of American rangers.

The Gulf of Salerno has roughly the shape of a half-circle twenty-one miles long and eight deep at the center. It is divided into two unequal parts by the river Sele. About two-thirds of the bay's shore lies to the north of this river. That was to be the sector of 10 Corps, represented on D-day by the 46th and 56th Infantry Divisions, accompanied by the commandos and rangers. The 10 Corps was to seize the town of Salerno, the airfield at Montecorvino, the rail and road center of Battipaglia, and the bridge at Ponte Sele, fourteen miles inland. On D plus 5 the 7th Armoured Division would come ashore in 10 Corps' sector to lead the drive on Naples. The American VI Corps, represented on D-day by only the 36th Infantry Division, was to occupy the smaller sector south of the Sele. Its mission was to protect the right flank of the Allied force by seizing the high ground dominating the Gulf of Salerno to the south and east. Two regiments of the 46th Infantry Division constituted the floating reserve. The 1st Armoured and the 3d and 34th Infantry Divisions were to land at Naples after its scheduled capture on D plus 13.

The 82d Airborne Division was withdrawn from the invading force after the drop it was scheduled to make was shown to be tactically unsound.[2]

The Northwest African Air Forces began planning for the invasion of Italy in late June.[3] A complex air plan was ready by late August. In essence, it recast for an amphibious operation the three-stage design for combined-arms offensives pioneered by the British in Africa. The Northwest African Air Forces, with some help from the IX Bomber Command of the Ninth Air Force, still stationed in North Africa, had primary responsibility for air superiority and interdiction.[4] From August 18 through September 2 the Strategic Air Force was to attack airfields in central and southern Italy to drive the *Luftwaffe* out of range of Salerno. Forces not necessary for this mission, or freed by its progressive accomplishment, were to be directed against the enemy's lines of communication, which would become the primary target after September 2.

The air plan provided that two squadrons of A–36s, nineteen of Spitfires, and four of Beaufighters would provide close air support for the landing forces and air cover for the invasion fleet. All these aircraft would come from the Tactical Air Force's XII Air Support Command. They were to be augmented by three groups of long-range P–38s from the Strategic Air Force. This arrangement provided for a total of 528 day fighters and 32 night fighters at normal rates of serviceability. But of this impressive number of aircraft only a small percentage could be in orbit over the battlefield at any given daylight hour because of the extreme distance from their Sicilian bases. Because of this limitation the British provided one fleet and four escort carriers; together they carried 110 Seafires (the naval version of the Spitfire). Even so, there would be on average only fifty-four aircraft over the Gulf of Salerno at any time during the day. Planners feared that this total would prove inadequate if the *Luftwaffe* attacked resolutely.[5]

The Desert Air Force, charged with providing air support for BAY-TOWN, controlled the Northwest African Tactical Air Force's Tactical Bomber Force, composed primarily of B–25s, B–26s, and A–20s, until the Eighth Army's D-day of September 3. Thereafter the XII Air Support Command would control most of its units for the support of AVA-LANCHE. Planners anticipated, however, that the Strategic Air Force

---

2. *Ibid.*, 19–45.

3. For the organization of the Northwest African Air Forces, see Table 1, page 34.

4. Shortly after the invasion of Italy the Ninth Air Force redeployed to the United Kingdom to become the American tactical air force for OVERLORD.

5. Wesley Frank Craven and James Lea Cate, eds, *The Army Air Forces in World War II*, 7 vols (Chicago, 1948–57; Washington, 1983), vol 2: *Europe: TORCH to POINTBLANK*, 488–502.

would have to perform most of the bombing. Unescorted missions were hazardous for the light and medium bombers of the Tactical Bomber Force, and most fighters that could otherwise have provided escort would be either part of the air cover for the invasion force or else out of range to the south with the Eighth Army.[6] For the same reason, the mission of interdiction fell primarily to bombers rather than to fighters.

In September 1943 the *Luftwaffe*, though still the object of anxious calculation on the part of the Allies, was but a shadow of its former self. Throughout the Mediterranean theater—southern France, Greece, Crete, Sardinia, Corsica, and Italy—it could muster only about 625 aircraft. In central and southern Italy it disposed only about 120 fighters (predominantly Messerschmitt Bf 109s) and approximately 50 fighter-bombers (Focke-Wulf FW 190s). An undetermined but certainly small number of twin-engine bombers—Junkers Ju 88s based in Italy and Heinkel He 111s from southern France—were also available to oppose the Allied landings. The Germans' numerical inferiority was partially offset by the proximity of their airfields to Salerno, but even so the *Luftwaffe* proved capable of not many more than 100 sorties a day over the beachhead. Maj. Gen. Heinrich von Vietinghoff, whose *Armeeoberkommando 10* (*AOK 10—Tenth Army*) had responsibility for the defense of central and southern Italy, based his plans on the premise that "effective support of the Army by the Navy or Air Force could not be expected." The Italian air force still numbered about 900 aircraft, but this demoralized and largely obsolete organization had effectively ceased operations by the time aerial preparations for AVALANCHE began in late August. Italy's secretly negotiated surrender to the Allies on September 8 removed whatever slight danger Italian airmen might have posed to the invaders of their homeland.[7]

Von Vietinghoff's *AOK 10*, which was to bear the entire brunt of AVALANCHE, numbered 135,000 men, 60,000 of whom had been evacuated from Sicily. It was divided into two corps. In Calabria, the Italian "toe," was the *LXXVI Panzer Corps*, composed of the *26th Panzer* and the *29th Panzer Grenadier Divisions*. To the north, three divisions of the *XIV Panzer Corps* guarded the area of Naples. By the Gulf of Gaeta, its sector stretching from Terracina to the mouth of the Volturno River, was

---

6. Allied Tactical Air Force, "Notes on Conference on Operation 'AVALANCHE' Held at Tactical Air Force Headquarters on 19th August 1943," 655.430-1.
7. Craven and Cate, *TORCH to POINTBLANK*, 510–11; British Air Ministry, *The Rise and Fall of the German Air Force (1933–1945)* (London, 1948), 261; Air Historical Branch of the British Air Ministry (AHB/BAM), "The Campaign in Italy," 1947, Translation VII/98, 1950 [from the original by Heinrich von Vietinghoff], 512.621, ch 6, 8.

the *15th Panzer Grenadier Division*. The *Hermann Göring Panzer Parachute Division* occupied a sector immediately to the south that reached from the Volturno to Castellammare di Stabia on the northern shore of the Sorrentine peninsula. Occupying the shore of the Gulf of Salerno itself as far south as Agropoli was the *16th Panzer Division*. Independent of the two corps, but still under *AOK 10*, was the *1st Parachute Division*, so situated as to seal the "heel" of the Italian peninsula. The *16th Panzer Division* alone was at nearly full strength; all the other divisions of *AOK 10* were undermanned and short of equipment.[8]

The Germans were uncertain what the Allies would do after Sicily fell. They thought an invasion of the Balkans likely—and feared the prospect because the resources of the region were essential to them and the communications of the forces stationed there were vulnerable. When aerial reconnaissance of Allied shipping showed Italy to be the objective, Calabria seemed the most likely site for a landing because of its closeness to Sicily. But the possibility of a landing as far north as Rome was not discounted. On August 29 the German Commander in Chief, South, Field Marshal Albert Kesselring, pronounced the Allies' intentions "entirely unpredictable."[9]

Wherever the blow fell, the Germans had scant hopes of being able to repel it with the forces available in central and southern Italy. Kesselring's plan was to make a stand on a shortened front in the Apennine Mountains southeast of Rome. While there would be every effort to crush the invasion, the Germans were prepared to claim success if they contained it long enough to allow the withdrawal of their forces from southern Italy. The *LXXVI Panzer Corps* received orders to move north on September 2 when BAYTOWN seemed imminent. After Montgomery crossed the Strait of Messina the next day, the *LXXVI Panzer Corps* avoided major combat by resorting extensively to demolitions to slow the British advance—a practice to which the broken terrain of southern Italy readily lent itself. The pace of retreat accelerated on September 7 when German pilots spied a fleet headed for central Italy. By the next day it was clear that the Allied objective was either Naples or Salerno. Von Vietinghoff placed the *XIV Panzer Corps* on alert, but because of his uncertainty about the Allies' exact goal, he kept its divisions at their dispersed stations.[10]

The counterair campaign against the *Luftwaffe* represented an extension of the effort begun in April for HUSKY. The end of the Sicilian Campaign on August 18 found nearly all airdromes in central and south-

---

8. Blumenson, *Salerno to Cassino*, 67.
9. *Ibid.*, 62–66.
10. AHB/BAM, "Campaign in Italy," ch 6, 3.

ern Italy neutralized save for those around Foggia, sixty miles northeast of Salerno. That Foggia posed a threat was demonstrated on the night of August 17 when as many as ninety German bombers raided Bizerte where part of the invasion fleet was assembling. The attackers succeeded in damaging two ships and one landing craft. A force of similar size struck Bizerte again the next night and damaged two more ships. The Allies retaliated by attacking Foggia on August 25. After 140 P–38s of the Mediterranean Allied Air Forces' Strategic Air Force had strafed the installation, 136 B–17s loosed 240 tons of bombs, both high explosive and fragmentation. Poststrike photography showed forty-seven aircraft destroyed and another thirteen damaged. German attacks on Allied bombers thereafter declined markedly—but primarily because the *Luftwaffe* was husbanding its remaining strength for the impending invasion. The size of the airfield complex at Foggia made disabling the runways exceedingly difficult, and the surrounding terrain, unlike that of Sicily, permitted the parked aircraft to be dispersed properly. That the base remained operational was proved on August 27 when forty bombers attacked Algiers, and again on September 6 when seventy-nine German bombers reattacked Bizerte. Neither raid succeeded in damaging any ships, but the raids stung the Allies into reattacking Foggia with 147 B–17s on September 7, with disappointing results. The runways remained serviceable, and only ten aircraft incurred bomb damage. The German aircraft that attacked the Allied invasion fleet two days later flew from Foggia.[11]

The Allies had begun to attack Italy's railways during the North African campaign. The principal early targets were the marshaling yards of Naples, Palermo, Messina, Reggio, and San Giovanni. During the battle for Sicily, all types of railroad targets came under more sustained attack. The high point of the intensified effort was a raid of July 19, 1943, on Rome's marshaling yards by more than 500 heavy and medium bombers. Also struck were the marshaling yards at Naples and Foggia, lesser yards elsewhere, and many bridges. With the fall of Sicily and the imminent invasion of the mainland, the attacks grew heavier still. (*Map 6*) The principal interdiction mission of the Strategic Air Force was to attack the communications north of the line Sapri-Trebisacce in order to slow the movement of reserves southward to Salerno.[12]

Allied planners had ample reason to make railroads the focus of the strategic interdiction campaign. According to contemporary intelligence estimates, 96 percent of Italy's oil and 80 percent of her coal were im-

---

11. Craven and Cate, *TORCH TO POINTBLANK*, 503-11; AHB/BAM, "R.A.F. Narrative (First Draft): The Italian Campaign, 1943-1945," vol 1: "Planning and Invasion," 90-92, 97-99.
12. Craven and Cate, *TORCH TO POINTBLANK*, 463-65.

Italian Bombing Targets

- Jul 10-Aug 17, 1943
- Aug 18 - Sep 8, 1943
- Both Periods

0   50   100 Miles

LUXEMBOURG

POLAND

FRANCE

GERMANY

SWITZERLAND

HUNGARY

Bolzano

YUGOSLAVIA

Bologna

Pisa

ITALY

ADRIATIC
SEA

CORSICA

Viterbo
Rome

Foggia

Bari

SARDINIA

Naples

Sapri

Trebisacce

TYRRHENIAN
SEA

Cosenza

Crotone

San Giovanni
Messina

Palermo

Reggio

SICILY

IONIAN
SEA

TUNISIA

MALTA

Map 6.

ported by rail. And only by rail could German troops in large numbers be brought quickly from points north. Ten lines entered the country. (*Map 7*) Of these the route through the Brenner Pass from Austria was for several reasons the most important. It carried no less than 50 percent of Italy's railborne imports, and afforded the most direct route from Germany of all the lines that did not pass through Switzerland. This last consideration was crucial because the Swiss guarded their neutrality jealously and permitted only nominally nonmilitary supplies such as coal to pass through their territory. The alternatives to the Brenner line were unsatisfactory because they were too long and underdeveloped. The measure of this is that the two Swiss lines carried 38 percent of what Italy imported by rail. Without the Brenner line, then, troops and military equipment would have to be carried by seven routes that among them normally carried only 12 percent of Italy's imports by rail.[13]

More than 75 percent of Italy's industry lay in the northern part of the country, particularly in the vicinities of Milan, Genoa, Turin, Brescia, Pavia, and Ravenna. Northern Italy was accordingly heavily tracked, and the number of alternative lines between most places was sufficiently great that at no time during the war were the Allies wholly able to paralyze rail traffic in the region.[14] This was to trouble the Allies later in the war, but more fortunate planners of AVALANCHE were able to ignore the thickly woven web of northern Italy's railways. The most promising railroad targets in the north were Verona, Milan, Turin, Trieste, and Fiume, all sites of large marshaling yards.[15]

Of these, only Verona, the southern terminus of the Brenner line, was attacked, and it but lightly. (*Table 2*) This indifference to targets at no great range from bases in Sicily is explained by the glaring weaknesses of the railroads of central and southern Italy that made them particularly vulnerable to attack. South of Bologna, industry was relatively sparse, and the need for railroads correspondingly less. The mountainous terrain, moreover, limited the number of possible routes and increased construction costs.

In peace, coastal shipping largely supplanted railroads in serving the

---

13. A–2 Section, Northwest African Air Forces, "Air Intelligence Weekly Summary," No. 41 (Aug 21–27, 1943), 612.607, 27–28; Studies, Mediterranean Air Command, "Capacity of the Principal Rail Routes into Italy," Sep 3, Oct 8, 1943, 655.454–1.

14. Brig Gen Karl Theodor Körner, "Rail Transportation Problems in Italy," MS DO–10, Record Group (RG) 338, National Archives and Records Administration (NARA), 12.

15. A–5 Section, Northwest African Allied Air Forces, "Bombing of Communications (in Support of Army Operations)—Central and Southern Italy (from Rome to the Gulf of Taranto)," Sep 4, 1943, 612.425.

Map 7.

Table 2. Bombing Missions of the Northwest African Air Forces, August 17–September 30, 1943

Target	Tons of Bombs	Number of Sorties*
Amorosi	110	75M
Angetola	210	150M
Aversa	250	50H, 150M
Battipaglia	150	75H, 50M
Benevento	250	225M
Bologna	425	175H
Bolzano	75	85H
Cancello	400	250M
Capua	125	100M
Caserta	375	50H, 200M
Castelnuovo	50	50H
Civitavecchia	100	75M
Foggia	250	100H
Formia	100	75M
Grottaminarda	75	50M
Leghorn	100	50H
Littorio	450	100H, 150M
Lorenzo	450	100H, 100M
Marina di Catanzaro	50	50M
Mignano	200	150M
Minturno	100	50M
Orte	110	50H, 50M
Pisa	575	225H
Salerno	210	25H, 110M
San Martino	50	50H
Sapri	425	300M
Sibari	75	50M
Staletti	100	75M
Sulmona	210	75H
Terni	375	150H
Terracina	50	25H
Torre Annunziata	150	50H, 50M
Trebisacce	110	75M
Trento	50	20H
Verona	15	19H
Villa Literno	150	50H, 75M

*An *M* in this column indicates sorties flown by medium bombers (Wellingtons, B-25s, and B-26s); and *H* indicates those flown by heavy bombers (B-17s). SOURCE: *Impact*, Nov 1943.

commercial needs of central and southern Italy. But by the latter part of 1943 the Tyrrhenian Sea had been all but swept clean of Axis shipping, leaving German forces south of Bologna heavily dependent on three railroad lines and motor transport, of which the Germans were perennially short.[16] One of the three railroads ran down the eastern coast, removed from the site of the invasion and of limited capacity. The other two lines were major routes. One ran down the west coast, the other down the center of the country as far as Rome, where it turned west and then south, parallel to the western coastal route. This was the major supply route for German forces in southern Italy because south of Naples the western coastal road became a secondary line of limited capacity. The connecting roads running across the country were few and unable to handle heavy traffic. For this reason, all trains south of Bologna had to pass through Rome, Naples, or Foggia. South of Naples, moreover, only ten marshaling yards, excluding those in Apulia, the Italian "heel," existed to assemble trains. And in all of central and southern Italy there were only four shops to repair locomotives.[17]

The priority given to marshaling yards reflected the influence of the British scientist Solly Zuckerman, who advised Air Chief Marshal Sir Arthur W. Tedder, commander of the Mediterranean Air Command. During the planning for the invasion of Sicily, Zuckerman had thought intensively about how railroads might best be damaged from the air. He concluded that bridges—theretofore the favorite target of Allied planners—were too expensive to be primary targets because of the high tonnages of bombs required to ensure hits. When struck, moreover, they were difficult to damage but generally easy to repair because their piers tended to survive even the most devastating blasts. Tracks were also elusive targets readily restored. Zuckerman reasoned that attacks were better directed at marshaling yards, the nodal points of rail systems. There rolling stock, highly vulnerable to blast and splinter damage, could be destroyed en masse. And, more important still, it was in these rail centers that trains were made up and engines repaired and maintained. The loss of these services would reduce the efficiency, and therefore the capacity, of the entire system. Tedder, swayed by these arguments, amended the target lists to reflect Zuckerman's analysis of the Italian rail system even before the Allies landed in Sicily.[18]

---

16. Körner, "Rail Transportation Problems in Italy," 5–6; "Air Intelligence Weekly Summary," No. 41 (Aug 21–27, 1943), 27–28. The war diary of *AOK 10* described the situation of the army with respect to vehicles as serious but "not hopeless." *Kriegstagebuch Armeeoberkommando 10/Ia* (*KTB AOK 10/Ia*), Aug 22, 1944, Roll 85, Microfilm Pub T–312, NARA.

17. Craven and Cate, *TORCH to POINTBLANK*, 504.

18. Solly Zuckerman, *From Apes to Warlords* (New York, 1978), 197–98, 203; Ltr, Solly Zuckerman to Air Chief Marshal Sir Arthur Tedder, Dec 28, 1943, enclosing his Rpt, "Air Attacks on Rail and Road Communications," 519.425–1, v–vi, 41–47, 53, 55–58, 59–60.

Zuckerman has received severe criticism for having overstated the difficulty of destroying bridges and underestimating the time required to repair them.[19] While these criticisms were shown later in the war—and in quite different circumstances—to have a certain validity, his advice was well taken in 1943. The successful attacks on bridges during STRANGLE and OVERLORD adduced by his critics were the work of fighter-bombers and medium bombers; heavy bombers were never adept at the task.[20] But before HUSKY, Allied aircraft had to stage from North Africa, and only B-17s and B-24s had the necessary range. During AVALANCHE, medium bombers based in Sicily could help with the attacks on the railroads, but they were still fitted with the British Mark IX bombsight which had not the accuracy of the Norden sights used later.[21]

The paucity of marshaling yards in southern Italy made the region's rail system particularly susceptible to the kind of attack that Zuckerman urged. After Sicily fell, the scientist assembled a team of experts to study the effects of bombing on rail and road communications. In a report submitted to Tedder on December 28, 1943, Zuckerman showed that "the Sicilian and Southern Italian railroads had become practically paralyzed by the end of July 1943," almost entirely as a result of attacks at six marshaling yards: Naples, Foggia, San Giovanni, Reggio, Palermo, and Messina. This effect, as predicted, had been achieved chiefly through "the destruction and damaging of rolling-stock and repair facilities." Bridges had proved "uneconomical and difficult targets," generally not worth attacking except when urgent tactical considerations demanded their destruction.[22]

Shortly before AVALANCHE the Allied air forces began to attack the roads over which German divisions would have to pass to reach Salerno. The principal targets of the tactical effort, which began on September 7, were possible choke points: bridges, junctions in difficult terrain, and vil-

---

19. Henry D. Lytton, "Bombing Policy in the Rome and Pre-Normandy Invasion Aerial Campaigns of World War II: Bridge-Bombing Strategy Indicated—and Railyard-Bombing Strategy Invalidated," *Military Affairs* 47 (Apr 1983):53–58. While correctly remarking later successes in attacks on bridges, Lytton inaccurately states that Zuckerman argued that marshaling yards were harder to repair than bridges. In fact, Zuckerman conceded that the yards were easy to repair; his argument for attacks on them rested on the contention (true for southern Italy) that rolling stock could be destroyed in them en masse. See, for example, Rpt, Zuckerman, "Air Attacks on Rail and Road Communications," 31–41.

20. Wesley Frank Craven and James Lea Cate, eds., *The Army Air Forces in World War II*, 7 vols (Chicago, 1948–57; Washington, 1983), vol 3: *Europe: ARGUMENT to V-E Day, January 1944 to May 1945*, 157–59.

21. Mediterranean Allied Air Forces, "Air Force Participation in Operation SHINGLE," n.d. [1944], 168.61-1, 9–10.

22. Rpt, Zuckerman, "Air Attacks on Rail and Road Communications," ii–vii.

A large formation of B–17 Flying Fortresses over the Mediterranean is on its way to targets in Italy.

lage roads that might be blocked with the rubble of bombed-out houses. Attacks on motor transport were few. The fighter-bombers most suitable for this task were either out of range of the mainland or else engaged in providing air cover for the fleet and beachhead. That German aircraft employing radio-controlled glide bombs damaged three cruisers on the third day of the invasion did nothing to encourage an early reassignment of the long-range fighters.[23]

Three reinforced Allied divisions, at least 60,000 men, landed in the Gulf of Salerno early in the morning of September 9, 1943. A formidable fleet of warships that included two battleships, twelve cruisers, and more than fourteen destroyers supported this force. Only the *16th Panzer Division* opposed the invaders. As the division's front of nearly twenty miles precluded continuous defensive works, its commander had organized a series of small strongpoints on the shore; he held several combat teams inland to attack the invaders almost as soon as they came ashore. But the attacks were piecemeal and easily repelled with the help of naval gunfire. Had the disparity between the opposing forces not been so great, the mountains surrounding the Gulf of Salerno would have been advantageous to the defenders. But the Germans had little artillery, while the waters of the gulf were gray with Allied warships. The German counterattacks, delivered downhill, were therefore exposed to a withering and unanswerable fire from the fleet.

The size of the landing convinced von Vietinghoff that no third landing was in the offing. He quickly decided to concentrate his forces to

---

23. Samuel Eliot Morison, *History of United States Naval Operations in World War II*, 15 vols (Boston, 1947–62), vol 9: *Sicily-Salerno-Anzio*, 283, 290–91, 296–97.

repel the invasion. General Clark afterwards wrote that this effort might have succeeded, had the concentration been effected rapidly.[24] The obstacles, however, were too numerous. Human indecision was not the least among them. The commander of the *XIV Panzer Corps*, nearest Salerno, feared that the landing was only a diversion for another nearer Naples and only hesitatingly obeyed von Vietinghoff. He assembled a combat team from the *15th Panzer Grenadier Division* but held it near the mouth of the Volturno River to await developments. He also ordered the *Hermann Göring Panzer Parachute Division* to assemble a combat team, but dispatched immediately only the reconnaissance battalion. This unit entered action on the evening of September 9, followed several hours later by the combat team.[25]

Slower still to reach the battlefield were the two divisions of the *LXXVI Panzer Corps* to the south. Both were retreating slowly north just ahead of the Eighth Army, which they kept at a safe distance through the extensive use of mines and demolitions. On September 9, the *26th Panzer Division* was breaking contact with the British in the vicinities of Cosenza and Paola.[26] The *29th Panzer Grenadier Division* was completely out of contact with Montgomery's forces. Its main body was near Castrovillari, about 130 miles by road southeast of Salerno.[27]

Upon learning of the Allied landing, von Vietinghoff ordered both divisions of the *LXXVI Panzer Corps* to make for Salerno. He expected the northernmost of two, the *29th Panzer Grenadiers*, would reach the battlefield on the night of September 9–10. He did not know that the division was immobilized at Castrovillari by a shortage of gasoline. The quartermaster of Kesselring's headquarters afterwards attributed the deficiency to "the interference with road and rail transport in southern Italy brought about by the Allied air forces."[28] This testimony, however, should be qualified. Von Vietinghoff, who had been closer to the scene, afterwards wrote, and contemporary documents confirm, that supplies of fuel in southern Italy were adequate to move the *LXXVI Panzer Corps* to Salerno.[29] The recently organized *AOK 10* had as yet no quartermaster

---

24. General Mark W. Clark, *Calculated Risk*, (New York, 1950), 201.
25. Blumenson, *Salerno to Cassino*, 85–86.
26. AHB/BAM, "Campaign in Italy," ch 6, 10.
27. *Ibid.*
28. AHB/BAM, "The Supply Situation," 1947, in "The Campaign in Italy: Special Subjects," Translation VII/100, 1950 [from the original by Col Ernst Fändrich], K512.621, 7.
29. On August 27, the fuel in *AOK 10*'s dumps was described as sufficient "for all planned battle-movements." On September 14 all the divisions of the *LXXVI Panzer Corps* had either two or three *Verbrauchsätze* of fuel (a *Verbrauchsatz* was the amount of fuel necessary to move all vehicles in a unit 100

of its own. It depended on Kesselring's staff in Rome, which sent it inaccurate and incomplete information about the locations of stores of fuel in Calabria. The quartermaster of the *LXXVI Panzer Corps*, moreover, had incorrectly calculated allocations of fuel by failing to account for the mountainous nature of the terrain to be covered and the worn state of the engines of the corps' vehicles. Finally, and most serious of all, the captain of a German tanker at Sapri, upon misreading an ambiguous signal, thought that the Allies were at hand and dumped his cargo into the sea. By various methods some fuel was shipped to the *LXXVI Panzer Corps* from the north; more was taken from the dumps of the disintegrating Italian Army. In this way enough was procured to move the *29th Panzer Grenadiers* to Salerno by battalions. Most of the division had arrived at the front by September 11, but, still hampered by shortages of gasoline, it could not enter combat until the next day. This division was at about half strength, but augmented by two battalions of paratroops from the *1st Parachute Division* which had been diverted from a march from Naples to rejoin their division in Apulia. The *26th Panzer Division* was similarly handicapped in its efforts to reach the fray. Starting from a point farther south, it did not reach Salerno until September 13, having traveled the same route used by the *29th Panzer Grenadiers*. Owing to various detachments its strength about equaled a brigade's.[30]

The delay of the *LXXVI Panzer Corps* in reaching the battle was critical; von Vietinghoff called it "perhaps decisive" to the outcome of the battle.[31] For this result the strategic interdiction campaign of the Allies may be partially responsible: Had the railroads been working, the several errors that deprived it of the fuel it needed to reach Salerno on time *might* not have been so critical.[32] The tactical interdiction campaign, on the other hand, was clearly ineffective. The divisions from the south moved openly by day, when they found gasoline to move at all. The commander of one of the two battalions of paratroops who traveled with

---

kilometers)—an adequate if not generous amount. *KTB AOK 10/Ia*, Aug 27 and Sep 14, 1943.

30. AHB/BAM, "Campaign in Italy," ch 6, 12–13, 17; *"Besprechung bei O.B. Süd/F.A. am 11.9.43,"* appended to *KTB AOK 10/Ia*; *"Rückblick auf die ersten 3 Tage der Schlacht bei Salerno,"* Sep 12, 1943, *ibid.*; Blumenson, *Salerno to Cassino*, 98; Heinrich von Vietinghoff, *"Der Feldzug in Italien,"* MS T–1a, RG 338, *Kapitel 6, Skizze* 2. This last document is the German original of the first-mentioned source, which in translation is unaccompanied by the sketched maps with which von Vietinghoff illustrated his manuscript.

31. AHB/BAM, "Campaign in Italy," ch 6, 13.

32. German records are explicit that disrupted railroad service was the principal reason for disrupted fuel distribution. Order, von Vietinghoff to *AOK 10*, Sep 3, 1943, subj: *Sparsamkeitsmassnahmen, bes. Betriebstoff*, appended to *KTB AOK 10/Ia*.

the *29th Panzer Grenadier Division* later wrote that the effort of the Allied air forces over Calabria was "astonishingly small."[33] Once the troops marching to Salerno were beyond the range of the Desert Air Force's P–40s, few fighters strafed them—demands for air cover over the beachhead absorbed most of the sorties of the Sicily-based fighters having range to operate over the mainland.[34] Neither were the efforts of the medium and heavy bombers great in Calabria. Against points south of Salerno, 504 Allied sorties dropped 730 tons of bombs, while north of the battle, 1,041 sorties dropped 2,060 tons.

The reason for the disparity between the efforts north and those south of Salerno lay in the disposition of the German forces in Italy—about which Allied intelligence was well informed, from both ULTRA and information supplied by Italian emissaries secretly negotiating with the Anglo-Americans.[35] While the divisions of *AOK 10* were divided about equally between the *XIV* and the *LXXVI Panzer Corps*, the northern units were much closer to Salerno. In northern Italy, moreover, was *Heeresgruppe B*—seven well-equipped divisions and several independent brigades under the command of the redoubtable Erwin Rommel. And at Rome, directly controlled by Kesselring, were the *3d Panzer Grenadier Division* and the *2d Parachute Division*.[36] All this Allied intelligence officers knew; they also surmised—correctly—that the Italian railroads were functioning as far south as Naples, no great distance from Salerno.[37]

As even a small part of the German forces under Rommel's command north of Rome could have driven the invaders into the sea, the Northwest African Air Forces directed its most strenuous efforts at blocking German movement south. The Allies could not know, however, that Rommel held the firm opinion that central and southern Italy should *not* be defended; he feared the Allies would use their command of the sea to bypass and entrap any forces committed to those regions. And he

---

33. Colonel Rudolf Böhmler, quoted in General Wolfgang Dickert, "The Impact of Allied Air Attacks on German Divisions and Other Armed Forces in Zones of Combat," K113.107-84, 19.

34. It was not until Sep 12 that P–40s based in southern Italy escorted bombers as far north as the road between Auletta and Lagonegro; not until Sep 14 did they fly missions over the battlefield. Intel and Ops Summaries, Northwest African Strategic Air Force, Sep 12, 14, 1943, 615.307-1.

35. F.H. Hinsely *et al., British Intelligence in the Second World War*, 5 vols (London, 1979–), vol 3, pt 1, 104, 108.

36. *Ibid.*

37. A–2 Section, Northwest African Allied Air Forces, "Air Intelligence Weekly Summary," No. 44 (Sep 11-17, 1943), 24-25; AHB/BAM, "The Transport Situation," 1947, in "The Campaign in Italy: Special Subjects," Translation VII/100, 1950 [from the original by Col Klaus Stange], K512.621, 9.

had so persuaded Hitler. Apparently blind to the great moral effect of crushing the first Allied invasion of the continent, Rommel refused Kesselring's urgent entreaties for several divisions. Neither could the Allies know that Kesselring, faced with an uncertain political situation in Rome and fearful of further landings, believed himself able to dispatch only one regiment of the *3d Panzer Grenadiers* to Salerno.[38]

While strikes on the roads south of Salerno were few, they were well located. (See *Map 7*) Of the six points attacked, two—Potenza and Trebisacce—were on routes likely to be used by the *1st Parachute Division*, either to proceed directly to Salerno or to join with the *LXXVI Panzer Corps* in Calabria. The Allies did not know that this division was to be used as a rearguard against the small British landing, called SLAPSTICK, at Taranto on September 9. The four remaining targets—Eboli (September 8, 9, and 14), Sala Consilina (September 13), Lauria (September 7 and 8), and Auletta (September 14)—were all squarely on the route used by both the *26th Panzer* and the *29th Panzer Grenadier Divisions* to reach Salerno. Bearing in mind that the divisions began to move on 9 September and had arrived at Salerno by September 13, it will be seen that the timing of these attacks was probably correct, save for the last one on Eboli and the single strike at Auletta. Since we know that the *LXXVI Panzer Corps* was hindered only by a lack of fuel, it is evident that these attacks failed to block the roads sufficiently to impede the march of the German divisions to Salerno from the south.

Nothing in the German records suggests that the divisions of the *XIV Panzer Corps* were similarly slowed by shortages of fuel. Indeed, the *16th Panzer Division* was sufficiently well provided with gasoline that even in the thick of the fighting on September 9 it could send a portion of its store to the *29th Panzer Grenadiers*.[39] Whether the comparatively heavy tactical strikes on the roads north of Salerno hindered the march of the *XIV Panzer Corps* or that of the regiment of the *3d Panzer Grenadier Division* that Kesselring dispatched from Rome remains to be investigated.

The *Hermann Göring Panzer Parachute Division* was, in common with most of the other German divisions that fought at Salerno, badly understrength; it had approximately the strength of a reinforced brigade.

---

38. Blumenson, *Salerno to Cassino*, 97; Albert Kesselring, *Kesselring: A Soldier's Record* (New York, 1954), 223.

39. Blumenson, *Salerno to Cassino*, 98. The *Hermann Göring Panzer Parachute Division* experienced some problems with fuel on its approach march. But these seem not to have been at all serious, as the movement was completed quickly. Lt Gen Wilhelm Schmaltz, "An Account of the 'Herman Goering' Division at Salerno, 9–17 September 1943," appended to ch 6 of AHB/BAM, "Campaign in Italy," 63; *Tagesmeldung AOK 10/O Qu*, Sep 6, 1943, Roll 85, T–312.

Having left its billets at Caserta during the day of September 9, it made contact with the invaders that very evening at a point north of Cava. The route the unit took is uncertain, but the last leg of its journey was on the road that ran southeast through Cava into Salerno.[40] There are five probable routes from Caserta to Cava, the shortest about forty miles and the longest about fifty-four. (*Map 8*) On each route one place was bombed: roads and road junctions at Pompeii (*see* Routes 1 and 4, September 13 and 14), the highway bridge at Torre del Greco (*see* Routes 1 and 5, September 13), and the bridges at Cancello across the Volturno (*see* Route 3, September 9). Allied photographic reconnaissance showed damage to all three targets, but it was nowhere so severe as to render a route impassable.[41] More important, only the bridges at Cancello were attacked before the division entered the battle. Its commander later wrote an account of the unit's march to Salerno which mentions no Allied interference before it encountered naval gunfire near Cava.[42]

Upon hearing of the landing at Salerno the commander of the *XIV Panzer Corps* deployed most of the *15th Panzer Grenadier Division*, badly understrength at 12,000 men and seven tanks, at the mouth of the Volturno to guard against an invasion of the Gulf of Gaeta.[43] According to the war diary of *AOK 10*, the corps began to move its reserves to Salerno on September 10 as the threat of another invasion diminished.[44] One battalion of the *15th Panzer Grenadiers* went into action on the night of September 10–11. The rest of the division, organized into a regimental combat team, followed. Whatever its date of departure, the main body of the *15th Panzer Grenadiers* reached the battlefield on September 13.[45]

The route this unit followed from the mouth of the Volturno has also not been recorded, but the sketches that General von Vietinghoff prepared for his postwar campaign history show that it approached the battlefield on the route that ran south through the village of Baronissi to Salerno.[46] There are five probable routes from Castel Volturno at the mouth of the Volturno to Baronissi. (*Map 9*) One place was bombed on two of these routes: Pompeii (*see* Route 1) and Torre del Greco (*see*

---

40. Schmaltz, "Account of the 'Herman Goering' Division at Salerno," 63.

41. Northwest African Photo-Reconnaissance Wing, "Attacks on Railroad and Road Communications: Italy, 1 September–31 October 1943," Nov 7, 1943, 650.03–1, 7a, 9–10.

42. Schmaltz, "Account of the 'Herman Goering' Division at Salerno," 63, 65.

43. Blumenson, *Salerno to Cassino*, 86, 97.

44. *KTB AOK 10/Ia*, Sep 10, 1943.

45. AHB/BAM, "Campaign in Italy," ch 6, 16; Blumenson, *Salerno to Cassino*, 117.

46. Von Vietinghoff, "*Der Feldzug in Italien*," Kapitel 7, Skizze 3.

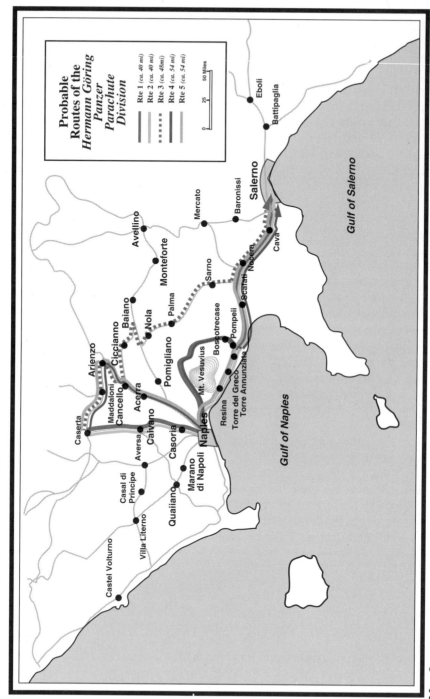

Probable
Routes of the
Hermann Göring
Panzer
Parachute
Division

Rte 1 (ca. 40 mi)
Rte 2 (ca. 40 mi)
Rte 3 (ca. 48mi)
Rte 4 (ca. 54 mi)
Rte 5 (ca. 54 mi)

0   25   50 Miles

Gulf of Salerno

Eboli
Battipaglia

Salerno

Baronissi

Mercato

Cava

Avellino

Monteforte

Nocera

Scafati

Sarno

Palma

Baiano

Nola

Ciccianno

Arienzo

Pomigliano

Pompeii

Boscotrecase

Mt. Vesuvius

Caserta

Maddaloni
Cancello

Acerra

Caivano

Aversa

Casoria

Resina
Torre del Greco
Torre Annunziata

Naples

Marano
di Napoli

Quaiiano

Casal di
Principe

Villa Literno

Castel Volturno

Gulf of Naples

Map 8.

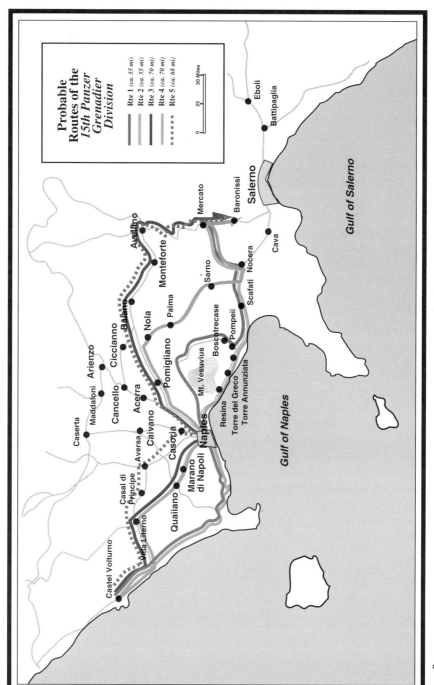

Probable Routes of the 15th Panzer Grenadier Division

Rte 1 (ca. 55 mi)
Rte 2 (ca. 55 mi)
Rte 3 (ca. 70 mi)
Rte 4 (ca. 70 mi)
Rte 5 (ca. 68 mi)

0   25   50 Miles

Gulf of Salerno

Gulf of Naples

Eboli
Battipaglia
Salerno
Baronissi
Mercato
Cava
Nocera
Scafati
Sarno
Avellino
Monteforte
Baiano
Palma
Nola
Cicciano
Arienzo
Maddaloni
Caserta
Cancello
Acerra
Caivano
Casoria
Pomigliano
Boscotrecase
Pompeii
Mt. Vesuvius
Resina
Torre del Greco
Torre Annunziata
Naples
Marano di Napoli
Qualiano
Casal di Principe
Aversa
Villa Literno
Castel Volturno

Map 9.

Route 2). As noted in the discussion of the march of the *Hermann Göring Panzer Parachute Division*, neither of these targets was blocked; both, moreover, were bombed only after September 13, the day the *15th Panzer Grenadier Division* reached Salerno.

The regimental combat team of the *3d Panzer Grenadier Division* was sent from Rome to the Gulf of Gaeta on September 10 against the possibility of an Allied landing there. When this seemed unlikely, the combat team was shifted to Salerno where it arrived on September 13 ahead of the *15th Panzer Grenadiers*.[47] No German source states the division's route of march from Rome to the region of the Gulf of Gaeta and thence to Salerno. But inasmuch as it traveled farther than either of the two divisions of the *XIV Panzer Corps* and it arrived before either one, there is no reason to suppose that Allied air power impeded the division. Confirming the conclusion of failure in this and the other instances of attempted tactical interdiction is the finding of Zuckerman's team of researchers who, having studied the effects of the bombing of roads and associated engineering features in Sicily and Italy, concluded that the practice was certain to fail to halt traffic in all but the most favorable of circumstances. Rarely could bombs block routes, and few were the places where no detour was possible.[48]

The failure of Allied efforts at tactical interdiction is recorded somberly in the U.S. Army's official history of the Salerno campaign: "The Fifth Army found itself at the edge of defeat on the evening of 13 September for one basic reason: The army could not build up the beachhead by water transport as fast as the Germans, for all their difficulties, could reinforce their defenders by land."[49] The caution of Allied ground commanders had, as German officers later testified, forfeited an opportunity to pierce the thin perimeter of the *16th Panzer Division* on September 9. The first attempts of the Anglo-Americans to push beyond the beachhead established on D-day were repulsed by German counterattacks on September 10. Reinforced, the defenders pressed their attacks on September 12 and recaptured many critical terrain features that the Allies had taken on D-day.

The skillful delaying action of the *16th Panzer Division* had prevented a firm linkup of the British and American units separated by the river Sele. On September 13 the Germans exploited this situation with an attack down the northern bank of the river to annihilate one American battalion and rout another. The situation was desperate. Amid scenes of

---

47. Blumenson, *Salerno to Cassino*, 97, 117.
48. Rpt, Zuckerman, "Air Attacks on Rail and Road Communications," 53–54.
49. Blumenson, *Salerno to Cassino*, 118.

confusion and panic, General Clark gave some thought to reembarking his troops. Late on September 13, American artillerymen, firing almost point-blank, barely staved off disaster.

On September 14 the Germans staged probing attacks at many points around the now-shrunken beachhead. (*Chart 1*) They were repelled by heavy shelling from the great flotilla of warships in the Gulf of Salerno and by more than 2,000 sorties by heavy and medium bombers of the Northwest African Strategic Air Force which, operating tactically, struck at roads and suspected concentrations of enemy troops on the battlefield. Certain areas of the battlefield received as many as 760 tons of bombs per square mile. A measure of the desperateness of the hour is that the P–38s that had been providing air cover for the fleet and beachhead were sent to strafe on and about the battlefield, even though the *Luftwaffe* was still flying 100 or more sorties a day against the invasion fleet and sank a merchant ship that very day. The bombers flew about 1,400 sorties on September 15.[50]

Many claims have been made for this flurry of aerial activity. For the first time the Germans found their movements severely hindered by aerial attacks—never before had they conducted a major attack under nearly total Allied air supremacy.[51] But what impressed German commanders most was the intensity and accuracy of the naval gunfire.[52] Von Vietinghoff decided to break off the attack on the beachhead on the afternoon of September 16 after his last attacks had been broken up by heavy shelling from the warships. Montgomery's Eighth Army, moreover, was by now alarmingly close.[53]

The strategic interdiction campaign that preceded the invasion of Italy may have contributed slightly to the success of AVALANCHE. Allied bombers certainly succeeded in seriously disrupting railroad service south of Naples. In attacking the rail system the Northwest African Air Forces enjoyed great advantages: Its aerial supremacy was scarcely contested, and few of man's handiworks are more identifiable from the air than railroads. Neither was intelligence a problem. ULTRA and disaffected Italians provided the complete German order of battle; most of the rest of what the Allies needed to know to plan their attacks on the rail sys-

---

50. Craven and Cate, TORCH to POINTBLANK, 534–35.
51. Blumenson, *Salerno to Cassino*, 118.
52. See, for example, AHB/BAM, "Campaign in Italy," ch 6, 18; Schmaltz, "Account of the 'Herman Goering' Division at Salerno," 65; Kesselring, *Kesselring*, 226.
53. AHB/BAM, "Campaign in Italy," ch 6, 19.

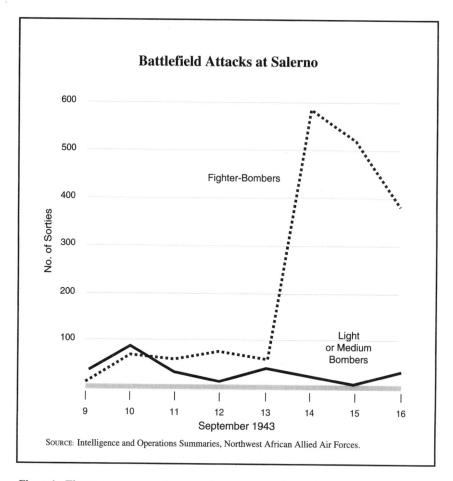

Battlefield Attacks at Salerno

Fighter-Bombers

Light
or Medium
Bombers

No. of Sorties

September 1943

SOURCE: Intelligence and Operations Summaries, Northwest African Allied Air Forces.

Chart 1. These curves must be regarded as approximate because the summaries from which the data were obtained are not always clear as to the purpose of missions.

tem, they found in atlases. The task of destruction was made still easier by the small number of rail centers in southern Italy.

The problems with fuel that slowed the Germans' concentration at Salerno were primarily of their own making, for there was in Calabria enough fuel to move the *LXXVI Panzer Corps* to the beachhead expeditiously. The possibility cannot be excluded, however, that, had the railroads been operating, the gasoline sent south from the dumps of the *16th Panzer Division* and points farther north might have arrived sooner. A railroad line passed through Castrovillari, where the main body of the *29th Panzer Grenadier Division* was located on September 9 and through which the *26th Panzer Division* passed on its march to Salerno. Had the

The twin-engine Lockheed P–38 Lightning proved valuable both for long-range air superiority and ground-attack strafing missions.

railroads been able to move the fuel faster, the *LXXVI Panzer Corps* might have reached the battle sooner, though with what effect none can say. We have seen, however, that both Generals Clark and von Vieting-hoff have opined that a quicker concentration of the German forces might have turned the tide. This question, like that of the rain on the eve of Waterloo, must remain one of the enduring questions of military history.

No such uncertainty surrounds the tactical interdiction campaign that accompanied AVALANCHE. It failed. The German divisions marched to Salerno openly by day, marveling that the Allies' air forces were so little in evidence.[54] The reason for the failure of tactical interdiction is not obscure. The whole effort was predicated on the theory that heavy bombardment of roads and bridges could deny them to the enemy. But roads proved almost impossible to close and bridges, with the aircraft available, were far too difficult to destroy.[55] In later campaigns strafing

54. Siegfried Westphal, supplement to ch 6, but appended to ch 7, of AHB/BAM, "Campaign in Italy," Translation VII/98, 5.
55. Rpt, Zuckerman, "Air Attacks on Rail and Road Communications," v–vi.

fighter-bombers proved an effective instrument of tactical interdiction. This was foreshadowed at Salerno, where the Germans began to complain of difficulties of movement only when the P–38s were released from providing air cover, and P–40s from southern Italian fields could at last reach the battlefield.[56] But this was too late to affect the movement of German divisions to the beachhead.

---

56. Blumenson, *Salerno to Cassino*, 133.

Chapter 4

---·◆·---

Anzio
January 2–February 19, 1944

During the Anglo-American landing at Anzio, the Allied air forces failed in their primary mission—to retard the movement of German divisions to the beachhead. But the effect of air attacks on German supply was considerable. Railroads were essential to the logistical systems of all the belligerents. The Germans, chronically short of motor vehicles, particularly depended upon them. The Allies capitalized upon this weakness by directing a two-pronged attack against the German logistical system. Their attacks on bridges and marshaling yards drove the German railheads back from the front. This of itself sufficed to strain the *Wehrmacht's* inadequate supply of motor transport. Strafing fighters simultaneously made matters worse by forcing convoys to seek the shelter of night. The result was logistical constriction, the chief manifestation of which was a critical shortage of artillery ammunition. This was the first demonstration of the strategy that the Allies would employ for the rest of the war to interfere with the resupply of German armies.

Map 10.

After their landing at Salerno, the Allies advanced slowly to the north, Naples falling to them on October 1, 1943. The satisfaction the Anglo-Americans took from this accomplishment was dimmed by the growing realization that the German retreat had been tactical. Hitler had initially ruled that his armies should defend only northernmost Italy, where Field Marshal Erwin Rommel commanded *Heeresgruppe B* (*Army Group B*). The decision owed much to Rommel, who warned against making a stand where the Allies could exploit their command of the sea to outflank German defenses. The counsel of Field Marshal Albert Kesselring was different. Always air-minded, this officer of the *Luftwaffe* argued that at all costs American bombers should be kept as far as possible from the *Reich*. He urged a stand in the formidable Apennine Mountains at the point where, 100 miles south of Rome, the Italian peninsula is narrowest.[1]

The *Führer*, long drawn to Kesselring's inveterate optimism, was newly appreciative of his generalship, for he had shown impressive skill in conducting the retreat from southern Italy. In late September, Hitler provisionally accepted Kesselring's strategic recommendation. He signaled his final approval in November by removing Rommel from Italy. While remaining Commander in Chief, South, Kesselring was named by the Führer to head the newly organized *Heeresgruppe C* (*Army Group C*) which comprised *Armeeoberkommando 10* (*AOK 10—Tenth Army*) and *Armeeoberkommando 14* (*AOK 14—Fourteenth Army*), newly formed from units previously assigned to Rommel's *Heeresgruppe B*.[2]

---

1. Unless otherwise noted, all details of the ground fighting are from Martin Blumenson, *Salerno to Cassino* [U.S. Army in World War II: The Mediterranean Theater of Operations] (Washington, 1969).

2. *Heeresgruppe B*, or rather the headquarters thereof, went with Rommel to

After Salerno, Kesselring delayed the Allies long enough to prepare positions in the Apennines, which the Germans occupied after the American Fifth Army forced the Volturno River on the night of October 12, 1943. The Gustav Line, as the main line of resistance was called, generally followed the courses of the Sangro and Garigliano Rivers. It was anchored at Monte Cassino, about seventy-five miles southeast of Rome. This prominence commanded the most direct approach to Rome, the Liri Valley. (*Map 10*) By early November the Allied advance had stalled before the German fortifications. To the Allies, the looming prospect of a prolonged stalemate was scarcely more inviting than defeat. They had invaded Italy to draw German divisions from France and Russia. In that they had succeeded. But if the Germans remained long in the Apennines they might strengthen their positions sufficiently to be able to withdraw divisions from Italy for use against OVERLORD, the invasion of northern France scheduled for spring 1944. Among the Allied leadership, moreover, were those who, like Prime Minister Winston S. Churchill, ardently desired Rome as a symbol of both victory and personal vindication. And beyond the Eternal City beckoned the Po Valley, from which Allied aircraft could range widely over France and Germany.

The obvious answer to the Allied predicament was the landing in force behind the German lines that Rommel had feared. In early November, General Dwight D. Eisenhower and his lieutenants decided upon a plan, SHINGLE, for just such a stroke. As originally conceived, SHINGLE was to follow a breakthrough into the Liri Valley. When the drive had reached the town of Frosinone, about forty-five miles southeast of Rome, the Fifth Army would land two divisions at Anzio, barely thirty miles south of the city. From there the invaders were to strike out for the Alban Hills, possession of which would put them astride two highways crucial for the supply of the Gustav Line and deny to the Germans the last natural barrier between Rome and the Allied army advancing from the south. In this way, it was thought, Kesselring would be either trapped or forced into a general retreat.

The plan almost foundered upon German resistance. A British attack across the Sangro had done little but lengthen the casualty lists, and the Allied armies were near exhaustion. Seeing little chance of breaking into the Liri Valley, Lt. Gen. Mark W. Clark of the Fifth Army recommended on December 18 that SHINGLE be canceled. Time was in any

---

France in anticipation of an Allied invasion of northwestern Europe. In the German Army, army groups and armies had an existence independent of the armies and divisions they commanded. Army headquarters were organizations of substantial size that might incorporate not only the commander and his staff but every manner of service unit.

event running out, as virtually all the landing craft in the Mediterranean were due to be surrendered to other theaters by January 15. Churchill, the tutelary spirit of the Mediterranean campaign, vehemently opposed abandoning the operation that promised the early capture of Rome. He summoned the Allied commanders to meet with him upon Christmas Day at Carthage, and there persuaded Eisenhower to reconfirm SHINGLE. An appeal to President Franklin D. Roosevelt postponed for a month the departure of the landing ships required for the operation.

The resurrected SHINGLE differed from the original plan in one crucial respect. The landing was to be nearly coincident with the offensive in the south, rather than to follow a breakthrough into the Liri Valley. The change was tacit tribute to the strength of the Gustav Line. SHINGLE, formerly to be the beneficiary of a breakthrough at Cassino, was now to make a breakthrough possible. The calculation, or rather the hope, was that the landing at Anzio would draw enough Germans from the Gustav Line to allow the Fifth Army to break into the Liri Valley.[3] It is evidence of Churchill's force of personality that the new plan, so much more a gamble than the first, was accepted. Most American officers, Eisenhower among them, were openly skeptical.[4] So, too, but more discreetly, were many Britishers.[5] Particularly vocal among the skeptics were the intelligence officers of the Fifth Army, who believed that the Germans would continue to resist stubbornly at Cassino while ruthlessly concentrating every available man at Anzio in an attempt to extirpate the beachhead.[6] The determined improvisation of the Germans at Salerno was evidence for this point of view, against which SHINGLE's advocates could adduce only their hope that the enemy would panic when confronted with a landing behind his lines. Clark came to share this happy expectation, telling one of his division commanders that SHINGLE "would cause the Germans so much concern that they would withdraw from the southern front."[7]

The debate over the merits of SHINGLE turned only slightly upon

3. Blumenson, *Salerno to Cassino*, 293–304. SHINGLE's rationale as interpreted by General Sir Harold Alexander, commander of the ground forces in Italy, is presented in Nigel Nicholson, *Alex: The Life of Field Marshal Earl Alexander of Tunis* (New York, 1973), 229–330.
4. Dwight Eisenhower, *Crusade in Europe* (Garden City, 1948), 212–13; Lucian K. Truscott, Jr., *Command Missions—A Personal Story* (New York, 1954), 291–92, 298, 306.
5. Among them, apparently, were General Alexander and, most definitely, General Sir Gerald Templer, commander of the only British division at Anzio. Nicholson, *Alex*, 232–33.
6. Blumenson, *Salerno to Cassino*, 353–54; Mark Clark, *Calculated Risk* (New York, 1950), 286.
7. Truscott, *Command Missions*, 291.

differing calculations of the effectiveness of aerial interdiction. General Sir Harold L. Alexander's Allied Force Headquarters (AFHQ), drawing on signals intelligence supplied by ULTRA, understood that the Germans had two divisions in reserve near Rome (the *29th* and the *90th Panzer Grenadier Divisions*) with which to oppose the landing. Alexander's intelligence officers counted on air attacks to slow the movements of these units so much that they would be unable to oppose the SHINGLE force effectively. The intelligence staff of the Fifth Army was more pessimistic. The Americans predicted that the Germans would respond resolutely with "all the resources and strength available to the German High Command in *Italy*." They estimated that the two divisions from Rome would arrive at Anzio within several days and expected a third division from the quiet Adriatic sector of the Gustav Line on D plus 3. The arrival of two more divisions from northern Italy was anticipated within two weeks.[8] But even this pessimistic calculation of five German divisions within two weeks made no allowance for the arrival of German formations from outside Italy. Such was the general confidence that the air forces could cripple Italy's railroads sufficiently to make a major concentration at Anzio impossible.[9]

Because the revived SHINGLE was no longer to follow gains at Cassino, the landing force had to be strengthened beyond the two divisions originally allotted: the American 3d Infantry Division and the British 1st Infantry Division. Now included were an American airborne regiment, two battalions of British commandos, and the Ranger Force—an elite American organization of three battalions somewhat patterned after the British commandos. More American units were added at the last minute: most of the 1st Armored Division, a regiment of the 45th Infantry Division, and several batteries of artillery. In all, SHINGLE gave 110,000 men as hostages to fortune.

As it was apparent that even the augmented SHINGLE force would be unable to hold the Alban Hills unless the Germans were routed at Cassino, Clark's orders to its commander, Maj. Gen. John P. Lucas, were deliberately ambiguous. Lucas was first to establish a secure beachhead and then to advance on the Alban Hills. It was left to Lucas to decide on the scene whether "on" meant "toward" or "to."

SHINGLE was the first major operation undertaken by the Mediterra-

---

8. Blumenson, *Salerno to Cassino*, 353–54 (emphasis added); F.H. Hinsley *et al.*, *British Intelligence in the Second World War*, 5 vols (London, 1979–), vol 3, pt 1, 184–85.

9. See, for example, Nicholson, *Alex*, 228; Blumenson, *Salerno to Cassino*, 353; Clark, *Calculated Risk*, 286; Truscott, *Command Missions*, 305–6.

Lt. Gen. Ira C. Eaker served as the commander of the Mediterranean Allied Air Forces during AVALANCHE, succeeding Air Chief Marshal Sir Arthur W. Tedder in that role.

nean Allied Air Forces (MAAF). Organized in December 1943, MAAF for the first time brought all Allied air forces in the Mediterranean under a single command by uniting the Northwest African Allied Air Forces with the Mediterranean Air Command and a congeries of British units, among them Royal Air Force Malta and Royal Air Force Middle East. MAAF's first commander was Air Chief Marshal Sir Arthur W. Tedder, formerly of the Mediterranean Allied Air Command. In mid-January, however, Tedder departed for England to participate in OVERLORD. His replacement was Lt. Gen. Ira C. Eaker, previously commander of the American Eighth Air Force in Great Britain.

The Northwest African Tactical and Strategic Air Forces were incorporated unchanged within MAAF. The responsibility for devising SHINGLE's air plan fell to the former organization. While the Strategic Air Force was to play an important role, its primary mission was the Combined Bomber Offensive against Germany.[10] (*Chart 2*)

SHINGLE's air plan, like AVALANCHE's, was a straightforward application of the three-phase strategy for a combined arms offensive developed in North Africa: air superiority, interdiction, and close air support. The Tactical Air Force issued the first operational directive for SHINGLE on December 30, 1943. The air plan came into force on January 1, 1944.

---

10. Wesley Frank Craven and James Lea Cate, eds., *The Army Air Forces in World War II*, 7 vols (Chicago, 1948–57; Washington, 1983), vol 2: *Europe*: *TORCH to POINTBLANK, August 1942 to December 1943*, 554–55.

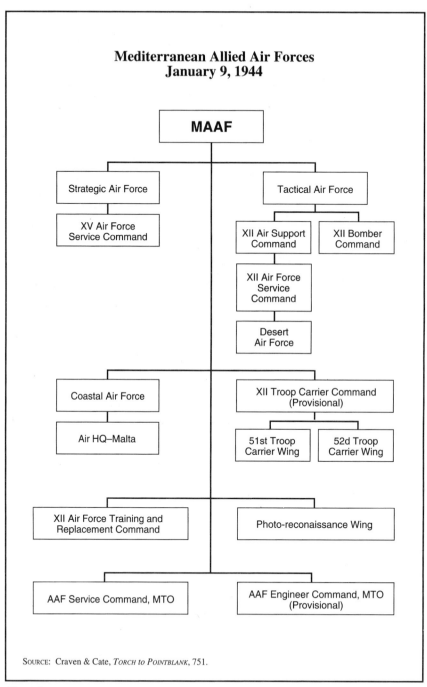

**Mediterranean Allied Air Forces
January 9, 1944**

MAAF

Strategic Air Force

XV Air Force
Service Command

Tactical Air Force

XII Air Support
Command

XII Bomber
Command

XII Air Force
Service
Command

Desert
Air Force

Coastal Air Force

Air HQ–Malta

XII Troop Carrier Command
(Provisional)

51st Troop
Carrier Wing

52d Troop
Carrier Wing

XII Air Force Training and
Replacement Command

Photo-reconaissance Wing

AAF Service Command, MTO

AAF Engineer Command, MTO
(Provisional)

SOURCE: Craven & Cate, *TORCH TO POINTBLANK*, 751.

Chart 2.

A supplementary order specifying targets appeared on January 4, 1944. Counterair operations began almost immediately.

Since AVALANCHE, Allied air superiority had grown even more pronounced. On January 21, 1944, MAAF disposed a total of slightly more than 7,000 aircraft, exclusive of gliders. The Germans had but 575 aircraft of all kinds in the entire Mediterranean theater, 200 fewer than at the time of AVALANCHE. Only 370 of these were in the central and western Mediterranean. There were only about 225 German fighters in all Italy—about 200 Messerschmitt Bf 109s and 25 Focke-Wulf FW 190s. The greatest concentration of German fighters was at Rome, well within range of Anzio. The *Luftwaffe*, husbanding its dwindling strength for the defense of the *Reich*, had ceased to send reinforcements to Italy. The Germans had no night fighters in the theater and few medium bombers, six groups of Junkers Ju 88s (about 180 aircraft) having been withdrawn from the Mediterranean in December for use against England. There remained fifty Ju 88s in Greece and Crete, while in southern France there was a mixed force of about sixty Ju 88s and Heinkel He 111s.[11]

In addition to these combat aircraft, the *Luftwaffe* maintained at Perugia a standing force of twenty Ju 88s and Me 410s for long-range reconnaissance. The destruction of this unit was one of the chief objectives of the counterair campaign, which opened on January 7 with an attack on the Perugia airdrome by forty-eight B-25s. Repeated attacks on this base culminated with a raid by twenty-eight B-24s on January 19. The German reconnaissance force remained out of action for four days, which allowed the Allied fleet to approach Anzio undetected on January 22.[12]

A raid on the German airdrome at Villaorba on the night of January 8 marked the beginning of an intensive effort to drive the *Luftwaffe* into northern Italy, out of range of Anzio. Several of the counterair attacks were carried out on a very large scale. On January 13, 100 B-17s, 140 B-24s, and 68 B-25s dropped more than 400 tons of bombs on German airfields near Rome at Guidonia, Centocelle, and Ciampino. During a se-

---

11. Mediterranean Allied Air Forces (MAAF), "Weekly Report of Status of Aircraft and Combat Crews," Jan 2, 1944, 622.245-4; Air Historical Branch of the British Air Ministry (AHB/BAM), "R.A.F. Narrative (First Draft): The Italian Campaign, 1943-1945," vol 1: "Planning and Invasion," 00895748, 241-43; British Air Ministry, *The Rise and Fall of the German Air Force (1933-1945)* (London, 1948), 259; Williamson Murray, *Strategy for Defeat: The Luftwaffe, 1933-1945* (Maxwell Air Force Base, Ala., 1983), 165. On January 2, 1944, MAAF had 1,772 Spitfires alone.

12. Wesley Frank Craven and James Lea Cate, eds., *The Army Air Forces in World War II*, 7 vols (Chicago, 1947-57; Washington, 1983), vol 3: *Europe: AR-GUMENT to V-E Day, January 1944 to May 1945*, 342-43; AHB/BAM, "Italian Campaign," 1:241-42, 245.

Bombing raids on the airfield at Ciampino reduced buildings to rubble *(left).* **Some had their steel skeletons exposed** *(upper left).* **Wrecked aircraft littered the field** *(upper right).*

ries of raids on January 19–20, B–17s dropped 700 tons of bombs on the same airfields. The common tactic was for the first wave of bombers to drop demolition bombs in order to crater the runways so that fragmentation bombs loosed by following aircraft would have a better chance of destroying stranded fighters. Neither the large raids nor many smaller ones destroyed many aircraft, the Germans having become adept at dispersal. But the attacks did succeed in denying to the *Luftwaffe* the use of its finest fields near Anzio for the crucial first days of SHINGLE.[13]

The interdiction phase of SHINGLE's air plan closely resembled AVALANCHE's in conception. It was to be implemented in three overlapping subphases. The purpose of the preparatory subphase, January 1–14, was the disruption of rail communications through central Italy, chiefly through the planned destruction of seven bridges and eleven marshaling yards. During the second subphase, January 15–21, the strategic interdiction of central Italy was to be supplemented by a more focused tactical interdiction to isolate the future beachhead from the hinterland—but not yet so focused as to reveal that Anzio was the Allied objective. The principal tactical interdiction targets were railroads and roads north of Rome and the highways between Rome and the Gustav Line. With D-day, January 22, the third subphase would begin: maximum interdiction consonant with the requirements for close air support of the roads leading directly to Anzio. The strategic interdiction of central Italy was to be maintained through this phase as well.[14]

The importance attached to the destruction of marshaling yards represented a change in emphasis from recent operations. During the fighting along the Gustav Line in the fall there had been a period when bridges, tunnels, and viaducts had been favored as targets. Allied intelligence had then estimated that each of the static German divisions needed only forty tons of supplies a day, which meant that the logistical requirements of *AOK 10* could be met if the railroads it employed functioned at a mere 5 percent of capacity. The nearly simultaneous destruction of engineering features had seemed the only way to cut into this modest requirement, for the portion of Italy's railroads remaining under German control was too well provided with rolling stock and marshaling yards for there to be much chance of cutting the efficiency of the system a full 95 percent solely by destruction of cars and service facilities.[15] But marshaling yards returned to the fore as targets with the approach of SHINGLE because of the low probability that a given bridge could be destroyed within a short period, whereas well-timed attacks on marshaling yards were thought certain to interrupt vital services and destroy at least some rolling stock. One of MAAF's staff studies put the case thus:

---

13. Craven and Cate, *ARGUMENT to V-E Day*, 342–42; AHB/BAM, "Italian Campaign," 1:241–42.

14. AHB/BAM, "Italian Campaign," 1:240; Assistant Chief of Staff, A–2, HQ U.S. Army Air Forces in Europe, "The Contribution of Air Power to the Defeat of Germany," vol 3, pt 11, sec 2 (no pagination), 519.601C.

15. The abortive experiment of the fall is discussed in Chapter 5.

> In choosing marshalling yards in preference to large engineering features, relatively greater probability of hitting and cutting is achieved at the expense of any expectancy of long-term interdiction. In support of a landing effort, *certainty* must take precedence over duration. . . . When it is desired to compel the retreat of strong and stabilized enemy force, by interdicting his line of supply, the *duration* of the cutting is the salient consideration.[16]

The concentration and supply of a large German force at Anzio, moreover, would require a considerably greater portion of the railroad system's capacity than the mere 5 percent utilized to support the static divisions of the Gustav Line.

Notwithstanding the considerable responsibilities of the Strategic Air Force in the air war against Germany and Germany's Balkan satellites, it cooperated closely with the Tactical Air Force in executing the air plan for SHINGLE. Attacks on engineering features and other point targets generally fell to those medium bombers in both air forces that had been recently fitted with the more accurate Norden bombsight. Area targets such as marshaling yards were the province of heavy bombers and those medium bombers still equipped with the older British Mark IX sight. A signal difference from AVALANCHE was that the establishment of air bases in Italy permitted the extensive use of fighter-bombers to strafe motor transport. During AVALANCHE, Allied fighters had been based in Sicily, and their limited range had precluded their making a major effort against German vehicles.

Throughout the preparatory bombardment, Allied planners carefully balanced two objectives: interdiction and deception. Since the preparations for a major landing operation could scarcely be hidden, the Allies strove to convince the Germans that the objective of the gathering force was Civitavecchia, about forty miles northwest of Rome. To that end, the planners ordered heavy attacks on rail communications along Italy's western coast from Pisa to Genoa and on Civitavecchia itself. They also arranged for demonstrations at sea and ostentatiously gathered ships at Corsica and Sardinia while the real invasion force assembled at Naples.

To disrupt German communications throughout Italy in such a way as to conceal that Anzio was the objective, MAAF struck hard at Italy's central and western rail lines, although it also repeatedly attacked the marshaling yard at Ancona, on the eastern coastal line. A glance at the railroad map of Italy will show that this emphasis was justified by both

---

16. MAAF, "Role of Strategic Air Force in Interdiction of Rail Traffic in Support of Anzio Operation," in MAAF, "Air Force Participation in Operation SHINGLE," n.d. [1944], 168.61–1 (emphases in the original).

The harbor (*above*) and marshaling yards (*right*) in Ancona on Italy's Adriatic coast south of the Pisa-Rimini line in central Italy show evidence of Allied attempts to interdict supplies to the Germans on the Anzio and Cassino fronts. Little rolling stock was destroyed or damaged in the marshaling yards; destruction of track outside the yards apparently caused more delays.

the proximity of the western and central lines to Anzio and their greater capacities relative to the eastern line.[17] (See *Map 7*)

During the first subphase of the prelanding bombing campaign, B–25 and B–26 medium bombers of the Tactical Air Force flew about 340 sorties, chiefly against the marshaling yards at Grosseto, Arezzo, Siena, Foligno, Lucca, Pontedera, and Fabriano. Also attacked were bridges at Orvieto and Giulianova and three ports important to the German's coastal traffic: Ancona, San Benedetto, and Civitavecchia. The raids on the latter two places were the work of fighter-bombers, which

17. Mediterranean Tactical Air Force, "Operations Directive for Operation SHINGLE No. 2," Dec 30, 1943, and "Operational Directive for Operation SHINGLE No. 4," Jan 4, 1944, both in "Air Force Participation in Operation SHINGLE." See also MAAF, "Role of Strategic Air Force," in "Air Force Participation in Operation SHINGLE," 6–10.

also flew armed reconnaissance against rail and road traffic north of Rome, and between Rome and the Gustav Line. The Strategic Air Force bombed Turin's marshaling yards on January 3 and those of Reggio Emilia on January 8.[18]

In the period January 13–22, strategic interdiction continued, both for its own sake and to maintain the deception that the Allies were preparing to descend on Civitavecchia. But there now began the series of attacks specifically targeted to disrupt the operation of those rail lines that the Germans would have to use to move troops from Rome and the Gustav Line to Anzio. The Tactical Air Force's area of operations, accordingly, shifted south. (*Chart 3*) Of the nearly 800 sorties the medium bombers flew in this period, most were south of Perugia. Hit hardest were the lines from Rome to Arezzo, Viterbo, and Leghorn, particularly the marshaling yards at Terni, Foligno, Orte, Piombino, Avezzano, and Chiarvalle and the bridges around Orvieto, Orte, Montalto di Castro, and Terni. South of Rome, medium bombers attacked bridges at Roccasecca and Pontecorvo, as well as the Liri River and Isoletta dams, which were bombed in an unsuccessful attempt to create flooding that would impede the movement of troops from the Gustav Line. The Tactical Air Force's fighter-bombers were also active, flying more than 1,000 sorties against rail and road targets, principally between Rome and the Gustav Line.[19] In the same period, the heavy bombers of the Strategic Air Force directed more than 700 sorties against the northern lines. The marshaling yards at Pisa, Arezzo, Pistoia, Prato, Pontedera, Rimini, Certaldo, Pontassieve, Civitanova, and Poggibonsi drew most of the sorties. British Wellingtons flew 110 night sorties to disrupt repair of the rail centers. In all, the Allied air forces dropped 5,400 tons of bombs on communications targets between January 1 and 22.[20]

The few German fighters left in Italy posed only a small threat to Allied bombers. They were either committed to the front or, after January 22, used for attacks on the Allies at Anzio. Neither was flak a serious obstacle to MAAF's interdiction campaign for SHINGLE. Most of the Germans' mobile antiaircraft artillery was assigned to infantry divisions along the Gustav Line or, after SHINGLE, to units at Anzio. For political reasons the heavy flak had been sent to the defense of Italian cities and factories in 1942. These assignments were not changed until the latter part of March 1944 when, in response to intensified Allied attacks on

---

18. MAAF, "Central Mediterranean Operational Summaries," Jan 1 through 14, 1944, 622.01–13.

19. *Ibid.*, Jan 14 through 23, 1944.

20. *Ibid.*; Mediterranean Tactical Air Force, "Operation SHINGLE—Bombing Plan," Jan 15, 1944, in "Air Force Participation in Operation SHINGLE."

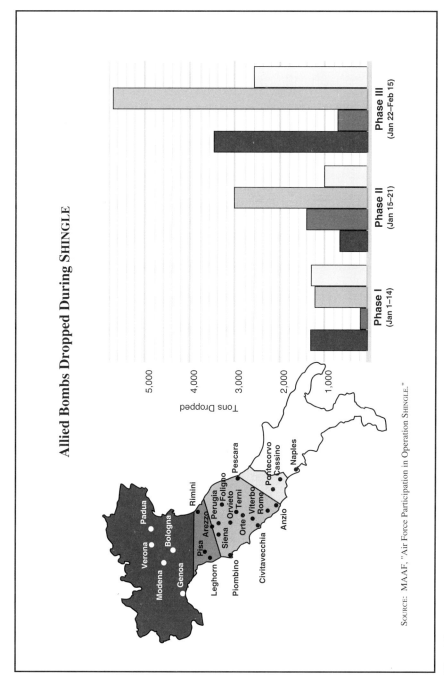

Allied Bombs Dropped During SHINGLE

SOURCE: MAAF, "Air Force Participation in Operation SHINGLE."

Chart 3.

their communications (Operation STRANGLE), the Germans for the first time heavily committed antiaircraft artillery to the defense of the railroads.[21]

On January 12 the Allies began the offensive designed to carry them into the Liri Valley. Three Allied corps faced the Germans near Monte Cassino. The British 10 Corps was on the left along the southern bank of the Garigliano River. The American II Corps was in the center, occupying high ground that overlooked the flooded plain of the Rapido River which, just south of Cassino, joins the Liri to form the Garigliano. On the Allied right was the French expeditionary force of two divisions that had replaced VI Corps, withdrawn for the landing at Anzio.

The French led the assault. They gained several miles before being stopped by German resistance and nearly impassable terrain. The Americans took Monte Trocchio, just south of the Rapido, on January 15. Two days later the British crossed the Garigliano and advanced four miles into the German positions before they too were stopped. On the night of January 20, the American 36th Division attempted to cross the Rapido and break into the Liri Valley just beyond. It suffered a disastrous repulse. At great cost the Allies had made some gains, but the Gustav Line held.

As survivors of the 36th Division straggled back across the Rapido on the morning of January 21, VI Corps sailed from Naples. A roundabout course to deceive the enemy brought the fleet to Anzio during the first hours of January 22. Thanks to the blinding of the *Luftwaffe*'s reconnaissance force and the fortuitous breakdown of the German radar network on the night of January 21–22, tactical surprise was total. But the Germans, having long expected a landing somewhere behind their lines, had made preparations: An alert force of two divisions, the *29th* and the *90th Panzer Grenadiers*, stood ready at Rome. A third division, the *4th Parachute*, was being formed near Terni to join them. In France and Yugoslavia other divisions stood ready to move to Italy on several hours' notice. Routes had been marked, fuel stocked, and crews detailed to clear mountain passes of snow.[22]

Unredressed, however, was the weakness of German intelligence. As the battles of January developed along the Gustav Line, Kesselring asked

---

21. Max Ritter von Pohl, "Commitment of Flak and Fighters to Protect the German Routes of Supply in Italy (1944–1945)," MS D–191, Record Group (RG) 338, National Archives and Records Administration (NARA), 4; British Air Ministry, *Rise and Fall of the German Air Force*, 266.

22. German Military Documents Section, Military Intelligence, War Department, "The German Operations at Anzio: A Study of the German Operations at Anzio Beachhead from 22 January to 31 May 1944," Apr 9, 1946, 170.2271, 5–6, 11–13; Wynford Vaughn-Thomas, *Anzio* (New York, 1961), 53.

the head of German military intelligence, Admiral Wilhelm Canaris, whether agents had reported preparations in Naples for an amphibious operation in the near term. Receiving Canaris's assurance that none was in evidence, Kesselring committed the *29th* and the *90th Panzer Grenadier Divisions* to bolster his sagging front along the Garigliano.

So it happened that the morning of January 22 found Lucas ashore unopposed and an appalled Kesselring bereft of the larger part of his alert force. The roads to the Alban Hills and even to Rome lay open. But Lucas was blind to his opportunities, and Kesselring equal to his peril. By 0500 the German commander had ordered the *4th Parachute Division* to move to Anzio from Terni. By 0600 he had requested and received reinforcements from Hitler: Within hours the *715th Infantry Division* had been ordered to Anzio from Avignon and the *114th Infantry Division* from northern Yugoslavia. Another division, the *92d*, was to be formed from training units in northern Italy. At 0710 Kesselring ordered *AOK 14*, responsible for the occupation of Italy north of the Gustav Line, to send every available unit to Anzio. By 1900 the *65th Division* (less one regiment) had set forth from Genoa, the *362d Division* (less one regiment) from Rimini, and elements of the *16th SS Panzer Division* from Leghorn. At 0839 came the hardest decision of all: Kesselring commanded hard-pressed *AOK 10* to send whatever it could to Anzio. That day the *3d Panzer Grenadier Division* (less one regiment), the *71st Infantry Division*, and elements of the *Hermann Göring Panzer Parachute* Division began to march. The *26th Panzer Division* and parts of the *1st Parachute Division* were under way by evening. By 1700 an improvised headquarters was at work in the Alban Hills, guiding the arriving units into a perimeter around the beachhead.[23]

The *Luftwaffe*'s reaction was also quick and efficient. Between January 22 and 31, 135 aircraft (mostly Ju 88s) moved to Italy from Germany, France, and Greece. Simultaneously, from fifty to sixty Dornier Do 217s and He 177s equipped with radio-controlled glide bombs reinforced the antishipping force in southern France. The *Luftwaffe* was, however, able to increase the fighter force in Italy by only about fifty aircraft in late January and another forty in late February. Thus, while German air strength increased by about 35 percent in the month following the landing at Anzio, the increase was unbalanced and bombers attacking the beachhead did so without adequate escort.[24]

Of the Germans' energetic response the Allies were for the moment ignorant. MAAF's intelligence analysts estimated that all rail communi-

23. Craven and Cate, *ARGUMENT to V-E Day*, 349–50.
24. AHB/BAM, "Italian Campaign," 1:248–49.

B–26 Marauders *(left)* **were a mainstay of medium bomber efforts against Nazi forces in Italy. With Florence still in Axis hands, a silver Marauder of the 1st Tactical Air Force** *(below)* **flies over the railyard to inspect the damage. From such intelligence, analysts believed that no rail communication was possible across the Pisa-Rimini line.**

cations north of Rome had been completely severed along a line from Pisa to Florence to Rimini, a condition believed to have existed since January 20. Confidence that Anzio was nearly isolated from the hinterland persisted until January 28, when the weather began to hamper MAAF's efforts.[25] "I feel now that the beachhead is safe and I can plan for the future with some assurance," Lucas wrote in his diary on Janu-

---

25. A.C.M.F. Intel Summary No. 32, Feb 16, 44, Appendix B, "Effect on Enemy Operations at Anzio of Allied Air Attacks on His L. of C.," in MAAF, "Air Force Participation in Operation SHINGLE"; MAAF, "Air Intelligence Weekly Summary," No. 67, Feb 28, 1944, 612.607.

Florence not only suffered Allied bomb damage; in retreat, the Germans attempted to knock out the last remaining road bridge across the Arno River *(above)*. Debris and desolation pervade as clouds of smoke rise from German shells. Evidence of the earlier Allied bombing is a locomotive left in a crater caused by a 1,000-pound bomb *(right)*.

ary 25. Nothing in the intelligence estimates he received indicated that VI Corps faced dangers greater than anticipated.[26]

The isolation of the beachhead was an illusion, but one sustained by strenuous efforts to make it a reality. From D-day through the end of the month, the fighter-bombers of the Tactical Air Force flew a daily average of 700 sorties in support of SHINGLE. Most were directed against German lines of communication, as there were few calls for close air support at Anzio before heavy fighting began there on January 30. In the

26. Blumenson, *Salerno to Cassino*, 386–87.

two weeks after D-day the medium bombers of the Tactical Air Force divided their efforts nearly equally between rail and road targets, weather permitting. (Poor weather forced cancellation of virtually all missions on January 24 and 26 and for the six days following January 30.) The bombing of roads was designed to block routes in and around the Alban Hills. The principal targets were junctions at Frascati, Albano, Palestrina, Marino, Mancini, Lariano, and Genzano. In attacking railroads, the Tactical Air Force concentrated on the lines from Rome to the north, particularly to Florence. The Strategic Air Force continued to attack marshaling yards all the way from Terni north to Verona on the line from the Brenner Pass. The principal targets were Bologna, Verona, Pontedera, Siena, Arezzo, Rimini, Civitanova, Terni, Foligno, Poggibonsi, Ancona, and Fabriano.[27]

German attacks on Allied shipping at Anzio were heaviest between January 23 and 29. The *Luftwaffe* dedicated as many as 150 daily to this purpose—all at night because of the strength of the Allies' daytime fighter force. Flak and night fighters soon took a toll of the more experienced and aggressive German crews, and the effectiveness of the *Luftwaffe*'s attacks declined rapidly even before bad weather closed over the beachhead at the end of the month and curtailed bomber operations on both sides. The bombing of German airfields at Villaorba, Udine, Maniago, and Lavariano on January 30 may also have contributed to the decline in German antishipping sorties. Between January 23 and February 19 the *Luftwaffe* sunk three naval vessels (a hospital ship, a destroyer, and a landing ship) and damaged five; one merchant ship was also lost and another seven were damaged.[28]

Lucas was a cautious and pessimistic man. He devoted the first nine days at Anzio to consolidating the beachhead. Historians have long debated the merits of an early advance to the Alban Hills. The consensus is that a rapid advance, appealingly bold as it might seem, would have dangerously extended Lucas's force. By January 28, in any event, intelligence from ULTRA had reinforced Lucas's native caution; it had been learned that perhaps eight German divisions were converging on Anzio, including one from France.[29] But even if Lucas's concern to render his beachhead secure may be counted wise, it remains curious that he waited until January 30 to take the villages of Cisterna and Campoleone that lay

---

27. Craven and Cate, *ARGUMENT to V-E Day*, 349-50.

28. AHB/BAM, "Italian Campaign," 1:248-49, 253; Samuel Eliot Morison, *History of U.S. Naval Operations in World War II*, 15 vols (New York, 1955-62), vol 9: *Sicily-Salerno-Anzio*, 342, 366.

29. F.H. Hinsley *et al., British Intelligence in the Second World War*, 5 vols (London, 1979-), vol 3, pt 1, 187-88.

scarcely four miles from positions occupied on D-day. Possession of these places was necessary for the strongest possible defense of the beachhead. And the psychological impact of the landing would have been magnified by their capture, for only seven miles northwest of Campoleone was Albano, a vital link in *AOK 10*'s communications with Rome. But by the time Lucas felt ready to grasp these neighboring prizes, they were firmly in the hands of an enemy whose approach had gone unnoticed. The Allies were greatly surprised when they encountered the *Hermann Göring Panzer Parachute Division* at Cisterna on January 30; neither ULTRA nor scouts had provided any warning about the approach of this formidable unit. The Allied repulse was bloody.[30] From the two ranger battalions that led the advance, not more than six men returned to the beachhead. Lucas had achieved an ultimately useful enlargement of his shallow beachhead, but the initiative had passed to the Germans.

Writing of the American disaster after the war, Maj. Gen. Wolf Hauser, *AOK 14*'s chief of staff, aptly observed that the Allies "had not reckoned on meeting resistance from more than advanced German units" because they had "relied too much on the effectiveness of their air attacks on railways." The proof of this is to be seen in a letter that Clark sent to Lucas on January 27. Reflecting the preinvasion estimate of what the Germans could move to Anzio (which ULTRA was just beginning to belie), Clark urged speed on his subordinate because there were no more than three German divisions near Anzio.[31] In fact, there were elements of *fourteen* German divisions at Anzio as Clark wrote, and more were on the way. (*Table 3*) Far from having been impeded, the buildup had proceeded so smoothly that Kesselring ordered the *715th Infantry Division*, speeding from France, to slow down and conserve its vehicles.[32]

The Germans had been able to invest the beachhead rapidly because their railroads had not been severed nearly so far south as the Allies had believed. Trains had ceased to run south of Rome by the end of 1943, and by mid-January they rarely ventured south of Terni and Orte.

---

30. ULTRA decrypts before February 2, 1944, contain no mention of the *Hermann Göring Division*. *Ibid.*, vol 3, pt 1, 188.

31. AHB/BAM, "The *Fourteenth Army* in Action at Anzio-Nettuno Up to 11 May 1944," 1947, Translation VII/99, 1950 [from the original document by Maj Gen Wolf Hauser *et al.*], K512.621, 8; Blumenson, *Salerno to Cassino*, 388. Clark's postwar judgment was the same as Hauser's. Clark, *Calculated Risk*, 286.

32. General Siegfried Westphal, "Army Group's Comments," in AHB/BAM, "*Fourteenth Army* in Action at Anzio-Nettuno," 31. The discrepancy between Clark's estimate of three divisions and the reality of fourteen was not so great as the bald numbers imply because few of the German divisions were at full strength or complete. Nonetheless, the underestimation of German strength was clearly serious.

Table 3. Major German Units Present at the Anzio Beachhead by January 31, 1944

Origin of Travel	Unit	Time of Departure	Arrival at Anzio
North of Rome			
Rimini	362d Infantry Division*	Jan 22–23	By Jan 25
Terni-Spoleto	4th Parachute Division	Jan 22	By Jan 25
Avignon (France)	715th Infantry Division	Jan 23–24	Jan 30
Yugoslovia	114th Infantry Division	Jan 23–24	By Jan 25
Genoa	65th Infantry Division*	1900 hrs, Jan 22	Jan 25 or 26
Leghorn	16th SS Panzer Division*	1900 hrs, Jan 22	By Jan 25
Berlin	Infantry and artillery demonstration regiments	Jan 23–24	Jan 30–31
South of Rome			
Gustav Line	90th Infantry Division	?	By Jan 25
Gustav Line	3d Panzer Grenadier Division*	Jan 22	Before noon, Jan 23
Gustav Line	71st Infantry Division*	?	Before noon, Jan 23
Gustav Line and Rome	Hermann Göring Division*	Jan 22	After noon, Jan 23
Adriatic Front	26th Panzer Division	?	By Jan 25
Adriatic Front	1st Parachute Division*	?	By Jan 25
Gustav Line	15th Panzer Division	?	After noon, Jan 23
Gustav Line	90th Panzer Grenadier Division	?	By Jan 25

*Not at full strength

SOURCES: *Kriegstagebuch Armeeoberkommando 14/Oberquartiermeister, Roll 485, Microfilm Pub T–312, NARA*; Blumenson, *Salerno to Cassino.*

Shortly before SHINGLE the destruction of bridges at Orte and Orvieto closed the central line for several weeks. The western line the Germans had already abandoned because of its extreme vulnerability, but the eastern suffered only brief blockages. Most night trains were able to proceed at top speed via Rimini, Ancona, and Foligno to Terni and Orte, where troops and supplies were loaded onto trucks. A few continued on the eastern line as far south as Pescara, proceeding nearly as far as Rome by way of Sulmona and Tivoli.[33]

---

33. AHB/BAM, "The Transport Situation," 1947, in "The Campaign in Italy: Special Subjects," Translation VII/100, 1950 [from the original by Col Klaus Stange], K512.621, 11–12; AHB/BAM, "*Fourteenth Army* in Action at Anzio-Nettuno," 4.

The Germans had prepared comprehensively for keeping the railroads functioning under aerial attack. Upon Italy's defection in September 1943, they seized the railroads and operated them for the rest of the war through the *Wehrmachtsverkehrsdirektion* (*WVD*) which employed 10,000 employees of the German National Railway. Most Italian workers stayed at their posts and worked for the Germans. The Italian railwaymen committed little sabotage, but their morale sagged as the intensity and frequency of Allied attacks increased. Cooperation of the Italians was essential, for the Germans were too few and too unfamiliar with the Italian system to run it by themselves. The *WVD* was commanded by Brig. Gen. Karl Theodor Körner, who had at his disposal a special railway engineer regiment. In January 1944 the regiment consisted of three repair battalions, each comprising seven companies. Italian laborers, recruited without difficulty, assisted with repair. The repair companies, strategically distributed along the principal railway lines, achieved a high degree of proficiency. They always opened marshaling yards to through traffic in one to three days; bridges took somewhat longer to repair. When lines were severed, the Germans resorted to what they called "island traffic": Locomotives and cars were kept on concealed sidings along the more vulnerable lines. This reduced the likelihood that any segment of a line would be devoid of rolling stock and allowed for the shuttling of men and supplies from one point of rupture to the next, where they could be loaded onto another train beyond the break. Of the situation that prevailed *north* of Terni and Orte, General Körner wrote, "All operating blocks could be ignored. Of course, in doing so one frequently had to put up with transloading by truck for short distances."[34]

South of Terni and Orte, however, the Germans could not keep pace with the destruction wrought by Allied aircraft. And that, taken with their perennial shortage of motor transport, was a source of intermittent logistical constriction. The overland distance from the supply depots near the railheads at Terni and Orte to Anzio was nearly 100 miles. Allied fighters, omnipresent by day, forced the German convoys to travel mostly at night. This nearly doubled the motor transport required for this route. Even with some help from *Heeresgruppe C, AOK 14*'s transport sufficed to move supplies from the depots to Anzio only at the expense of an equally vital operation: the movement of supplies from the railheads to the supply depots.[35]

---

34. AHB/BAM, "Transport Situation"; Maj Gen Karl Theodor Körner, "Rail Transportation Problems in Italy," MS DO-10, RG 338.

35. Kesselring complained to Berlin on January 26 that supply trains were not reaching Rome and that motor transport was accordingly insufficient for daily needs. German supply records show why this was so. On February 1 *AOK*

The problems the Germans faced in moving troops and supplies were real, but MAAF's intelligence officers considerably overestimated them. They subsequently claimed that, but for interdiction, the German buildup at Anzio would have been completed by January 28.[36] As it was, virtually all German divisions were in place by February 1, the date that Maj. Gen. Eberhard von Mackensen of the *AOK 14* had chosen for his attack upon the beachhead.[37] The German practice of running trains only at night or in bad weather had hindered the Allies in their attempts to assess the effectiveness of their attacks, but a more basic reason for their deluded optimism was slowness to understand that the bombing of marshaling yards, which had been so devastating in southern Italy, was less effective under the conditions that obtained in January 1944. To a degree, this was a matter of numbers: South of Naples there were only ten major marshaling yards; north of Rome there were forty-eight. More important, however, was the different way in which the railroads had come to be used. Before AVALANCHE, they had been under the control of the Italian authorities, who naturally tended to give a certain precedence to the needs of the civilian population. The few marshaling yards in the south had to be used to shuffle cars because military shipments were often commingled with civilian goods, and the latter had to be dispersed among many centers of population. After Italy's defection, the Germans took over the railroads and used them solely to meet their own military requirements. Trains were made up north of the Alps and run straight through to railheads near the front. Under this regime marshaling yards were little more than switching stations, when they were not stretches of thoroughfare distinguished only by the presence of a dozen or so tracks

---

14 had a daily supply requirement of about 1,000 tons. Because of the distance involved and the requirement to move mostly by night, 2,000 tons of motor transport were required to convey supplies from depots. Of this amount, the divisions of *AOK 14* could supply 1,500 tons. *AOK 14*'s own transport companies had to supply the remainder; they also had to provide another 500 tons of transport space daily for operations in and around the supply depots. The transport companies fell short of having the required 1,000 tons of transport space; it was still unclear on February 1 whether *Heeresgruppe C* would be able to make good the deficit. The situation probably grew worse as new units joined *AOK 14* and the fighting intensified. Hinsley *et al., British Intelligence in the Second World War*, vol 3, pt 1, 189; "*Beurteilung der Versorgungslage (Stand 1.2.1944),*" appended to *Kriegstagebuch AOK 14/Oberquartiermeister* (hereafter *KTB AOK 14/O Qu*), Roll 485, Microfilm Pub T–312, NARA.

36. See, for example, A.C.M.F. Intel Summary No. 32, Feb 16, 1944, app B, "Effect on Enemy Operations at Anzio of Allied Air Attacks on His L. of C.," in MAAF, "Air Force Participation in Operation SHINGLE"; MAAF, "Air Intelligence Weekly Summary," No. 67, Feb 28, 1944.

37. In fact, of the German divisions that fought at Anzio during the first month of the battle, *only* the *29th Panzer Grenadier Division* arrived after January 31.

in parallel.[38] The Italian rail centers, in short, were not so central to the functioning of the rail system as they had been the preceding summer when Professor Solly Zuckerman had directed the attention of the Allied air forces to them. And no longer were the Allies presented with dense clusters of rolling stock that could be destroyed wholesale.[39]

MAAF's intelligence summaries rarely claimed the destruction of trains. They often claimed, however, that whole lines were blocked because of the destruction of tracks in marshaling yards. Apparently forgotten was Zuckerman's admonition that marshaling yards should *not* be bombed to create blockages: "Only in very special cases," he had written in his report to Tedder, "would it be worthwhile to attack a railway center with the primary object of interrupting traffic for a day or two."[40] MAAF could have kept the rail centers closed only through an expenditure of resources it could not have afforded, even had it realized the need. (As previously noted, the Germans were reopening bombed yards in one to three days. Before long, MAAF would admit to a figure of two to four days.[41]) During January only twenty-eight of the forty-eight major yards in German hands were bombed, and the average interval between attacks was *eighteen days.* During the two weeks which saw the Germans begin and complete their buildup at Anzio, the average interval between attacks was *12.2 days.*[42] The extent to which MAAF overestimated the effect of its attacks, presumably because of faulty photo-

---

38. "Headquarters, 2677 Headquarters Company Experimental, U.S. Army" [Office of Strategic Services, Caserta], "Air Attacks on Bridges and Marshalling Yards in Italy—Is Experience Prior to the Fall of Naples a Reliable Guide for Attack in 1944?" Mar 7, 1944, 622.454-1, 1-9.

39. *Ibid.,* 3, 7-9. For the theories of Professor Zuckerman and their influence upon Allied bombing operations, see Chapter 3.

40. Ltr, Solly Zuckerman to Air Chief Marshal Sir Arthur Tedder, Dec 28, 1943, enclosing his Rpt, "Air Attacks on Rail and Road Communications," 519.425-1, 41.

41. P.H. Coombs, Target Consultant, A-2 Section, MAAF, "Considerations Concerning Air Attack on Enemy Rail Communications in Italy," Mar 16, 1944, 622.454-1, 2.

42. During the period December 31, 1943, to February 4, 1944, the twenty-eight yards struck were bombed an average of two times, or once every eighteen days. During the critical period, January 24 to February 4, the interval was 12.2 days, but only seventeen of the twenty-eight yards on the target list (51 percent of those on the target list; 35 percent of all marshaling yards in German-occupied Italy) were attacked. The targets were generally well chosen. The abandoned western line was attacked at only four points, three of which fed the central and eastern lines, which were very much in use. Two of the three places most attacked, Terni and Orte (9 and 5 attacks, respectively), were the railheads for the German forces at Anzio and the Gustav Line, while the third, Foligno (5 attacks), was a principal marshaling yard on the eastern line that the Germans used most heavily. MAAF, "Air Intelligence Weekly Summaries," Nos. 60-64 (Jan 10 through Feb 7, 1944), 622.01-6.

graphic reconnaissance, is especially striking because between December 31 and February 4 it claimed the destruction of only two bridges, both on the central line.[43]

It would be incorrect, however, to conclude that MAAF's interdiction campaign was without effect on the German buildup. The war diary of *AOK 14* complained on January 29 that the arrival of forces at Anzio had been "delayed, as the railroad system in Italy has been crippled by enemy air raids." The assault on the beachhead was to have taken place on January 28, but von Mackensen delayed it until February 1 so that certain special-purpose units then en route from Germany by train could participate. As these reinforcements were not scheduled to reach the Brenner Pass before January 26 and 27, it is an open question how much the delay was due to the damaged railways and how much to their late dispatch from Germany.[44] However occasioned, the postponement of the offensive had this important consequence: It allowed General Lucas unwittingly to preempt the German counterattack planned for February 1 with his own abortive advance of January 30, which cost the Germans enough in ground lost and ammunition expended to force them to delay their general assault on the beachhead for more than an additional two weeks.[45]

The events of January 30 made it plain to all that the estimate that the Germans would be able to move only about three divisions to Anzio in the time since D-day had been wildly wrong. But MAAF's confidence remained unshaken. Indeed, it later claimed that it had delayed the German assault on the beachhead until February 16.[46] Interdiction by itself, however, was at most partially responsible for delaying the attack by several days. The additional sixteen days of postponement were chiefly the result of Lucas's attack of January 30. But to the extent that interdiction

---

43. MAAF, "Air Intelligence Weekly Summaries," Nos. 60–64 (Jan 10 through Feb 7, 1944). German sources agree that damage to the bridges at Orvieto and Orte closed down the central line for part of January. This forced the Germans to rely primarily on the Rimini-Ancona-Foligno-Terni routes during their buildup at Anzio. But the important marshaling yard at Foligno was attacked only twice during the twelve days from January 24 to February 4. Assuming an average repair time of two days, the line was closed for only four of twelve days—and possibly only for hours, depending upon the effectiveness of the attacks.

44. "War Diary of the *Fourteenth Army*," Jan 29, 1944, in German Military Documents Section, Military Intelligence, War Department, "German Operations at Anzio."

45. *Ibid.*, Jan 31, 1944.

46. A.C.M.F. Intel Summary No. 32, Feb 16, 1944, app B, "Effect on Enemy Operations at Anzio of Allied Air Attacks on His L. of C."; MAAF, "Air Intelligence Weekly Summary," Feb 28, 1944; Craven and Cate, ARGUMENT to V–E Day, 53.

contributed to the initial delay of four days that had allowed Lucas to launch his attack, it performed a real service. General Clark, greatly concerned that the estimates of the speed with which the Germans could build up their forces had proved so wrong, ordered Lucas on February 2 to go on the defensive and to strengthen his positions with barbed wire and minefields. Both measures were carried out on an extensive scale in the following days, and on February 16 the beachhead was far better prepared to withstand the storm that broke against it than it would have been earlier.

Though repulsed at Cisterna and Campoleone, the Allies had gained a finger-shaped salient that extended through the German positions toward Campoleone. Within the salient was the village of Aprilia, which sat at the heart of a network of roads important to the German plan for attacking the beachhead. Von Mackensen attacked the salient on February 3 with the object of regaining Aprilia. On the night of February 4 the salient's British defenders withdrew from their more exposed positions, but Aprilia remained in Allied control. The Germans returned to the attack on February 9. After three days of heavy fighting, which saw many Allied counterattacks, the German commander had recaptured the ground he needed for his assault on the beachhead. In order to allow his soldiers several days for rest and reorganization, von Mackensen set the attack for February 16.

As the Germans edged into position around the beachhead, MAAF continued its raids on their lines of communication. Weather was bad from February 3 to 5, and again on February 7, but daylight hours of the clear days saw fighter-bombers fly hundreds of sorties in search of trains and motor vehicles. The heavy and medium bombers continued to attack the railroads. Particularly hard hit were the marshaling yards at Verona, Siena, Prato, Orte, Modena, Perugia, Padua, Piombino, and Pisa. Railway bridges were bombed at Civita Castellana, Manziana, Monterotondo, Fratta Todina, and Perugia.[47] (See *Chart 3*)

Logistical demands imposed by the greatly increased fighting around the beachhead after January 30, added to those of the Gustav Line where fighting still raged at Cassino, began to strain a supply system constricted by the delays imposed by damage to the railroads, the need to rely on trucks to bridge the gap between the railheads north of Rome and the fighting forces, and the inability to operate either trucks or trains by day. Shortages of all kinds began to afflict the Germans, but one was critical

---

47. MAAF, "Central Mediterranean Operational Summaries," Feb 2–16, 1944. During the period February 5–18, when the weather was not good, only sixteen marshaling yards were struck; the attacks averaged one every 7.5 days. MAAF, "Air Intelligence Weekly Summaries," Nos. 65, 66 (Feb 14, 21, 1944).

and possibly decisive: artillery ammunition. The attack on the beachhead could not succeed without heavy artillery support. Always essential for offensive operations, it was particularly important at Anzio because the Germans lacked the strong naval and air support enjoyed by the Allies. The shortage of ammunition was the more keenly felt because the situation of the German artillery at Anzio was otherwise good. For the first weeks of the fighting the Germans had more guns than the Allies.[48] The beachhead, moreover, was a gunner's dream of a target. Because of Lucas's failure to capture Cisterna and Campoleone, the position lacked adequate depth. Although it stretched for fourteen miles along the coast, the Allied enclave was nowhere more than twelve miles deep. Along the principal axis of the German attack of February 16, Allied front lines were scarcely six miles from the sea. German artillery, therefore, could without displacement support the projected advance for virtually its entire length. And from their positions in the Alban Hills the Germans had a clear view of everything in the beachhead.

In planning for his attack, von Mackensen was plagued by three worries that several times induced him to submit his resignation to Kesselring, who refused it. The first was the inexperience of most of his troops; few were veterans. The second was that his command fell far short of having the advantage of three to one desirable for offensive operations against an entrenched foe: On February 16, 125,000 Germans attacked 100,000 Anglo-Americans. The shortage of men was the result of Germany's overextended strategic position—every available reinforcement had been sent from Germany, and even as he prepared for the attack of February 16 von Mackensen had to send troops to shore up the Gustav Line. The German general's third worry was the shortage of ammunition. The war diary of *AOK 14* is clear about the reason for it: The entry for January 31 states, "Because of the difficult rail situation, we . . . doubt whether an ammunition issue can be assured for the *Fourteenth Army*, especially since the *Tenth Army* requires a great deal of ammunition at Cassino."[49]

These forebodings were amply borne out. Throughout the fighting at Anzio, a German artilleryman subsequently wrote, the German guns had "a bare average of two issues of ammunition"—less than the tactical situation demanded. (*Table 4*) The Allies, on the other hand, benefited from "a quantitative superiority in ammunition that was horrifying," fir-

---

48. Maj Gen Walther Kühn, "The Artillery at Anzio-Nettuno," 171.3–14, 11–12.

49. "War Diary of the *Fourteenth Army*," Jan 31, 1944, in German Military Documents Section, Military Intelligence, War Department, "German Operations at Anzio."

Table 4. Ammunition Status (in *Ausstattungen*) of *AOK 14*, February 15, 1944, 1800 Hrs

Ammunition Type	Issues in the:	
	Divisions	Depots
Machinegun	0.88	—
8-cm mortar	0.91	0.15
12-cm mortar	1.75	0.37
Light infantry gun	1.19	0.51
Heavy infantry gun	1.19	0.66
Light field howitzer 18	1.76	0.15
Heavy field howitzer	1.52	0.05
10-cm cannon	1.42	1.10
21-cm mortar	2.18	0.74
17-cm mortar	2.09	—
15-cm *Nebelwerfer*	1.36	0.46
21-cm *Nebelwerfer*	1.08	1.82
Field cannon	2.06	2.63
Unknown	0.79	—
Light field howitzer 16	1.57	—
22-cm mortar	1.9	1.71

SOURCE: *Anlage 2* to untitled *Anlage 191, KTB AOK 14/O Qu.*

ing, according to German estimates, twelve to fifteen shells for each shot at them.[50] This calculation accords well with the figures given in the history of the Fifth Army for the week before the Germans' attack, when the Anglo-Americans fired 25,000 rounds daily and received but 1,500.[51]

The Germans' lack of ammunition handicapped their attack in several dire ways. A rolling barrage that had been deemed essential to clear a path through the Allies' fortifications had to be canceled for lack of

---

50. Kühn, "Artillery at Anzio-Nettuno," 12–13. The German issue, the *Ausstattung*, was roughly the equivalent of the American basic issue. It was determined by a number of considerations: experience, the weapon's rate of fire, its tactical employment, and the weight of its ammunition. One issue supposedly sufficed for ten days of normal—that is to say, light—combat. But in support of a major attack as many a five or six issues might be fired in a day or two (see General Wesphal's comments in the text that follows). Brig Gen Kurt Scheffler, "Strength and Composition of German Artillery During World War II," MS P-057, RG 338, 11–12, 14–15, 17; G-2 Section, Allied Force Headquarters, "The German System of Supply in the Field: Italy, 1943-1945," Feb 1946, German Naval Records Collection, Operational Archives Branch, Naval History Division, Office of the Chief of Naval Operations, 99. For a detailed accounting of the German ammunition situation at Anzio, see the untitled *Anlage 191* to *KTB AOK 14/O Qu*, Mar 19, 1944, T-312, Roll 485.

51. U.S. Fifth Army, "Fifth Army History," pt 4, "Cassino and Anzio," n.d., 680.01, 126.

shells. All that was possible was "a brief preparatory barrage against known points of resistance," with fires thereafter "only on selected visible targets."[52] This ruled out effective counterbattery fires, which was particularly unfortunate for the Germans because Hitler had ordered a massive assault along a single axis in place of the infiltrating attacks along several axes that von Mackensen had originally planned to counteract the Allied advantage in artillery. As it was, the Germans drove deeply into the beachhead and, despite their headlong charge across open terrain, inflicted casualties equal to those they sustained. Their own losses were almost entirely caused by artillery fire.[53]

Allied interdiction seems to have contributed to the inadequacy of German artillery support, and therefore to the outcome of the battle, in yet another way. General Siegfried Westphal, Kesselring's chief of staff, wrote afterwards that the German army in Italy had developed a " 'poor man' complex" from its persistent shortages of virtually everything. It was first an official requirement, and then a psychological compulsion, to expend supplies and ammunition as sparingly as possible. During the attack of February 16 the German command was misled by incomplete reports from the artillery regiments that nearly all the issue of ammunition reserved for that most important day had been fired. Ever fearful of shortages, the artillery commander ordered an immediate conservation of ammunition, for there remained scarcely another issue for the rest of the engagement, which was expected to last several days. Only after the Germans had stopped their advance for the day was it learned that the report from the batteries had referred only to that portion of the issue slated for firing for February 16 stored at the guns; fully half the issue remained unfired in the dumps or with the supply companies. Westphal, who witnessed the attack, later wrote that "even at the time it seemed that a decisive success could have been achieved if a complete allocation [issue] of ammunition had been expended in the operations on 16 February."[54]

The attack of February 16 was the German army's only real chance to fulfill Hitler's order to "lance the abscess" that was SHINGLE. Another assault on February 29 fell far short of the near success of the first

---

52. "War Diary of the *Fourteenth Army*," Feb 13, 1944, in German Military Documents Section, Military Intelligence, War Department, "German Operations at Anzio"; AHB/BAM, "*Fourteenth Army* in Action at Anzio-Nettuno," 14.

53. Blumenson, *Salerno to Cassino*, 424; "War Diary of the *Fourteenth Army*," Feb 16–20, 1944, in German Military Documents Section, Military Intelligence, War Department, "German Operations at Anzio."

54. Westphal, "Army Group's Comments," in AHB/BAM, "*Fourteenth Army* in Action at Anzio-Nettuno," 33–34.

effort. Even the official history of the Fifth Army, not given to minimizing successes, describes the second attack as having shown "both timidity and lack of co-ordination."[55] Like the first, it was plagued by the shortage of ammunition that bedeviled the Germans until they were driven from Anzio in May.[56]

The second attack on the beachhead was not defensible in strictly military terms. It was made because of the great importance that Hitler attached to defeating SHINGLE in the hope that OVERLORD would then be canceled or postponed. Fearing that the *Führer* would insist on a third attack that would gut the German army in Italy, Kesselring entrusted Westphal with the delicate mission of explaining matters in Berlin. To the great surprise of his entourage, Hitler listened patiently as Westphal explained why no third attack was possible. When the general came to the question of ammunition, Hitler asked "how many allocations [issues] of ammunition . . . would be required to throw the enemy back into the sea." Westphal replied that "four or five allocations [issues] would be necessary but that it was impossible to bring them to the front owing to the daily severance of rail communications in Italy by bombing attacks." This was so manifestly true that the willful dictator had to admit that his forces could not attack again.[57]

The measure of success for an interdiction campaign must be its effect on the ground battle. By this standard, interdiction was successful at Anzio, albeit not nearly so much so as MAAF boasted. The consequences of the Germans' shortage of artillery ammunition were great: It gravely handicapped two attacks and obviated a third. It is also possible that interdiction contributed somewhat to delaying the first attack the Germans planned on the beachhead long enough for it to be preempted by the Allied attack of January 30 which, though it failed, gained a respite of sixteen days during which time the Anglo-Americans strongly entrenched themselves. That respite, however, was wholly a function of the situation on the ground, and MAAF's claims to the contrary notwithstanding, air power made no contribution to it beyond the quite conjectural role it may have played in moving the date of the planned German assault from January 28 to February 1.

55. U.S. Fifth Army, "Fifth Army History," pt 4, 157.
56. "War Diary of the *Fourteenth Army*," Feb 29, 1944, in German Military Documents Section, Military Intelligence, War Department, "German Operations at Anzio." See also *ibid.*, Feb 10–14, 1944.
57. Westphal, "Army Group's Comments," in AHB/BAM, "*Fourteenth Army* in Action at Anzio-Nettuno," 35. See also Siegfried Westphal, *Erinnerungen* (Mainz, 1975), 252–53.

Neither did air power seriously retard the movement of German divisions to Anzio. MAAF's claim to have severed the Italian railroads along a line running from coast to coast through Pisa, Florence, and Rimini was erroneous; the ability of the Allies to damage the railroads was never decisively greater than the ability of the Germans to repair them north of Terni and Orte. MAAF's efforts were further hampered by its inability to operate at night and in bad weather. The effect of interdiction during the Anzio campaign, then, was clearly not that nearly hermetic isolation of the battlefield promised by the less restrained enthusiasts of air power. Its contribution to the victory of the ground forces lay rather in a marginal reduction in the flow of supplies to the Germans which, at a critical juncture, rendered them weaker than they would otherwise have been. Against the claims made for interdiction both before and after SHINGLE this was not much. But it was enough.

Chapter 5

———◆———

Operation STRANGLE
March 19–May 10, 1944

Operation STRANGLE remains unique among strategic interdiction campaigns. Except for the first week of the operation, there was little fighting in Italy during STRANGLE, and
the consumption of the two German armies subject to interdiction was minimal. The Allied air forces nonetheless seriously curtailed German resupply, although they did not
achieve their objective of forcing the evacuation of the
Gustav Line. That STRANGLE had the effect it did was
largely due to the Germans' usual logistical liabilities—a serious shortage of motor transport and the resultant dependence on railroads. The Allies, enlarging on the strategy they
had effectively employed at Anzio, deliberately and skillfully
exploited these weaknesses. They drove German convoys
from the road by day while crippling the railroads of central
Italy with a newly intensive effort against bridges and other
engineering features. The demands on German motor transport soon soared to impossible levels.

Map 11.

Operation STRANGLE, observed a historian of the Mediterranean Allied Air Forces (MAAF), "emerged from the frustration of Anzio and the stalemate before Cassino."[1] The landing at Anzio had represented the Allies' last chance of flanking the strongly entrenched Germans from the sea, for OVERLORD soon after drained the Mediterranean of shipping. The Germans' rapid investment of the beachhead and the coincident repulse of the Allies before Cassino confirmed the Italian stalemate. No one was more disturbed than the commander of the U.S. Army Air Forces, General Henry H. Arnold, in distant Washington. He wrote in early March to the commander of MAAF, Lt. Gen. Ira C. Eaker, that "we are all very greatly disturbed here at the apparent 'bogging down' " of the Italian campaign because it threatened to furnish "ammunition to the advocates who decry the use of air power except as artillery." And that, the general feared, might imperil the relative independence of action that the air arm had acquired in North Africa.[2]

Arnold recommended that MAAF's heavy bombers be massed to break the German front at Cassino. In his reply of March 6, Eaker explained that just such an attack had already been planned and would be executed as soon as the weather permitted.[3] He was, however, more confident of another project:

---

1. Mediterranean Allied Air Forces (MAAF), "Operations in Support of DIADEM," n.d., 622.430–3, 1:5.
2. Ltr, General Henry H. Arnold, to Lt Gen Ira C. Eaker, n.d. [Mar 3, 1944], Box 22, vol 1, Eaker-Arnold Correspondence, Papers of Ira Eaker, Library of Congress (LC).
3. The Allies had on February 15, 1944, bombed and destroyed the famed abbey of Monte Cassino in the mistaken belief that Germans were inside. The operation to which Eaker referred, which was executed on March 15, 1944, entailed bombardment of the German lines in and around the town of Cassino. This bombing was spectacular but failed to dislodge the Germans, who easily repulsed a closely following infantry assault.

> The air phase of the plan which will win Rome for us and eventually force the enemy back to the Pisa-Rimini line has been carefully worked out also. It calls for cutting lines of communication, road and rail, and the destruction of enemy coastal shipping to the point where he cannot possibly supply his 17–20 divisions South of that line. We have sufficient air force to carry out this plan in good weather. It is not a novel or original idea. It is the same old plan which pushed Rommel out of Africa.[4]

Eaker would have been more accurate to state that the operation contemplated was a replay upon a larger scale of an effort made the previous fall. In October and November 1943 the Allies had attempted to starve the Germans of supplies by systematically attacking their railroads. Engineering features—bridges, viaducts, and tunnels—had been the main targets. Bad weather and other demands on the air forces had been the primary reasons for the early and inconclusive end of the project. Also influential, however, had been a certain disillusionment with the number of sorties that bombers had required to destroy bridges. Their inefficiency had seemed to confirm the position of the British scientist, Professor Solly Zuckerman, that bridges were unsuitable targets for aerial attack except when urgent tactical needs justified the expense of their destruction. Zuckerman had argued that railroads could be crippled more quickly and more completely by bombing marshaling yards, where rolling stock could be destroyed en masse with vital switching, repair, and signaling facilities. Near the end of 1943, the scientist finished a lengthy study of what had happened after the Northwest African Air Forces had, at his urging, begun to bomb the rail centers of southern Italy the previous summer. The treatise, which conclusively showed that the attacks had paralyzed the entire rail system south of Naples, greatly impressed Air Chief Marshal Sir Arthur W. Tedder, who had been named to head MAAF upon its creation in December 1943. Tedder relinquished command to Eaker within days, but not before making Zuckerman's precepts its doctrine for strategic interdiction. Henceforth, Tedder ruled, attacks against Italy's railroads were to be limited to the marshaling yards at Rimini, Foligno, Verona, Genoa, Turin, Vicenza, and Voghera.[5]

---

4. Ltr, Eaker to Arnold, Mar 6, 1944, Box 22, vol 1, Eaker-Arnold Correspondence, Papers of Ira Eaker. MAAF's former deputy commander, Lt Gen Carl A. Spaatz, shared Eaker's confidence. He wrote to Arnold after a visit to Italy that the success of the impending interdiction operation was "just as inevitable as was the Tunisian Campaign." Ltr, Spaatz to Arnold, Feb 25, 1944, *ibid.*
5. For the influence of Zuckerman on operations in the Mediterranean theater, see Chapter 3. The abortive interdiction campaign of the fall is covered in Wesley Frank Craven and James Lea Cate, Jr., eds, *The Army Air Forces in World War II*, 7 vols (Chicago, 1948–57; Washington, 1983), vol 2: *Europe: TORCH to POINTBLANK, August 1942 to December 1943*, 554–58, 580–81. For

The failures of the fall and Tedder's patronage of Zuckerman notwithstanding, there remained advocates of another effort to cut the enemy's lines of communication through the destruction of engineering features.[6] Their chief stronghold was MAAF's A-2 (intelligence) Section. On the very day that Tedder officially endorsed Zuckerman's approach to interdiction, the intelligence officers proposed the isolation of the German front by the *"complete, simultaneous* and *continuous* interdiction of rail traffic. . . ."[7] Evidence for their proposal appeared within days. About the turn of the year an Italian officer, one General D'Aurelio, defected to the Allies from the Fascist forces still fighting with the Germans to claim that the bridge-bombing of the fall had seriously disrupted communications. D'Aurelio related that the *Oberquartiermeister* of Field Marshal Albert Kesselring's *Heeresgruppe C (Army Group C)* had told him that it would be impossible to hold Rome if bridges continued to be destroyed apace. The defector added that by the end of November, when the experimental interdiction campaign had ended, German communications with Rome had depended upon two minor loop lines. Had they been severed, the city must soon have fallen.[8]

Two predictions soon followed that SHINGLE's air plan, which reflected MAAF's understanding of Zuckerman's recommendations, would fail. On January 5, the G-2 Section of Allied Force Headquarters argued that the directive stressed marshaling yards too much, as the Germans had some time before begun to make up their supply trains in the *Reich* itself.[9] There was therefore little point in bombing rail centers unless they could be so thoroughly demolished as to block traffic through them. On January 15 the A-2 of the Twelfth Air Force observed that MAAF's

---

Tedder's order, see the Air Historical Branch of the British Air Ministry (AHB/BAM), "R.A.F. Narrative (First Draft): The Italian Campaign, 1943 to 1945," vol 1: Planning and Invasion, 00895748, 307.

6. During the war this approach was often designated "interdiction" to distinguish it from "the Zuckerman Theories" because it stressed the cutting of lines of communication in conscious opposition to the British scientist's preference for introducing systemic inefficiencies into the enemy's railroad system through the destruction of rolling stock and service facilities. This study considers both strategies to have been interdiction inasmuch as their common aim was to reduce the flow of supplies to the German front.

7. MAAF, A-Section, "Special Intelligence Report No. 64: Communications (Italy)," Dec 24, 1943, in MAAF, "Operations in Support of DIADEM," vol 7, Tab F.

8. MAAF, "Air Intelligence Weekly Summary," No. 61 (Jan 17, 1944), 622.01-6. For the identity of the informant, see Wesley Frank Craven and James Lea Cate, Jr., eds, *The Army Air Forces in World War II*, 7 vols (Chicago, 1948-57; Washington, 1983), vol 3: *Europe: ARGUMENT to V-E Day, January 1944 to May 1945*, 372. German records do not support D'Aurelio's statement.

9. Ltr, Col Ford to Grp Capt Luard, Jan 5, 1944, in MAAF, "Operations in Support of DIADEM," vol 4, Tab I.

force of bombers was too small to keep the marshaling yards blocked, the Germans having shown they could restore traffic through bombed rail centers in a few days.[10]

Events soon confirmed these doubts. On February 4, MAAF's A-2 released a detailed report of its findings for the critical week of January 27–February 3, when the Germans had rushed divisions to Italy to contain the Allied beachhead at Anzio. Although many marshaling yards had been heavily damaged, at least one rail line had remained open through most of them. At no time had Rome been isolated from northern Italy.[11] MAAF could plausibly claim that during this and the preceding week it had delayed the concentration of the German divisions at Anzio by imposing lengthy detours around damaged marshaling yards and several destroyed bridges.[12] But after the German counterattacks of February the considered opinion within the Allied air forces was that the bombing of the marshaling yards had had little effect on German communications.[13] The ground commanders, in whom ultimate authority resided, could not have agreed more.[14]

The failure to prevent the transfer of strong German forces to Italy led MAAF's deputy commander, Air Marshal Sir John Slessor, to wonder if the Allies could not turn the enemy's recent augmentation to their advantage. On February 11, 1944, he addressed a long memorandum to the director of operations, Brig. Gen. Lauris Norstad:

> There are now some seventeen German divisions in Italy south of Rome. I do not believe the Army—even with our support—will move them. But I think it is more than possible that the Hun, by concentrating all his forces so far south has given us—the Air Forces—an opportunity. He has been able up to now just to support his small armies on the present line in spite of our air attacks on his communications. I find it hard to believe, that by increasing those forces, he has not put a load on his communications which they will not be able to stand if we really sustain a scientifically planned offensive against the *right places* in his L. of C. [lines of communication].[15]

---

10. A-2 Section, Twelfth Air Force, "A Suggested Plan for Making Impossible the Military Utilization of the Italian Railways by the Enemy," Jan 15, 1944, 650.454–3, 55–57.

11. *Ibid.*

12. See Chapter 4.

13. A-2 Historical Section, Twelfth Air Force, "Report on Operation STRANGLE, March 13–May 11, 1944," n.d., 650.454–5, 8.

14. See, for example, Lucian K. Truscott, Jr., *Command Missions—A Personal Story* (New York, 1954), 305–6, 353–54; Mark Clark, *Calculated Risk* (New York, 1950) 286–87.

15. Sir John Slessor, *The Central Blue: The Autobiography of Sir John Slessor, Marshal of the RAF* (New York, 1956), 566; Memo, Slessor to Brig Gen

Slessor concluded with a series of questions that implicitly questioned the emphasis given to marshaling yards. Norstad replied on February 13 with a memorandum that was little more than a précis of Zuckerman's arguments *for* bombing rail centers. He did, however, concede the possibility of "other targets which, accepting the Zuckerman conclusions, are of equal or greater importance [than marshaling yards] and which, at the same time, may cause effective temporary disruption and the destruction of supplies critical to the current battle."[16]

In response to Slessor's initiative, MAAF's Bombing Policy Committee met on February 14 to prepare recommendations for taking "advantage of the enemy build-up south of ROME to force him to withdraw at least to the PISA-RIMINI line by making impossible the supply of his Armies in the south." The committee foresaw no need to change the role of the Strategic Air Force, which was to bomb the six northern Italian rail centers that Zuckerman had deemed critical: Padua, Verona, Bolzano, Turin, Genoa, and Milan. It did, however, suggest that the Tactical Air Force attack targets of an unspecified nature "with the object of effecting current interruption with supply even though," the minutes noted with a deferential nod toward Zuckerman, "the effects could only be fleeting. . . ." The committee saw marshaling yards as a strictly secondary target for the Tactical Air Force.[17]

The actual operations instructions promulgated on February 18 reversed the priorities for the Tactical Air Force: Its targets were to be "marshalling yards, railroad repair facilities and other railroad targets," the purposes being "first, to destroy railway facilities . . . and second, to stop rail movements."[18] Despite its reaffirmation of established policy,

---

Lauris Norstad, Feb 11, 1944, in MAAF, "Operations in Support of DIADEM," vol 7, Tab K.

16. Memo, Norstad to Slessor, subj: Interdiction of Italian Rail Communications, Feb 13, 1944, in MAAF, "Operations in Support of DIADEM," vol 7, Tab L.

17. Memo, Bombing Policy Committee, subj: Bombing Policy: Memorandum of Meeting 14.2.44, in MAAF, "Operations in Support of DIADEM," vol 7, Tab M.

18. The continuing emphasis on marshaling yards probably reflects the influence of Norstad who, as operations officer, issued the order. In a memorandum of March 16, for example, Norstad attempted to persuade Eaker that precisely because the enemy had been able to put bombed marshaling yards "back into operation almost immediately" and moved the marshaling of trains "farther north," MAAF should *continue* to give priority to the rail centers. All this, he reasoned, supported "our earlier conclusion that cutting a railway line, whether it is a marshaling yard or a bridge, does not stop traffic except for a very limited period of time. For this reason, our current bombing directive [of February 18] was based upon destruction of the enemy's means of transportation [rolling stock] rather than upon the temporary expedient of merely cutting rail lines." Concluding with yet another echo of Zuckerman, Norstad asserted that only

Martin B-26 Marauders strike north along the Tyrrhenian Sea *(above)* **to blast German targets in Italy. In the Allied drive on Rome, the bombers had to cross these rugged mountains to make their attacks. The rail line entering northern Italy through the Brenner Pass in the Alps played a vital role in the supply of the German Army throughout the Italian campaign. A B-25 and two P-47s** *(right)* **fly low over a bridge, inspecting bomb damage done to the rail line there by planes of the Twelfth Air Force.**

the new directive was marked by a signal innovation: There was now to be an attempt to force the Germans into retreat by attacking their railroads "at about 100 miles from the front so as to increase the strain on the enemy's already inadequate motor transport."[19] This was to be the central idea of Operation STRANGLE. The directive of February 18 also marked the commitment of the Allied commanders, both ground and air, to a novel attempt to break the Italian stalemate solely through air power—through an aerial siege of the Gustav Line. "My general plan for Italy," declared the supreme commander for the Mediterranean theater, General Sir Henry Maitland Wilson, "is to use the air to deprive the enemy of the ability either to maintain his present positions or to withdraw his divisions out of Italy in time for OVERLORD." With luck and good weather, Wilson thought, "it is not unreasonable to expect that the effect

---

"pressing tactical considerations" could justify "cutting lines at critical points." Memo, Norstad to Eaker, Mar 16, 1944, Box 24, Mediterranean Allied Air Forces File, Papers of Ira Eaker.

19. "Operations Instructions No. 8," Feb 18, 1944, in MAAF, "Operations in Support of DIADEM," vol 17, Tab G. Though it cannot be demonstrated with available records, it is likely that this decision reflected intelligence information about the strain under which German motor transport was already laboring (see Chapter 4).

will make itself felt by the end of April. That effect should be to compel the enemy to withdraw at least to the Pisa-Rimini line." But, as one of MAAF's historians noted some months later, "there was still no general agreement as to the specific targets to be hit."[20]

The advocates of line cutting soon resolved the question in their favor. In a paper of February 29, MAAF's A-2 Section observed that all now agreed that the enemy marshaled his supply trains north of the Alps. Recent experience, moreover, had shown the extreme difficulty of blocking the marshaling yards. The only remaining reason for continuing to attack them was to destroy locomotives and rolling stock. But Italy's yards were no longer being used to make up trains, and it was difficult to see how bombing them could destroy much rolling stock. The Germans, in any case, were building locomotives in such numbers throughout occupied Europe that they could "afford to send into Italy each day the number of locomotives required to haul the 15 trains of military supplies to the front, and discard each locomotive at the end of the haul." Nor were they short of rolling stock, as they could draw at will upon the continent's stock of 2,000,000 cars. Recent surveys had shown, moreover, that even in the extraordinarily favorable conditions that had obtained during HUSKY, no more than 5,000 cars had been destroyed in all the attacks upon the marshaling yards of Sicily and southern Italy. And, the intelligence officers continued, "in the 19 weeks since the capture of Naples, Allied bombers (all types) have dropped a total of 8,258 tons of bombs on 47 marshalling yards without critically weakening the enemy supply position." In conclusion, the A-2 Section once more called for "a policy of bombing designed to sever all rail lines to the front and thus interdict completely the flow of necessary military equipment by this means of transportation."[21]

Strong support for the A-2 Section came from the American intelligence organization, the Office of Strategic Services (OSS). In a paper of March 7, the OSS stated that Zuckerman had erred in arguing that it was more economical to attack marshaling yards than it was to attack bridges. Between October 22, 1943, and January 22, 1944, 428 tons of

---

20. Msg, Field Marshal Sir Henry Wilson to Field Marshal Sir Harold Alexander, Feb 25, 1944, C/S Directives, 622.01-8; MAAF, "Operations in Support of DIADEM," 7:8.

21. Memo, A-2 Section to MAAF A-3 Section, MAAF, subj: Current Intelligence Considerations in Interdiction of Rail Traffic to Italian Peninsula, Feb 29, 1944, in MAAF, "Operations in Support of DIADEM," vol 7, Tab N. That this criticism of an attritional approach was new is evident from the fact that the Twelfth Air Force's interdiction plan of January 15, 1944, criticized attacks on rail centers for destroying rolling stock that the Allies could later use themselves. See note 10 above.

bombs had been required to block a marshaling yard for one or two days, but only 196 (as opposed to Zuckerman's estimate of 500 to 1,000) tons were needed to destroy a bridge that might remain down for weeks. The scientist's influential study, the OSS claimed, had also greatly overestimated the difficulties of destroying bridges by supposing all bridges to be steel, when many were in fact masonry, easier to destroy but harder to repair than steel.[22] "It can be . . . asserted," the OSS concluded, "that nothing in the record to date shows that a simultaneous interdiction of all north-south rail lines by bombing bridges is beyond the capabilities of MAAF, given a scale of effort comparable to that currently being expended against other transport targets."[23]

These arguments, operating in the climate of disillusionment created by the patent failure of the air forces to prevent the concentration of German forces at Anzio, resolved the contest between rival theories of interdiction in favor of cutting railroad lines by demolishing engineering features.[24] With that decision, the rest of Operation STRANGLE was dictated by the topography of Italy and the state of German transport, as it appeared to Allied intelligence.[25] The strategy was that of the operation instructions issued February 18: to place an insupportable burden upon the enemy's transport by blocking the railroads at a distance from the front, 100 miles or more, too great to be bridged with the trucks at his command. This element of continuity notwithstanding, STRANGLE is properly dated from a series of directives issued on March 19. Not until after February 18 were the decisive arguments against marshaling yards

22. Events would show that while the spans of masonry bridges might be easier to destroy than those of steel bridges, masonry bridges were in general easier to keep in operation. This was because their massive piers tended to be little damaged by even direct hits. Their piers were also more closely spaced than those of steel bridges. Therefore it was a comparatively simple task for competent engineers to replace the destroyed spans. During the battle for Normandy the Allies failed to close the masonry bridges of the Loire, but they did block the bridges across the Seine, which were predominantly of steel.

23. "Headquarters, 2677 Headquarters Company Experimental, U.S. Army" [Office of Strategic Services, Caserta], "Air Attacks on Bridges and Marshalling Yards in Italy—Is Experience Prior to the Fall of Naples a Reliable Guide for Attack in 1944?," Mar 7, 1944, 622.454-1.

24. See, for example, MAAF, "Operations in Support of DIADEM," 7:3-10, 22-24; Ltr, Ira C. Eaker to Jacob Devers, Apr 1, 1944, ibid., Tab R; Mediterranean Allied Tactical Air Force (MATAF), "Report on Operation STRANGLE," Jul 24, 1944, 626.430-15, 2-6; A-2 Historical Section, Twelfth Air Force, "Operation STRANGLE, 4-5, 7-10.

25. The name STRANGLE was conferred when the operation was completed. General Norstad subsequently wrote that it first came into use in May after DIADEM began, apparently as a way of distinguishing between interdiction before and after the Allied offensive. The origin of the name, he observed, was "obscure." Rpt, Brig Gen Lauris Norstad, "Air Force Participation in DIADEM," Jul 31, 1944, in MAAF, "Operations in Support of DIADEM," vol 7, Tab FF, 622.430-3.

advanced and accepted. Nor was it until after the failure of the Allied offensive at Cassino on March 15, which featured the spectacular but useless bombardment upon which Arnold had pinned his hopes, that most of MAAF's tactical aircraft became available for interdiction, as STRANGLE's concept of operations required. The weather, finally, was too inclement before the latter part of March to permit an aerial campaign of sustained intensity.[26]

From the southern reaches of Italy to about the latitude of Rome, the Apennines form a central spine to the Italian peninsula. Near the capital, they curve northeast and run along the Adriatic coast until they reach the vicinity of Rimini. From there they arc generally northwest across the country until, in the vicinity of La Spezia, they meet the Ligurian Sea. The Po Valley is in this way separated from the regions to the south by a rampart of mountains stretching from La Spezia to Rimini. Below this barrier the land is broken by foothills and spurs; through many of the intervening valleys, moreover, flow rivers that drain the Apennines. Foremost among these is the Tiber, Italy's greatest river after the Po. Because of the serpentine path of the mountains, these secondary features have axes of all azimuths, and are therefore as likely to impede travel east to west as north to south. (*Map 11*)

Italy's variform geography had made her railroads and highways heavily dependent upon engineering features of every kind; tunnels, bridges, viaducts, and embankments abounded. Where arteries ran north to south through the Apennine chain and its spurs, their number was necessarily reduced, and transverse connecting lines were few or none. Allied planners distinguished several zones of vulnerability wherein a paucity of lines and a heavy dependence upon engineering features rendered the railroads particularly susceptible to attack. The first of these was the Frontier Zone, in which railways from France, Switzerland, and Austria debouched from the Alps and crossed the Po. Next was the La Spezia–Rimini Zone, wherein the northern Apennines traversed the peninsula. Immediately to the south was the Central Italian Zone, sometimes divided into the Cecina–Fano and the Montalto di Castro–Orvieto–Pedaso Zones. Here the chief obstacle was the Tiber and its many tributaries.[27]

The distance of the Frontier Zone from the airfields of the Allies ruled out its becoming the target of STRANGLE. So too did the consideration that the major German supply dumps lay farther south. They were believed to be sufficiently well stocked that interdiction of the Frontier

---

26. MATAF, "Report on Operation STRANGLE," 1.
27. A–2 Section, Twelfth Air Force, "Suggested Plan for Making Impossible the Military Utilization of the Italian Railways by the Enemy," 7–54.

Zone would have no early effect on the supply of the armies to the south. The La Spezia–Rimini Zone was in many respects the best suited to interdiction. The relatively few rail lines in the northern Apennines depended heavily upon bridges and viaducts, while the general ruggedness of the terrain had precluded the construction of many transverse connecting lines and would make the transshipment of supplies around cuts difficult. This zone, however, was excluded because it was beyond the range of the fighters that were to escort bombers and harry motor transport.[28]

There remained the Central Italian Zone, a large area roughly quadrangular in shape, defined by Pisa, Ancona, Pescara, and Rome. This was to be the battlefield of Operation STRANGLE. There was no narrow and neatly defined belt of interdiction across Italy. A plot of the places attacked during STRANGLE shows why contemporary accounts of the operation simply defined the area of interdiction as generally south of a line between Pisa and Rimini and, to the extent possible, 100 miles or more from the closest front.[29] (*Map 11*)

Several characteristics of the Central Italian Zone favored the Allied design. It lay south of the larger German dumps in northern Italy and within the range of the fighter-bombers. The country was broken, and engineering features were common. But the Central Italian Zone was not so mountainous as the La Spezia–Rimini Zone, and was accordingly better provided with railroads. No fewer than twelve first-class lines ran north to south and east to west, and there were many minor bypass lines and a well-developed net of highways to facilitate transshipment around severed lines.[30]

Eaker described STRANGLE for Lt. Gen. Carl A. Spaatz in a letter of April 23, 1944:

> Our general plan of operations has called for: (A) the destruction of marshalling yards south of the Pisa-Rimini line by the Tactical Air Force; (B) destruction of bridges by mediums and fighter bombers in the same area so as to effectively block all rail lines leading to the Rome area; (C) when circumstances permit, employment of heavy bombers against congested marshalling yards north of the cited line.[31]

Marshaling yards south of the Pisa-Rimini line were to be bombed only when there were indications that they were being used for the ordering of

---

28. A–2 Historical Section, Twelfth Air Force, "Operation STRANGLE," 10–11.
29. *Ibid.*, 6, 12.
30. *Ibid.*, 11–12.
31. Msg, Eaker to Spaatz, Apr 23, 1944, Roll 58, Records of the MAAF, "Bombing Policy, Part 2," United States Air Force Historical Research Center, Maxwell Air Force Base, Ala.

trains. By far the largest number of attacks would be aimed at cutting lines—principally through the destruction of engineering features but also through the cratering of roadbeds in remote areas where the breaks might take long to repair. Each line was to be cut in several places; all cuts were to be kept under surveillance and reattacked as necessary to maintain the blocks.[32]

The heaviest burden fell on the Tactical Air Force, the Strategic Air Force being heavily engaged in attacking Germany and the Balkans. This was not a limitation, for once equipped with accurate Norden bomb-sights, medium bombers (B–25s and B–26s) had proved better for attacking point targets than larger aircraft because their size permitted tighter formations and therefore denser concentrations of bombs. The medium bombers were assigned to the larger bridges and viaducts, while fighter-bombers were to attack smaller structures, crater railbeds, and fly armed reconnaissance in search of motor transport. The B–17s and B–24s of the Strategic Air Force would be called on to bomb marshaling yards north of the Pisa–Rimini line if blocked lines to the south had created a jam of supply-laden trains.[33]

The Tactical Air Force's "Bombing Directive No. 2" of March 19, 1944, assigned areas of responsibility to subordinate commands. Two wings of medium bombers—the 42d, based in Sardinia, and the 57th, based in Corsica—were to attack targets south of, but including, the Pisa–Florence–Pontassieve railroad line and west of, but including, the line Pontassieve–Arezzo–Orte. The XII Air Support Command, which, except for the 57th Fighter Group, was located around Naples, was assigned the following lines: Rome–Orte–Terni, Orte–Orvieto, Viterbo–Rome, Rome–Montalto di Castro, and all routes south of Rome to the battle area. The Desert Air Force, based around Termoli on the Adriatic coast, was assigned the lines Terni–Perugia, Terni–Foligno–Fabriano, Pescara–Ancona, and Terni–Sulmona–Pescara.[34]

The 57th Fighter Group, detached from the XII Air Support Command (successor to the XII Support Command) and placed under the direct control of the Tactical Air Force, flew from Corsica. It had three zones of responsibility: Zone 1 ran down the Italian coast from La Spezia to Montalto di Castro; it extended ten miles out to sea and embraced the isle of Elba. Zone 2 consisted of all rail and road communications south of, but including, the Pisa–Florence–Pontassieve line and west of,

---

32. A–2 Historical Section, Twelfth Air Force, "Operation STRANGLE," 12–13.

33. *Ibid.*, 12–13, 23–24.

34. HQ MATAF, "Bombing Directive No. 2," Mar 19, 1944, in MATAF, "Report on Operation STRANGLE," annex B.

Photo reconnaissance of German supply routes shows the Germans' reliance on roads, less vulnerable but also less capacious than the railroads that the Allies succeeded in effectively interdicting. The train carrying the German tanks *(left)* was photographed east of Pescara, near Italy's Adriatic coast. Typical of German motor columns is this truck convoy *(below)*.

but including, the Arezzo and Chiusi junctions. All rail and road communications north of the Pisa–Florence–Pontassieve line as far as Parma fell into Zone 3. The group was to expend 80 percent of its effort in Zone 2 and the remainder in Zone 1. Zone 3 was to be attacked when the weather precluded operations in Zones 1 and 2.[35]

STRANGLE was launched only after intensive efforts to establish the logistical requirements of the two German armies south of the Pisa–Rimini line—*Armeeoberkommando 14 (AOK 14—Fourteenth Army)* at Anzio and, to the south, *Armeeoberkommando 10 (AOK 10—Tenth Army)* on the Gustav Line.[36] There seems, however, to have been considerable uncertainty among intelligence analysts as to what the enemy's needs were, for their estimates varied widely, even when allowance is made for changes in the number of German divisions in Italy and the

---

35. Msg, Lt Gen John Cannon to Brig Gen Gordon Saville, subj: Employment of 57th Fighter Group, Mar 26, 1944, in MATAF, "Report on Operation STRANGLE," annex B.

36. F.M. Sallagar maintains the contrary in his well-known study of STRANGLE, *Operation "STRANGLE" (Italy, Spring 1944): A Case Study of Tactical Air Interdiction* (The Rand Corp., R–851–PR, Santa Monica, 1972), 27.

ebb and flow of battle. In December 1943 MAAF's A-2 Section estimated that fourteen German divisions south of the Pisa–Rimini line needed 5,000 tons of supplies daily.[37] In January the A-2 of the Twelfth Air Force put the figure at 3,250 tons for the same number of divisions.[38] On February 13 Norstad quoted a figure of 3,250 tons for seventeen divisions.[39] Shortly before STRANGLE began, the OSS seconded an estimate by the G-2 of Allied Force Headquarters that the divisions south of the Pisa–Rimini line, which were then thought to number eighteen, needed 4,500 tons a day.[40] As this last figure appears in a document from MAAF's A-2 Section dated February 29, it is probable that it was used to plan STRANGLE, although a document from the same source with a date of April 27 gives a figure of 4,000 tons daily.[41]

From the information available to them through ULTRA, photographic reconnaissance, and the interrogation of prisoners, Allied intelligence analysts drew up a substantially accurate model of the German supply system: Of the supplies sent to the two German armies south of the Pisa–Rimini line, 85 to 90 percent reached the main depots around Terni and Orte by rail. This traffic, however, represented only a fraction of the rail system's capacity—5 percent in early estimates and 10 to 15 percent in later ones. STRANGLE's concept of operations required, accordingly, that *all* lines be permanently blocked 100 miles or more from the front. If this was accomplished, and from all indications MAAF began STRANGLE in high hopes that it would be, the logistical position of the Germans would become insupportable because they lacked an alternative means of transport sufficiently capacious to substitute for the railroads between the railheads and the fronts to the south. The Allies believed that their enemies shipped about 500 tons a day by sea. This figure, they calculated, could be raised to not more than 1,500 tons. If the balance of the daily requirement—something like 3,000 tons—was to reach *AOKs 10* and *14*, it would have to be conveyed by more trucks

---

37. MAAF, A-2 Section, "Special Intelligence Report No. 64."
38. A-2 Section, Twelfth Air Force, "Suggested Plan for Making Impossible the Military Utilization of the Italian Railways by the Enemy," 10.
39. Memo, Norstad to Slessor, Feb 13, 1944.
40. HQ, 2777 HQ Company Experimental, "Air Attacks on Bridges and Marshalling Yards in Italy," 5.
41. Memo, MAAF A-2 to MAAF A-3, Feb 29, 1944; A-2 Section, MAAF, "Appreciation of Air Attack Against Enemy Communications and Supply in Italy," Apr 27, 1944, 622.552-2. This uncertainty may seem surprising, considering the advantage of ULTRA. It was probably due partly to the fact that only a portion of the German messages were intercepted and partly to the nature of the messages themselves. The German logistical reports were little more than collections of numbers, exceedingly hard to interpret without a guide. The Allies never learned to read them in their entirety. Chapter 6 includes a discussion of this point.

than the Germans were thought to have. MAAF therefore concluded that "no more than a fraction of [the enemy's requirements] could be met in this manner without severe strain. Moreover, in hauls [of] over 100 miles, the operational overhead [fuel and tires, for example] would tend to subtract severely from the system's carrying capacity and render it highly uneconomical."[42]

STRANGLE was much hindered by weather, which grounded the medium bombers for nearly half of the operation's fifty-three days.[43] There was compensation for this, however, in the feebleness of the *Luftwaffe*, which as a fighter force had been thoroughly defeated in the Mediterranean theater.[44] With little to fear from the enemy in the air, the medium bombers often flew unescorted and sometimes in flights of as few as four aircraft. Allied fighters, lightly burdened with missions of escort and ground support, were unusually free to participate in the interdiction campaign.[45] Until the last ten days of April, Allied aircraft encountered only light antiaircraft fire, even over targets repeatedly attacked. Then, increasingly stung, the Germans began to withdraw antiaircraft weapons from cities and factories to protect bridges on their principal supply routes. Occasionally intense flak was thereafter encountered over some targets, but Allied losses were never serious. During the period of STRANGLE, MAAF lost 365 aircraft in 65,003 sorties (a rate of 5.6 aircraft per 1,000 sorties), though not all of these were lost over Italy or on missions of interdiction.[46]

No figures definitively establish how many sorties MAAF devoted to interdiction. MAAF itself published no data, and subsequent studies defined interdiction variously.[47] One study, defining interdiction targets as marshaling yards, rail and road bridges, military transports, dumps, har-

42. Memo, MAAF A–2 to MAAF A–3, Feb 29, 1944.
43. Craven and Cate, *ARGUMENT to V–E Day*, 379.
44. The *Luftwaffe*, wrote Norstad of STRANGLE and DIADEM, was "wholly without influence on either the air or land battles." Rpt, Norstad, "Air Force Participation in DIADEM." German bombers were still quite active, but were principally directed against Allied ports and shipping.
45. Craven and Cate, *ARGUMENT to V–E Day*, 379.
46. MAAF, "Operations in Support of DIADEM," vol 7, Tab V table: Summary of MAAF Effort; General Max Ritter von Pohl, "Commitment of Flak and Fighters to Protect the German Supply Routes in Italy," MS D–191, Record Group (RG) 338, National Archives and Records Administration (NARA), 3.
47. Craven and Cate, for example, given a round figure of 50,000 while a study done internally for the Air Force's Assistant Chief of Staff, Studies and Analysis, states that there were 34,000. AF ACS, S&A, *The Uncertainty of Predicting Results of an Interdiction Campaign* (Washington, 1969). The discrepant figures result from the failure of MAAF to break down its sorties finely by type of mission in any of the STRANGLE or DIADEM reports. The figures used in the text subsequent are derived from a careful reading of daily operations reports.

bors, docks, shipping, and miscellaneous military installations, concludes that MAAF flew 21,688 sorties against German communications and dropped 25,375 tons of bombs on them between March 15, the first day of the weekly reporting cycle in which STRANGLE began, and May 10.[48]

The targets attacked for the most part lay south of the Pisa–Rimini line. On targets it classified "lines of communication," MAAF dropped 6,567 tons north of the Pisa–Rimini line, and 15,838 to the south.[49] For the first two weeks of STRANGLE, MAAF attacked marshaling yards more heavily than engineering features: The former class of targets drew 1,316 sorties and 2,917 tons of bombs; the latter, 1,272 sorties and 1,470 tons.[50] This reflects not so much Professor Zuckerman's lingering influence as the temporary freedom of the Strategic Air Force from its obligations to the Combined Bomber Offensive against Germany. During the last ten days of March the Strategic Air Force delivered a series of very heavy attacks against marshaling yards in northern Italy, which included its first "thousand-ton" raid. Thereafter, with a change in the weather over Germany and the Balkans, the participation of the Strategic Air Force's heavy bombers declined.[51]

With the departure of the heavy bombers, the statistics for STRANGLE reflect the view, which Eaker strongly defended in a letter of April 1, that the campaign's targets of priority should be bridges and other engineering features.[52] After the first two weeks of the operation, marshaling yards claimed 2,346 sorties and 4,506 tons of bombs as opposed to 10,075 sorties and 9,551 tons for engineering features.[53] Most of the bombing was done by the medium bombers of the Tactical Air Command. The fighter-bombers of the XII Support Command (now redesignated the XII Tactical Air Command) and the Desert Air Force, theretofore engaged with supporting the ground forces at Cassino, joined STRANGLE in a major way early in April. They attacked all manner of targets, but were principally active against rail lines and bridges. The American P-47 Thunderbolt soon proved itself especially suited to

48. Historical Evaluation and Research Organization (HERO), *Tactical Air Interdiction by U.S. Army Air Forces in World War II: Italy* (Dunn Loring, Va., n.d.), VII-8.

49. MAAF, "Operations in Support of DIADEM," vol 7, Tab V table: Summary of MAAF Effort.

50. HERO, *Tactical Air Interdiction by U.S. Army Air Forces in World in World War II*, VII-8.

51. Craven and Cate, ARGUMENT to V–E Day, 380.

52. Ltr, Eaker to Devers, Apr 1, 1944, in MAAF, "Operations in Support of DIADEM," vol 7, Tab R.

53. HERO, *Tactical Air Interdiction by U.S. Army Air Forces in World War II*, VII-9.

The Republic P–47 Thunderbolt *(upper left)* proved itself especially suited to bridge bombing. Notable among Operation STRANGLE targets was the Bucine viaduct *(above right)*, located near Arezzo, south of the Pisa-Rimini line. On one of the central rail lines to Rome, it was smashed while a train was crossing it.

bridge-bombing. As the Germans were forced to shift from rail to motor transport, the fighters concentrated ever more on armed reconnaissance.[54]

By the end of March, MAAF claimed that photographic reconnaissance verified a daily average of 25 cuts in the targeted railroad lines. By mid-May this figure had risen to 75, and on some days the verified cuts exceeded 100. MAAF asserted that all the lines between Rome and northern Italy were severed by March 24 and remained so throughout STRANGLE, claiming that supply trains rarely approached closer to the Italian capital than 125 miles, save for brief periods when repairs permitted approaches of about 50 miles.[55]

MAAF's claims were on the whole conservative.[56] They have not, however, gone unchallenged. One influential study of STRANGLE minimizes the damage to the rail system by quoting one of the German officers responsible for its operation, to the effect that "it was possible to repair all these damages within a comparatively short period of time and

---

54. *Ibid.*; Craven and Cate, *ARGUMENT to V–E Day*, 377–78.
55. MATAF, "Report on Operation STRANGLE," 9.
56. See note 61 below.

in an adequate manner to permit railroad operations to continue and the trains required by the *Heeresgruppe* to be moved in." But in context it is clear that this passage refers *only* to the Strategic Air Force's bombing of the marshaling yards north of the Pisa-Rimini line.[57] Elsewhere in his manuscript, this officer discusses the effect of STRANGLE within the area of interdiction: After only a few days "all the lines to the south on the level of Pisa-Florence-Rimini were cut in several places. . . . On all the lines—through Siena, through Florence to Orte, through Rimini to Ancona and through Florence to Orte, bridges were attacked and damaged while some were completely destroyed." Additionally, "another form of attack now made itself felt, which, in addition to causing heavy damage, was extremely unpleasant. This was the activity of the fighter bombers. From this time, all lines south of the Apennines were threatened all day long by fighter-bomber attacks." The *Jabos*, as the Germans called them, strafed trains and bombed small bridges and even open stretches of track; then they slowed repairs by harassing work crews.[58]

By the beginning of April the Germans had been forced to unload their supply trains at Florence, about 125 miles north of Rome. From there trucks carried the goods to the front. The Germans realized that if the supply of their armies was to be assured, "arrangements had to be made to bring trains into the area Arezzo, Chiusi, Perugia and Foligno and Terni." They brought four or five companies of railroad engineers from France, improved the methods of reporting damage, and created a number of mobile workshops. By concentrating these resources on the main line from Florence to Orte and the loop lines Siena-Chiusi and Ancona-Orte "it was always possible to reopen the lines for several hours or nights and thus spasmodically to get trains to the Lake Trasimeno area and to Chiusi, and on the east coast lines as far as the Foligno-Terni area."[59] MAAF, in short, had succeeded in its plan to drive back the

---

57. Sallagar, *Operation "STRANGLE,"* 46, after Col Klaus Stange, "Railroad Situation from January 1944 Up to the Beginning of the May Offensive (Italy)," MS D-049, RG 338, NARA. As the NARA translation is awkward and incomplete, subsequent references to Stange's memoir will be to the translation done by the British Air Ministry, a copy of which is in the records of the United States Air Force Historical Research Agency. AHB/BAM, "The Transport Situation," 1947, in "The Campaign in Italy: Special Subjects," Translation VII/100, 1950 [from the original by Col Klaus Stange], K512.621.
58. Stange, "Railroad Situation," 14–15.
59. *Ibid.* Another writer goes to the opposite extreme and assumes that the cessation of rail traffic south of Florence was permanent. Col T.N. Dupuy, *Numbers, Prediction, and War: Using History to Evaluate Combat Factors and Predict the Outcome of Battles* (Indianapolis, 1979), 80.

German railheads about 100 miles from the fronts at Anzio and Cassino.[60]

The rigors that STRANGLE imposed on the German logistical system contrasted markedly with the conditions that had obtained immediately before the operation's inception. On March 4, for example, the *Oberquartiermeister* of *AOK 14* had written that the efficiency of the railroads had improved throughout February and that supplies could be carried as far as Rome. But on March 23, with STRANGLE little more than a week old, he reported that "because of air attacks in the rear areas of the Army in Upper and Middle Italy all rail lines have been cut for periods of up to ten days." By May 3 he had despaired of being able to use the lines within the army's area of operations: Bridges, he observed ruefully, were destroyed again as soon as they could be rebuilt.[61] The records of *AOK 10* show that STRANGLE dramatically cut the number of trains arriving at its depots.[62]

The Germans, as Allied analysts had predicted, lacked the motor transport wholly to replace the railroads for any considerable distance.[63] The enforced retreat of the railheads to the north, therefore, had serious consequences for them. They were not, as their enemies had planned,

---

60. Records of the Italian Ministry of Communications, examined after the Allies had taken Rome, generally corroborate MAAF's claims. The claims may be compared with the records for a period of 79 days during STRANGLE and its successor, DIADEM. Of the 1,122 cuts claimed, investigators verified no fewer than 848. And while there were only 62 instances of damage overestimated, there were 212 instances of underestimation. During STRANGLE the Florence–Chiusi segment of the much-attended line between Florence and Orte was blocked for 50 of 57 days. On the western-loop line, the segment Siena–Chiusi was closed for at least 27 days, and the segment Chiusi–Rome, for no fewer than 57, making Chiusi, about 80 miles from Rome and 115 miles (by a straight line) from Anzio, the major railhead for both the central line and its western loop. On the eastern-loop line, Ancona–Orte, the segment Ancona–Foligno was closed for at least 28 days, and that of Foligno–Orte, for at least 54, making Foligno, 70 miles from Rome and 110 and 120 miles (by straight lines) from Anzio and Cassino, respectively, the major railhead for the eastern-loop line. MATAF, "Report on Operation STRANGLE," 10.

61. "*Beurteilung der Versorgungslage (Stand 1.3.1944),*" Mar 4, 1944, and "*Beurteilung der Versorgungslage (Stand 1.5.44),*" May 3, 1944, both appended to *Kriegstagebuch (KTB) Armeeoberkommando 14/Oberquartiermeister (AOK 14/O Qu)*, Roll 485, T–312, RG 242; *KTB AOK 14/O Qu*, Mar 23, 1944, Roll 484, T–312.

62. In the period February 2–March 25, 1944, 537 carloads of supplies arrived at the right station within the area of *AOK 10*, while 1,248 carloads had to be unloaded farther north. In the period March 24–April 23, only 48 carloads arrived at the right station, while 666 had to be unloaded farther north. "*Beurteilung der Versorgungslage,*" Apr 3, 1944, appended to *KTB Armeeoberkommando 10/Oberquartiermeister* (hereinafter *AOK 10/O Qu*), Roll 103, T–312.

63. See, for example, Stange, "Railroad Situation," 15.

starved into retreat. But after the onset of STRANGLE they ceased to be supplied at a rate sufficient both to cover current consumption and to permit the stockpiling of fuel and artillery ammunition that their commanders thought necessary to meet the Allies' predictable spring offensive, DIADEM.

This conclusion is starkly at variance with the findings of several other studies of STRANGLE. The most influential of these asserts that "the outstanding fact to emerge from the German records is that there were no critical supply shortages, either during STRANGLE or even during DIADEM."[64] This conclusion rests upon two arguments. The first is that in postwar memoirs both Kesselring and one of his quartermaster officers recalled that the situation of *Heeresgruppe C* with respect to supply had been "satisfactory" when the Allies struck.[65] These retrospective remarks, however, are contradicted by the contemporary comments of officers on the scene—among them Kesselring himself, who stated on April 23, 1944, that he was worried about ammunition.[66] The second argument is that the Germans' aggregate stocks of ammunition rose during STRANGLE, as did the *AOK 14*'s holdings of fuel. The combined ammunition stocks of the two German armies rose between March 15 and May 11 from 32,743 to 37,456 metric tons, the latter figure representing thirty days of consumption at the rate that prevailed during DIADEM.[67]

---

64. Sallagar, *Operation "STRANGLE,"* 45. See also HERO, *Tactical Air Interdiction by U.S. Army Air Forces in World War II*, VII-16, and AF ACS, S&A, *Uncertainty of Predicting the Results of an Interdiction Campaign*, 11–15.

65. Sallagar, *Operation "STRANGLE,"* 45, 47.

66. In reply to an expression of concern about the ammunition supply from the commander of *AOK 10*, General Heinrich von Vietinghoff, Kesselring said, *"Die Munitionfrage macht mir auch Sorgen* [The question of ammunition also worries me]." Tele con, Kesselring/von Vietinghoff, transcript appended to *KTB AOK 10/Operationsabteilung* (hereafter *AOK 10/Ia*), Apr 23, 1944, Roll 90, T-312.

67. Sallagar, *Operation "STRANGLE,"* 54. In the same period *AOK 14*'s holdings of fuel rose from 3,372 metric tons to 4,428. Those of *AOK 10*, however, fell from 3,129 metric tons to 1,809. Certain that the increasing stocks of ammunition prove the failure of STRANGLE as logistical interdiction, Sallagar declines to ascribe the decline of *AOK 10*'s stock of fuel to Allied interdiction. He speculates plausibly that the *AOK 14* received a larger allocation of fuel because it contained three of the four mobile divisions that constituted *Heeresgruppe C*'s strategic reserve. In fact, for part of STRANGLE all four of the divisions of the strategic reserve were attached to *AOK 14*. It is therefore quite certain that that organization was favored in the allotment of fuel. But this does not explain why the aggregate holdings of both armies should have fallen from 6,500 to 6,246 in the course of a failed interdiction campaign that saw almost no fighting on the ground. The figures are calculated from Sallagar. Sallagar, *Operation "STRANGLE,"* 83–86 tables 2 and 3. For Sallagar's analysis, see pp 56–57 of the same source.

The increased stock of ammunition does not of itself prove that STRANGLE failed to hinder the supply of the German armies. The heavy fighting of February and March at Cassino and Anzio had depleted German stocks, even as Allied air attacks and bad weather complicated resupply. As the *Oberquartiermeister* of *AOK 14* noted on March 4, "Unfortunately, it has developed that the Army has been able to hold no reserves of supplies, or only minimal reserves, in its depots." The plight of the *AOK 10* was similar, its *Oberquartiermeister* describing February as a logistical "low point."[68] Given the depleted state of German stores at the beginning of STRANGLE, the failure of the operation cannot be proved merely with a demonstration that stocks increased during its course. It must rather be shown that the increase was sufficient to free German commanders from logistical constraints as they prepared to meet the Allied spring offensive. All available evidence demonstrates that this was not the case.

This assertion might appear to be contradicted by the observation that at the end of STRANGLE the Germans had reserves of ammunition for thirty days at the rate of expenditure that prevailed during DIADEM. But that argument is circular in that it implicitly assumes the sufficiency of German reserves during the Allied offensive. It begs the question of STRANGLE's effectiveness, in other words, by failing to distinguish between actual and optimal expenditures, for it posits no operational requirements other than the actual consumption of a defeated army.

A better approach is to see what the Germans said about their requirements and then to measure their stated needs against the recorded inventories. The German unit of measure for ammunition was the *Ausstattung*, a concept roughly equivalent to the American "basic load." Each weapon had an *Ausstattung*, and the *Ausstattung* for a unit was the sum of all its weapons' *Ausstattungen*.[69] The Germans calculated that a field army defending against a major enemy offensive should have about

---

68. "*Beurteilung der Versorgungslage (Stand 1.3.1944)*," Mar 4, 1944, appended to *KTB AOK 14/O Qu*, Roll 485, T–312; "*Beurteilung der Versorgungslage*," Apr 3, 1944, appended to *KTB AOK 10/O Qu*, Roll 103, T–312.

69. The *Ausstattung* for a given weapon was determined by the experience of the First World War, the principles governing its tactical employment, its rate of fire, and the weight of its ammunition. While nominally adequate for ten days of normal combat, the *Ausstattung* bore no necessary implication of tactical sufficiency; it was essentially an accounting unit. For a discussion, see G-2 Section, Allied Force Headquarters, "The German System of Supply in the Field: Italy, 1943–1945," Feb 1946, German Naval Records Collection, Operational Archives Branch, Naval History Division, Office of the Chief of Naval Operations, 99. This work written from German supply records with the help of former German supply officers affords much information about logistical operations in Italy not to be found elsewhere.

three *Ausstattungen* on hand. None of the German armies, to the great concern of their commanders, attained this level. *AOK 10*, in fact, never exceeded 1.5 *Ausstattungen*.[70]

A further difficulty with the arguments from aggregate tonnages is the failure to distinguish between types of ammunition in constant demand and types less used, the supply of which posed fewer problems because expenditure was less.[71] Much of the ammunition in the German dumps and depots, for example, was captured Italian ammunition, usable only in the small number of Italian weapons that the Germans retained, or was small-arms ammunition, which the German army in Italy had in surplus. Both the booty and the small-arms ammunition counted toward the aggregate tonnage of ammunition held by each army. But as

---

70. This information was supplied by Charles von Lüttichau of the U.S. Army Center for Military History, a German veteran of the world war. See also the U.S. War Department's *Handbook on German Military Forces*, TM-E 30–451 (Washington, 1945; reprint, Baton Rouge, La., 1990), 300–301, and Brig Gen Kurt Scheffler's "Strength and Composition of German Artillery During World War II," MS-057, RG 338, 11–12, 14–15, 17. As much can be deduced from the anxious conversations about ammunition between *AOK 10* and *Heeresgruppe C* at the end of April. On April 29, for example, Kesselring's chief of staff, Brig Gen Siegfried Westphal, informed General von Vietinghoff that a major effort was under way to raise *AOK 10*'s stock of ammunition to more than two *Ausstattungen*—to as much, in fact, as nearly two and a half *Ausstattungen* for certain calibers. Von Vietinghoff's reply was appreciative but hardly ecstatic: "*Dann wird es ja etwas besser* [Then it will be somewhat better]." Tele con, Westphal/von Vietinghoff, transcript appended to *KTB AOK 10/Ia*, Apr 29, 1944, Roll 90, T–312.

71. Sallagar seems to dispose of this problem by noting that the ammunition status reports of the *AOK 10* show that for most weapons the ammunition on hand was at least equal to the amount "required." This, however, reflects a misunderstanding of the German supply records. As Chart 4 shows, the *Istbestand* (inventory) for *AOK 10*'s artillery ammunition was throughout STRANGLE equal to or greater than the *Soll* (the amount of ammunition required to be on hand). But this is just what one should expect, for the *Istbestand* consisted of the *Soll* plus whatever was available for expenditure. The *Soll* was used, first, to apportion the ammunition available among units according to their missions and, second, to insure that reserves were maintained for major actions. Ideally, therefore, there would have been a correspondence between the *Soll* for a unit and the estimate of what the unit needed to perform its mission. This, however, was not the case in Italy where transport was so seriously disrupted and the actual role of the *Soll* was to apportion scarce resources. Chart 4 shows that the *Soll* for each type of ammunition varied with the *Istbestand*, and therefore with the state of communications. That an *Istbestand* in excess of the *Soll* was no guarantee of a tactically sufficient reserve of ammunition is shown in the upper graph in Chart 4. The *Istbestand* for 10-cm shells was throughout STRANGLE always at least equal to the *Soll*, but *AOK 10*'s Chief of Staff, Brig Gen Friedrich Wentzell, worried about a shortage of ammunition for the 10-cm cannons, the only weapon with a range sufficient to harass and interdict Allied movements behind the front lines. Tele cons, Wentzell/Westphal, transcripts appended to *KTB AOK 10/Ia*, Apr 23, 24, 1944, Roll 90, T–312.

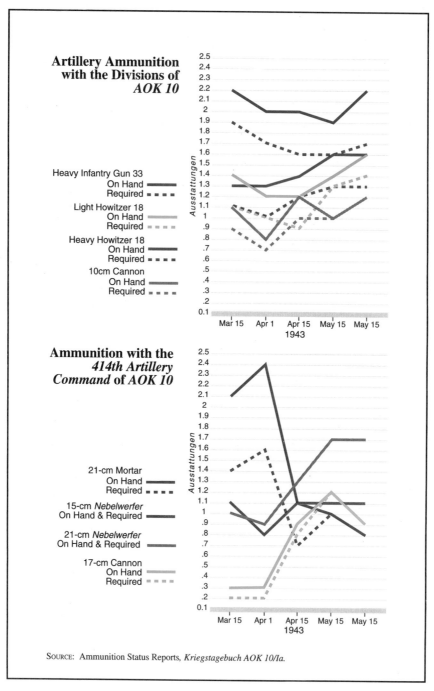

Artillery Ammunition with the Divisions of AOK 10

Heavy Infantry Gun 33
On Hand
Required
Light Howitzer 18
On Hand
Required
Heavy Howitzer 18
On Hand
Required
10cm Cannon
On Hand
Required

Ausstattungen

Mar 15 Apr 1 Apr 15 May 15 May 15
1943

Ammunition with the 414th Artillery Command of AOK 10

21-cm Mortar
On Hand
Required
15-cm *Nebelwerfer*
On Hand & Required
21-cm *Nebelwerfer*
On Hand & Required
17-cm Cannon
On Hand
Required

Ausstattungen

Mar 15 Apr 1 Apr 15 May 15 May 15
1943

SOURCE: Ammunition Status Reports, *Kriegstagebuch AOK 10/Ia*.

Chart 4. The figures presented in the top graph for the divisions of *AOK 10* do not include issues for the *90th Panzer Grenadier Division*, which left *AOK 10* in April 1943. **Solid lines** represent the on-hand actual holdings (*Istbestand*) of the various ammunition types; **broken lines** represent required, or authorized, amounts (*Soll*).

the one type was of little consequence and the other was taken for granted, neither was among the critical ammunition types, the stocks of which were reported to the commander at the end of each day. On the first day of the Allied offensive, May 12, the noncritical types accounted for fully 39 percent of all the ammunition held by *AOK 10*.[72]

While the Allies had correctly calculated that they could overburden the Germans' motor transport by driving their railheads north, they erred in supposing that they could curtail the Germans' supply routes sufficiently enough to compel them to retreat. One reason for their miscalculation was an overestimation of the Germans' logistical requirements. It will be recalled that MAAF had estimated that *AOK 10* and *AOK 14* together required 4,500 tons of supplies daily. On April 15, the latter organization put its total requirement at 1,350 tons a day, of which from 940 to 980 tons were for the divisions. As this allowed for some stockpiling, it was clearly not the minimum that the army needed to subsist. (*Chart 5*) Twelve days earlier, the *Oberquartiermeister* of *AOK 10* had written that his army required 45,000 tons monthly, or about 1,500 tons a day.[73] As this also allowed for some stockpiling, it is probably not wide of the mark to conclude that the two German armies south of the Pisa-Rimini line consumed approximately 2,850 tons of supplies daily to meet minimal logistical objectives, even less merely to subsist.[74]

On April 15, 1944, *AOK 14* had 2,226 tons of service-ready transport devoted to supply (*Versorgungstonnage*) and about 1,900 tons reserved for tactical movements (*Nottonnage*).[75] *AOK 10*, which had a

---

72. Calculated from the ammunition status reports appended to *KTB AOK 10/Ia* of May 12 through 25, 1944, Roll 90, T–312.

73. "*Beurteilung der Versorgungslage,*" Apr 3, 1944.

74. This estimate pertains to *AOKs 10* and *14* only. There were units of both the *Kriegsmarine* and the *Luftwaffe* south of the Pisa-Rimini line. They were small, however, and would not have required much transport for their support. But *Heeresgruppe C* had assumed responsibility for the provisioning of Rome, which must have required many vehicles. It is possible that a failure to understand the extent of the German commitment to Rome caused the Allies to overestimate the logistical requirements of *AOKs 10* and *14*.

75. Table 5 shows the *Versorgungstonnage* and *Nottonnage* of *AOK 14* as of May 20, 1944. On that date, the composition of the Army was as it had been on April 15, except for the *26th Panzer Division*, which had been withdrawn and sent to *AOK 10*. Comparing the *Versorgungstonnage* of April 15 (*Chart 5*) with that of May 20, it will be seen that the difference is 328 tons. This difference can be accounted for by the departure of the *26th Panzer Division*, which on April 15 had a *Versorgungstonnage* of 378 tons. As, therefore, the *Versorgungstonnage* of *AOK 14*, corrected for the withdrawal of the *26th Panzer Division*, changed little between April 15 and May 20, it is probable that the *Nottonnage* was also much the same on the two dates, again making allowance for the *26th Panzer Division*. The statement that the *Nottonnage* was about 1,900 tons on April 15 is based on the figure of May 20 (1,443.5 tons) plus 500 tons, the approximate *Nottonnage* of the *29th Panzer Grenadier Division* on May 1. The comparison is conservative

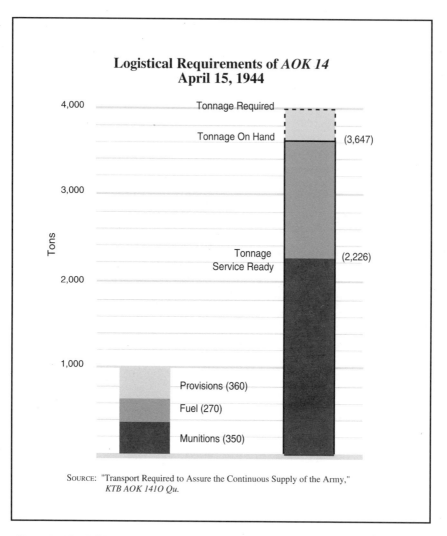

Logistical Requirements of *AOK 14*
April 15, 1944

Tonnage Required

Tonnage On Hand — (3,647)

Tonnage Service Ready — (2,226)

Provisions (360)

Fuel (270)

Munitions (350)

Tons

4,000

3,000

2,000

1,000

Source: "Transport Required to Assure the Continuous Supply of the Army,"
KTB AOK 14 IO Qu.

Chart 5. The lefthand column shows that on this day the divisions needed 980 tons of supplies daily. Ordinarily, the ports and railheads would have been no farther from the divisional depots than one or two days' travel. The service-ready transport (2,226 tons) at the disposal of the army would therefore have more than sufficed (2 × 980 = 1,960 tons). By mid-April, however, STRANGLE had forced the railheads north and restricted daytime movements. The length of a round trip from the railheads or ports required 4 × 24 hours because the supply convoys could move only at night. The delivery of 980 tons to the front would have required an unavailable 4,000 tons (4 × 980 = 3,920 tons) of transport space. The result was logistical constriction.

Table 5. Supply and Emergency Tonnage of *AOK 14*, May 20, 1944

Unit	Supply Tonnage (Versorgungstonnage)		Emergency Tonnage (Nottonnage)	
	Actual Holdings	Service Ready	Actual Holdings	Service Ready
I Parachute Corps				
3d Panzer Grenadier Division	350	259	190	131
4th Parachute Division	394	289	228	189
65th Infantry Division	138	68	80	60
Corps	120	100	—	—
Total	1,002	716	498	380
LXXVI Panzer Corps				
362d Infantry Division	90	55	50	25
715th Infantry Division	118	54	856	425
Corps	116.5	89	195	110
Total	324.5	198	1,101	560
29th Panzer Grenadier Division*	450	210	450	450
92d Infantry Division†	90	73	90	53.5
Army	1,346	741	—	—
Grand Total	3,212.5	1,938	2,139	1,443.5

*The *29th Panzer Grenadier Division* is represented outside the corps structure because of its impending departure from *AOK 14*.

†The *92nd Infantry* is listed independently because its mission was to guard the western coast north of the front.

SOURCE: "*Versorgungs- und Nottonnage*" from *KTB AOK 14/O Qu.*

much larger area of operations than *AOK 14*, probably had a comparable establishment of vehicles, even though it had fewer mechanized divisions.[76] The Germans assigned to their trucks an average capacity of

because a *Panzer* division had more vehicles than a *Panzer Grenadier* division. The comparison is made with the *29th Panzer Grenadier Division* rather than with the *3d Panzer Grenadier Division* because in accounts of the Italian campaign the *26th Panzer* and the *29th Panzer Grenadier Divisions* are bracketed with the *90th Panzer Grenadier* and the *Hermann Göring Panzer Parachute Divisions* as the only German armored divisions with anything like authorized levels of strength. As can be seen from Table 5, the *3d Panzer Grenadier Division* was not among this select group. For the *Versorgungstonnage* of the *26th Panzer Division* on April 15, see "*Transportraumübersicht AOK 14 (Stand 15.4.44)*," appended to *KTB AOK 14/O Qu*, Roll 485, T–312.

76. Between March 15 and April 12 one of the three corps of *AOK 10*, the *XIV Panzer Corps*, disposed of an average of 954 tons of service-ready *Versorgungstonnage* and 375 of *Nottonnage*. *Tagesmeldungen Quartiermeister*, Mar 12–Apr 12, 1944, appended to *KTB Generalkommando XIV Panzer Corps/Ia*, Roll 459, T–314.

three tons.[77] Their probable *Versorgungstonnage* of about 4,500 tons, while representing only about 1,500 vehicles, was nonetheless about what Allied intelligence thought would be required to replace the railroads if *AOK*s *10* and *14* required 4,000–4,500 tons of supplies a day. The quartermaster units of *Heeresgruppe C*, finally, disposed of at least 10,000 tons of transport space, although the larger part of this was devoted to provisioning Rome.[78]

Given, then, the Germans' supply of trucks and lower than expected consumption, STRANGLE would have failed to affect the supply of their armies to any appreciable extent, were it not for the effects of armed reconnaissance. Soon after most of MAAF's fighters were assigned to interdiction in late March, the Germans' losses of vehicles became insupportable. Shortly before April 5, *Heeresgruppe C* ordered that supply columns should move only at night.[79] From that time forward, the German convoys could no longer make their round trips in a day, which effectively increased the amount of transport space required to haul the armies' supplies. Two other factors added to the squeeze on German transport: So much of *Heeresgruppe C*'s transport was dedicated to the support of Rome that by late April as little as 800 tons of transport space a day was left to support the armies on some days.[80] On April 3, moreover, the *Heeresgruppe* informed *AOK 14* that because of the pressing needs of the less favorably situated *AOK 10*, it could thereafter deliver only two-thirds of the army's supplies.[81] *AOK 14*'s *Oberquartiermeister* later wrote that with this communication the *Heeresgruppe* withdrew its transport almost entirely from the support of the army. *AOK 14* thereafter had to use its limited supply of trucks to fetch sup-

---

77. Thus General von Vietinghoff wrote to *Heeresgruppe C* on April 22, 1944, "The delivery of eighty service-ready trucks to the *90th Panzer Grenadier Division*, ordered by telephone on April 14, 1944, and now in progress, raises the number of trucks given up by the army to about 260—about 800 tons." Ltr, von Vietinghoff to *Heeresgruppe C*, Apr 22, 1944, appended to *KTB AOK 10/O Qu*, Roll 103, T–312.

78. After the heavy losses of the spring offensive, but with the addition of transport from various civilian agencies and military formations, *Heeresgruppe C*'s own transport units controlled about 10,725 tons of service-ready transport in June. "*Versorgungslage in Juni 1944*," Aug 5, 1944, appended to *KTB Heeresgruppe C*, Roll 279, T–311.

79. The order banning travel by night was repeated on April 5 because of repeated violations. Cable, Kesselring to *AOK 10* and *AOK 14*, appended to *KTB AOK 10/O Qu*, Apr 5, 1944, Roll 107, T–311.

80. Lt Col Ernst Eggert, "Supply During Allied Offensive, May 1944, and Pursuit Fighting to the Apennines," MS D–128, RG 338, NARA, 2–3.

81. Cable, *Heeresgruppe C to AOK 14*, appended to *KTB AOK 14/O Qu*, Apr 3, 1944, Roll 485, T–312.

plies from the depots of the *Heeresgruppe* and then to distribute them among its divisions, as the latter did not have enough vehicles to perform this service for themselves.[82]

The retreat of the railheads, the ravages of the fighter-bombers, and the heavy commitment of *Heeresgruppe C*'s transport to the civilian population combined to impair the supply of the German armies. Chart 5 is instructive in this connection. From the fact that on April 15 the supply convoys, traveling only at night, required four days for their round trips, it can be deduced that the trips would have required but two days, had movement by day been possible. In that case, 1,960 tons of *AOK 14*'s 2,226 tons of service-ready *Versorgungstonnage* would have sufficed to move the desired total of 980 tons from the ports and railheads to the divisions. At this time, in other words, the enforced migration of the railheads to the north was not of itself sufficient to reduce the army's ability to supply itself; the effect of the fighter-bombers in forcing the convoys to travel only at night meant the entire service-ready *Versorgungstonnage* of the army could deliver only about 555 tons to the front daily. The deficit was doubtless reduced at the expense of tactical mobility by use of the *Nottonnage*, a practice the *Heeresgruppe* condoned when it announced the withdrawal of transport from the army. But it would have taken all of the *Nottonnage* to close the gap of nearly 1,800 tons between the available *Versorgungstonnage* and the amount of transport space required to move 980 tons of supplies to the divisions. Since much of the *Nottonnage* was with the three divisions of the strategic reserve then assigned to *AOK 14*, prudence dictated a limit to the number of tactical vehicles diverted to supply. Kesselring, indeed, stressed that these divisions had to be ready to move upon several hours' notice.[83]

AOK 14's logistical situation had worsened by May 8. (*Table 6*) The army's organic transport of 900 tons was wholly occupied with various tasks in its rear area. There remained 2,330 tons of *Versorgungstonnage* with the units to move their daily requirement of 940 tons of supplies. Even with travel around the clock, supply convoys would have required three days to complete a full cycle, and the result would still have been a shortfall of 490 tons (2,820 tons minus 2,330 tons) of transport space. But with the round trips requiring six nights, the effective deficit was

---

82. By the end of April the *Heeresgruppe* was carrying only 7 percent of the supplies arriving at the depots of *AOK 14*. "*Beurteilung der Versorgungslage (Stand 1.5.1944)*," appended to *KTB AOK 14/O Qu*, May 3, 1944, Roll 485, T–312.

83. On May 9, for example, Kesselring ordered "that in no case can it be permitted to employ the tactical vehicles of the motorized divisions to such an extent that the degree of mobility required of them cannot be guaranteed." *KTB AOK 14/O Qu*, May 9, 1944, Roll 484, T–312.

Table 6. Logistical Requirements of *AOK 14*, May 8, 1944*

Transport Space	Amount in Tons
Required for reshipments within the rear area of the army	
To ship to the depots the 1,350 tons of supplies brought daily to *AOK 14* by the three supply trains of *Heeresgruppe C*'s supply columns	300
To apportion supplies among depots	300
To reship 1,200 tons daily from the harbors of Civitavecchia and San Stefano	300
Total	900
Required for supply of the units	
For a unit's daily supply of	
Ammunition	300
Fuel	300
Provisions	200
Fodder	120
Weapons and equipment	20
Total	940
	×6
For a convoy's round trip of six nights' duration	5,640
Total requirement	6,540
Available for transport of the	
AOK 14	900
LXXXVI Panzer Corps	
Corps tonnage	90
26th Panzer Division	650
90th Panzer Grenadier Division	200
29th Panzer Grenadier Division	300
92d Infantry Division	60
Total	1,300
I Parachute Corps	
Corps tonnage	150
4th Parachute Division	400
65th Infantry Division	60
3d Panzer Grenadier Division	300
363d Infantry Division	60
715th Infantry Division	60
Total	1,030
Total available	3,230
Net shortage of transport space	3,310

*A somewhat more complete breakdown of *AOK 14*'s needs and assets than the document reproduced in Chart 5, this table shows that conditions had worsened since mid-April. The railheads had been driven farther north, and six days were now required for a supply convoy to complete its round trip. The deficit of transport space had therefore increased since April 15.
SOURCE: *KTB AOK 14/O Qu.*

3,310 tons. Under these conditions the *Versorgungstonnage* of the army sufficed to deliver only about 388 of the required 940 tons of supplies. On May 8 *AOK 14* probably had about 2,400 *Nottonnage*.[84] Even if the army had been allowed to cripple the mobility of the strategic reserve by devoting all the *Nottonnage* to supply, only about 788 tons of the required 940 would have reached the units. But there was no total diversion of *Nottonnage*: At a planning exercise of May 9, during which Kesselring emphasized the paramount importance of maintaining the mobility of the reserves, *AOK 14* estimated that it could deliver only about 400 tons a day to its units with the transport available.[85]

These estimates of the capability of the *AOK 14* to deliver supplies to its units are only rough approximations. The actual rate surely varied greatly with the rail situation and the weather, to the extent that the latter hampered the activity of the fighters and permitted travel by day. It is also not possible to tell how much *Nottonnage* was diverted to supply or how many tons of supplies were carried in defiance of orders by day in good weather. It is evident from Kesselring's several reiterations of his order banning travel by day that the practice was widespread—impressive testimony to the perilous logistical plight of an army not noted for insubordination.[86]

The transport of *AOK 14*, then, was insufficient to cope with the conditions that STRANGLE created. No comparably detailed information has survived about the transport problems of *AOK 10*. But the reports filed by the *Oberquartiermeister* of that organization indicate that its problems were of comparable gravity. In an appreciation of the supply situation written on April 3 the quartermaster described "the increased strain on motor transport caused by the departure of the *90th Panzer Grenadier Division* and its vehicles [for *AOK 14*], the unloading of trains ever farther to the north, the shortening of the nights [when the convoys traveled] and the increased deterioration of the roads [especially from cratering]." By means of "severe rationing reserves of fuel and ammunition had been increased slightly as compared with the low point of February," although reserves of fodder had fallen. The reserves of ammunition were sufficient only "if measured by the needs of the fighting at Cassino, limited both in extent and duration." The *Oberquartiermeister* plainly viewed the future with apprehension, reporting the need for "still

---

84. The calculations for this statement are the same as those found in note 75, with the addition of 500 tons of *Nottonnage* for the *90th Panzer Grenadier Division*, which joined *AOK 14* on April 27 but left on May 14.
85. *KTB AOK 14/O Qu*, May 9, 1944, Roll 484, T-312; "*Planspiel am 9 Mai 1944*," appended to *KTB AOK 14/O Qu*, Roll 485, T-312.
86. See, for example, Kesselring to *AOK 10* and *AOK 14*, April 5 and 15, 1944, appended to *KTB AOK 10/O Qu*, Roll 107, T-311.

more stringent rationing of ammunition" because the transport situation could only be expected to grow worse. Even rationing could not ensure sufficient motor transport to supply the army as long as the railroads remained unrepaired.[87]

The *Oberquartiermeister* was even less sanguine in his report of April 28. The condition of the railroads was worse, "for in the course of the current reporting month many bridges have been so thoroughly destroyed that their repair is not conceivable." Transport space had been insufficient to retrieve from the railheads all the supplies allocated to the army; much still remained at Florence from early in the month when trains had been unable to proceed farther south. The effects had been grave:

> In spite of the unusual quiet on the front our logistical difficulties prevent an increase in stocks. Insofar as a temporary and insignificant increase of reserves did result, it was at the cost of other categories of supply (e.g., the decrease of fodder). Reserves of ammunition now stand at 1.5 *Ausstattungen*.[88]

There were other problems. Because of the transport situation, *AOK 10*'s reserves of fuel were "*völlig unzureichend*"—"wholly inadequate." It had been impossible to raise the reserves of fuel above 3.5 *Verbrauchssätze*,[89] whereas 5 *Verbrauchssätze* were necessary. The *Oberquartiermeister* reported that to conserve the reserves of fuel that had been amassed, he had had to curtail "every kind of movement."[90] As it had taken all the available transport to haul the fuel and ammunition allocated to the army, *AOK 10*'s reserves of fodder and provisions had dropped. The *Oberquartiermeister* described the army supplies of food "insufficient" on May 4.[91]

---

87. "*Beurteilung der Versorgungslage*," appended to *KTB AOK 10/O Qu*, Apr 3, 1944, Roll 103, T–312. On the same day that he wrote his report, the *Oberquartiermeister* lamented in his journal that because of the crisis in transport all the chief categories of ammunition were in short supply and that "a small army reserve" could be maintained only by refusing to cover fully the expenditures of the units. *Ibid*.

88. "*Beurteilung der Versorgungslage*," appended to *KTB AOK 10/O Qu*, Apr 28, 1944, Roll 103, T–312.

89. One *Verbrauchssatz* was the amount of fuel required to move a unit 100 kilometers. It was the equivalent for fuel of the *Ausstattung*.

90. See note 88 above.

91. *KTB AOK 10/O Qu*, May 4, 1944, Roll 103, T–312. Throughout STRANGLE the *Quartiermeister* of the corps defending Cassino recorded pressing shortages of fodder, potentially serious because the German infantry depended heavily on horses to move supplies and artillery. *KTB LI Gebirgekorps/Qu*, Mar 15–May 10, 1944, Roll 1270, T–314.

Daily reports filed by *AOK 14*'s *Oberquartiermeister* during STRAN-
GLE usually began with the succinct formula, "*Versorgungslage gesich-
ert*"—"supply situation secure." The reference, however, was to current
requirements. In his monthly reports this officer showed the same concern with the longer term as his counterpart on the southern front. The
first of his reports filed during STRANGLE, dated April 5, was relatively
optimistic. During March supply had improved continuously and was assured for all categories but fuel. Insufficient shipments of this commodity were directly attributed to cuts in the railroad during the previous two
weeks, that is, since the inception of STRANGLE. The *Oberquartiermeister*
anticipated, however, that increased shipments by sea and conservation
would allow reserves to be raised to the necessary level of five *Verbrauchssätze*. Within four days he had abandoned this hope, writing in
his journal on April 9 that "an improvement in the fuel situation is not
to be expected because of the catastrophic state of the railroads."[92]
Probably the immediate reason for this pessimism was *Heeresgruppe C*'s
announcement of April 5 that it would withdraw some of its transport
from the support of *AOK 14*.

AOK 14's monthly report of May 3 concluded that while the supply
of fuel for current consumption was secure, stocks had not increased and
would, indeed, "probably decrease because of the longer supply routes
and further reductions in transport space." Because of the *Heeresgruppe*'s heavy commitment of transport to *AOK 10*, it had carried only
7 percent (rather than the promised two-thirds) of the supplies from its
depots to those of *AOK 14*. It had therefore been necessary for the
army's own transport units, as well as for the vehicles of its corps and
divisions, to travel to the depots of the *Heeresgruppe*, some of which
were as far north as Florence:

> The conveyance of supplies, especially of ammunition, has accordingly
> suffered in the past reporting month. The ever mounting aerial activity
> of the enemy, moreover, has forced the supply columns to move only at
> night. Supply trips, therefore, require increasingly more time, so that
> columns sent for ammunition and fuel from dumps lying far to the
> north may be on the road as long as eight days. The result is the de-
> creased availability of transport space on hand. The ability of the
> *Panzer* and *Panzer Grenadier Divisions* to move upon four hours' notice

---

92. "*Beurteilung der Versorgungslage (Stand 1.4.44)*," appended to *KTB
AOK 14/O Qu*, Apr 5, 1944, Roll 485, T–312; *KTB AOK 14/O Qu*, Apr 9, 1944,
Roll 484.

has been called into question. The motor vehicles, moreover, are losing their combat-worthiness through constant use and the shortage of tires.[93]

The *Oberquartiermeister* voiced concern that supplying the force would present "the greatest difficulties" with the resumption of heavy fighting because too little transport was available for the task.[94] That his worries were not without foundation was shown during a planning exercise conducted on May 9 in the presence of Field Marshal Kesselring. The premise of the session was that an Allied effort to break out of the beachhead would be accompanied by a new landing on the western coast between Castiglione and the mouth of the Tiber. *AOK 14*'s staff had calculated that the defeat of the Allies would require the expenditure of 0.75 *Ausstattung* by the entire army during the first day of combat and of 0.33 *Ausstattung* each day thereafter. But such an expenditure, he concluded, "would be possible only with difficulty because of insufficient transport space," the principal reason for the insufficiency being the sixfold increase necessitated by the conditions imposed by Allied interdiction.[95]

Because the planners assumed an Allied landing would accompany a sally from the beachhead, they envisioned that all of *AOK 14*'s divisions would be engaged from the first day. The expenditures of ammunition calculated reflected this assumption, which proved pessimistic because no new landing occurred. Soon after the exercise, however, a staff study showed that the desired expenditure of 0.75 *Ausstattung* would be impossible even if only those divisions investing the beachhead became engaged (excluding, that is, the three divisions then assigned to the strategic reserve and one infantry division on coastal guard), because the army's reserves of four types of artillery ammunition were insufficient.[96]

As DIADEM approached, both General Heinrich von Vietinghoff of *AOK 10* and his chief of staff, Brig. Gen. Friedrich Wentzell, grew increasingly concerned over the shortage of ammunition. On April 23 von Vietinghoff explained to Kesselring that the army had conserved as much as it could through drastic rationing and that increased supply was now imperative. Kesselring replied that he would try to help. "The question

---

93. *"Beurteilung der Versorgungslage (Stand 1.5.1944),"* May 3, 1944, appended to *KTB AOK 14/O Qu,* Roll 485, T–312.

94. *Ibid.*

95. *KTB AOK 14/O Qu,* May 9, 1945, Roll 484, T–312; *"Planspiel am 9 Mai 1944,"* appended to *KTB AOK 14/O Qu,* Roll 485, T–312.

96. *"Schusszahlberechnung,"* n.d. [May 9–19, 1944], appended to *KTB AOK 14/O Qu,* Roll 485, T–312. The fourth division of the reserve was at Anzio.

of ammunition also worries me," he added.[97] Later the same day Wentzell explained to Kesselring's chief of staff, Brig. Gen. Siegfried Westphal, that inadequate stocks of ammunition had reduced *AOK 10* to
watching helplessly as the Allies reinforced their front, perhaps for the
long-expected offensive. "Ammunition! Ammunition!," he cried out at
one point. Both Wentzell and von Vietinghoff were particularly dis-
tressed by the shortage of shells for their 10-cm cannon, their only
weapons with the range to harass and interdict Allied forces as they
massed for the offensive.[98]

On April 29 Westphal informed von Vietinghoff that a major shipment of ammunition to *AOK 10* was under way, for which purpose no
less than 2,000 tons of motor transport had been diverted from various
military construction projects in northern Italy. The plan was to raise
AOK 10's reserves of artillery ammunition to about 2.5 *Ausstattungen*.
Westphal added, "We hope that we still have the time to forward everything. . . . But the railroad situation is still very bad."[99] The Germans
lost their race with time. Between April 29 and May 10, the last full day
before the Allies struck the Gustav Line, stocks of ammunition held by
the divisions and in the corps dumps declined, while the overall reserves
of the army increased a mere 6 percent over the worrisome level of 1.5
Ausstattungen.[100] Since the beginning of STRANGLE when *AOK 10*'s reserves were depleted from the winter's heavy fighting at Cassino, the aggregate tonnage of the ammunition it held had increased by only 7 percent. Indeed, when the Allies attacked in May, *AOK 10* was not so well
provided with ammunition as it had been in January when the Allies first
tried to take Cassino. At that time *AOK 10* had faced only three divisions; in May it confronted twelve. *AOK 14* had done better, but its increase of 22 percent was still unimpressive, as it too had entered STRAN-
GLE with depleted stocks.[101] (*Table 7*)

Although STRANGLE failed to dislodge the Germans from the Gustav
Line and the entrenchments around Anzio, it nonetheless prepared the
way for DIADEM by restricting the rate at which *AOKs 10* and *14* were
resupplied. This was significant because the heavy fighting of the winter,
at Cassino and at Anzio, had left both armies with depleted stores of

---

97. Tele con, von Vietinghoff/Kesselring, transcript appended to *KTB AOK
10/Ia*, Apr 23, 1944, Roll 90, T–312.

98. Telephone con, Wentzell/Westphal, *ibid.*

99. Telephone con, von Vietinghoff/Westphal, transcript appended to *KTB
AOK 10/Ia*, Apr 29, 1944, Roll 90, T–312.

100. *Tagesmeldungen AOK 10/O Qu*, Apr 29 and May 19, 1944, Roll 103,
T–312.

101. Calculated from Sallagar, *Operation "STRANGLE,"* 83–86 tables 2, 3.

Table 7. Changing Ammunition Status, by Ammunition Type, as a Percentage of an Issue: AOKs 10 and 14, January–May 1944

Recipient	Ammunition Type, as Percent of Issue															
	Machine-gun	8-cm Mortar	12-cm Mortar	Light Infantry Gun	Heavy Infantry Gun	Light Field Howitzer	Heavy Field Howitzer	10-cm Cannon	21-cm Mortar	17-cm Mortar	15-cm Nebelwerfer	21-cm Nebelwerfer	Unknown	Mountain Gun	Mountain Howitzer	22-cm Mortar
AOK 10																
Jan 24, 1944																
Units	105	165	192	167	196	117	117	126	214	113	95	105	unl§	unl	unl	unl
Depots	61	65	248	113	91	68	69	116	542	58	100	100	unl	unl	unl	unl
Total Holdings*	166	230	440	280	287	185	186	242	756	171	195	205	unl	unl	unl	unl
Mar 15, 1944																
Units	145	99	110	174	228	135	116	91	142	17	76	91	38	176	73	82
Depots	59	42	150	107	134	23	53	120	84	10	81	247	1,138	284	118	172
Total Holdings†	204	141	260	281	362	158	169	211	226	27	157	338	1,176	460	191	254
May 10, 1944																
Units	145	101	32	166	148	162	145	146	112	81	141	157	unl	150	108	84
Depots	33	3	57	16	128	57	75	40	111	14	89	89	unl	226	245	103
Total Holdings	178	104	89	182	276	219	220	186	223	95	230	246	unl	376	353	187

AOK 14

Mar 15, 1944															
Units	111	122	118	187	154	164	199	186	298	72	100	152	427	unl	190
Depots	13	8	9	45	59	23	60	45	84	61	127	157	333	unl	109
Total Holdings‡	124	130	127	232	213	187	259	231	382	133	227	309	760	unl	299
May 10, 1944															
Units	125	115	234	201	278	217	214	171	370	104	267	359	unl	unl	252
Depots	2	2	31	2	97	14	31	43	217	68	unl	unl	unl	unl	417
Total Holdings	127	117	265	203	375	231	245	214	587	172	267	359	unl	unl	669

*Of the twelve critical ammunition types that can be compared for January 24 and May 10, seven declined and five increased.

†Of the fifteen critical ammunition types that can be compared for March 15 and May 10, nine declined, five increased, and one remained essentially the same.

‡Of the eleven critical ammunition types that can be compared for March 15 and May 10, four declined, six increased, and one remained essentially the same.

§Unlisted.

SOURCES: *Tagesmeldungen AOK 10/O Qu* and *Tagesmeldungen AOK 14/O Qu.*

fuel and ammunition. STRANGLE showed for the first time just how vulnerable to interdiction railroads are when an attacker exploits their greatest weakness, channelization, by systematically destroying choke points like bridges and viaducts, and reattacking them as often as necessary to prevent repairs. The Allies effectively constricted German supply by forcing the Germans to abandon the capacious but vulnerable railroads for trucks, less vulnerable but also less capacious. They could not choke off German motor transport because the roads were many and resistant to damage. But because of the far-ranging armed reconnaissance of Allied fighter-bombers, German convoys could take advantage of the redundant and durable road network only at night, which effectively reduced transport space below that necessary to provide both for current consumption and adequate stockpiling. STRANGLE's success was due primarily to this last effect, for the Germans' holdings of trucks were sufficient to supply their armies adequately, had their convoys been able to move by day. On the eve of DIADEM, *AOK 10* had reserves of ammunition of about 1.5 *Ausstattungen*, about half of what was desirable in its circumstances and less than would have been at its disposal but for Allied interdiction. The reserves of *AOK 14*, although larger, were still not sufficient to sustain the rate of fire its staff thought necessary to contain the expected spring offensive of the Allies. In a theater where more than 60 percent of all casualties were caused by artillery fire, this was clearly an important accomplishment for interdiction.[102] Neither army had been able to raise its reserves of fuel to necessary levels. These results are all the more impressive because of the unusual quiet that reigned on both Italian fronts during STRANGLE.

---

102. Gilbert W. Beebe and Michael E. De Bakey, *Battle Casualties: Incidence, Mortality, and Logistical Considerations* (Springfield, Ill., 1952), 135 table 5.

Chapter 6

Operation DIADEM: Interdiction and the Battle for Rome
May 11–June 10, 1944

Operation STRANGLE and the immediately succeeding inter-diction operation present a semblance of paradox. Among students of interdiction, probably no point has commanded greater allegiance than this—that heavy consumption by a force subject to interdiction is a virtual necessity for its logistical posture to be significantly impaired. STRANGLE, as the previous chapter demonstrated, seriously reduced the rate at which the two German armies south of Rome could be resupplied. It did so when the fronts were notably quiet. During DIADEM—the Allied offensive that led to the capture of Rome—the Anglo-American air forces continued and even extended the program of interdiction begun with STRANGLE. Yet the effect on German supply was considerably less than that of STRANGLE, even though a great battle raged. The key to the seeming paradox lies in the way in which DIADEM's scheme of maneuver and the interdiction plan worked at cross-purposes. The offensive did of course greatly increase German consumption, but the German logistical system was not pitched into crisis. The Allied armies attacked on a narrow front, enabling the Germans to concentrate their motor transport to support the endangered section of their line, a luxury denied them during STRANGLE, when they were uncertain where their enemy would strike.

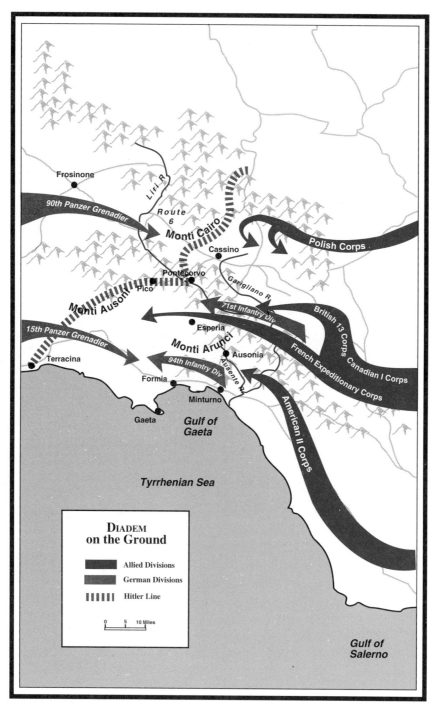

Frosinone

90th Panzer Grenadier

Liri R.

Route 6

Monti Cairo

Cassino

Polish Corps

Pontecorvo

Pico

Garigliano R.

Monti Ausoni

71st Infantry Div

15th Panzer Grenadier

Esperia

British 13 Corps Canadian I Corps

Terracina

Monti Arunci

Ausonia

French Expeditionary Corps

Formia

94th Infantry Div

Ausente R.

Minturno

Gaeta

Gulf of
Gaeta

American II Corps

Tyrrhenian Sea

DIADEM
on the Ground

Allied Divisions

German Divisions

Hitler Line

0   5   10 Miles

Gulf of
Salerno

Map 12.

T he supreme commander of Allied forces in the Mediterranean, General Sir Henry Maitland Wilson, initially shared the confidence of his airmen that interdiction could break the Italian stalemate. On February 25, 1944, he cabled the commander of the ground forces in Italy, General Sir Harold Alexander, that it was "not unreasonable" to expect that by the end of April Operation STRANGLE would force the Germans to retreat "at least to the Pisa-Rimini line." Alexander and his staff were much less confident, and their pessimism seems to have affected Wilson. In an appreciation of March 20 Alexander predicted that a month of hard fighting would be required in the spring to relieve the beachhead at Anzio.[1]

Planning for the spring offensive, Operation DIADEM, was accordingly unaffected by the heady optimism with which STRANGLE was launched. Alexander's chief of staff, General Sir John Harding, developed DIADEM's concept of operations in late February. The British Eighth Army was to storm the Gustav Line at Cassino and then advance through the Liri Valley along Route 6, the highway between Cassino and Rome, driving most of the right flank of the *Armeeoberkommando 10 (AOK 10—Tenth Army)* before it. Simultaneously, the main body of the American Fifth Army would sweep aside the remainder of *AOK 10*'s right flank and move rapidly along the Tyrrhenian coast toward Anzio. As it approached the Allied beachhead, the remainder of the Fifth Army, besieged at Anzio since February, would break out through the encircling *Armeeoberkommando 14 (AOK 14—Fourteenth Army)* and join the main body for a drive east to Valmontone. Route 6, the escape route of

---

1. Msg, General Sir Hugh Maitland Wilson to General Sir Harold Alexander, Feb 25, 1944, C/S Directives, 622.01-8; W.F.G. Jackson, *The Battle for Italy* (New York, 1967), 205-6, 219-20.

the German forces retreating from Cassino before the Eighth Army, would thus be severed, and much of *AOK 10* could then be pinned against a spur of the Apennines and ground to pieces. Only then did Harding envision an advance on Rome.

The preparations for DIADEM were extensive and ultimately pushed D-day back to May 11. To gain the requisite numerical advantage, additional divisions had to be brought into Italy from the Middle East, North Africa, and the United States. There were major changes in the composition of the Allied forces at Cassino. The Eighth Army redeployed to that sector from the Adriatic front, where its place was taken by an independent British corps. The repeatedly defeated New Zealand Corps was withdrawn from the line and subsequently disbanded. The Polish Corps replaced the French Expeditionary Corps, which was then attached to the Fifth Army in the coastal sector.[2]

Two cover plans were implemented to deceive the Germans. The purpose of one was to create the impression that the offensive could not occur before June. As the redeployment of the Eighth Army could not possibly be disguised, most of its divisions remained in training areas far behind the front, to move forward for the assault under cover of darkness only forty-eight hours before D-day. The object of the second ruse was to cause Field Marshal Albert Kesselring to fear that another Anzio was in the offing, so that he would be reluctant to commit his strategic reserve when the Allies attacked his southern front. To that end, American and Canadian troops conspicuously practiced landings near Naples.[3]

During April the leadership of the Mediterranean Allied Air Forces (MAAF) quickly abandoned its earlier confidence that STRANGLE would dislodge the Germans from the Gustav Line. Its commander, Lt. Gen. Ira C. Eaker, wrote on April 7 that "there is no question in our minds but that we are keeping the enemy's supply below the minimum for successful combat." But the plan, of course, had been to hold the Germans below the level of supply they needed to *maintain* their forces, even under the quiet conditions that prevailed along the front during STRANGLE. Eaker plainly thought that this had not been achieved: "Actually, what we now need more than anything is some Army support. . . . What we ask the Army to do is to put enough pressure on the enemy to force him to discharge some ammunition and further reduce his reserves of fuel and ammunition."[4]

2. Jackson, *Battle for Italy*, 202–4, 223–24.
3. *Ibid.*, 225–26.
4. Ltr, Lt Gen Ira C. Eaker to General Henry H. Arnold, Apr 7, 1944, Box 22, Eaker-Arnold Correspondence, Papers of Ira C. Eaker, Library of Congress.

In Naples harbor, Allied troop exercises were held to divert attention from the preparations under way for operation DIADEM.

One reason for Eaker's pessimism was that the Germans, for all the destruction of their railroads and harrying of their motor transport, did not seem to be seriously short of supplies. An assessment completed about May 1 by the Office of Strategic Services (OSS) summarized Allied perceptions with a bluntness from which Eaker might have shrunk in his correspondence with the notoriously impatient General Henry H. Arnold: "Up to April 28 the [interdiction] campaign has produced no visible effect on enemy front line strength." Prisoners had told of shortages of ammunition, but the OSS discounted the reports because at Anzio "the enemy has not hesitated to engage in artillery duels, even after a month of railroad interdiction." Neither did the Germans seem to suffer from a shortage of fuel, as traffic behind their lines was heavy. "Measured in terms of siege warfare not accompanied by assault, the campaign has so far produced no substantial results."[5]

Another reason for pessimism was the interpretation that Allied intelligence put upon the information from ULTRA. This can be seen by reading between the lines of an estimate prepared on April 27 by MAAF's A-2 Section, which relied heavily on signals intelligence in planning STRANGLE.[6] The intelligence officers estimated that the Germans

5. Office of Strategic Services (OSS), "Railroad Traffic Interdiction—Central Italy—March–April 1944," n.d. [May 1944], annex J to Mediterranean Allied Tactical Air Force (MATAF), "Report on Operation STRANGLE," 626.430–15.

6. Reports from the G-2 Section of the War Department General Staff on the use of ULTRA in the Mediterranean theater show clearly how important aerial operations were. The officers in MAAF's A-2 Section who were responsible for the interpretation and dissemination of information from ULTRA were, by and

had been able to meet their minimum requirements, and had on hand
reserves of ammunition sufficient for "thirty days of sustained operations" and fuel enough for ten. The analysts held out hope, however,
that once the spring offensive had begun the Germans would be unable
to convey to the front the additional 1,000 tons a day they would then
require, and that after an unspecified period a "critical situation" would
develop, especially with respect to fuel. The OSS was more cautious,
stating only that "it seems unlikely that so long as present pressure can
be maintained preparations for handling of any heavy additional load
will be possible."[7]

ULTRA did not open quite so wide a window into German logistics
as its triumphs in other applications might suggest. Before the beginning
of DIADEM, the Government Code and Cipher School at Bletchley Park,
where German radio traffic was deciphered, sent to Italy fragmentary
daily quartermaster reports from *AOK 10* for thirteen of STRANGLE's
fifty-eight days. From *AOK 14* there were three complete and twelve partial reports.[8] These sufficed to show that the overall ammunition reserves

---

large, the same who had designed STRANGLE. One visitor from Washington
found "no lack of appreciation of Special Intelligence in the Mediterranean
Theater," where intelligence officers admitted "that it won the Battle for North
Africa for them and that it is the most important single intelligence factor available." The same officer noted that at the time of his visit (March–April 1944),
ULTRA was being used to determine target priorities for STRANGLE. Another visitor from Washington, in fact, worried "that there seems to be a tendency in
practice to rely too heavily upon ULTRA to the exclusion of all else." MAAF distributed information from ULTRA to subordinate commands according to need-
to-know. Intelligence officers from commands selected to receive ULTRA were
brought into MAAF's A-2 Section for several weeks of indoctrination and training. At the time of STRANGLE/DIADEM, both the Strategic and the Tactical Air
Forces had ULTRA-indoctrinated officers, as did their principal subcommands,
the XII Tactical Air Command, the Desert Air Force, and the Fifteenth Air
Force. National Security Agency, SRH-031, "Trip Reports Concerning Use of
ULTRA in the Mediterranean Theater, 1943–1944," Record Group (RG) 457, National Archives and Records Administration (NARA), 6–8, 12, 19, 25, 28, 30–31,
35, 38, 45, 49–51.
  7. A-2 Section, MAAF, "Appreciation of Air Attacks Against Enemy Communications and Supply in Italy," Apr 27, 1944, 655.552-2.
  8. For *AOK 10*, see DEFE 3/36: KV 335, Apr 6, 1944, Roll 15, "ULTRA"
(New York: Clearwater Microfilms, 1979–); DEFE 3/40: KV 1298, Apr 18, 1944,
KV 1460, Apr 20, 1944, and KV 1487, Apr 20, 1944, all Roll 16, *ibid.*; DEFE
3/43: KV 2007, Apr 25, 1944, and KV 2052, Apr 26, 1944, both Roll 17, *ibid.*;
DEFE 3/45: KV 2669, May 2, 1944, Roll 18, *ibid.*; DEFE 3/151: VL 9318, Mar
24, 1944, VL 9484, Mar 26, 1944, VL 9430, Mar 26, 1944, and VL 9431, Mar 26,
1944, all Roll 14, *ibid.*; DEFE 3/152: VL 9668, Mar 28, 1944, Roll 14, *ibid.*; and
DEFE 3/153: KV 3342, May 10, 1944, Roll 19, *ibid.* For *AOK 14*, see DEFE
3/35: KV 217, Apr 4, 1944, Roll 15, *ibid.*; DEFE 3/38: KV 777, Apr 12, 1944,
Roll 16, *ibid.*; DEFE 3/40: KV 1469, Apr 20, 1944, Roll 16, *ibid.*; DEFE 3/42:
KV 1912, Apr 24, 1944, Roll 17, *ibid.*; DEFE 3/43: KV 2153, Apr 27, 1944, Roll
17, *ibid.*; DEFE 3/44: KV 2400, Apr 20, 1944, and KV 2485, Apr 30, 1944, both

of both armies had increased slightly, as had *AOK 14*'s holdings of auto-mobile fuel. They could not show, however, that *AOK 10*'s holdings of this commodity dropped precipitously before STRANGLE's end, because the last deciphered message from that army that Bletchley sent to Italy before DIADEM began dated from April 20, when *AOK 10*'s supply of fuel stood at a temporary peak, before falling sharply. (*Chart 6*)

The quartermaster reports presented a further difficulty for Allied intelligence analysts in that they were predominantly numerical and wholly uncaptioned. Allied intelligence could nonetheless tell with relative ease how much fuel was available to the German armies. Each daily supply return stated the current size for an issue for fuel in cubic meters, and gave the number of issues actually on hand. The vital clue to the identity of these figures was that they were all in two columns—one for automobile fuel, the other for diesel. The daily reports also stated in tons the current issue for ammunition, first as an aggregate figure, then broken down by the most critical types. Ammunition on hand was reported similarly. The problem for the Allies was that they did not understand the letter codes used to designate each type.[9] They therefore resorted to the approach used by later students of STRANGLE and calculated the German reserves in terms of aggregate tonnages. The A–2 Section, for example, derived its estimate of days of ammunition expenditure available to the German armies by dividing the average of the aggregate tonnages they had on hand during STRANGLE by an estimated daily expenditure of 600 tons a day, a figure apparently based on reports intercepted during the winter's heavy fighting.

The difficulty with the approach was that, measured in tons, most of the ammunition in the German depots was *not* of the types deemed sufficiently critical to be reported to the operations section of the army staff at the close of each day. (*Table 8* shows the critical types.) On May 12, the first full day of DIADEM, noncritical types accounted for no less than 39 percent of all ammunition with *AOK 10*, though they constituted only 13 percent of the total expended during the following two weeks of

---

Roll 17, *ibid.*; DEFE 3/45: KV 2684, May 3, 1944, and KV 2528, May 11, 1944, both Roll 18, *ibid.*; DEFE 3/47: KV 3223, May 9, 1944, Roll 18, *ibid.*; DEFE 3/150: VL 9082, Mar 22, 1944, Roll 14, *ibid.*; DEFE 3/151: VL 9447, Mar 26, 1944, and VL 9396, Mar 25, 1944, both Roll 14, *ibid.*; and DEFE 3/153: VL 9555, Mar 27, 1944, and VL 9614, Mar 28, 1944, both Roll 19, *ibid.*

9. Bletchley Park tentatively identified some of the letter codes, as follows: a = small arms other than machinegun; b = machinegun; c = 8-cm mortar; d = 12-cm mortar; e = light-infantry gun; f = heavy-infantry gun; g = light howitzer; h = medium howitzer; and i = 10-cm gun. All these were wrong, as a comparison with Table 8 will show. Bletchley declined even to guess at the identify of the others. DEFE 3/130: VL 4168, Jan 17, 1944, Roll 7, *ibid*.

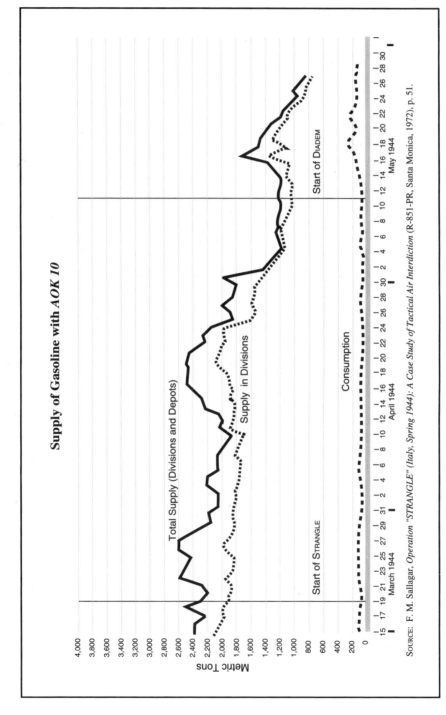

Supply of Gasoline with *AOK 10*

Metric Tons

Total Supply (Divisions and Depots)

Supply in Divisions

Consumption

Start of STRANGLE

Start of DIADEM

15 17 19 21 23 25 27 29 31 2 4 6 8 10 12 14 16 18 20 22 24 26 28 30 2 4 6 8 10 12 14 16 18 20 22 24 26 28 30
March 1944   April 1944   May 1944

SOURCE: F. M. Sallagar, *Operation "STRANGLE" (Italy, Spring 1944): A Case Study of Tactical Air Interdiction* (R-851-PR, Santa Monica, 1972), p. 51.

Chart 6.

fighting.[10] Thus, by calculating German reserves as they did, MAAF's analysts underestimated STRANGLE's effect. For at the actual rates of expenditure that prevailed during DIADEM, *AOK 10* had on April 27, the day of the A–2 Section's appreciation, ammunition reserves of the critical types for eighteen days; the corresponding figure for *AOK 14* was twenty-two days.[11]

Even these latter figures seem quite high until one looks at the individual types of ammunition. As Chapter 5 demonstrated, the general effect of STRANGLE was to thwart the plans of the Germans to raise their stocks of ammunition and fuel to meet the Allied offensive, sure to come with spring. Neither German army had been able to raise its reserves of artillery ammunition to an appropriate average of three *Ausstattungen* (issues), although this level was exceeded for a few calibers.[12] *AOK 10* suffered more, as it was farther from the depots of the *Heeresgruppe* and, unlike its sister organization at Anzio, had an extensive front to defend. While most of *AOK 14*'s holdings of the critical types increased, most of *AOK 10*'s declined or remained about the same, notwithstanding an increase in the overall tonnage of ammunition in its depots.[13] Indeed, *AOK 10* was, in respect of artillery ammunition, not so well prepared for DIADEM than it had been for the first assault on Cassino in January, when it had had to contend with only three divisions, not the twelve hurled against it during DIADEM. *AOK 14*'s situation, while better, was still constrained. In planning for the Allied offensive, its staff found it had to reduce the planned expenditure of artillery ammunition for D-day

---

10. As noted in Chapter 5, noncritical types consisted primarily of ammunition taken from Italian depots, for which the Germans had only a limited use, or of small-arms ammunition, of which they had an abundance.

11. *Tagesmeldungen AOK 10/Oberquartiermeister (AOK 10/O Qu)* appended to *Kriegstagebuch (KTB) AOK 10/O Qu*, Apr 28 and May 12, 1944, Roll 103, T–312, NARA; *Tagesmeldung*, appended to *KTB AOK 14/O Qu*, Apr 27, 1944, Roll 484, *ibid*. The rate of expenditure for *AOK 10*, May 12–25, was 543 tons a day. The rate for *AOK 14*, May 23–30, was 615 tons a day. The figures for *AOK 10*'s expenditure of ammunition given in the studies by RAND and the Historical Evaluation and Research Organization (HERO), cited below, are inaccurate. They were taken from Section 1 of the daily quartermaster report which gives estimated consumption (*"Gëschätzter Tagesverbrauch"*) of fuel and ammunition for the day not yet finished. Section 2 of the report, however, gives exact figures for the consumption of ammunition on the previous day. Section 3 gives the corresponding figures for fuel.

12. For a discussion of the *Ausstattung*, see Chapter 5.

13. On March 15 *AOK 10* had total ammunition reserves of 16,722 tons; on May 10, of 18,102. The figures for total tons of ammunition in *AOK 10* given by RAND and HERO are accurate but are predated by a day because the researchers failed to note that the data given in Section 2 of the daily reports pertain to the previous day. The same problem does not occur for *AOK 14*; all data in its reports are of the same day as the report.

Table 8. Changing Ammunition Status, by Ammunition Type, as a Percentage of an Issue: AOKs 10 and 14, May 12–30 1944

Recipient	Ammunition Type, as Percent of Issue															
	Machine-gun	8-cm Mortar	12-cm Mortar	Light Infantry Gun	Heavy Infantry Gun	Light Field Howitzer	Heavy Field Howitzer	10-cm Cannon	21-cm Mortar	17-cm Mortar	15-cm Nebelwerfer	21-cm Nebelwerfer	Unknown	Mountain Gun	Mountain Howitzer	22-cm Mortar
AOK 10																
May 12, 1944																
Divisions	146	115	58	165	150	147	149	143	100	69	123	158	unl*	167	98	30
Depots	32	26	35	11	178	67	90	72	368	4	41	81	unl	109	122	158
Total Holdings	178	141	93	176	328	214	239	215	468	73	164	239	unl	276	220	188
May 19, 1944																
Divisions	131	113	51	115	103	135	146	97	217	36	25	37	unl	168	81	40
Depots	183	62	13	36	113	48	52	50	30	24	38	64	unl	91	109	113
Total Holdings	314	175	64	151	216	183	198	147	247	60	63	101	unl	259	190	153
May 25, 1944																
Divisions	118	127	52	113	98	117	122	72	202	18	22	42	unl	173	71	84
Depots	10	8	7	24	76	60	76	4	135	70	6	22	unl	67	109	206
Total Holdings	128	135	59	137	174	177	198	76	337	88	28	64	unl	240	180	290

AOK 14

May 23, 1944																
Divisions	132	125	355	192	325	237	256	174	369	137	unl	unl	150	unl	unl	252
Depots	26	5	28	unl	130	14	49	109	230	unl	unl	unl	unl	unl	unl	unl
Total	158	130	383	192	455	251	305	283	599	137	unl	unl	150	unl	unl	252
Holdings																
May 30, 1944																
Divisions	72	72	112	111	179	141	118	44	211	98	119	unl	174	unl	unl	238
Depots	1	2	unl	158	unl	2	2	unl	252	unl	386	unl	15	unl	unl	unl
Total	73	74	112	269	179	143	120	44	463	98	505	unl	189	unl	unl	238
Holdings																

*Unlisted.

SOURCES: *Tagesmeldungen AOK 10/O Qu* and *Tagesmeldungen AOK 14/O Qu.*

from three-quarters of an *Ausstattung* to one-half.[14] Germany's production of ammunition was at near record levels and continued to increase until September 1944. Shortages on the western fronts before that date were due to the transportation problems caused by Allied air power.[15]

Allied estimates of fuel held by the German armies in Italy were quite accurate: On April 27 *AOK 10* had reserves of both automobile and diesel fuel for ten days at the rate of consumption that prevailed from May 12 to 25, while *AOK 14* had reserves of the former commodity for eleven days and of the latter for twelve, at the rate of consumption for the period May 23–31.[16] These figures, like those for ammunition, seem sufficient until they are put into the context of operational requirements. By the beginning of DIADEM neither German army had raised its reserves of fuel to the level planned at the beginning of STRANGLE—five issues, or *Verbrauchsätze* (*VS*).[17] Even *AOK 14*, favored to receive supplies because of its responsibility for the divisions of the strategic reserve, had its supply of diesel fuel reduced to a marginally adequate 3.5 *VS*. *AOK 10*'s supply of diesel fuel was lower yet, while its reserves of automobile fuel had plummeted from 4.25 to 2.3 *VS*. *AOK 14* had managed to hold the reserves of three of the four divisions of the strategic reserve at 5 *VS*, but reserves of the fourth division and of several small armored units assigned to the reserve were at worrisome levels.[18] The German quartermasters attributed their fuel problems entirely to interdiction. Germany's production of fuel had peaked in March. It began to decline rapidly in May because of the effects of strategic bombing, but shipments to the field armies were nonetheless maintained from stocks at previous levels until August.[19]

Little in the intercepted supply returns gives much sense of the Germans' operational requirements. Past consumption was a poor guide,

---

14. Ltr, *Oberst* Fieger to *Oberst* Hauser, subj: Ammunition Supply, May 15, 1944, appended to *KTB AOK 14/O Qu*, Roll 485, T–312.

15. U.S. Strategic Bombing Survey, *The Effects of Strategic Bombing on the German War Economy* (Washington, Oct 31, 1945), 183, 188; Brig Gen Kurt Scheffler, "Strength and Composition of German Artillery During World War II," 1947, MS P–057, RG 338, NARA.

16. Calculated from the same sources cited in note 11.

17. For a discussion of the effects of STRANGLE on German supply, see Chapter 5.

18. Ltr, *Oberst* Fieger to *Oberst* Fähndrich, subj: *Betriebstoffbevorratung der beweglichen Grossreserven, in Sonderheit der 90. Pz. Gr. D.*, appended to *KTB AOK 14/O Qu*, May 14, 1944, Roll 485, T–312.

19. U.S. Strategic Bombing Survey, *Effects of Strategic Bombing on the German War Economy*, table 41, 79; U.S. Strategic Bombing Survey, *Oil Division Final Report: German Oil, Chemical, Rubber, Explosives, and Propellants Industries* (Washington, Aug 25, 1945), figure 15 facing page 20. See Chapter 5 for German logistical appraisals of STRANGLE.

though it was better for fuel than for ammunition because the former could not be rationed so stringently as the latter. The fronts were quiet during STRANGLE, but supply convoys still had to ply their long routes to the depots of *Heeresgruppe C.* The heavy fighting of the winter along the Gustav Line afforded Allied intelligence little guidance, as it had not been nearly so intense as that which the spring would bring.

There was, accordingly, a marked contrast between Allied and German assessments of STRANGLE. The Allies feared the operation had failed; the Germans were concerned that their supply would prove inadequate once fighting resumed. In the Allied camp there were various explanations of why the interdiction campaign so hopefully begun had soon disappointed its authors. On April 16, MAAF's deputy commander, Air Marshal Sir John Slessor, repeated Eaker's complaint that the army had not forced the Germans to consume their supplies. This was accurate enough, as was the deputy commander's observation that the German soldier lived far harder than his British or American counterpart did. Not so correct were the British officer's other reasons for what he saw as the failure of STRANGLE: that the Germans shipped a fair percentage of their requirements (about 500 tons daily) by sea, and that they had been able to stock their forward depots during February and early March when Allied planes had been grounded by poor weather. Slessor's estimate of what the Germans sent by sea was quite exact, but the ports where the supplies were unloaded, primarily San Stefano on the west coast and Ancona on the east, were so far to the north that maritime shipments had not relieved the strain on motor transport that was the root cause of the Germans' logistical problem. Neither had they stocked their forward dumps during February and March, both the weather and the fighting of those months having frustrated their efforts to do so.[20]

The OSS opined that STRANGLE's zone of interdiction had been insufficiently deep to overtax the Germans' motor transport. While the OSS overestimated the supplies the German armies required, it so underestimated the burden on German motor transport as to make the whole interdiction campaign seem a trifling inconvenience. It did, nonetheless, identify a reason for STRANGLE's not having had a greater effect:

---

20. Between Jan 1 and Apr 1, 1944, the Germans shipped an average of 400 to 600 tons a day by sea to both armies. G-2 Section, Allied Force Headquarters, "The German System of Supply in the Field: Italy, 1943–1945," Feb 1946, German Naval Records Collection, Operational Archives Branch, Naval History Division, Office of the Chief of Naval Operations, 155; Sir John Slessor, *The Central Blue: The Autobiography of Sir John Slessor, Marshal of the RAF* (New York, 1956), 571–75.

MAAF's failure, or rather inability, to bomb as heavily in the mountainous region between La Spezia and Rimini as had originally been planned.[21]

The principal result of April's pessimistic estimates of STRANGLE was to shift the justification for continued interdiction from forcing a German withdrawal to helping the ground forces during the approaching offensive. MAAF and its subordinate organizations later asserted in campaign histories that this had been STRANGLE's sole object all along. Maj. Gen. Lauris Norstad, MAAF's Director of Operations, was more candid. STRANGLE, he wrote the following summer, had not been wholly successful: "The enemy was not forced to withdraw all or even part of his forces due to strained supply problems."[22]

MAAF issued the outline air plan for DIADEM on April 28, 1944. The actual operations order of May 12 derived from a draft prepared by the commander of the Tactical Air Force, Maj. Gen. John Cannon. The plan envisioned three stages. A chastened STRANGLE appeared innocuously as the Preparatory Phase. From April 25 to D-day—May 11—attacks on the enemy's rail and road bridges, motor transport, and harbors were to be intensified. So, too, were the raids on his supply dumps and depots, the locations of which were generally known from ULTRA. Those holding fuel, the Germans' greatest logistical weakness, were to be attacked first, followed by those with ammunition, and then by those containing supplies of other kinds. Also planned for the final days of the Preparatory Phase was a greatly amplified counterair campaign.[23] Of all the tasks that faced MAAF, the harrying of the residuum of German air power in Italy was probably the easiest. By DIADEM there were no more than 350 German aircraft of all kinds in Italy; there were also about 150 medium bombers in southern France, periodically available for the support of *Heeresgruppe C*. All in all, no more than 700 German aircraft of all types were available for service in the Mediterranean theater. MAAF, by contrast, disposed 3,960 combat aircraft on May 12.[24]

---

21. "Railroad Traffic Interdiction, Central Italy, March–April 1944." The OSS estimated that the German armies needed no more than 4,000 tons of supplies a day (of which 3,500 tons were moved overland), that they had 13,500 tons of transport space for this task, and that the round trips of the convoys required no more than four days. For a more detailed discussion, see Chapter 5.

22. Rpt, Brig Gen Lauris Norstad, "Air Force Participation in DIADEM," Jul 31, 1944, vol 7, Tab FF, in MAAF, "Operations in Support of DIADEM," n.d., 622.430-3.

23. Headquarters Mediterranean Allied Tactical Air Force (HQ MATAF), "Outline Plan for Air Participation in DIADEM," Apr 27, 1944, Memo, Cannon to Eaker, Apr 27, 1944, and MAAF, "Operations Order No. 35," May 12, 1944, *all* in MAAF, "Operations in Support of DIADEM," vol 1.

24. "Air Situation, 12 May 1944," in MAAF, "Operations in Support of

The Assault Phase was to commence with D-day. The Strategic Air Force and some of the medium bombers of the Tactical Air Force were directed to attack a long list of German headquarters, the locations of which had been identified through ULTRA. Counterair operations were to be continued, if needed, and interdiction was to be sustained. MAAF's planners drew no distinction between logistical and countermobility interdiction. All German movements were the quarry: "Interruption of communications," the outline air plan directed, "will be maintained to prevent supplies and reinforcements [from] reaching the German Armies and, in the case of early success, to prevent the withdrawal of the enemy to the north."[25] The last stage of the air plan, the Sustained Offensive Phase, was to follow a breakthrough on the southern front. At that time, the Strategic Air Force would revert to its normal emphasis upon missions over Germany and the Balkans, leaving the Tactical Air Force to continue with its responsibilities for interdiction and close air support. Throughout all three phases the mission of the Coastal Air Force was to attack enemy shipping.

DIADEM's interdiction campaign was conceptually a continuation of STRANGLE. There were, however, two significant differences. In response to the OSS's criticism of the earlier operation, the zone of interdiction was deepened to include all rail lines crossing the northern Apennines. The object was to put 140 miles, rather than STRANGLE's 100, between the German railheads and the front in order to increase still more the burden on German motor transport. The second innovation was a greater emphasis on interdiction by night. This mission fell to the light bombers of the Tactical Air Force.

Apart from a limited number of attacks on harbors and headquarters, the role of the Strategic Air Force was confined, as it had been during STRANGLE, to attacks on marshaling yards north of the Pisa-Rimini line. All interdiction to the south was the responsibility of the Tactical Air Force. XII Tactical Air Command had an area of operations that ran

---

DIADEM," vol 1, Tab C. The numbers given in this appreciation are presumed accurate because they were based upon ULTRA. German sources located after the war give a strength of 750 to 775 aircraft on March 1, 1944. British Air Ministry, *The Rise and Fall of the German Air Force (1933–1945)* (London, 1948), 267.

25. HQ MAAF, "Outline Air Plan for Air Participation in DIADEM," Apr 27, 1944, in MAAF, "Operations in Support of DIADEM," vol 1, Tab I. F.M. Sallagar, in his well-known study of Operations STRANGLE and DIADEM, states the latter was merely a continuation of STRANGLE; "supply denial remained the sole objective. . . ." F.M. Sallagar, *Operation "STRANGLE" (Italy, Spring 1944): A Case Study of Tactical Air Interdiction* (The Rand Corp., R-851-PR, Santa Monica, 1972), 61. This is contradicted not only by the draft operations order but by other evidence as well. See, for example, the letter from Slessor to Portal, written April 16, 1944. Slessor, *Central Blue*, 574.

Evidence of the restrictions imposed by Allied bomb damage on the ability of the Germans to move their divisions and concentrate their land forces is seen *(clockwise from the top left)* on the roads of Bologna, the harbor at Leghorn, the docks of Civitavecchia, and the rail lines at Littorio and at Foggia.

in a broad strip down the center of the peninsula from Lake Trasimene south to the front. Added to this was the Tyrrhenian coast between the front and Lake Bolsena. The 87th Fighter Wing, based in Corsica, was allotted the western coast north of Lake Bolsena, the eastern demarcation of its responsibilities being the line Lake Trasimene–Arezzo–Florence. To the Desert Air Force fell a zone of operations bounded on the east by the Adriatic and on the west by the areas of XII Tactical Air Command and 87th Fighter Wing; the northern limit was Fano, the southern the latitude of Rome. Also allotted to the interdiction campaign were two wings of medium bombers directly under the control of General Cannon, the 42d and the 57th. For night operations the peninsula was roughly divided in two, between the latitudes of Cassino and Fabriano, the eastern half falling to the Desert Air Force, the western to XII Tactical Air Command. This plan was implemented without modification, except for the periodic extension of the overall zone of interdiction northward as the German armies retreated in order to maintain the stipulated 140 miles between their railheads and the front.

To carry out the missions assigned it by the air plan, the Strategic Air Force had about 1,200 heavy bombers. The Tactical Air Force disposed approximately 575 fighter-bombers and nearly 700 light and medium bombers.[26] At no time after May 11, however, could the Tactical Air Force give its undivided strength to interdiction because of its responsibility for close air support. XII Tactical Fighter Command was assigned to aid both the Fifth and the Eighth Armies, while Desert Air Force was to help the British 5 Corps, which held the sector on the Adriatic front vacated by the Eighth Army.

DIADEM began with a barrage of 2,000 guns shortly before midnight on May 11. The attack caught the Germans by surprise, so successful had been the ruse of holding most of the Eighth Army to the rear until just before D-day. Not only the commander of *AOK 10*, General Heinrich von Vietinghoff, but also the supremely able commander of the *XIV Panzer Corps*, Maj. Gen. Frido von Senger und Etterlin, was on home leave. The suddenness of the blow was not without logistical conse-

---

26. None of the sources tells how many aircraft were assigned to each component of MAAF. These estimates have been extrapolated from a list that gives the types of aircraft stationed at various places in Italy and an order of battle that gives the types of aircraft assigned to each major subdivision of MAAF. The margin of uncertainty comes from the fact that the former document is not broken down very finely. "Air Situation, May 12, 1944," in MAAF, "Operations in Support of DIADEM," vol 1, Tab C; Order of battle appended to HQ MAAF, "Outline Plan for Air Participation in DIADEM," Apr 27, 1944, in MAAF, "Operations in Support of DIADEM," vol 1, Tab I.

quences, for *Heeresgruppe C* had only just begun a major effort to increase *AOK 10*'s reserves of ammunition.[27]

Twelve Allied divisions crowded forward on a narrow front between Cassino and the Tyrrhenian Sea, a distance of about twenty-five miles. Three German divisions (*1st Parachute, 71st Infantry*, and *94th Infantry*) opposed them with a fragment of a fourth (*305th Infantry*). Part of *AOK 10*'s reserve, the *15th Panzer Grenadier Division*, was held behind the sector attacked. Four other Allied divisions on the southern front had little role in the fighting, nor did the remaining five divisions of the *AOK 10*. In all, the Allies had twenty-two divisions, sixteen on the southern front and six in the beachhead in Anzio. Not counting the *von Zangen Group*, a motley force of four second-rate divisions training and chasing partisans in northern Italy, *Heeresgruppe C* had eighteen divisions. Ten of these were in *AOK 10*, the remaining eight in *AOK 14*. Of these eight, however, four formed *Heeresgruppe C*'s strategic reserve. Only one reserve division, the *3d Panzer Grenadiers*, was at Anzio. The *29th Panzer Grenadier Division* was at Viterbo, 30 miles north of Rome. In the immediate vicinity of Rome were the *90th Panzer Grenadier* and the *26th Panzer Divisions*. In an emergency, Kesselring could also call upon the *Hermann Göring Panzer Parachute Division*, which was not part of *Heeresgruppe C* but was rather under the direct control of the *Oberkommando der Wehrmacht (OKW)*. This division was at Leghorn, about 200 miles from the southern front. The overall Allied advantage in men was about two to one, but it exceeded three to one around Cassino where the blow fell.[28]

Their surprise notwithstanding, the Germans resisted the Allies fiercely and with some success. The Polish Corps failed to take Cassino, while the rest of the Eighth Army made little progress in the Liri Valley. Also thwarted was the American Fifth, with the notable exception of the French Expeditionary Corps, composed largely of fierce tribesmen from Morocco. Advancing through terrain that commanders on both sides had considered impossible, these hardy mountaineers broke into the Ausente Valley and took Ausonia, driving a wedge between the German *71st* and *94th Infantry Divisions* that soon made possible a general advance by the Fifth Army. (*Map 12*)

DIADEM had thus developed very differently from Alexander's plan. The breakthrough had come not at Cassino, where the Eighth Army

---

27. See Chapter 5 for details of the Germans' last-minute effort to resupply *AOK 10*'s dwindling stock of artillery ammunition.

28. Secondary works give surprisingly different orders of battle for the German forces, especially as regards the composition of the strategic reserve. The information given here is taken directly from German sources.

faced the German *LI Mountain Corps*, but farther west in the sector of the *XIV Panzer Corps*, the commander of which was still absent. Kesselring was thus faced with the virtual collapse of his right flank. But the German commander's fears of a landing behind his lines were eased by the magnitude of the Allied offensive, and he began to send his reserves south. By May 16 Kesselring had ordered the *26th Panzer* and the *90th Panzer Grenadier Divisions* south to *AOK 10*. The *29th Panzer Grenadiers* followed on May 18, which left only the *3d Panzer Grenadiers* to support *AOK 14*.

The attack of the Eighth Army began at last to gain momentum on May 15, just as Ausonia was falling to the French. On the night of May 17–18 the German *1st Parachute Division*, its flanks endangered by British advances, abandoned Cassino. The Eighth Army then began to move up the Liri Valley, but quickly stalled before the Hitler Line, a secondary position not much above the Gustav Line. The Fifth Army, meanwhile, spearheaded by the French Expeditionary Corps, continued its advance in the west, slowed but not stopped by the piecemeal arrival of the German reserves. After the Eighth Army breached the Hitler Line on May 25, *AOK 10* began a general retreat.

Once most of the German reserves had been committed, Alexander signaled a breakout from Anzio. The attack of May 23 was immediately successful against the weakened *AOK 14*. The sally reunited the Fifth Army, which, as Alexander had planned, thereupon began a drive on Valmontone to trap *AOK 10*. Then it stopped. Alexander had not allowed for the independence of Lt. Gen. Mark W. Clark of the Fifth Army, who was determined that he and his troops should have the glory of capturing Rome. Well short of Route 6, Clark's command turned toward the Italian capital, leaving only a single division to continue the attack on Valmontone. Kesselring had meanwhile obtained permission from the *OKW* to commit the *Hermann Göring Panzer Parachute Division*, which he ordered south to defend Valmontone. As the urgency of the hour required, it marched by day and suffered grievous punishment from fighter-bombers. But Kesselring's decision had been correct: The division arrived in time to block the threat to Valmontone, and so saved *AOK 10*. Clark argued in justification of his decision to make for Rome that the spur of the Apennines against which Alexander had hoped to pin the German army afforded escape routes. And so it did. But General von Senger, who returned from Germany in time to conduct the retreat of his corps, has confirmed the validity of Alexander's plan by observing that the mountain roads to which the vainglorious Clark pointed were "of

German defenders anchored their positions on Italian hill towns and fought a steadfast delaying action. Once the British Eighth Army breached the Hitler Line and Fifth U.S. Army advanced past the Gustav Line, the race for Rome was on.

doubtful and limited value in view of the enemy's overwhelming air superiority."[29]

MAAF attacked the Germans relentlessly throughout DIADEM. Early in the morning of May 12 the Strategic Air Force bombed the headquarters of *Heeresgruppe C* and *AOK 10*. The former, dug into a mountain, seems to have escaped damage, but operations at the latter were disrupted for some portion of D-day.[30] The Tactical Air Force bombed the headquarters of the *1st Parachute, 44th Infantry*, and *15th Panzer Grenadier Divisions*, apparently without much effect.[31] From May 12 through 14 the Tactical Air Force harried German transport immediately behind the front to hinder the movement of reserves and supply. One effective tactic was to bomb towns so that the debris from demolished buildings buried roads and road junctions.[32]

---

29. Frido von Senger und Etterlin, *Neither Fear Nor Hope* (New York, 1964), 249. For a brief but very clear account of the fighting during DIADEM, see Jackson's *Battle for Italy* (230–46). For a detailed account, see Ernest F. Fisher, Jr., *Cassino to the Alps* [U.S. Army in World War II: The Mediterranean Theater of Operations] (Washington, 1977), 1–226.

30. A captured German document stated that "a strong air raid (of 4 engined bombers) destroyed the Headquarters of an Army completely, and rendered it absolutely useless." The headquarters of *Heeresgruppe C* suffered only a disruption of its wire communications. HQ, MATAF, "Operation DIADEM, 11 May to 4 August 1944," n.d., 626.430-8, 15.

31. The captured document cited above mentions no damage to the divisional headquarters; neither do memoirs.

32. See, for example, *KTB AOK 10/O Qu*, May 22–26 and 28, 1944, Roll 103, T–312; *KTB AOK 10/Ia*, May 26, 28, 1944, Roll 91, T–312. The account of DIADEM by the Tactical Air Force, by contrast, does not mention the tactic in its account of DIADEM. This was perhaps because bridge-bombing and strafing left more evidence of their effectiveness. The appended account of the 42d and the 57th Bombardment Wings, however, shows that they expended a great deal of effort in creating roadblocks, chiefly by bombing towns. "Operations of the

On May 15 the Tactical Air Force's medium bombers returned to the railroads, while the fighter-bombers continued to be predominantly occupied with the battlefield. With the fall of the Hitler Line on May 25, the fighters turned to the armed reconnaissance that was to be their primary activity throughout the rest of DIADEM. The heavy bombers of the Strategic Air Force bombed the marshaling yards of northern Italy very heavily during the first week of the offensive; their efforts then fell off considerably until the week of June 1. The most complete statistical breakdown of MAAF's effort suggests that between May 11 and June 7 MAAF devoted approximately 22,500 sorties and slightly more than 31,000 tons of bombs to interdiction. The weather was generally good except for May 20–23. With the exception of a highly successful raid of May 12 on a base of medium bombers in Corsica, the *Luftwaffe* was, as anticipated, a negligible factor. It never mounted even 200 sorties a day. MAAF's loss rate during DIADEM was about what it had been during STRANGLE: 5.9 aircraft per 1,000 sorties. Nearly all Allied aircraft lost between May 12 and June 22 were victims of flak.[33]

Except for the periodic adjustments of the depth of the zone of interdiction to keep the stipulated 140 miles between the German armies and their railheads, the plan of interdiction drawn up by the Tactical Air Force remained unmodified. There was, indeed, nothing to prompt modifications in the reports of success that came to MAAF from the ground forces, who everywhere found hundreds of destroyed German vehicles in the course of their advance, or in the deciphered German signals from Bletchley Park. On May 16, for example, the *1st Parachute Division*, truly the keystone of German resistance, reported that its artillery had supported the "defensive fighting as far as [the] ammunition situation allowed." Two days later *AOK 10* signaled that "difficulties of supply, especially of ammunition, remain unchanged." And on June 5 the *15th Panzer Grenadier Division*, covering the flank of von Senger's retreating corps, reported itself virtually devoid of fuel and ammunition.[34]

42d and 57th Medium Bombardment Wings in Operation DIADEM, 11 May to 23 June 1944," annex F to MATAF, "Operation DIADEM."

33. "Summary of MAAF Effort," n.d., in MAAF, "Operations in Support of DIADEM," vol 7, Tab V. The breakdown of sorties is from HERO, *Tactical Air Interdiction by U.S. Army Air Forces in World War II: Italy* (Dunn Loring, Va., n.d.), table 8-8.

34. For the first three weeks of the battle MAAF's assessments of the results of the interdiction campaign were restrained and tentative. By the beginning of June, however, MAAF was convinced that the campaign had been a major success. MAAF claimed to have destroyed 5,194 trucks and armored vehicles in the period May 12–June 10 and in the fourth weekly installment of its chronicle of the battle claimed that "in the battle area and beyond the enemy can neither bring in nor take out large quantities of ammunition or materials. His forward

Throughout DIADEM the Germans suffered from a dire crisis of transportation. This was in the first instance the effect of their extraordinarily long supply lines, the fruit of MAAF's relentless efforts to drive northward the railheads that supported *AOK*s *10* and *14*. Speaking to von Vietinghoff over the telephone on May 26, Kesselring was disturbed to detect for the first time a note of pessimism in the voice of *AOK 10*'s commander: "But until now you have always been such an optimist in spite of everything. What's different now?" "I am still an optimist," von Vietinghoff replied, "but my supply lines are too long."[35]

The distance between the fronts and the railheads greatly increased the German armies' need for transport space, as did the necessity of moving convoys only at night to avoid the attentions of Allied fighters. This was as it had been during STRANGLE. But with the resumption of heavy fighting during DIADEM, the demand for transport space grew greatly. Only the *Panzer* and the *Panzer Grenadier* divisions had establishments of vehicles sufficient to fetch their own supplies from the depots of the armies and to move themselves. German infantry divisions had to be supplied and moved by the transport of the army headquarters. When the Allies attacked, the consumption of supplies increased considerably, as did the need for troop movements. As the transport of the armies had not sufficed for supply even during STRANGLE, with DIADEM troop movements could only be carried out at the expense of supply, or vice versa. On some days the transport of *AOK 10* was wholly employed moving divisions and hauling supplies to them from its own depots, leaving no vehicles to carry supplies from the depots of the *Heeresgruppe*. Although *AOK 14* seems not to have been pressed quite so hard, closer as it was to its sources of supply, it nonetheless appealed in vain to the *Heeresgruppe* for another transport battalion. During its retreat, *AOK 14* abandoned a hospital full of wounded at Civita Castellana, apparently for want of transport, and on one occasion was unable to supply vehicles to evacuate the staff of a logistical facility about to be abandoned to the advancing Allies.[36]

Even as the demands of battle increased the need for transport space, the fighting reduced its availability, both absolutely and effectively. The pressures of supply and troop movement often forced travel

---

elements are short of supplies." MAAF, "Operations in Support of DIADEM," Jun 2–8, vol 4; DEFE 3/156: KV 4155, May 17, 1944, and DEFE 3/157: KV 4372, May 18, 1944, both Roll 20, "ULTRA"; DEFE 3/166: KV 6583, Jun 6, 1944, Roll 23, *ibid*.

35. Tele con, Kesselring/von Vietinghoff, transcript appended to *KTB AOK 10/Ia*, May 28, 1944, Roll 93, T–312.

36. See, for example, *KTB AOK 10/O Qu*, May 15, 1944, Roll 103, T–312; *KTB AOK 14/O Qu*, May 31, and Jun 6, 9, 1944, Roll 484, T–312.

by day, which increased losses to strafing and artillery fire.[37] German records speak for the first time during DIADEM of effective night attacks by flare-dropping aircraft. At one point these drops were so successful in several mountain passes that Kesselring proposed moving a supply column in late afternoon to avoid them.[38] Troop commanders, desperate for transport, sometimes hijacked empty supply columns.[39] The availability of transport space was reduced still more by bombing attacks that destroyed roads or piled the rubble of demolished towns on them, creating enormous traffic jams. Local commanders were directed to clear all such obstructions at all costs.[40]

The seriousness of the transportation problem notwithstanding, at no time did *AOK 10*'s problems with its supply of ammunition, and still less those of *AOK 14*, reach a stage of general crisis. That *AOK 14* escaped logistical catastrophe is perhaps not surprising: It had suffered less from STRANGLE than *AOK 10*, was closer to the depots of the *Heeresgruppe*, and had a compact area of operations at Anzio. But STRANGLE had decidedly impaired *AOK 10*'s plans to meet the Allied offensive. Why, then, did the similar and no less intensive interdiction of DIADEM not lead to crisis? During STRANGLE, *AOK 10* had expended a daily average of only 143 tons of ammunition of all types. During the critical first two weeks of DIADEM that figure climbed to 453 tons.

The basic answer to the question is that the Allies lacked a truly unified plan for their combined arms offensive. DIADEM's concept of operations was in essence a relentless concentration of overwhelming mass upon a narrow sector of the Gustav Line, to be followed after some weeks by a sally en masse from the invested beachhead at Anzio. Had the Allies wished to do so, they could hardly have devised a plan better

---

37. On one unusually bad day, for example, the *I Parachute Corps* of *AOK 14* lost 100 trucks to strafing attacks. "*Versorgungslage am 29.5.1944*," appended to *KTB AOK 14/O Qu*, Roll 484, T-312. In early June *AOK 10* estimated that it was receiving about 100 tons of new transport daily while losing 200–250 tons. *KTB AOK 10/O Qu*, Jun 6, 9, 1944, Roll 103, T-312. The primary source for the replenishment of German motor transport was the Italian motor industry, which was being operated at this date entirely for the support of the German armed forces.

38. See, for example, *KTB AOK 10/O Qu*, May 17, 1944, Roll 103, T-312; *KTB AOK 10/Ia*, May 18, 1944, Roll 91, T-312; tele con, Kesselring/Wentzell, May 31, 1944, transcript appended to *KTB AOK 10/Ia*, May 31, 1944, Roll 91, T-312. Allied accounts of the campaign are curiously silent about night operations, save for the barest statistics about sorties and the establishment of areas of operation, as described in the text above.

39. See, for example, *KTB AOK 10/O Qu*, May 25, 1944, Roll 103, T-312.

40. See, for example, *KTB AOK 10/Ia*, May 28, 1944, Roll 91, T-312. Alluding to these problems on May 21, von Vietinghoff said, "The traffic on the roads is insane." Tele con, Kesselring/von Vietinghoff, transcript appended to *KTB AOK 10/Ia*, May 21, 1944, Roll 93, T-312.

calculated to ease the problem of transport space than their own interdiction plan had created for the Germans.

A few numbers tell the story. *Table 9* shows the amount of ammunition expended by units of *AOK 10* between May 13 and 25 when the Allies had won the battle for the Gustav Line and put von Vietinghoff's army to flight.[41] Together a mere four divisions, with their supporting artillery, accounted for 76 percent of all ammunition expended—5,774 of 7,499 tons, decidedly more than the 3,818 tons delivered to *AOK 10* between May 12 and 25.[42] The *1st Parachute Division* at Cassino alone accounted for nearly a third of all expenditure. The *71st* and the *94th Infantry Divisions* that opposed the Fifth Army, together with the *15th Panzer Grenadier Division* (the division of the army's reserve sent to their relief) and the local artillery command (the *451st*), expended 40 percent of the total. Most of the other divisions of *AOK 10* required little or no resupply of ammunition during the first two weeks of battle, greatly relieving the burden on the army's transport battalions. And since the transport of *Heeresgruppe C* was wholly committed to *AOK 10* before May 23, throughout the decisive phase of the battle on the southern front a substantial portion of all the German transport in Italy was supporting a mere four divisions with their attached artillery. *There was, in short, no logistical constriction in spite of the high consumption that DIADEM imposed on the Germans, who wanted not for ammunition but for transport*.

Though Allied interdiction did not produce a general crisis, it did cause the Germans to have problems with their supply of ammunition. The unrelenting pressure on their supply lines that reduced their transport space made the flow of ammunition to the front inelastic; that is, deliveries could not be raised commensurately with expenditure. The General for Transport, Italy, reported not long after the battle that throughout the encounter supplies necessary to support the armies had reached northern Italy without difficulty. "But the conveyance of imme-

---

41. The war diary of the *AOK 10*'s *Ia* (operations) section contains no breakdown for May 12—quite possibly because of the disruption caused by the bombing attack upon the army's headquarters that day.

42. Derived from the formula $[S - (E_1 + E_2)] + (D_1 + D_2) = F$, where S is the starting amount of a given kind of commodity, F the finishing, D_1 deliveries through logistical channels, D_2 the amount brought into the into the organization by transferring units, E_1 expenditure or consumption, and E_2 the amount carried away by units transferring from the organization. In the case of ammunition, D_2 and E_2 are put at one issue for the transferred unit, a figure supported by the testimony of the war diary of the *AOK 14*'s *Oberquartiermeister*. Since the issue of the army was equal to the issues of all the units from which it was formed, the issue of a transferring unit can be told from the corresponding change in the army's issue, which is given in each day's quartermaster report. The data for the present calculation are drawn from *Tagesmeldungen O Qu*, appended to *KTB AOK 10/O Qu*, May 12, 15, 1944, Roll 103, T–312.

Table 9. Ammunition Expenditure of *AOK 10*, by Unit, May 13–25, 1944*

Army Unit	Ammunition Expended	
	Metric Tons	Percent of Total
1st Parachute Division	2,226	30
44th Infantry Division	250	3
71st Infantry Division	501	7
94th Infantry Division	924	12
114th Infantry Division	28	0
305th Infantry Division	77	1
334th Infantry Division	107	1
5th Mountain Division	224	3
15th Panzer Grenadier Division	994	13
26th Panzer Grenadier Division†	432	6
90th Panzer Grenadier Division‡	607	8
414th Artillery Command	432	6
451st Artillery Command	697	9

*Ammunition records are incomplete for the first two days of DIADEM, May 11–12. Army units **underlined** were engaged from the first day, having been on the line when the Allies attacked. The *15th Panzer Grenadier Division*, although an army reserve, entered the battle on the first day. The other two *Panzer Grenadier* divisions were part of *Heeresgruppe C*'s reserve and joined the fighting only after some days. The underlined units expended 5,774 metric tons of ammunition, or 76% of the total.

An indication of the Germans' uncertainty about Allied intentions, and their consequent dispersion of transport and supplies during STRANGLE, may be seen in the low expenditure of the *44th Infantry Division*. Although it participated hardly at all in the fighting during DIADEM, it was logistically the best prepared of any unit, having as many as seven *Ausstattungen* of some kinds of ammunition.

†Entered battle on May 22.

‡Entered battle on May 16.

SOURCE: Ammunition status reports, *KTB AOK 10/Ia*.

diately needed supplies to the front suffered extraordinarily from the serious destruction wrought by the enemy. Because of the nearly complete isolation of the region south of Bologna–Pisa–Rimini [to rail traffic] only a small portion of the supplies reached the front."[43] The inelasticity of *AOK 10*'s ammunition supply is evident from the following: With DIADEM, its daily consumption went up by 380 percent (from 143 tons to 543), but deliveries through logistical channels increased but 162 percent

43. *General des Transportwesens, Italien*, "*Beiträge zum Kriegstagebuch für den Monat Juni*," June 1944, appended to *KTB Heeresgruppe C/O Qu*, Roll 279, T–311.

(from 169 tons a day to 272, about half the average daily expenditure). Not surprisingly, *AOK 10*'s chief of staff complained on May 16 of "living hand to mouth."[44]

Between May 12 and 25 the total tonnage of munitions in *AOK 10*'s dumps declined only slightly, from 18,187 to 16,496. As noted earlier, most of the ammunition in the army's depots (on May 12, 5,235 of 8,337 tons, or 63 percent) consisted of munitions other than the critical types that accounted for fully 87 percent of expenditure during DIADEM. A further problem with any argument from aggregate tonnages is that it makes no allowance for the fact that the composition of *AOK 10* changed steadily throughout DIADEM. Much of the ammunition brought into the army between May 12 and 25 (2,036 of 5,304 tons, or 35 percent) came along with the reserve divisions sent from the *AOK 14*. These units strengthened *AOK 10*, but the ammunition they brought represented no real increase to its reserves because its needs went up proportionally with the arrival of each new division. The *Ausstattung*, by contrast, was a flexible unit of measurement that took into account holdings relative to requirements because a division's *Ausstattung* was determined by the *Ausstattungen* of its individual weapons, an army's *Ausstattung* by the *Ausstattungen* of its divisions. The so-called *Erste Ausstattung* (first issue) therefore changed as new divisions arrived to join the army. When *AOK 10*'s holdings of ammunition are plotted in *Ausstattungen*, a steady decline is evident. (*Chart 7*) This is not surprising. Between May 12 and 25, *AOK 10* expended 7,499 tons of ammunition and received but 3,818.[45]

The inelasticity of *AOK 10*'s supply of ammunition made inevitable shortages of those types already scarce as a result of STRANGLE, especially mortar shells and rounds for the rocket projectors, or *Nebelwerfer*. Also affected were certain types for which consumption tended to be heavy, such as the light infantry gun, the most common artillery piece with the German armies. The war diary of *AOK 10*'s *Oberquartiermeister* attests to recurrent shortages. By May 14, for example, the army's reserves of ammunition for the 15-cm *Nebelwerfer* and the light infantry gun were gone. On May 17 the depots could cover only 50 percent of the previous day's expenditure of all types of ammunition. Many shortages proved temporary, but they were not insignificant. For a few days around May 19 the defense of Cassino was weakened by a virtual dearth of ammunition for the *Nebelwerfer*.[46] Because of the tight supply of am-

---

44. Tele con, Wentzell/Fähndrich, transcript appended to *KTB AOK 10/Ia*, May 16, 1944, Roll 92, T–312. Calculations, as in note 42.
45. Calculations, as in note 42.
46. *KTB AOK 10/O Qu*, May 14, 17, 19, 1944, Roll 103, T–312. The war

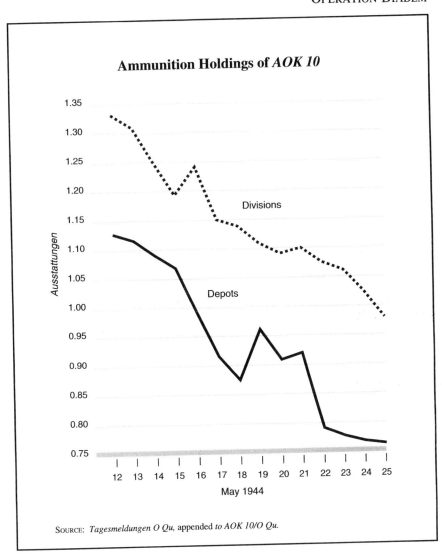

Ammunition Holdings of *AOK 10*

SOURCE: *Tagesmeldungen O Qu,* appended *to AOK 10/O Qu.*

Chart 7.

diary of the *LI Mountain Corps* specifically attributes the shortage of *Nebel-werfer* ammunition to transportation problems. *KTB LI Gebirgekorps/O Qu,* May 19, 1944, Roll 1270, T–312. Between May 12 and 19 the supply of 15-cm *Nebelwerfer* ammunition with the *451st Artillery Command* (the principal con-sumer) plummeted from an already low 1.2 *Ausstattungen* to 0.06 *Ausstattung,* and ammunition for the 21-cm *Nebelwerfer* fell from a healthy 3.7 *Ausstattungen* to 0.2 *Ausstattungen. KTB AOK 10/Ia,* May 12, 19, 1944, Roll 92, T–312.

munition, moreover, expenditure had to be rationed. General von Viet-inghoff subsequently testified that this "severe restriction on the expenditure of ammunition naturally prejudiced management of the battle."[47] The ammunition reserves of *AOK 14* also declined after it became involved in the fighting on May 23, and it too suffered from occasionally serious spot shortages of certain types of ammunition.[48]

The fuel situation was desperate for both German armies throughout DIADEM because neither had been able to amass adequate reserves during STRANGLE. By May 14 the depots of *AOK 10* were "practically empty of fuel" and the situation on the right flank, where the *15th Panzer Grenadier Division* had to come to the aid of the *71st* and the *94th Infantry Divisions*, was "critical." By May 25 the *Oberquartiermeister* had come to fear that the mobility of the entire army had been called into question; the next day he noted that receipts did not even approximate consumption. *AOK 14* began its battle with a perilous shortage of fuel because so much of what it had amassed was sent off with the reserve divisions dispatched to the southern front. On May 25, after only two days of combat, the army was saved from complete immobility only by a last-minute shipment of fuel from the *Heeresgruppe*.[49]

In the opening phases of DIADEM fuel had not limited German tactical movements. Three divisions of the *Heeresgruppe* strategic reserve had moved expeditiously (albeit by night) to relieve *AOK 10*, and *AOK 10* itself had been able to move its reserve division, the *15th Panzer Grenadiers*, in time to shore up the sagging *71st* and *94th Infantry Divisions*. Fuel had been tight, but quantities sufficient to move the reserves had been husbanded. By early June, when both armies had been in retreat for more than a week, the situation was quite different. As *AOK 10* retreated north of Rome, it used its motorized units to screen the plodding infantry divisions from the Fifth Army, a constant threat to von Vietinghoff's right flank. A shortage of fuel seriously affected this defense. By

---

47. "*Diese starke Beschränkung beim Verbrauch von Artilleriemunition war natürlich für die taktischen Handlungen ein grosser Nachteil. Sie verhinderte in besonders die—an sich erforderlich—planmässig Bekämpfung des allierten Aufmarsches, der sich fast ungestört vollziehen konnte.*" Heinrich von Vietinghoff-Scheel, "*Stellungnahme zu den Kapitel* [The German Situation]," *in dem Band* "The Drive on Rome" *von Dr. Sydney T. Mathews aus der Reihe* "The United States Army in World War II," RG 242, NARA.

48. See, for example, *KTB AOK 14/O Qu*, May 25 and Jun 11, 1944, Roll 484, T–312; "*Beurteilung der Versorgungslage (Stand 1.6.1944)*," appended to *KTB AOK 14/O Qu*, Roll 486, T–312. It was, in fact, shortages of certain kinds of ammunition that led *AOK 14* to adopt the dangerous expedient of running empty convoys on their return trips by day. *KTB AOK 14/O Qu*, May 30, 1944, Roll 484, T–312.

49. *KTB AOK 10/O Qu*, May 14, 25–26, 1944, Roll 103, T–312; *KTB AOK 14/O Qu*, May 25, 1944, Roll 484, T–312.

June 6, the army was making its moves piecemeal—a unit would move, exhaust its fuel, and wait for resupply. *AOK 10* was saved only by the fact that it was withdrawing through hilly terrain well suited to rearguard actions. "If only the country were more open we would make hay of the whole lot," Alexander signaled to London on June 4, the day Rome fell to the Fifth Army.[50]

In contrast to the logistical problems that DIADEM caused, the Germans' loss of tactical mobility has been widely noted. The war diaries of both German armies incessantly lament the need to move at night, the damage to roads and bridges, and the traffic jams that resulted. Rapid and coherent movement was impossible; schedules were no sooner drawn up than discarded.[51] Little need be added to General von Senger's post-mortem: "In a battle of movement a commander who can only make the tactically essential movements by night resembles a chess player who for three moves of his opponent has the right to make only one."[52]

But if the logistical effects of STRANGLE and DIADEM have been underestimated, their effects on German mobility have been exaggerated. Even as no position was lost for want of ammunition, so no essential movement went unexecuted.[53] In one of the most brilliant maneuvers of the war, for example, von Senger was able after the fall of Rome to move his *XIV Panzer Corps* across the entire front of *AOK 14* to check the Fifth Army, an action that probably saved *AOK 14* from destruction.

---

50. *KTB AOK 10/O Qu*, Jun 4, 6, 1944, Roll 103, T–312; Jackson, *Battle for Italy*, 246.

51. See, for example, *KTB AOK 10/Ia*, May 17–18, 21–23, 26–28, and 30, 1944, Roll 91, T–312; *KTB AOK 10/O Qu*, May 14, 16, 21–26, and 29–31, and Jun 1–10, 1944, Roll 103, T–312.

52. Von Senger, *Neither Fear Nor Hope*, 66.

53. In his study of STRANGLE/DIADEM Sallagar incorrectly states that the movement of the divisions of the strategic reserves to the front was greatly hindered by interdiction. This was true only to the extent that they had to move by night. He identifies only two of the four divisions of the reserve: the *26th Panzer Division* and the *29th Panzer Grenadier Division*. Claiming that their movements were slow, he strongly suggests that air attacks and bad roads were responsible for their tardiness. The latter of these two divisions was ordered south on May 16 (not May 14, as Sallagar states) and was fully deployed by the 19th. This is hardly excessive, considering that the division had to move tanks and horse-drawn artillery. Roads may have caused some slight delay, but not air attacks. It is quite clear from the account of its commander that the division experienced no air attacks before June 5 and when they came they were "surprisingly ineffective." Road damage also failed to hamper the retreat of the division at that time. The movement of the *26th Panzer Division* was slow, but only because the commander of *AOK 14*, General von Mackensen, was loathe to release it; this was one of the principal reasons for his subsequent relief. Sallagar, *Operation "STRANGLE*," 70–72; Fisher, *Cassino to the Alps*, 80, 86, 94; Smilo von Lüttwitz, "The Employment of the *26th Panzer Division* from 15 May to 12 July 1944 in Italy," MS D–312, RG 242, NARA.

As one historian has noted, and as any reading of the campaign will confirm, it was "the ability of the Germans, despite harassment by a daily average of 2,000 Allied air sorties, to shift major units from one sector to another and to bring important reinforcements from northern Italy to man the several delaying lines north of Rome" that was "largely responsible for the failure of the two Allied armies to cut off and destroy significant parts of either of the two German armies."[54] The principal reason that MAAF did not interfere more effectively with German movement was technological: Allied air forces could not mount large-scale tactical air operations at night when the Germans moved. Nocturnal sorties were limited to several dozen a night by aircraft that, lacking the means to acquire targets on the ground, seem to have been effective mainly by chance or when German movements were highly channelized, as through mountain passes. It was a great handicap to be forced to move only at night; but in the end it was probably the cloak of darkness that saved the German armies from destruction.

Assessments of the effectiveness of interdiction during DIADEM have ranged widely. At the time, Allied airmen, perhaps still smarting from the doubts that clouded the later stages of STRANGLE, virtually claimed to have won the battle for Rome by themselves.[55] The commanders of the ground forces, whose faith in interdiction had not been great since the rapid German concentration after the landing at Anzio, were naturally disposed to assert that air power had been only marginally effective, and not a few historians have taken their side.[56] Others have praised interdiction for crippling German tactical movements while denying that it affected supply. The truth seems to be that MAAF's great exertions during DIADEM adversely affected both supply and tactical movements but crippled neither. Interdiction doubtless hastened the pace of the Allied advance and saved the lives of Allied soldiers, who would otherwise have had to face a stronger foe, but it did not win the battle.

STRANGLE seriously impeded the preparations of *AOK 10* for DIADEM, but the army's stocks of fuel and ammunition nonetheless sufficed to stave off logistical starvation, although not serious shortages, during the Allied offensive. That the Germans fared as well as they did was largely the result of the Allied plan of attack which, while sophisticated in its accompanying deceptions, was rudimentary as a scheme of maneu-

---

54. Fisher, *Cassino to the Alps*, 250.
55. See, for example, Slessor, *Central Blue*, 581.
56. The historian, and staff officer during DIADEM, W.F.G. Jackson, for example, dismisses STRANGLE as a failure and neglects even to mention interdiction during the final battle for Rome in his otherwise excellent *Battle for Italy*.

ver. As the Allies concentrated their divisions upon a very narrow sector of the front, so their enemy was able to concentrate his limited supply of transport, a task made easier by the interval of two weeks that elapsed between the attack on the Gustav Line and the sally from Anzio. The plan of attack was to no small degree dictated by geography.[57] But it is a question of considerable theoretical interest whether diversionary attacks elsewhere along the southern front, or an earlier breakout from the beachhead, might not have rendered the Germans' transportation problems insuperable. The possibility cannot be excluded. As it was, *AOK 10* was barely able to cover half its expenditure of ammunition and rather less of its consumption of fuel.

The other great problem for the Allied plan of interdiction was that MAAF lacked a significant capacity for night operations. DIADEM, like STRANGLE, overreached the available technology. Darkness was therefore a privileged sanctuary through which men and supplies could be moved with relative impunity. While a plan of attack for the ground forces designed to exploit the problems that interdiction had created for the Germans conceivably might have greatly compounded their logistical problems, MAAF's inability to fight at night precluded any hope of paralyzing German tactical movements. The terrain of Italy prevented sweeping maneuvers by the Allied armored divisions; this slowed the pace of battle sufficiently that the Germans found the time during the hours of darkness to carry out even such ambitious maneuvers as von Senger's *tour de force* during the retreat north of Rome.

---

57. See, for example, Fisher, *Cassino to the Alps*, 12–15.

Chapter 7

———•••———

Operation OVERLORD: The Invasion of Northwestern France
March 25–June 30, 1944

The Allied invasion of Normandy in 1944 was aided by the most intensive interdiction campaign yet waged. The purpose of this great effort, as in earlier landings, was to prevent the Germans from concentrating their forces more quickly by land than the Allies could by sea. The success of the Allies in slowing the movement of the German strategic reserves was certainly much greater than it had been at Salerno or Anzio, and the effect on German supply probably more severe than it had been during STRANGLE. These results can be viewed as proof of the old adage that practice makes perfect, for little was new about Allied interdiction in Normandy—it was, indeed, a kind of summation of all that had gone before. In its broadest outlines, the Allied plan was an application of the three-phase design for a combined arms offensive that the British had pioneered in North Africa. The strategic interdiction effort saw both the extensive bombing of marshaling yards *and* a STRANGLE-like effort against bridges. The approach to tactical interdiction also drew upon the experience gained in Italy: Towns were flattened to create roadblocks while swarms of strafing fighters drove German transport from the roads by day. Once more the fatal dependence of the Germans upon railroads was exposed as their railheads were driven back a distance that could not be bridged by their inadequate stock of motor transport.

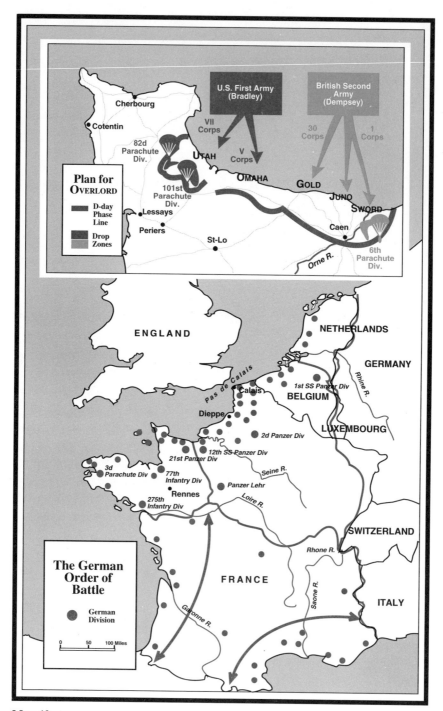

Plan for OVERLORD

- D-day Phase Line
- Drop Zones

Cherbourg
Cotentin
82d Parachute Div.
101st Parachute Div.
Lessays
Periers
St-Lo

U.S. First Army (Bradley)
VII Corps
V Corps
UTAH
OMAHA

British Second Army (Dempsey)
30 Corps
1 Corps
GOLD
JUNO
SWORD
Caen
Orne R.
6th Parachute Div.

ENGLAND

NETHERLANDS
GERMANY

Pas de Calais
Calais
1st SS Panzer Div
Rhine R.
BELGIUM
Dieppe
2d Panzer Div
LUXEMBOURG
12th SS Panzer Div
21st Panzer Div
Seine R.
3d Parachute Div
77th Infantry Div
Panzer Lehr
Rennes
275th Infantry Div
Loire R.

SWITZERLAND
Rhone R.

The German Order of Battle

● German Division

0   50   100 Miles

FRANCE
Garonne R.
Saone R.
ITALY

Map 13.

The adjective "decisive" has been much misused in the writing of military history, but few are likely to begrudge its application to the Anglo-American invasion of France in 1944. If the Allies had failed in their great endeavor, material factors would have compelled a long delay before another attempt, and political developments might have forbidden one. It is in retrospect as easy to underestimate the war-weariness of the peoples of the western powers as it is to exaggerate their commitment to the principle of unconditional surrender. For Germany, the test in France represented the last chance for a stalemate. The defeat of the Allies would have gained her a long respite during which many of the fifty-odd divisions in France could have been transferred to the east, perhaps to check the advance of the Red Army. Triumph over Stalin was no longer possible. But during the deadlock that had prevailed on the eastern front between the Battles of Stalingrad and Kursk (January–July 1943), the Soviet dictator had shown signs of a willingness to conclude a separate peace with Hitler.[1] He might bargain again. And it was an open question whether the unnatural alliance between the western democracies and Bolshevism, already strained by the long delay of the invasion, could survive a defeat in France.

From the first days of American participation in the war, President Franklin D. Roosevelt and the U.S. Army favored an early invasion of France. While not disputing the need for an eventual landing in northern Europe, the British counseled that Germany should first be weakened by attacks on the weaker flanks of her empire. Anglo-American strategy developed as a compromise between these two approaches. In 1942, under

---

1. For the most complete treatment of Soviet-German diplomatic contacts during the world war, see Ingeborg Fleischhauer, *Die Chance des Sonderfriedens: Deutsch-Sowjetische Geheimgespräche 1941–1945* (Berlin, 1986).

the code name BOLERO, American forces began to concentrate in Great Britain for an early crossing of the English Channel. But at the Casablanca Conference (January 1943) the British, arguing that an insufficiency of shipping precluded a major invasion during the year just begun, successfully urged an interim measure: a descent upon Sicily to force Italy from the war. The Combined Chiefs of Staff did, however, name a British officer, Lt. Gen. Frederick E. Morgan, to be chief of staff to the as yet unnamed Supreme Allied Commander (COSSAC) for the invasion of France now projected for 1944. It was Morgan's task to plan for the operation soon to be known as OVERLORD.[2]

Notwithstanding the considerable progress that Morgan made in this task during the remainder of 1943, Prime Minister Winston S. Churchill and the British Chiefs of Staff refused at the Cairo Conference (November 1943) to set a firm date for the invasion. But where the Americans failed, the Soviets succeeded. Stalin, who had with mounting anger and impatience importuned a "second front" since early 1942, forced Churchill at the Teheran Conference (December 1943) to accede to a date of May 1944. He also demanded the prompt appointment of a commander for OVERLORD. Roosevelt, who in earlier talks with the British had forced them to accept an American for the post, shortly thereafter named General Dwight D. Eisenhower. Upon his arrival in London early in 1944, Eisenhower replaced COSSAC with SHAEF—Supreme Headquarters, Allied Expeditionary Force—and Morgan with his old chief of staff from the Mediterranean theater, Lt. Gen. Walter Bedell Smith. Morgan became deputy chief of staff, but remained important in the final shaping of OVERLORD.

Eisenhower accepted COSSAC's design for the invasion in its essentials. Morgan and his staff had selected a site for the invasion. Several considerations had dictated their choice. As aerial supremacy was essential, the beachhead had to be within the range of fighters based in the United Kingdom. The beaches could not be too readily defensible; either heavy fortifications or natural obstacles might fatally break the momentum of the assault. The place had to permit rapid reinforcement of the landing force once an initial lodgment had been gained. This necessitated a well-sheltered roadstead with a port in close proximity. The range of Allied fighters restricted the area of consideration to the French coast between the Belgian border and Cherbourg. Within that stretch there were only three suitable beaches: on the Pas de Calais, at Dieppe, and in Nor-

---

2. For the most comprehensive discussion of the background of, and the planning for, the invasion of France, see Gordon A. Harrison, *Cross-Channel Attack* [U.S. Army in World War II: The European Theater of Operations] (Washington, 1951), 1–267.

mandy. The first two were closest to Britain. The Germans had accordingly fortified them heavily, and neither offered a good roadstead. That left Normandy.

The final plan for OVERLORD was essentially this: The assault forces were to be organized into the 21 Army Group under the command of General Sir Bernard Law Montgomery. This organization comprised the American First Army under Lt. Gen. Omar Bradley and the British Second Army commanded by Lt. Gen. Sir Miles Dempsey. The landing zone would extend west from the river Orne, which flowed through Caen, to the base of the Cotentin Peninsula, which would shelter the invasion fleet. Five divisions, several independent brigades, and small detachments of commandos were to form the first wave of the assault. The American VII Corps would make the westernmost landing on UTAH beach. To the east were OMAHA, where the American V Corps would come ashore; GOLD, for the British 30 Corps; and JUNO and SWORD for the British 1 Corps. Two American airborne divisions were to land behind UTAH to protect it from immediate counterattack, while a single British division was to drop near Caen to block whatever reinforcements the German *Fifteenth Army, Armeeoberkommando 15 (AOK 15)*, in the Pas de Calais might send to its *Seventh Army, AOK 7*, which defended Normandy. *(Map 13)*

Once the four Allied corps were ashore in strength, the plan called for them to push inland, linking up as they did so, to provide space for the hundreds of thousands of reinforcements to follow. VII Corps would clear the Cotentin and capture the port of Cherbourg no later than D plus 15, while V Corps secured the line Lessay-Periers-Saint-Lô. With the fall of Cherbourg, First Army was to advance to the line Avranches-Domfront. By D plus 20 the beachhead would thus have been made sufficiently deep that the Allies could form up in depth for a push through the encircling Germans. In preparation for this drive, two new armies, the United States Third and the Canadian First, would become operational, while Eisenhower's SHAEF assumed control of the front. Montgomery's 21 Army Group would then comprise the British Second and the Canadian First Armies, while the newly established 12th Army Group would control the American First and Third Armies. Commanded by Lt. Gen. George S. Patton, the Third Army was to spearhead the thrust inland.[3]

Strategic deception on a massive scale was an integral part of OVERLORD. The principal ruse was Operation FORTITUDE, which entailed the creation of a fictitious U.S. First Army Group under Patton to delude

---

3. *Ibid.*, 56–59, 71–82, 164–74, 180–207.

the Germans about the direction of the approaching invasion. Allied intelligence knew from ULTRA that the Germans considered the Pas de Calais to be the most likely site for the impending invasion. Patton's phantom force was therefore notionally located in southern England immediately opposite Calais to encourage the Germans in their false surmise. Every manner of dummy facility—parks of rubber tanks and trucks, empty tent cities, fields of wooden planes—was created, along with an extensive but spurious radio net. So effective was FORTITUDE that the Germans continued to believe for a month after D-day that the Allies might yet land in the Pas de Calais.[4]

On October 25, 1943, Field Marshal Gerd von Rundstedt, the *Oberbefehlshaber West* (*OB West*—Commander in Chief, West), submitted to Hitler a somber review of the state of his command.[5] He concluded that the German armies in France were entirely unprepared for the test to come. For two and a half years they had been bled of men and equipment to meet the demands of the Eastern Front; there had been little fortification. In all, the vaunted "Atlantic Wall" of German propaganda was a brittle crust that the Allies could anywhere break at will. There were no strategic reserves worthy of the name, and the coastal divisions, largely conscripted from men unfit for duty elsewhere and even Russian prisoners of war, were spread perilously thin. Divisional sectors averaged 50 miles, and in some places they exceeded 100. All the coastal divisions were deficient in armament and wholly without transport.[6]

Hitler had decreed the fortification of the French coast in 1942, but the program had languished as the war in Russia absorbed German resources. Von Rundstedt's report sharply returned the *Führer*'s attention to the West. On November 3, 1943, Hitler promulgated *Führer*-Directive No. 51 to redress the long neglect. He forbade further raids upon the manpower of the forces in France and called for renewed effort to fortify the Atlantic coast of his empire from Denmark to the French Riviera: "Only an all-out effort in the construction of fortifications, an unsurpassed effort that will enlist all available manpower and physical resources of Germany and the occupied areas, will be able to strengthen our defenses along the coasts within the short time that still appears left to us."[7]

Time was not the only obstacle. The Germans operated in a nearly

---

4. Chester Wilmot, *The Struggle for Europe* (London, 1953), 199–201; F.H. Hinsley *et al.*, *British Intelligence in the Second World War*, 5 vols (London, 1979–), vol 3, pt 2, 47–49.

5. Harrison, *Cross-Channel Attack*, 128.

6. *Ibid.*, 128–48.

7. *Ibid.*, 148, 464–67.

perfect intelligence vacuum. Only sporadically could they conduct aerial reconnaissance over England; all their agents had been captured and were broadcasting bogus information under the control of British counter-intelligence.[8] German commanders concluded that the Pas de Calais, *AOK 15*'s sector, was the most threatened because the English Channel was narrowest at that point, and the path to the *Reich* the most direct. The *Kanalküste*, as the Germans called the region, was therefore the most heavily fortified part of the French coast; at the time of von Rundstedt's report *AOK 15* was three times the size of *AOK 7*.[9] But confidence that the Allies would land in the Pas de Calais was never total, and at various times the Germans entertained fears of Allied landings as far afield as Portugal and Norway.[10] Even the *Führer*'s personal directives, finally, could not avert the demands of other fronts, particularly the Russian. In January 1944 the *715th Infantry Division*, one of the few units in France with a respectable complement of motor vehicles, was sent to Anzio, while in late March the entire *II SS Panzer Corps* went to Poland.[11]

Shortly after *Führer*-Directive 51 appeared, Hitler appointed Field Marshal Erwin Rommel to command a reserve army group headquarters that would deploy wherever the Allies landed.[12] Rommel was also charged with inspecting the coastal defenses of France and of Denmark. He arrived in France in late December. Both Rommel and von Rundstedt agreed that the anomalous position of the reserve army group headquarters outside the normal chain of command was inefficient. They proposed, and Hitler accepted, that Rommel's staff should become *Heeresgruppe B* (*Army Group B*) and command *AOK*s 7 and 15 in the region most endangered.[13]

His experiences in North Africa, the depleted state of the *Luftwaffe*, and the dubious quality of his command all shaped Rommel's conception of how France should be defended. Two years before, he had found that

---

8. Col Anton Staubwasser, "The Enemy As Seen by the *Oberkommando* of *Heeresgruppe B* Before the Invasion," MS B–675, RG 338, NARA; Hinsley *et al.*, *British Intelligence in the Second World War*, vol 3, pt 2, 43.

9. Harrison, *Cross-Channel Attack*, 234.

10. *Ibid.*, 138; Staubwasser, "The Enemy As Seen by the *Oberkommando* of *Heeresgruppe B* Before the Invasion."

11. Harrison, *Cross-Channel Attack*, 234.

12. In the German Army, in contrast to American and British practice, the headquarters of armies and army groups had an organizational existence apart from the divisions or armies they commanded, if they commanded any at all. Thus the possibility of a reserve army group headquarters was possible.

13. Lt Gen Fritz Bayerlein, "Invasion 1944," in *The Rommel Papers*, edited by B.H. Liddell Hart and translated by Paul Findlay (New York, 1953), 451–60; Maj Gen Hans Speidel, "Ideas and Views of Genfldm. Rommel, Commander, A. Gp. B, on Defense and Operations in the West in 1944," MS B–720, RG 338, 13.

the growing aerial superiority of the British had reduced his ability to engage in fast-paced armored warfare. Allied superiority in the air was now much greater, while even the best of his divisions was not up to the standards of the *Afrika Korps*. The sea power of the Allies concerned him no less than their air forces. With their great fleets they could, upon establishing a lodgment, build up their forces more rapidly than the Germans, even if the French railroads were working at normal capacity, which was doubtful. Rommel had also been impressed in Africa by the skill of the British at defensive antitank warfare, and this too was now greater than it had been. He concluded that if the Allies were not promptly ejected before they could gain a firm foothold, they would soon be present in overwhelming strength, and the war lost.

Only the *Panzer* divisions had the power to break even the first wave of the Allied invasion. The accepted principles of war dictated that German armor should be held in a central strategic reserve until it was clear where the enemy would land. But Rommel argued that such a disposition was inadvisable because the *Luftwaffe* had lost the battle for air superiority over France, and could not protect the strategic reserve as it moved toward the beachhead. He doubted that the armored divisions, subject as they would be to incessant aerial attack, could reach the front quickly enough to expel the landing force before it became too strong. He concluded that they should be held close to the coast—not massed, but rather spread out so that at least one or two divisions could attack within a few hours.[14]

Rommel threw himself furiously into preparing the beach defenses of his command. To contain the Allied landing force so that it could be dispatched by an armored counterattack, he planned a fortified belt extending four to six miles inland. In this area, strongly fortified resistance nests were to be built; mine fields and barbed wire would prevent their being bypassed. Rommel also designed underwater obstacles to be planted in vast arrays along the coast. He ordered fields where gliders could land to be flooded, or else staked and mined. These efforts began much too late for completion before D-day. They were, moreover, heavily concentrated in the Pas de Calais, which Rommel, too, thought most in danger. Throughout the spring *AOK 7*'s program of fortification lagged six weeks behind that of *AOK 15*.[15]

Rommel's strategy for repelling the Allied invasion began one of the most familiar military debates of the Second World War. German plan-

---

14. See, for example, Ltr, Rommel to Hitler, Dec 31, 1943, in *Rommel Papers*, 453–55.

15. Harrison, *Cross-Channel Attack*, 249–50; Friedrich Ruge, *Rommel in Normandy: Reminiscences by Friedrich Ruge* (San Raphael, Calif., 1979), 97.

ning in France, taking its cue from a *Führer*-Directive of 1942, had at first emphasized a strong perimeter defense based upon fortifications.[16] But von Rundstedt, believing his command was not nearly numerous enough to implement the established strategy, called in his report of October 1943 for the creation of a central armored reserve. Hitler adopted this concept in his directive of the following month.[17] *OB West* began to motorize a few of its infantry divisions, and importuned Berlin for armor. In November, von Rundstedt appointed General Leo *Freiherr* Geyr von Schweppenburg, one of the German Army's leading experts on armored warfare, to head *Panzergruppe West*, the planned strategic reserve.[18]

At this juncture, Rommel arrived on the scene to attack the whole conception of a central reserve. Rommel and Geyr von Schweppenburg were for reasons of personality the leading protagonists in the ensuing contest. Both were confident and opinionated; the elderly von Rundstedt was courtly and inclined to delegate. His advocacy of a central reserve notwithstanding, he was not opposed to some form of coastal defense. Geyr von Schweppenburg's position, however, was extreme: He urged that beaches be abandoned and all German forces concentrated far inland near Paris. There they could protect the French capital from paratroopers while waiting for the Allies to reveal their route of march inland from their beachhead, whereupon *Panzergruppe West* would move to engage them in a climactic battle. In devising his plan, Geyr von Schweppenburg drew, as Rommel did, upon past experience. He recalled that in Sicily and Italy, German counterattacks upon newly landed Anglo-American armies had been defeated primarily by naval gunfire. He did not minimize the potential of Allied air power but held it could be neutralized if *Panzergruppe West* moved and attacked under cover of darkness.[19]

The irony of the controversy between the two commanders is that while both were clearly right in certain respects, probably neither man's strategy could have worked. Rommel, it appears, never explained how his early armored attacks upon the beachhead would survive the storm of steel from the sea which, unlike air power, was as effective by night as by day. Soon after D-day, he was to write of the heavy naval guns "that

---

16. Harrison, *Cross-Channel Attack*, 136–37.
17. *Ibid.*, 154.
18. The name of this officer has caused some confusion among English-speaking writers. "*Freiherr*" (baron) was his title, and "Geyr von Schweppenburg" his complete last name.
19. Lt Gen Leo *Freiherr* Geyr von Schweppenburg, "History of *Panzergruppe West*," MS B–258, RG 338; Brig Gen Fritz Krämer, "*I SS Pz. Corps* in the West in 1944," MS C–024, RG 338.

their effect is so immense that no operation of any kind is possible in the area commanded by this rapid-fire artillery, either by infantry or tanks."[20] Nor did he explain how his thrusts could maintain mass and coherence in negotiating the obstacles that he was so busily constructing.

As Maj. Gen. von Senger und Etterlin would shortly show in Italy, the sweeping movements by night that Geyr von Schweppenburg advocated were feasible in the face of Allied air power. But Geyr von Schweppenburg never addressed Rommel's basic point: The Allies, with their great fleet, could soon overreach any conceivable German reinforcement. And, swarming ashore by the hundreds of thousands, they would surely not have obliged Geyr von Schweppenburg by moving inland for a decisive battle before their strength was overwhelming.

As it happened, neither Rommel's nor Geyr von Schweppenburg's strategy was actually implemented. The landing at Anzio led the *Oberkommando der Wehrmacht* (*OKW*) to believe that the Allies might make a series of landings to dissipate German strength before their supreme effort. Southern France, where *AOKs 1* and *19* stood guard, seemed a likely target. In April 1944 the *OKW* organized these two armies into *Heeresgruppe G* and assigned three of the ten armored divisions then in France to the new organization. Rommel's *Heeresgruppe B* also had three armored divisions, far too few to assure a prompt attack on an Allied beachhead. This left a less than overwhelming total of four divisions for the strategic reserve, one of which was distantly located in Belgium. Not only was this far from being the force that Geyr von Schweppenburg and von Rundstedt wanted, they did not even have direct control over it. Only the *OKW*, with Hitler's concurrence, could commit *Panzergruppe West* to action.[21]

While the German commanders contended, the Allies marshaled aircraft on an unprecedented scale in the United Kingdom. No fewer than four separate air forces supported OVERLORD. Two were strategic—the British Bomber Command (Air Chief Marshal Sir Arthur Harris) and the American Eighth Air Force (Maj. Gen. James Doolittle)—and the remaining were tactical—Ninth Air Force (Lt. Gen. Lewis Brereton) and the British Second Tactical Air Force (Air Marshal Sir Arthur Coningham). The tactical air forces were for operational purposes grouped into the Allied Expeditionary Air Forces (AEAF) under the air commander in chief for OVERLORD, Air Chief Marshal Sir Trafford Leigh-Mallory. In practice, however, Leigh-Mallory's control over Ninth Air Force was less than complete. The American officers with whom he had to deal tended

---

20. Appreciation by Rommel, Jun 10, 1944, in *Rommel Papers*, 477.
21. Harrison, *Cross-Channel Attack*, 257–58.

to resist British authority in general, and Leigh-Mallory's in particular, because of their dislike for his cold and overbearing personality. Ninth Air Force, moreover, was administratively subordinate to the U.S. Strategic Air Forces (USSTAF). The Americans had created the latter organization on January 1, 1944, primarily to coordinate the activities of Eighth Air Force with those of the Italian-based Fifteenth Air Force, but also to resist the British-dominated AEAF.[22] Nor was Leigh-Mallory's task made any easier by the fact that USSTAF was commanded by Lt. Gen. Carl A. Spaatz, who tended to regard OVERLORD as an annoying sideshow to the strategic air war against Germany. Although nominally subordinate to the chief of the British Air Staff until April 1, 1944, Spaatz was in practice nearly independent of every authority but that of the Washington-based General Henry H. Arnold, commanding general of the Army Air Forces. This did not change greatly even when the Supreme Allied Commander took control of the strategic air forces on April 1. Harris of Bomber Command, finally, was equally independent and no less convinced that strategic air power alone could win the war against Germany. (*Chart 8*)

Of the air forces' many responsibilities for OVERLORD, none was more crucial, nor more problematic, than impeding the movement of German reserves to the beachhead. "The crux of the operation," General Morgan observed, "is . . . likely to be our ability to drive off the German reserves rather than the initial breaking of the coastal crust."[23] All of COSSAC's studies envisioned a brief but intense interdiction campaign. Commencing a few days before the invasion, it was to isolate the Cotentin principally through the destruction of bridges and tunnels and the bombing of towns to create roadblocks.[24] Only a few days before COSSAC produced the last version of its interdiction plan, chief of the British Air Staff Air Chief Marshal Sir Charles Portal had officially adopted the conclusions that Professor Solly Zuckerman had derived from his study of attacks on communications targets in Sicily and southern Italy during HUSKY.[25] Zuckerman had come to favor a preeminently strategic approach to interdiction that stressed attacks on repair facilities

---

22. Intvw, Dr Bruce Hopper with Gen Carl A. Spaatz, May 20, 1945, Box 135, Papers of Carl A. Spaatz, Library of Congress (LC).
23. Morgan, as quoted in Max Hastings, *OVERLORD: D-Day and the Battle for Normandy* (New York, 1984), 27.
24. Air Historical Branch of the British Air Ministry (AHB/BAM), "R.A.F. Narrative (First Draft): The Liberation of North West Europe," vol 1: "The Planning and Preparation of the Allied Expeditionary Air Force for the Landings in Normandy," n.d., 00895753, 141; Harrison, *Cross-Channel Attack*, 76.
25. Ltr of instruction, Air Marshal R.H. Peck to [unidentified] Mediterranean Allied Air Forces (MAAF) officer, in MAAF, "Operations in Support of DIADEM," Feb 2, 1944, 622.430-3, vol 7, Tab C.

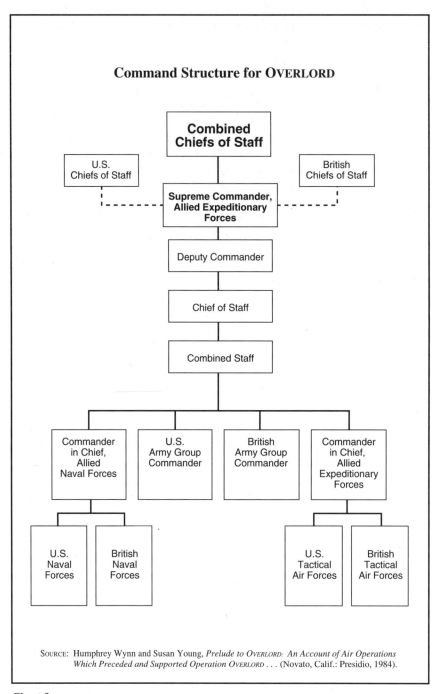

Command Structure for OVERLORD

Combined
Chiefs of Staff

U.S.
Chiefs of Staff

British
Chiefs of Staff

Supreme Commander,
Allied Expeditionary
Forces

Deputy Commander

Chief of Staff

Combined Staff

Commander
in Chief,
Allied
Naval Forces

U.S.
Army Group
Commander

British
Army Group
Commander

Commander
in Chief,
Allied
Expeditionary
Forces

U.S.
Naval
Forces

British
Naval
Forces

U.S.
Tactical
Air Forces

British
Tactical
Air Forces

SOURCE: Humphrey Wynn and Susan Young, *Prelude to OVERLORD: An Account of Air Operations Which Preceded and Supported Operation OVERLORD* . . . (Novato, Calif.: Presidio, 1984).

Chart 8.

and marshaling yards where locomotives and rolling stock could be destroyed en masse. He had also concluded that bridges were in general uneconomical targets because of the numbers of bombs necessary to destroy them. Further in contrast to COSSAC's plan, Zuckerman also deprecated attempts to create roadblocks by bombing, observing that only rarely could a town or defile be found that admitted of no bypass. Not surprisingly, therefore, the Air Staff quickly attacked COSSAC's plans for an unwise selection of targets. AEAF's Bombing Committee seconded these objections, powerfully supported by Leigh-Mallory, whose principal objection was that COSSAC's design for a brief tactical campaign against difficult targets unwisely presupposed an improbable run of good weather.[26]

Zuckerman himself had meanwhile returned to England and was participating in the deliberations of AEAF's Bombing Committee, where his criticisms had weighed heavily in the rejection of COSSAC's plan.[27] Aided by two railroad experts, E.W. Brant and Capt. C.E. Sherrington, the scientist developed a proposal for attacking repair centers and marshaling yards throughout France and Belgium to create a "railway desert" through which the Germans could move troops and supplies only with the greatest difficulty. "What is principally aimed at," Zuckerman wrote,

> is not the cutting of communications in the sense that an artery is cut, but the widespread destruction of the means of communication, and the means of maintaining the railway system in operation. . . . In any event, the effect will be such that the subsequent movement by rail of major reserves into France should almost be impossible.

By February 1, Eisenhower had expressed his preliminary approval of this plan, which called for the destruction of 101 rail centers over a period of ninety days with 45,000 tons of bombs.[28] (*Map 14*)

Thus was the "Transportation Plan" introduced into Allied councils, and a strategic debate joined that was to prove no less famous than the contemporary controversy between Rommel and Geyr von Schweppenburg. The Transportation Plan was not offered as a complete interdiction plan for OVERLORD.[29] It was intended, as Zuckerman carefully explained, to complement a purely tactical plan of interdiction, such as

---

26. AHB/BAM, "Liberation of North West Europe" 1:141–42.
27. *Ibid.*
28. Solly Zuckerman, *From Apes to Warlords*, (New York, 1978), 232; AHB/BAM, "Liberation of North West Europe," 1:142–46.
29. See, for example, W.W. Rostow, *Pre-Invasion Bombing Strategy: General Eisenhower's Decision of March 25, 1944* (Austin, Tex., 1981), 14.

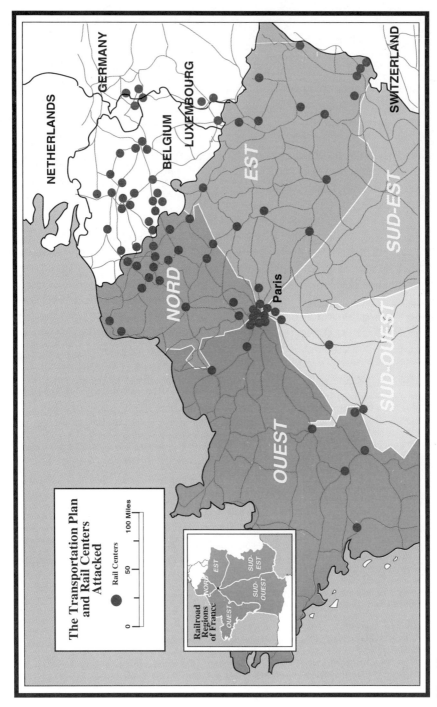

The Transportation Plan and Rail Centers Attacked

● Rail Centers

0   50   100 Miles

Railroad Regions of France

NETHERLANDS

GERMANY

BELGIUM

LUXEMBOURG

SWITZERLAND

EST

NORD

Paris

OUEST

SUD-EST

SUD-OUEST

Map 14.

the one that COSSAC had proposed. Destruction of the rail centers, he argued, would channelize rail movements, thereby easing the work of the strafing fighter-bombers employed under the tactical plan. The Transportation Plan's reduction in the overall capacity of the French rail system, moreover, would make such trains as might occur all the more valuable, and their destruction correspondingly more damaging.[30] Much of the retrospective controversy over the Transportation Plan has revolved around Zuckerman's skepticism about the costs of bridge-bombing. This was not, however, the issue in the early months of 1944. For while the scientist had not receded from his position that bridges were uneconomical targets, by February 15 the Transportation Plan had been amended to call for the bombing of bridges in the lodgment area shortly before the invasion.[31] Had the debate revolved around this or any other technical point, it would probably not have aroused the heat that it did. The rub was rather that the Transportation Plan, unlike COSSAC's tactical scheme, required a massive and lengthy diversion of the strategic air forces. The 45,000 tons of bombs for which Zuckerman had called was nearly half of what all the Allied air forces were expected to drop on Europe between February 1 and D-day. As the tactical air forces could deliver no more than a fraction of that amount, the strategic air forces would have to curtail operations against Germany in the interest of the Transportation Plan.[32] This was a prospect that neither Spaatz nor Harris, each obsessed with his own vision of victory through air power, relished.[33] Conversely, both Leigh-Mallory and Eisenhower's deputy supreme commander, Air Chief Marshal Sir Arthur W. Tedder, saw in the Transportation Plan not only an intrinsically meritorious project, but a means of gaining some control over the nearly autonomous fiefdoms of the bomber barons.

The opposition of the strategic commanders to the Transportation Plan was immediately evident when Leigh-Mallory briefed them about it

---

30. AHB/BAM, "Liberation of North West Europe," 1:144–45; Zuckerman, *From Apes to Warlords*, 233.

31. Zuckerman, *From Apes to Warlords*, 233.

32. The preinvasion bombing program at this time called for a total of 108,000 tons of bombs. Zuckerman anticipated reducing Eighth Air Force's contribution to POINTBLANK, the campaign against the German aircraft industry, to a mere 20 percent of its preinvasion effort. AEAF, " 'OVERLORD' Employment of Bomber Forces in Relation to the Outline Plans," Feb 12, 1944, Box 14, Spaatz Papers.

33. Even before the Transportation Plan became an issue, Spaatz feared that the diversion of strategic air forces to support OVERLORD would preclude "Air operations of sufficient intensity to justify the theory that Germany can be knocked out by Air power." Diary, Carl A. Spaatz, Jan 21, 1944, Box 14, Spaatz Papers.

Maj. Gen. Carl A. Spaatz *(above right)*, **a staunch advocate of strategic bombing, questioned the wisdom of using Allied resources, such as this squadron of B-17s** *(above left)*, **to bomb targets in France. He wanted to concentrate efforts against oil refining and transportation targets in Germany.**

on February 15. Spaatz's first line of defense was that it conflicted with the directives of the Combined Bomber Offensive laid down at the Casablanca Conference of 1943, which assigned paramount importance to the destruction of the German aircraft industry. He doubted that the *Luftwaffe* would rise to defend rail centers so that it could be destroyed in the air. The American airman showed in the clearest fashion his distaste for the prospects of USSTAF's subordination to AEAF any earlier than the date on which Eisenhower (and through him Leigh-Mallory) was to assume control of the strategic forces for direct support of OVERLORD. Spaatz asked Leigh-Mallory when he anticipated beginning to direct some portion of the strategic air forces to carry out the Transportation Plan. After the British officer replied "March the first," the American said, "That's all I want to know; I've nothing further to say." Harris based his opposition upon technical grounds: The railroad networks of northern Europe were too different from those of Italy for Zuckerman's theories to be applicable, and Bomber Command, trained for the indiscriminate bombardment of German cities, lacked the accuracy for the role assigned to it.[34]

---

34. Zuckerman, *From Apes to Warlords*, 233–35; Memo, Col Richard D'O. Hughes to Lt Gen Spaatz, Feb 15, 1944, subj: Conference Held at AEAF Head-

Within days the very concept of the Transportation Plan was under attack from several quarters, British and American. The British critics included the Committee of Four (composed of representatives from Air Intelligence, the Directorate of Transportation, the War Office, and the Ministry of Economic Warfare). Leading the American opposition was the Enemy Objectives Unit (EOU) of the American embassy in London. This organization, the joint creation of the Office of Strategic Services (OSS) and the Board of Economic Warfare, consisted of a team of economists under the direction of Col. Richard D'Oyly Hughes, a former British officer who had moved to the United States in the early 1930s and been commissioned in the Army Air Forces during the war. Two of the economists, Charles P. Kindleberger and W.W. Rostow, later became prominent both as scholars and as advisers to government. EOU's primary purpose was to develop targets for USSTAF, in which capacity it had a major influence on the strategic air war against Germany.[35]

EOU's critique of the Transportation Plan resembled that with which the OSS had attacked Zuckerman's legacy in Italy.[36] Reduced to essentials, it was that the Germans used so small a percentage of Europe's rail capacity for their military that no practicable program of attacking marshaling yards could seriously interfere with their operations. The economists calculated that not 81, but 500 rail centers would have to be attacked, and emphasized evidence from Italy that the Germans could open even the most heavily bombed marshaling yards to through traffic within days.[37]

Zuckerman replied that his critics' contention that his program would not stop all traffic was true but irrelevant. The destruction of marshaling yards would so reduce the capacity of the French rail system that what remained would suffice neither to supply nor to reinforce *AOK 7*. The Transportation Plan, moreover, did not preclude tactical interdiction close to D-day; it would in fact contribute to the success of interdiction in the ways noted earlier. The scientist also attacked his opponents' theoretical assumptions. Their concept of "surplus capacity," he asserted, was nonsensical. It was based upon a simplistic comparison of present holdings of locomotives with what one could expect to destroy. The argument ignored the systemic effects of the loss of repair, mainte-

---

quarters, Stanmore, Box 14, Spaatz Papers.

35. Rostow, *Pre-Invasion Bombing Strategy*, 15–24.

36. The OSS's critique is discussed in Chapter 5 in the context of Operation STRANGLE.

37. AHB/BAM, "Liberation of North West Europe," 1:149–51; Zuckerman, *From Apes to Warlords*, 237–41; Wesley Frank Craven and James Lea Cate, eds, *The Army Air Forces in World War II*, 7 vols (Chicago, 1948–57), vol 3: *Europe: ARGUMENT to V–E Day, January 1944 to May 1945*, 74–76.

nance, signaling, and marshaling facilities. Locomotives, for example, had to have their boilers flushed nearly daily. If the necessary facilities were destroyed, the fate of the locomotives themselves mattered little.[38] Zuckerman's supporters seem at no time to have been a majority of those party to the debate. But they included the crucial Tedder, who dismissed the scientist's critics as "special pleaders" for the strategic air forces.[39]

Even as Zuckerman struggled to win acceptance for the Transportation Plan, EOU and USSTAF were preparing an alternative. Seeking to capitalize on the punishing losses that Eighth Air Force had inflicted on the *Luftwaffe* during the Combined Bomber Offensive, EOU's economists drew up plans for a comprehensive assault on Germany's oil industry. Their paper, "The Use of Strategic Air Power after March 1, 1944," was completed on February 28. After some modification by Colonel Hughes and Brig. Gen. Charles P. Cabell of USSTAF's planning staff, the plan was presented to Spaatz on March 5. He accepted the study's conclusions that Germany's refineries were vulnerable to bombing and that a vigorous attack could bring dramatic results within a few months, as Germany's reserves of petroleum products were already seriously depleted.[40]

General Spaatz discerned another virtue in the "Oil Plan": He had long believed that the greatest contribution to the success of OVERLORD would be to destroy the *Luftwaffe* with his strong force of long-range fighters. But the enemy air force had first to be brought to battle, and that, Spaatz reasoned, could best be done by bombing assets so valuable that the Germans would be compelled to defend them. The Oil Plan, he believed, would have that effect, and the Transportation Plan would not. Spaatz set about persuading Eisenhower and Portal of this.[41]

---

38. AHB/BAM, "Liberation of North West Europe," 1:149–51; Zuckerman, *From Apes to Warlords*, 237–41. For a latter-day recounting of the debate between Zuckerman and the American economists, see Charles P. Kindleberger, "Zuckerman's Bomb: World War II Strategy," *Encounter* 51 (Nov 1978):39–42; Lord Solly Zuckerman, "Bombs & Illusions in World War II," *ibid*. 52 (Jun 1979):86–89; and W.W. Rostow, "The Controversy Over World War II Bombing: A Reply to Lord Zuckerman," *ibid*. 55 (Aug–Sep 1980):100–2.

39. AHB/BAM, "Liberation of North West Europe," 1:151.

40. Rostow, *Pre-Invasion Bombing Strategy*, 31–34; "Statement of Colonel R.D. Hughes, Assistant to Director of Intelligence," Jun 13, 1944, Box 135, Spaatz Papers. The authors of the Oil Plan estimated that the destruction of only four synthetic oil plants and thirteen refineries would rob Germany of over 80 percent of her synthetic fuel production and 60 percent of her refining capacity. Hughes statement, Jun 13, 1944.

41. Leigh-Mallory, on the other hand, believed that the Germans would husband their aircraft until D-day, and that the climactic battle for air superiority would follow D-day. Spaatz intvw, May 20, 1945; AHB/BAM, "Liberation of

The EOU did not see the Oil Plan as a complete alternative to the Transportation Plan. As the size of Germany's reserves of fuel was not precisely known, the economists could not be sure how long it would take for the Oil Plan to affect the mobility of her army. This led them to propose a strategic interdiction campaign based upon bridge-bombing and comprehensive attacks on supply depots, the locations of which were generally known from ULTRA.[42] Their scheme strongly resembled Operation STRANGLE, which was in the throes of gestation when EOU advanced its proposal on February 17. The resemblance to STRANGLE was not coincidental; EOU drew heavily upon the experience of the Mediterranean theater.[43] While in favor of attacking bridges shortly before D-day as part of a tactical plan, Zuckerman remained convinced that bridges were difficult and expensive targets, a position he maintained until at least early May.[44] He therefore regarded EOU's proposed strategic campaign as extravagant and liable to fail. EOU counterattacked with a paper produced by the OSS in Italy just before STRANGLE. This document purported to demonstrate that Zuckerman's influential study of the effects of bombing during HUSKY and AVALANCHE had exaggerated both the problems of attacking bridges and the benefits of bombing marshaling yards.[45]

Zuckerman's later statement that the question of whether to bomb bridges was a "trivial" feature of the preinvasion debate would therefore be misleading, were it not for one consideration: At no time before May did Spaatz advocate a French STRANGLE.[46] Leigh-Mallory's impatience to get on with the Transportation Plan had given the American airman a perfect opportunity to do so in March. Both Spaatz and Harris had frustrated Leigh-Mallory's efforts to extend the authority of AEAF over their commands in order to begin the Transportation Plan.[47] The air marshal at length prevailed upon Portal to break the impasse. Portal

---

North West Europe," 1:151–52; Craven and Cate, *ARGUMENT to V–E Day*, 76-77.

42. EOU was not at all specific when asked when the effects of the proposed attacks on the German oil industry would be felt. At the meeting of March 25, during which Eisenhower decided for the Transportation Plan, Maj Gen Frederick Anderson of USSTAF had to admit that there could be no guarantee that "the attacks of oil targets would have an appreciable effect during the initial stages of OVERLORD. . . ." Rostow, *Pre-Invasion Bombing Strategy*, 42; Ralph Bennett, *ULTRA in the West: The Normandy Campaign 1944–1945* (New York, 1980), 69.

43. See, for example, Rostow, *Pre-Invasion Bombing Strategy*, 38–41, 57–58.

44. *Ibid.*, 56–57.

45. *Ibid.*, 38–43.

46. Zuckerman, *From Apes to Warlords*, 257.

47. AHB/BAM, "Liberation of North West Europe," 1:148.

convened a conference on March 25 at which all the air commanders met with Eisenhower to decide how the preinvasion aerial campaign should be implemented. Tedder urged the Transportation Plan; Spaatz then extolled the Oil Plan, breathing not a word of EOU's plan for comprehensive attacks on bridges and depots. In the ensuing discussion the American was unable to demonstrate that the Oil Plan, even if immediately successful, would force von Rundstedt's command to dip into its reserve stocks of fuel before D-day. Eisenhower then decided for the Transportation Plan, observing that no one had shown how else the air forces could contribute to OVERLORD's success in the two months that remained before the beginning of tactical aerial operations in and around Normandy. "Thus," as W.W. Rostow observed, "on March 25 Eisenhower was presented with false alternatives: marshalling yards versus oil. The true alternatives were oil, plus a sustained systemic attack on bridges and dumps, versus marshalling yards."[48]

Spaatz did not press for EOU's plan because be believed that OVERLORD was likely to fail and he did not wish the record to show that he had not done all that Tedder and Eisenhower had asked of him. About a week before the conference of March 25, General Cabell and one of EOU's economists argued for the bridge campaign:

> After listening, Spaatz clapped his battered Air-Corps style cap on his head, rose from his desk, paced the room, and delivered himself of the following (more or less): "I won't do it. I won't take the responsibility _____ . This _____ invasion can't succeed, and I don't want any part of the blame. After it fails, we can show them how we can win by bombing."[49]

Eisenhower formally approved the Transportation Plan on March 26. He did allow, however, for a possible start on the Oil Plan, should

---

48. Rostow, *Pre-Invasion Bombing Strategy*, 43. See also "Final Minutes of the March 25 Meeting," *ibid.*, app A, 88–89.

49. Rostow adds that he believes that Spaatz was reluctant to prescribe for the tactical air forces, which were not under his command. *Ibid.*, 44–46. Spaatz offered his gloomy views on OVERLORD to Maj Gen Hoyt Vandenberg on April 10. The operation was "highly dangerous"; he feared that "the Allied forces might be batting their heads against a stone wall in the OVERLORD operation." Worse, it was "no longer necessary" because the strategic air forces had shown their prowess against Germany, especially since the introduction of the H2X bombing radar. If he were in charge of the campaign in Europe, Spaatz continued, he would invade Norway. Sweden would probably join the Allies, and then Germany could be attacked from all sides. (Spaatz assumed the ultimate success of the plan then being developed to station bombers in the Soviet Union.) "Why," he concluded, "undertake a highly dubious operation in a hurry when there is a sure way to do it as just outlined?" Notes on Spaatz-Vandenberg conf, Apr 10, 1944, Box 14, Spaatz Papers.

the Transportation Plan prosper. He made Tedder responsible for over-
seeing the implementation of the Transportation Plan. The British officer's major responsibility was to see that Eighth and Fifteenth Air Forces
devoted half their visual bombing to marshaling yards. Harris had
proved surprisingly cooperative since several demonstration attacks ordered by Portal had shown that Bomber Command, contrary to Harris's
expectations, could attack rail centers by night with reasonable accuracy.[50]

While allowing several large attacks on marshaling yards in April,
Prime Minister Churchill delayed full-scale inauguration of the Transportation Plan. He had serious misgivings about the political consequences
of Zuckerman's design because some British analysts foresaw heavy casualties among French civilians. The Foreign Secretary, Sir Anthony Eden,
explained the reason for Churchill's concern at a meeting of the War
Cabinet: Intelligence reports indicated that the peoples of occupied Europe were showing disquieting signs of looking to the Soviet Union for
political inspiration, and the projected collateral casualties of the Transportation Plan were scarcely likely to check that unwelcome trend in
France. But the firm insistence of Tedder and Eisenhower at length
swayed the British leader to accept the Transportation Plan on May 3,
provided it could be shown that no more than 10,000 French deaths were
likely to result. Still uneasy, Churchill imparted his concerns to President
Roosevelt on May 7. Roosevelt replied on May 11 that "however regret-
table the attendant loss of civilian lives" might be, he was "not prepared
to impose from this distance any restriction on military action by the responsible commanders that in their opinion might militate against the
success of OVERLORD." Churchill now finally and completely acceded to
the Transportation Plan. His lingering fears were presumably assuaged
somewhat by Zuckerman's demonstration that the more pessimistic estimates of civilian casualties derived from misapplication of formulas that
he had himself derived from his studies of German attacks on England in
1940.[51]

Eisenhower had assumed command of the strategic air forces at midnight, April 13, 1944. Four days later, SHAEF issued its master directive
for the strategic forces. While emphasizing the Transportation Plan, the
order showed that the supreme commander accepted Spaatz's argument

---

50. AHB/BAM, "Liberation of North West Europe," 1:154-55; Zuckerman, *From Apes to Warlords*, 241.
51. Zuckerman, *From Apes to Warlords*, 250, 252-53; AHB/BAM, "Liberation of North West Europe," 1:151-72; Craven and Cate, ARGUMENT to V-E
Day, 79; Winston S. Churchill, *The Second World War*, 6 vols (London,
1948-53), vol 5: *Closing the Ring*, 466-67.

that it was necessary to bring the *Luftwaffe* to battle. SHAEF therefore ordered USSTAF to continue daylight raids on the German aircraft industry as its first priority. Rail centers in France were the second priority: Eisenhower directed Spaatz to bomb all marshaling yards specified by the British Air Ministry. Bomber Command was to continue attacking German population centers while beginning forthwith its share of the Transportation Plan.[52]

SHAEF published the air plan for tactical operations in and around Normandy on April 23, although some of the operations it stipulated had been under way for several weeks. From D minus 50 to D minus 30, counterair operations against the *Luftwaffe* in northern France and Belgium had priority. From D minus 30, to D minus 1, the priorities were, in descending order, the *Luftwaffe*; rail centers; coastal batteries; and airfields within 130 miles of Caen, which were to be relentlessly hammered to obviate the Germans' ability to compensate for their inferior numbers by flying more sorties per aircraft than the Allies. At no time during the preparation for OVERLORD, in short, were Anglo-American airmen free to give interdiction the virtually undivided attention that the Mediterranean Allied Air Forces had given to STRANGLE. A further diversion of effort resulted from the demands of CROSSBOW, the campaign against the launching sites in France that the Germans were rushing to complete for their V-1 flying bombs.[53]

Implementation of the Transportation Plan fell most heavily on the two tactical air forces and on Bomber Command. Eighth Air Force joined the campaign on April 19 after considerable prodding by Tedder and Leigh-Mallory, both of whom considered Spaatz willfully tardy.[54]

---

52. "Directive by the Supreme Commander to U.S.S.T.A.F. and Bomber Command for Support of 'OVERLORD' during the Preparatory Period," Apr 17, 1944, Box 14, Spaatz Papers. Spaatz gave a clear explanation in May 1945 of how Eisenhower's directive affected his operations: "Although the Transportation Plan was agreed on, it was not given priority above getting control of the *air*, so that USSTAF did not come under Leigh-Mallory's operational control until just before the invasion took place. They were given a commitment in this Transportation Plan to attack the marshalling yards that were their share of the marshalling yards. The surplus bombing was directed to best advantage to obtain control of the air. Now, fortunately for all concerned, the weather was such that there was enough surplus to attack targets well in Germany—including oil—to force the Germans into the air fight necessary to (1) keep their air forces in being, and (2) keep them on the defensive back in Germany instead of them concentrating up forward to meet the invasion." Spaatz intvw, May 20, 1945 [emphasis in the original].

53. AHB/BAM, "Liberation of North West Europe," 1:81, 84–106, 138, 142.

54. The weather over Germany had been unusually good, and Spaatz had used the opportunity to pursue the campaign against the German aircraft industry and to begin the Oil Plan. In an interview that he gave shortly after the end of the war, Spaatz said, ". . . I think sometimes the oil enthusiasts get a little off

Fifteenth Air Force did not begin to fulfill its obligations under the Transportation Plan until May 25. In early June, Leigh-Mallory's staff estimated that fifty-one of the eighty rail centers on the final target list had been so completely destroyed that they needed no further attention beyond occasional dive-bombing to frustrate repair. In all, the Allies dropped 71,000 tons of bombs, far more than the 45,000 tons that Zuckerman had originally called for. (*Table 10*) Most of the bombing was concentrated in Belgium and *Régions Nord* and *Ouest* of the French railway system, although the raids extended throughout France and into Germany itself. (See *Map 14*) Antiaircraft fire was light throughout, and Allied losses were low; German fighters offered no significant opposition.[55] Casualties among French civilians totaled about 4,750.[56]

Fighter sweeps supplemented the devastation of the rail centers. Allied fighters had occasionally strafed trains since March, but on May 20 Leigh-Mallory ordered large-scale armed reconnaissance in the belief that civilian passenger traffic had ceased. The sweeps extended throughout northern France and Belgium, occasionally reaching into Germany and even Poland. The most ambitious of these operations was CHATTA-NOOGA CHOO-CHOO, which began on May 21 when 763 of AEAF's fighters ranged over northern France, while 500 fighters of Eighth Air Force attacked trains in Germany. The sweeps forced the Germans to curtail daytime rail service in France after May 26.[57]

Zuckerman had favored operations of this kind. What he most decidedly did not advocate, however, was the strategic campaign against bridges that began mid-May, occasioned by continuing skepticism about the effectiveness of the Transportation Plan. One stronghold of doubters was SHAEF's G-2 Section, which on May 20 would flatly declare that Zuckerman's scheme had failed "so [to] reduce the railway operating facilities as to impair the enemy's ability to move up reinforcements and maintain his forces in the West." The bombing had imposed delays on the Germans, SHAEF continued, but they still had four times the number of cars, eight times the number of locomotives, and ten times the number of servicing facilities needed to meet their essential requirements. Only a STRANGLE-like operation could cut into this margin of surplus capacity. Montgomery's 21 Army Group, long an advocate of bridge-

---

base in what they say about it. In my opinion, our Air Force would not have attacked oil targets any oftener than we did—if oil had been selected as first priority, or—qualifying that a little bit—we might have attacked them one or two days more than we did." Spaatz intvw, May 20, 1945.

55. Craven and Cate, *Argument to V-E Day*, 150–56.

56. Army Air Forces Evaluation Board in the European Theater of Operations (AAF Eval Bd/ETO), "The Effectiveness of Air Attack Against Rail Transportation in the Battle of France," Jun 1, 1945, 138.4–37, 164.

57. *Ibid.*, 156.

Table 10. Distribution of Bombs Dropped on Rail Centers During the Transportation Plan

Location	Prior to Apr 29, 1944		Apr 29–Jun 5, 1944		Total, Pre–D-day		Total, Post–D-day	
	Tons	Percent	Tons	Percent	Tons	Percent	Tons	Percent
Region								
Nord	13,463	41	8,350	22	21,813	31	8,589	17
Est	1,765	5	2,417	6	4,182	6	5,760	12
Ouest	5,371	16	6,662	18	12,033	17	13,015	26
Sud-Ouest	2,467	7	2,448	7	4,915	7	6,714	14
Sud-Est	2,067	6	3,104	8	5,171	7	7,195	14
Belgium	5,961	18	8,113	21	14,074	20	2,237	5
Other*	2,171	7	6,798	18	8,969	12	6,197	12
Total	33,265	100	37,892	100	71,157	100	49,707	100

*Includes Alsace-Lorraine, Luxembourg, and Germany.
SOURCE: Army Air Forces Evaluation Board in the European Theater of Operations, "The Effectiveness of Air Attack Against Rail Transportation in the Battle of France."

In gun-camera footage shot by an attacking Allied plane, a locomotive from a German supply train passes through northern France some months before OVERLORD.

bombing, associated itself with this conclusion, as did Spaatz, who returned from Italy impressed by first-hand observation of STRANGLE.[58]

Advocates of a like policy in France were further encouraged by the success of British Typhoon fighter-bombers in dropping several French and Belgian bridges on April 21. Leigh-Mallory, however, continued to resist, swayed by predictions, based on Zuckerman's earlier research in Italy, that 1,200 tons of bombs would be required to destroy each of the bridges across the Seine. At a target conference on May 6 he repeated these statistics but yielded to the plea of Air Marshal Coningham that there be at least some experimental bridge-bombing to determine the best method of attack, for it had long since been agreed that tactical interdiction in and around Normandy would require the destruction of bridges. Even Leigh-Mallory's entrenched doubts were swept aside on May 7 when eight P-47 Thunderbolts, using only a few tons of bombs, dropped the major railroad bridge at Vernon and damaged three lesser spans across the Seine. This heartening success was somewhat tarnished by a decrypted message from *Luftflotte 3* in France: Citing the evident Allied interest in the Seine, the message concluded, "From this the view of *Luftflotte 3*, already often expressed, that the landing is planned in the area Le Havre–Cherbourg is confirmed once more." This was uncomfortably close to the truth. On May 10, Leigh-Mallory, now converted to bridge-bombing, ordered the destruction of the bridges over the Meuse and the Albert Canal in Belgium, which would impede movement into Normandy while maintaining the deception that the Allied objective was

---

58. *Ibid.*, 156–57; Harrison, *Cross-Channel Attack*, 224; Msg, Spaatz to Arnold, Feb 25, 1944, Box 22, Papers of Ira Eaker, LC. The information from ULTRA was ambiguous, and both parties in the inter-Allied debate drew upon it to support their positions. Hinsley et al., *British Intelligence in the Second World War*, vol 3, pt 2, 111–15.

the Pas de Calais. There were to be no further attacks along the Seine until after the destruction of the slated Belgian bridges.[59]

SHAEF had meanwhile prepared an ambitious plan to ring Normandy with three lines of interdiction. The first and most important of these was defined for most of its length by the rivers Seine and Loire. The second line stretched from Étaples southeast to Fismes on the Vesle and thence south to Clamecy near the Loire. (*Map 15*) The third line, which started at Antwerp and ran across Belgium to Maastricht on the Meuse and thence down that river to Belfort near the Swiss border, was never systematically attacked. Although SHAEF did not officially promulgate its plan until June 7, the campaign against the Seine bridges began on May 24. For the most part, it followed the pattern developed in Italy. B–26 medium bombers attacked the larger structures with 2,000-pound bombs, while P–47 fighter-bombers dropped 500 pounders on the smaller ones. There was constant surveillance of the downed bridges, which were reattacked as often as necessary to frustrate repairs. All bridges across the Seine south of Paris had been destroyed by D-day, at a total cost of 4,400 tons of bombs—about one-fifth the tonnage that detractors of bridge-bombing had calculated. The bridges of the Seine north of Paris were spared for the moment so as not to compromise the deception of FORTITUDE. For the same reason, there were no attacks at all on the bridges of the Loire. Further to divert German attention from Normandy, the Allies bombed beach defenses most intensively in the Pas de Calais.[60]

Three circumstances combined to magnify the effect of the preinvasion bombing. The first was the debilitation of the French railway system even before it was struck by the might of the Allied air forces. By 1944, the Germans had confiscated for use outside France about 30 percent of the locomotives and 35 percent of the rolling stock. A long series of financial problems before the war, moreover, had led the French to defer repair and renewal. "These reductions in the aggregate supply of railroad materials and facilities were *not*," a careful American study of 1945 concluded, "matched by an equivalent reduction in aggregate demands for railroad services." French industry was too important to the German war effort to permit a curtailment of operations. The same could be said of the morale and welfare of the French people, both of which depended to

---

59. Hinsley *et al.*, *British Intelligence in the Second World War*, vol 3, pt 2, 58, 112; "Notes of Meeting Held in the A C.-in-C.'s Office, Headquarters, A.E.A.F., on Saturday, 6th May, 1944, to Discuss Bombing Targets," Box 15, Spaatz Papers.

60. Craven and Cate, ARGUMENT *to V–E Day*, 156–59; Harrison, *Cross-Channel Attack*, 229–30; AAF Eval Bd/ETO, "Effectiveness of Air Attack Against Rail Transportation in the Battle of France," Jun 1, 1945, 8, 24-26.

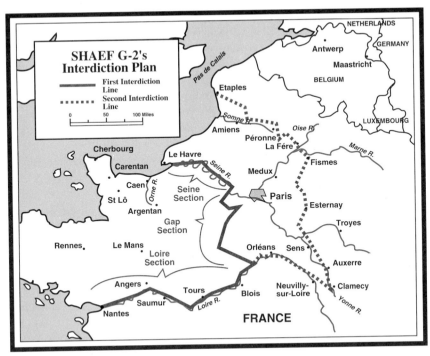

Map 15.

no small degree upon a high volume of railroad traffic. "The Allied air attacks hit a weakened system in which physical and economic circumstances made men, machines, and materials work under heavy stress and strain."[61]

The second circumstance was that the German Army, in France as elsewhere, lacked motor transport sufficient to compensate for gross disruptions of rail transport. The quartermaster of *OB West* calculated that in the event of invasion the units in France would need 50,000 tons of motor transport space, an estimate that presumably presupposed some destruction of the railroads. *OB West* itself controlled 5,000 tons; *AOK 15* had 15,000 tons, but *AOK 7* had only 1,300.[62] As it is unlikely that *AOK*s *1* and *19* on the Mediterranean coast were given a higher priority for transport than *AOK 7*, it is perhaps not far wrong to conclude that in France the German Army had only about 25,000 tons of motor trans-

61. AAF Eval Bd/ETO, "Effectiveness of Air Attack Against Rail Transportation in the Battle of France," Jun 1, 1945, 2-4 (emphasis in the original).
62. Col Otto Eckstein, "The Activity of the *Oberquartiermeister West* During the Time of Preparations for Warding off an Invasion and During the Initial Battles," MS B-827, RG 338, 22; Harrison, *Cross-Channel Attack*, 410-11.

port, or about half of what it required. Whatever the exact figure, the shortage of trucks showed itself once the fighting in Normandy began.

The final circumstance favoring the Allies was the inadequacy of the Germans' logistical preparations. Given their dependence on a weakened rail system and shortage of alternative transport, the Germans had done surprisingly little to prepare for a campaign against their communications that, given the Italian precedents, was predictable. They decentralized their supply depots to protect them from bombing, and increased the stocks of ammunition, fuel, and rations in forward positions.[63] But they attempted neither to build underwater bridges nor to decentralize facilities for the maintenance and repair of locomotives.[64]

The effects of Allied bombing on the French railroads were immediate and drastic. On March 1 the system was operating at about the rate of 1943. But between March 1 and D-day, total rail traffic declined by 60 percent. In *Région Nord* (see *Map 14*), the decline was steeper still: 75 percent. This loss of capacity was even more significant than it might appear. About two-thirds of all German military freight was carried in trains predominantly devoted to civilian purposes. The number of trains actually carrying military supplies and equipment was therefore considerably greater than might be supposed from the fact that 40 percent of the system's capacity was allotted to the *Wehrmacht*. Military traffic, furthermore, had to compete with civilian traffic. Even as the capacity of the system shrank under Allied attack, economic shipments for the German war industry continued to receive a share of transport space equal to that of the *Wehrmacht*—40 percent. Since shipments of this kind were obviously vital to the German war effort, little surplus capacity could be painlessly drawn upon as the performance of the rail system declined.[65] (*Chart 9*)

Losses of locomotives and rolling stock to Allied attacks were occasionally severe. On May 21, the first day of CHATTANOOGA CHOO-CHOO, fighters disabled fifty locomotives in the area of *AOK 7* alone. A raid on the large marshaling yard at Le Mans the previous day had destroyed or damaged 617 cars.[66] At no time, however, was there a general shortage of rolling stock, although the reduced circulation of traffic sometimes produced local shortages of particular kinds of cars.[67] The

---

63. Eckstein, "Activity of the *Oberquartiermeister West*," 12–13, 18.
64. AAF Eval Bd/ETO, "Effectiveness of Air Attack Against Rail Transportation in the Battle of France," Jun 1, 1945, 106.
65. *Ibid.*, 66.
66. Historical Evaluation and Research Organization (HERO), "Tactical Air Interdiction by U.S. Army Air Forces in World War II: France," ch 3, 34–35.
67. AAF Eval Bd/ETO, "Effectiveness of Air Attack Against Rail Transportation in the Battle of France," Jun 1, 1945, 60.

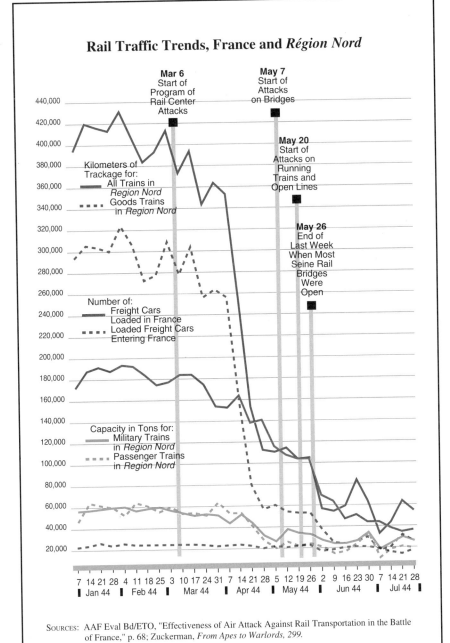

Rail Traffic Trends, France and *Région Nord*

Mar 6
Start of
Program of
Rail Center
Attacks

May 7
Start of
Attacks
on Bridges

May 20
Start of
Attacks on
Running
Trains and
Open Lines

May 26
End of
Last Week
When Most
Seine Rail
Bridges
Were
Open

Kilometers of
Trackage for:
All Trains in
Region Nord
Goods Trains
in *Region Nord*

Number of:
Freight Cars
Loaded in France
Loaded Freight Cars
Entering France

Capacity in Tons for:
Military Trains
in *Region Nord*
Passenger Trains
in *Region Nord*

440,000
420,000
400,000
380,000
360,000
340,000
320,000
300,000
280,000
260,000
240,000
220,000
200,000
180,000
160,000
140,000
120,000
100,000
80,000
60,000
40,000
20,000

7 14 21 28 4 11 18 25 3 10 17 24 31 7 14 21 28 5 12 19 26 2 9 16 23 30 7 14 21 28
▮ Jan 44 ▮ Feb 44 ▮   Mar 44   ▮   Apr 44 ▮   May 44 ▮   Jun 44   ▮   Jul 44 ▮

SOURCES: AAF Eval Bd/ETO, "Effectiveness of Air Attack Against Rail Transportation in the Battle
of France," p. 68; Zuckerman, *From Apes to Warlords, 299.*

Chart 9.

loss of locomotive power, however, was severe and contributed heavily to the system's loss of capacity. Strafing attacks rarely destroyed locomotives—their punctured boilers could be repaired. The same was true of splinter damage sustained during the bombing of the rail centers. What did make for a loss of traction was, as Zuckerman had projected, the loss of repair facilities. If, for example, the locomotives awaiting repair on June 15 could have been returned to service, the number of usable engines would have been about what it was before the beginning of the Transportation Plan.[68] (*Table 11*)

The transport officer for *OB West*, Colonel Hans Höffner, later testified that the chief cause of the loss of traction was the inability to utilize undamaged locomotives effectively. Here the effects of the Transportation Plan and bridge-bombing complemented each other, for it was chiefly the destruction of switching facilities in rail centers and the dropping of bridges that impeded the circulation of the locomotives. The increasingly grudging performance of the French train crews further reduced the efficiency of the rail system when it came under heavy attack. Their patriotic reluctance to help the Germans was compounded by fear for their own safety, especially after Allied fighters began to strafe trains and to set them ablaze by using their external fuel tanks as incendiaries.[69]

While the effects of the two modes of attack on the French rail system were mutually reinforcing, destruction of rail centers contributed most to the overall loss of capacity. The Army Air Forces Evaluation Board, which after the war exhaustively analyzed the records of the *Société Nationale des Chemins de Fer Française*, concluded that attacks on the rail centers, unaccompanied by any other form of attack, would by mid-July have reduced the capacity of the rail system to 43 percent of what it had been on March 1. The destruction of bridges, the strafing of locomotives, and the bombing of tracks would by themselves have reduced overall capacity only to 81 percent of the level of March 1.[70]

Because the Combined Bomber Offensive had defeated the *Luftwaffe* as a daytime fighter force, the Germans had no remedy for the devastating attacks on their communications. Only palliatives remained to them: *OB West* progressively banned nonessential traffic from the rail system to reduce the demands on its dwindling capacity. Efforts at repair

---

68. *Ibid.*, 98–105.

69. *Ibid.* Höffner later recalled, "During the course of this bombing operation, which we followed every day by our reports and on our maps, etc., we kept on saying, 'We couldn't do it any better ourselves'." Rpt, Combined Services Detailed Interrogation Center (CSDIC) (U.K.), "The Effect of Allied Bombing on the Western Front," S.R.M. 1256, Apr 8, 1945, Box 134, Spaatz Papers.

70. AAF Eval Bd/ETO, "Effectiveness of Air Attack Against Rail Transportation in the Battle of France," Jun 1, 1945, 109.

Table 11. Utilization and Repair of Locomotives, March–July 1944

Date	Region					All France
	Ouest	Nord	Est	Sud-Est	Sud-Ouest	
Number of Utilizable Locomotives						
Mar 4	1,806	1,574	1,147	2,732	1,542	8,801
May 20	1,712	830	906	2,647	1,496*	7,591
Jul 15	852	709	901	2,320†	1,131†	5,913
Percent Reduction of Utilizable Locomotives, Mar 4–Jul 15						
	53	55	21	15	27	33
Number of Locomotives Undergoing or Awaiting Repair of Damage Due to Bombing and Strafing‡						
Mar 4	6	10	1	2	4	23
May 20	81	642	173	23	75*	994
Jul 15	673	715	308	289†	336†	2,321

*Figures for May 13; no reports available for May 20.
†Figures for Jul 22; no reports available for Jul 22.
‡Inadequate repair capacity and the concomitant reduction in available motive power were due principally to the cumulative effects of bombing and strafing operations, which damaged locomotives much more rapidly than they could be repaired.
SOURCE: Army Air Forces Evaluation Board in the European Theater of Operations, "The Effectiveness of Air Attack Against Rail Transportation in the Battle of France."

were intensified but hindered by the loss of two of *OB West*'s five railroad repair battalions to the Italian front—one in January, the other in March. Before D-day, 28,000 workers were taken off the construction of the Atlantic Wall and put to work on the railroads.[71]

These measures did not stop the steady erosion of rail capacity. Already stretched taut, the system steadily contracted under Allied bombardment. Logistical consequences were immediate. As early as March, *AOK 7* reported that declining rail capacity had interacted with the shortage of motor transport to produce a situation in which "only the most urgently needed supply goods could be forwarded."[72] The conveyance of fuel and rations particularly suffered, but by D-day *OB West*'s forward

71. Harrison, *Cross-Channel Attack*, 227–28.
72. *Beurteilung der Versorgungslage*, appended to *Kriegstagebuch Armeeoberkommando 7/Oberquartiermeister*, Apr 5, 1944, Roll 1571, T–312, RG 242, NARA.

positions had been stocked with both to prescribed levels. Shortages of some kinds of ammunition, to be sure, persisted, but they owed more to the demands of other fronts and manufacturing problems in Germany than to interdiction. By D-day frontline stocks of ammunition were generally adequate, if not bountiful.[73] The preinvasion interdiction campaign, in short, hindered but did not cripple the supply of *OB West*.

The progressive loss of railway capacity did, however, slow Rommel's fortification of the Atlantic Wall. Even before the air raids began, cement had been in short supply. With the advent of the Transportation Plan, the shortage became acute. The damage to the rail system interfered with both the shipment of coal to the plants where the cement was made and the subsequent delivery of the finished product. By April the whole project had been so slowed by shortages of labor and materials that Rommel concentrated his resources on fortifying the beachfront, abandoning altogether the construction of reserve positions to the rear.[74] The exact contribution of the transportation crisis to the slowing of the hardening of the Atlantic Wall is difficult to assess, but it was doubtless significant. *Heeresgruppe B* reported in late May that while the coastal defenses had been "reinforced by increased construction operations and mining," problems of transport were "having a bad effect on the situation."[75]

The responsibility for devising OVERLORD's tactical interdiction plan fell to Montgomery's 21 Army Group. The final draft, "Delay of the Enemy Reserves," was completed on April 19. It greatly stressed the destruction of bridges and the creation of temporary roadblocks in the tactical area by the bombing of towns through which major arteries passed. To accomplish these purposes, Montgomery was so bold as to claim both strategic air forces in their entireties. Even with air support, the authors of the paper were pessimistic about blocking the advance of German reserves within the area enclosed by the Seine and the Loire—the network of roads within the region seemed too rich for the roadblocks to have more than a temporary effect. They accordingly emphasized destruction of the bridges across the Seine and the Loire. (See *Map 15*) The Royal Air Force, still dubious of the merits of bridge-bombing, immediately attacked the proposal. This debate was soon overtaken by SHAEF's successful insistence upon a like policy. The focus of the dispute about the

---

73. *Ibid.*, May 5, Jun 5, 1944, Roll 1571, T–312, RG 242; Eckstein, "Activity of the *Oberquartiermeister West*," 13, 56.

74. Harrison, *Cross-Channel Attack*, 263–64.

75. AHB/BAM, "Situation Reports by German Army Commanders in Normandy, May 15–October 11, 1944," Translation VII/73, Jul 31, 1948, 512.621, 6.

tactical plan then shifted to the list of twenty-six towns that the 21 Army Group wanted destroyed to create roadblocks.[76]

Leigh-Mallory generally took Montgomery's part, but Tedder, Spaatz, and Doolittle strenuously objected to the bombing of the French towns as both inhumane and ineffectual. Tedder claimed that such efforts had generally failed in Italy, and that the plains of Normandy offered fewer potential blocks than the mountains and defiles of the southern theater. Spaatz predictably objected that the diversion of the bombers from the *Reich* would give a dangerous respite to the *Luftwaffe*. A compromise resulted from a series of meetings held June 3 and 4: Twelve towns, not twenty-six, were to be attacked, their inhabitants warned by leaflets dropped an hour before the destruction began.[77]

Little disagreement surrounded the employment of fighter-bombers, whose effectiveness in suppressing enemy movements on and around the battlefield had been amply demonstrated in Italy. Leigh-Mallory successfully insisted that fighters to the greatest extent possible be used for armed reconnaissance rather than for air cover. The former mission fell primarily to the Thunderbolts and Mustangs of VIII Fighter Command, which in small but numerous formations were ordered to range widely over the battlefield. The tasks of providing air cover and close air support went in the main to IV Fighter Command and Second Tactical Air Force.[78]

The numerical odds that confronted German flyers on D-day were terrible. On June 6 the Allies disposed 3,467 heavy bombers; 1,545 medium, light, and torpedo bombers; and 5,409 fighters. To this overwhelming force, the Germans could on June 6 oppose only 319 aircraft of all types, the *Luftwaffe* having decided not to transfer any large number of aircraft to France before the invasion. By July 7 an additional 1,105 aircraft, nearly all single-engine fighters, had arrived from Germany.[79] But they accomplished little. The beachhead's effective air defenses—flak, barrage balloons, and interceptors—frustrated all attacks. The Germans thereafter used their fighters primarily to protect supply lines and to drive off Allied artillery-spotting planes. They were not ef-

---

76. AHB/BAM, "Liberation of North West Europe," vol 2: "The Administrative Preparations," n.d., 00895754, 179, 182.
77. *Ibid.*, 2:183–84.
78. AHB/BAM, "Liberation of North West Europe," 2:185; AHB/BAM, "The Liberation of North West Europe," vol 3: "The Landings in Normandy," n.d., 00895755, 11–20, 70.
79. AHB/BAM, "Liberation of North West Europe," 3:139; AHB/BAM, "The Normandy Invasion, June 1944," Aug 8, 1944 [prepared by the German Air Historical Branch (*8th Abteilung*)], Translation VII/31, Jun 23, 1947, 512.621.

OMAHA Beach, with Allied aircraft overhead, shows the glut of supply that supported the invasion. The *Luftwaffe* was unable to attack the flow of matériel delivered across the beaches until December 1944.

fective even in these limited roles. The Allies had destroyed most of the airdromes within 130 miles of Caen and many more to a distance of 350 miles, which deprived the reinforcements the fields prepared for their use. This forced German airmen either to stage from makeshift fields in Normandy, which the rains of summer often made unusable, or else to fly from airdromes in central France, unprepared and excessively distant from the coast. The *Luftwaffe* was therefore unable to compensate for its inferior numbers by flying more sorties per aircraft than the Allies.[80]

The few German aircraft present in France on D-day hindered neither the dropping of paratroopers in the first hours of June 6 nor the actual landings around 0630. No enemy craft was seen before late afternoon, when they flew about 100 sorties, mostly by strafing fighters. That night saw about another 175 sorties flown by bombers and torpedo planes. No attack inflicted much damage. The Allied strategic air forces,

---

80. AHB/BAM, "Normandy Invasion"; AHB/BAM, "Some Aspects of the German Fighter Effort During the Initial Stages of the Invasion of North-west Europe," Nov 18, 1944 [a survey written by the Air Historical Branch of the *Luftwaffe*], Translation VII/19, Jan 18, 1947, 512.621.

by contrast, flew 5,309 sorties on D-day in support of the invasion, and Allied tactical air forces flew an additional 5,276.

The staggering number of sorties on June 6 belies a crucial fact: On D-day the Allied air forces stumbled in their primary mission—to block the movement of the German armored divisions nearest the lodgment. June 6 was overcast, and the tactical air forces could not operate effectively before late afternoon, when the skies cleared.

Three *Panzer* divisions were within a day's march of the battlefield. The first was the *21st Panzer Division*. Attached to the reserves of *Heeresgruppe B*, it was stationed near Caen and was the only armored unit in Normandy. Fortunately for the Allies, it was much the weakest of the three, its tanks being captured French or older German models.[81] The other two, *12th SS Panzer* and *Panzer Lehr*, belonged to the reserve of *OB West*. The former, stationed at Evreux, was closest—about ninety miles by road from the landing. *Panzer Lehr* was garrisoned near Nogent-le-Rotrou, about 130 road-miles from the front. Both were very strong divisions.[82]

The *21st Panzer Division* delivered the only serious counterattack on D-day. Reports of airborne landings around 0100 alerted the Germans that Normandy was under attack. But the only armored division in the immediate vicinity received no orders and remained inactive until about 0800 when its commander decided on his own initiative to move against British paratroopers seen along the river Orne. While under way, he received instructions about noon to resist a developing British threat to Caen. The division changed direction quickly but soon discovered that all the bridges across the Orne save one had been destroyed. The need for the entire force to file across a single bridge presented the only impediment to its approach march. There were occasional strafing attacks, but none inflicted much damage. The skies remained leaden, and the tactical air forces were not yet out in strength. The *21st Panzer* attacked the British about 1600. One battalion broke through to the coast, but the rest of the division was forced into defensive positions with heavy losses. But the British drive on Caen had been blunted.[83]

The abortive counterattack of the *21st Panzer Division* underscores two important facts about the events of June 6: The response of the German command was hesitant in the extreme, and Allied tactical air power

81. Maj Gen Edgar Feuchtinger, "History of the *21st Panzer Division* from the Time of Its Formation Until the Beginning of the Invasion," MS B-441, RG 338, 11–12.

82. AAF Eval Bd/ETO, "Effectiveness of Air Attack Against Rail Transportation in the Battle of France," Jun 1, 1945, 122 table 8.

83. Feuchtinger, "History of the *21st Panzer Division*," 20–24; B.H. Liddell Hart, *History of the Second World War* (New York, 1971), 547.

was not a powerful presence on the battlefield before the passage of many hours. Several commanders who might have shown initiative were absent: Rommel was on his way to see Hitler, and General Friedrich Dollman of *AOK 7* was directing an exercise in Brittany. Worst of all, the *Führer* slept late and no one dared wake him. The chief of the operations staff of the *OKW*, Lt. Gen. Alfred Jodl, at 0730 refused von Rundstedt's entreaties for the release of *Panzer Lehr* and *12th SS Panzer*. When Hitler was finally awake he hesitated to commit the reserves of *OB West*, uncertain that Normandy was not a feint for a second landing in the Pas de Calais. Not until about 1600 were there orders to commit *Panzer Lehr* and *12th SS Panzer*.[84]

By then the skies were clear, and a valuable opportunity had been squandered.[85] The commander of *Panzer Lehr*, Maj. Gen. Fritz Bayerlein, urged that the march begin at dusk. But General Dollman of *AOK 7*, to whom *Panzer Lehr* had been subordinated, ordered him on. By dusk *Panzer Lehr* had lost twenty or thirty vehicles. Dollman insisted the march continue throughout the next day. Bombed road junctions slowed the pace, and a damaged bridge had to be repaired before it could bear the weight of tanks. And all the while there were the insistent attacks of the Allied fighters. "By noon it was terrible," Bayerlein recalled. "By the end of the day I had lost forty tank trucks carrying fuel and ninety others. Five of my tanks were knocked out, and eighty-four half-tracks, prime-movers and self-propelled guns." Because of the aerial attacks and damage to roads and bridges, the division averaged ten to twelve kilometers per hour—the usual rate for a road march was twenty-five to thirty. Two whole days were required to negotiate the 209 kilometers (130 miles) to the front; the march should have taken one.[86]

The *12th SS Panzer Division* also suffered what Rommel described as "sustained substantial losses from low-flying aircraft" on its way to the front. Even the time-consuming use of secondary roads was not sufficient to avoid the unwelcome attentions of Allied aircraft late in the day. More time was lost when, on the evening of June 6, the division had to circumvent the bombed town of Falaise, which was in flames and im-

---

84. Hart, *History of the Second World War*, 547; Harrison, *Cross-Channel Attack*, 333.

85. Maj Gen Max Pemsel, "The *Seventh Army* in the Battle of Normandy and the Fighting Up to Avranches (6 June to 29 July, 1944)," MS B-763, RG 338, 107-8.

86. Untitled list of questions put to Maj Gens Fritz Krämer and Fritz Bayerlein, Apr 28, 1948, MS B-814, RG 338; Krämer, "*I SS Pz. Corps* in the West," 20; Bayerlein, quoted in Milton Shulman, *Defeat in the West* (New York, 1948), 107. Planning figure is from Charles von Lüttichau of the U.S. Army's Center for Military History.

A B–26 Marauder over Normandy.

passable. The *12th SS Panzer*, like *Panzer Lehr*, was not committed to action until June 8; even then, elements of both divisions still straggled in.[87]

The most intensive phase of interdiction began with the lodgment in France. The weather was generally good after June 6. The pace of the attacks on marshaling yards and repair facilities slowed somewhat after the landing, but between D-day and July 31 the Allies nonetheless dropped about 35,000 tons of bombs on rail centers during 16,000 sorties. Bridge-bombing was much more emphasized, as there was no longer a need to conceal the site of the invasion. Allied aircraft now attacked the bridges of the Loire as well as those in the "Gap," the flyers' name for the region between the Loire and the Seine. Between June 6 and July 31 they flew 16,000 sorties against bridges large and small, dropping 24,500 tons of bombs.[88] VIII Fighter Command returned to escorting bombers, leaving IX Fighter Command and Second Tactical Air Force to carry on armed reconnaissance. This, too, was pursued massively. It took a heavy toll of German vehicles and, more important, confined resupply and reinforcement to darkness and bad weather. As there were sixteen hours of daylight, the Germans' ability to use their already limited supply of motor transport was cut by about two-thirds. So pervasive was the armed reconnaissance that a German officer observed ruefully that "the effect of Anglo-American air superiority on the Normandy front and as far as Paris is so great that . . . even single vehicles are used only by day in the most extreme emergencies."[89] The savaging of German communi-

87. Memo, Rommel to von Kluge, Jul 3, 1944, in *Rommel Papers*, 483–84; Krämer, "*I SS Pz. Corps* in the West," 10–13.
88. Craven and Cate, ARGUMENT *to V–E Day*, 214.
89. AHB/BAM, "Normandy Invasion," 2.

cations was supplemented by the systematic bombing of German supply centers, the locations of which were generally known from ULTRA. Losses of supplies in these attacks were small, however, because the dumps and depots were well concealed and dispersed.[90]

So comprehensive was Allied interdiction that *AOK 7* had, except for the brief respite on D-day, the greatest difficulty in moving its reserves comparatively short distances to the front. The *275th Infantry Division*, for example, stationed on the southern coast of Brittany (See *Map 13*), received on the morning of June 6 an order to send a battle group to the front. The distance by rail was about 120 miles, and the deployment of *Kampfgruppe Heintz*, as the detachment was known, should have required no more than two days. The force assembled in less than ten hours, but air attacks prevented it from entraining until the next day. Shortly after noon on June 7, five trains began to roll toward Normandy. Within an hour the first had stopped near Avranches because of reports that the line was blocked ahead. As it waited, dive-bombing fighters cut the tracks behind. Once the trouble ahead had cleared, the first train proceeded a few more miles to Folligny, where it was attacked and thoroughly demolished by fighter-bombers. (*Map 16*) All the equipment aboard was destroyed, and casualties were heavy. The second train, meanwhile, had reached Pontorson but was halted there by cut rails. While it waited for repairs, it too was strafed. There were more casualties, and an engineer company lost most of its equipment. Survivors were ordered to proceed on foot.

Aircraft had attacked the remaining trains by 1800; none had reached Rennes. Because all the lines between Rennes and Dol had been cut, a detour had to be arranged. It was then learned that the detour had been cut in *nineteen* places. On June 8, seven trains carrying the bulk of *Kampfgruppe Heintz* lay immobilized south of Rennes. Aerial attacks repeatedly frustrated attempts to load the divisional artillery onto two other trains. The last train did not get under way until late in the evening of June 8. As all the routes north of Rennes were still obstructed, a detour through Fougères was arranged, but on June 9 this line was also cut. At this point, the transportation officers bowed to the inevitable and ordered *Kampfgruppe Heintz* to proceed to the front on foot. Most of the unit had moved no more than thirty miles in two days and three nights. The road march to the front consumed another three to five days.[91]

---

90. Bennett, ULTRA *in the West*, 69; Eckstein, "Activity of the *Oberquartiermeister West*," 18.

91. Harrison, *Cross-Channel Attack*, 378–79.

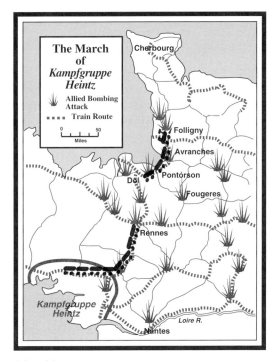

Map 16.

The ordeal of *Kampfgruppe Heintz* was not exceptional. Another of the divisions that *AOK 7* shifted into Normandy, the *3d Parachute*, required six days to reach Normandy from Brittany, a distance by road of about 150 miles. "By the time it arrived," Rommel wrote, "the attack it was due to launch on Bayeux was no longer possible, as strong enemy forces had already taken possession of the Forest of Cerisy."[92] The *77th Infantry Division*, stationed at St.-Malo and therefore much closer to the fighting than was the *3d Parachute*, also needed six days to reach the front in force.[93] (See *Map 13*).

By June 18, *AOK 7* had been reinforced by only *five* divisions. According to the mobilization plan of *OB West*, it should have received *seventeen* within several days of the Allied landing. Besides *Panzer Lehr* and *12th SS Panzer*, the five reinforcements included *2d Panzer* (June 13),

---

92. Memo, Rommel to von Kluge, Jul 3, 1944; AAF Eval Bd/ETO, "Effectiveness of Air Attack Against Rail Transportation in the Battle of France," Jun 1, 1945, 122 table 8.
93. AAF Eval Bd/ETO, "Effectiveness of Air Attack Against Rail Transportation in the Battle of France," Jun 1, 1945, 122 table 8; Memo, Rommel to von Kluge, Jul 3, 1944.

17th SS Panzer Grenadier (June 13), and *1st SS Panzer* (June 18).[94] All were fully motorized armored divisions; all were harassed from the air and forced to use circuitous routes that about doubled the time of their journeys.[95] The infantry divisions that should have reinforced *AOK 7* suffered delays of absurd lengths. As they lacked organic transport, the ruined state of the railroads forced them to reach Normandy on foot.[96] On June 18 it was evident, if it was not before, that the Allies were going to win the race for reinforcement. On that day the Allies had twenty divisions ashore. Opposing them were elements of eighteen German divisions, which had the strength of perhaps fourteen full divisions.[97] The odds against the Germans grew steadily worse because their communications remained precarious. *II SS Panzer Corps* (*9th* and *10th SS Panzer Divisions*) reached the front in late June, having been redeployed from Poland. The corps took longer to reach Normandy from its points of detrainment near Nancy than it had to reach Nancy from Poland. Only the tanks reached Paris by rail: Railroad congestion in the French capital caused by destroyed rail centers and downed bridges on the Seine forced the men to detrain at Nancy, about 175 miles east of Paris, and walk to the front.[98] By July 4 the Allies had landed 929,000 men, 586,000 tons of supplies, and 177,000 vehicles.[99] The day before, Rommel had written that all the reserves had "arrived far too late to smash the enemy landing by counterattacks. By the time they arrived the enemy had disembarked considerably stronger forces and himself gone over to the attack. . . ."[100]

---

94. Pemsel, "*Seventh Army* in the Battle of Normandy," 122. After the war, von Rundstedt recalled that after the first few days of fighting he lost all hope of victory: "The Allied Air Forces paralyzed all movement by day, and made it very difficult even at night. They had smashed the bridges over the Seine, shutting off the whole area. These factors greatly delayed the concentration of reserves there—they took three or four times longer to reach the front than we had reckoned." Basil H. Liddell Hart, *The German Generals Talk* (New York, 1948), 243–44.

95. Maj Gen Heinrich *Freiherr* von Lüttwitz, "Commitment of the *2d Panzer Division* in Normandy," MS B–257, RG 338; General Kurt Hallwachs, "*17 Panzer Grenadier Division 'Goetz von Berlichingen,' bis September 1944*," MS P–165, RG 338, 3; Harrison, *Cross-Channel Attack*, 349; James J. Weingartner, *Hitler's Guard: The Story of the Leibstandarte Adolf Hitler, 1933–1945* (Carbondale, Ill., 1974), 97, 120; AAF Eval Bd/ETO, "Effectiveness of Air Attack Against Rail Transportation in the Battle of France," Jun 1, 1945, 120.

96. Enemy Objectives Unit (EOU), "Amendment to Movement of German Divisions into the Lodgement Area, OVERLORD, D to D+50," Oct 3, 1944, 142.0422-14.

97. Wilmot, *Struggle for Europe*, 319.

98. General Wilhelm Bittrich, "Report on the Invasion Battles in Normandy (19 June to 24 July, 1944)," MS B–747, RG 338, 4.

99. Harrison, *Cross-Channel Attack*, 447.

100. Memo, Rommel to von Kluge, Jul 3, 1944.

The Army Air Forces Evaluation Board analyzed exhaustively the reasons for the excruciating slowness of the German buildup. It found that the destruction of rail centers had reduced the speed of troop trains to less than a third of normal; troop trains east of the French border traveled 200 miles a day, but only 60 once they crossed it. Because of the destruction of the Seine bridges, troop trains from the *Reich* and the Low Countries could not proceed directly to Normandy; they had to be funneled through Paris to the south. This lengthened their journeys and compounded the preexisting delay and congestion wrought by the Transportation Plan. The chaos in *Région Nord* was serious, but worse for the Germans was their inability to use the railroads of *Région Ouest*, which comprised Normandy and Brittany. As the experience of *Kampfgruppe Heintz* showed, only the most halting traffic was possible within the area enclosed by the Seine and the Loire. The Allies never succeeded in closing all the bridges across the Loire, which the Germans regarded as more important than those over the Seine.[101] Most were constructed of masonry and proved more resistant to bombs than the steel structures of the Seine. This was also true, in lesser degree, of the bridges in the Gap.[102] But this availed the Germans little. For even when these bridges were open, the omnipresent danger of strafing fighter-bombers usually forced divisions to detrain on the eastern bank of the river, whence they marched the remaining 100 miles to the front—at night. The short nights

---

101. The transport officer for *OB West* recalled, "The LOIRE bridges were the more important, for the LOIRE bridges at TOURS seriously interfered with out traffic towards the front, whereas the SEINE bridges interrupted movements to the flank." CSDIC (U.K.) Rpt, "Effect of Allied Bombing on the Western Front," S.R.M. 1256, Apr 8, 1945, Box 134, Spaatz Papers.

102. The Army Air Forces Evaluation Board used the concept of "route days" to describe the effectiveness of bridge attacks during the seventy days after D-day. There were, for example, four routes across the Seine that the Germans could have used for their buildup in Normandy. A day on which all four of these routes were open counted as four route-days. Calculated in this fashion, the bridges of the Seine were closed for 265 of a possible 280 route-days, or 94 percent of the time. Attacks against the six major routes in the Gap were markedly less successful. Between D-day and August 15, bridges in the Gap were closed for only 236 of 420 route-days, or 56 percent of the time. Ten bridges across the Loire served an equal number of routes. They were closed for 594 of 700 possible route-days, yielding a success rate of 85 percent. This figure is misleading, however. The Germans were principally concerned to keep open the three double-track bridges at Tours. Between D-day and August 5, when the Germans abandoned their attempts at repair, all three bridges were closed simultaneously for twenty-four of the sixty days compared, so that after D-day the Germans were able to send trains across the Loire on three days of five. The masonry bridges were easier to repair because their spans were shorter and their massive piers resisted total destruction even when hit directly. AAF Eval Bd/ETO, "Effectiveness of Air Attack Against Rail Transportation in the Battle of France," Jun 1, 1945, 41, 44.

of summer, together with the inevitable inefficiencies of movement in the dark, reduced the rate of travel to about 25 percent of normal for those units fortunate enough to have or to find motor transport. Within *Région Ouest* vehicular columns were rarely able to cover more than thirty miles a day, barely more than twice the rate achieved by those divisions—the majority—that had to proceed wholly on foot.[103]

Allied air supremacy inevitably had a serious effect on German supply. As early as June 10 Rommel reported that "every traffic defile in the rear areas is under continual attack and it is very difficult to get essential supplies of ammunition and petrol up to the troops."[104] The problems that confronted the Germans in France were essentially the same as those they had faced in Italy during DIADEM. The creation of a "railroad desert" in *Région Ouest* drove back their railheads, greatly increasing the distance to be bridged with motor transport. The destruction of road bridges over the Seine in particular lengthened the supply routes. Allied fighters, by denying the Germans use of the roads by day, effectively reduced their motor transport space by two-thirds or more.[105] Even with travel restricted to night and dusk, the loss of vehicles to aerial attacks was heavy. The artillery commander of the *I SS Panzer Corps* testified that losses occasionally reached 60 to 80 percent of the trucks in a convoy.[106] Urgent tactical movements could only be made at the expense of supply, or vice versa.[107]

Because of the demands of other fronts and the state of German industry, *OB West* began the battle with stocks of fuel and ammunition that would have been adequate only if communications with the *Reich* had remained unimpaired. But they did not, and the logistical position of the defenders of Normandy was from the first catastrophic.[108] On June

---

103. *Ibid.*, 117–19.

104. Appreciation by Rommel, Jun 10, 1944, in *Rommel Papers*, 474.

105. See, for example, Pemsel, "*Seventh Army* in the Battle of Normandy," 146; and Eckstein, "Activity of the *Oberquartiermeister West*," 54–60. The transport officer for OB West, Col Hans Höffner, stated to his interrogators that no more than thirty supply trains entered the area enclosed by the Seine and the Loire between D-day and the end of July. The Germans brought daily into this area about 1,900 tons of supplies—1,200 tons by truck, 700 tons by barge. Whether barge transport was affected by Allied tactical aviation as seriously as motor transport was is nowhere stated, but it is reasonable to suppose that it was. In any event, supplies carried by barge would usually have to make the last part of their journey by truck. AAF Eval Bd/ETO, "Effectiveness of Air Attack Against Rail Transportation in the Battle of France," Jun 1, 1945, 141.

106. Maj Gen Walter Staudinger, "*I SS Panzer Corps* Artillery (6 June to 30 July 1944)," MS B-832, RG 338, 12.

107. See, for example, AHB/BAM, "Telephone Log of the German *Seventh Army* from June 6 to June 30, 1944," 2245 hrs, Jun 15, 1944, Translation VII/70, 512.621.

108. Eckstein, Activity of the *Oberquartiermeister West*, 50.

14 the *Oberquartiermeister* of *AOK 7* reported that the army needed daily receipts of 1,500 cubic meters of fuel and 1,000 tons of ammunition; actual receipts were, respectively, 200 cubic meters and 100 tons.[109] On June 21 he told army headquarters that he could cover only a fifth of the units' ammunition requirements.[110] As serious as the Germans' plight had been in Italy, it appears that no position was lost for want of ammunition. In Normandy, however, soldiers of *AOK 7* had to yield Carentan to the American V Corps on June 12 because they completely exhausted their ammunition.[111] On June 20 *OB West* was unable to carry out an order from the *OKW* to counterattack the Americans near Balleroy: Not only had some of the divisions supposed to participate failed to reach the field, but the artillery lacked sufficient ammunition to permit even defensive operations.[112] The same day *AOK 7* reported that two detachments of heavy artillery had no ammunition at all; on June 21 several batteries were withdrawn for the same reason.[113] On June 26 *AOK 7* complained that of its 348 medium howitzers, only eighteen had ever had as many as eighteen rounds on hand at any time during the fighting; properly supplied, each would have fired several hundred rounds a day.[114]

The problems with fuel were as great. On June 10 detachments of the *3d Parachute* and the *17th SS Panzer Grenadier Divisions* ran out of fuel on their approach marches.[115] When *II SS Panzer Corps* finally reached the field, it could not employ all of its tanks in an attack of June 29 because it lacked sufficient fuel.[116] The effects of interdiction were magnified by the general lack of foresight that characterized so much German planning for the invasion. The Germans were plagued throughout the fighting by the shortage of small fuel tanks throughout France. They therefore had to rely on a small number of large facilities both vulnerable to aerial attack and distant from the tactical area. Throughout four years of occupation nothing had been done to rectify this.[117] Similarly, the artillery commander of the *I SS Panzer Corps*, whose vulnerable supply lines forced him to restrict concentrations on

---

109. HERO, "Tactical Air Interdiction by U.S. Army Air Forces in World War II: France," ch 4, 44.
110. AHB/BAM, "Telephone Log of the German *Seventh Army*," 1030 hrs, Jun 21, 1944.
111. *Ibid.*, 1040 hrs, Jun 12, 1944.
112. Harrison, *Cross-Channel Attack*, 442–43.
113. AHB/BAM, "Telephone Log of the German *Seventh Army*," 1400 hrs, Jun 20, 1944; Pemsel, "*Seventh Army* in the Battle of Normandy," 146.
114. Pemsel, "*Seventh Army* in the Battle of Normandy," 146.
115. AHB/BAM, "Telephone Log of the German *Seventh Army*," 1100 hrs, 1245 hrs, Jun 10, 1944.
116. *Ibid.*, 1340 hrs, Jun 29, 1944. See also *ibid.*, 0900 hrs, Jun 15, 1944.
117. Eckstein, "Activity of the *Oberquartiermeister West*," 17–18.

even the most promising targets to a single minute, found to his amazement that Normandy was honeycombed with abandoned mineshafts in which fuel and ammunition could have been safely stored—but had not.[118]

The Allied air forces were on balance highly successful during OVER-LORD in executing the mission of interdiction assigned to them. The principal task had been to assure that the Anglo-American buildup in Normandy proceeded faster than the opposing concentration of German divisions. This was achieved, and *OB West*'s mobilization plan was reduced to a shambles. The Allied air forces, with some assistance from the French underground, devastated the railroads upon which the Germans depended to move the unmotorized majority of their divisions.[119] Destruction of the railroads, with the constant threat of Allied fighters to motor transport, thoroughly disrupted German supply. "Supply difficulties during the invasion," wrote Hans Speidel, the chief of staff of *Heeresgruppe B*, "were insurmountable." The fighter bombers "paralyzed all movement by day and inflicted heavy losses."[120] The successes of Allied airmen were particularly important because stubborn German resistance soon fought the invaders to a standstill. Before the American First Army broke through the German lines at Avranches on the last day of July during Operation COBRA, all Allied gains were incremental. Caen, which Montgomery was to have taken on D-day, did not fall until July 9. OVERLORD, as B.H. Liddell Hart has written, "was an operation that eventually 'went according to plan' but not according to timetable."[121] Penned up for nearly two months within a small lodgment, the Allied armies were potentially more vulnerable to counterattack than COS-SAC's planners had feared. But the danger of expulsion from the lodgment never materialized because the Germans could not execute their scheduled concentration.

The record was not unmixed. The greatest worry of the Allied planners had been an early attack by German armored formations before the beachhead had been consolidated. The lack of early onslaught can be at-

---

118. Staudinger, "*I SS Panzer Corps* Artillery," 10–11.

119. For the contribution of the underground, see Harrison, *Cross-Channel Attack*, 204, 408–10.

120. Hans Speidel, *We Defended Normandy* (London, 1948), 62.

121. Liddell Hart, *History of the Second World War*, 543; Speidel, *We Defended Normandy*, 62; British Air Ministry, *The Rise and Fall of the German Air Force (1933–1945)* (London, 1948), 330–31; General Dwight D. Eisenhower, *Report by the Supreme Commander to the Combined Chiefs of Staff on the Operations in Europe of the Allied Expeditionary Force, 6 June 1944 to 8 May 1945* (Washington, n.d.), 20; AHB/BAM, "Normandy Invasion."

Generals Arnold and Bradley share a moment after the success of OVERLORD.
National Archives.

tributed less to Allied interdiction than to German muddle. Had the decisive Rommel with his direct line to Hitler been in France, *Panzer Lehr* and *12th SS Panzer* might have been ordered to the front in the early hours of June 6. In the murk that prevailed for much of the day they might well have reached the front in time and in sufficient strength to have delivered a concerted counterattack with *21st Panzer* on June 6 or, more probably, on the morning of June 7. The eminent Liddell Hart believed that the early arrival of the two powerful armored divisions might well have spelled disaster for the Allies.[122] We should then remember OVERLORD as interdiction's greatest failure.

---

122. Liddell Hart, *History of the Second World War*, 548. *12th SS Panzer* was alerted and was on the road even before the Allies landed. This was upon von Rundstedt's initiative. But the *OKW* soon halted the division. It remained stalled at Lisieux until around 1600 hrs when both it and *Panzer Lehr* were ordered to the front. There seems little reason to doubt that *12th SS Panzer* could have reached the lodgment area before evening on D-day. *Panzer Lehr*, had it left its cantonment in the early morning of D-day, should have been able to reach the front that night. Harrison, *Cross-Channel Attack*, 333.

As it happened, there is no cause to dispute the judgment of *OB West*'s chief of staff that "it was the mastery the Allies had in the air that was responsible for the most serious consequences in all spheres."[123] Allied air supremacy turned the dependence of the Germans upon railroads, the most channelized and easily disrupted of all means of transport, into a fatal liability. The Allies, when saddled with the wreckage of the railroads they had themselves destroyed, showed that motor transport could in large measure replace railroads, albeit at a cost that one American official historian pronounced "terrible."[124] But Hitler had begun his war without the foresight to build Germany's automotive industry to anything like the size required to equip a modern army.[125] Many of the other weaknesses from which the Germans suffered in Normandy were also self-inflicted: Indecision and divided command precluded effective employment of the armored divisions. The Germans failed to heed the lessons of Italy, where all the techniques of Allied interdiction had been amply demonstrated, and they had done astonishingly little during the long occupation of France to prepare for the day of reckoning.

The success of interdiction in Normandy has never been seriously questioned. The only real controversy has concerned the Transportation Plan. Many have argued that an earlier adoption of bridge-bombing would have obviated the need for attacks on rail centers, sparing bombs and aircraft for the Oil Plan.[126] In essence, this critique is a restatement of the argument from "surplus capacity" made by Zuckerman's critics before D-day. SHAEF's G-2 Section estimated that the Germans would need 175 trains weekly to effect their concentration in Normandy and to supply it. A greater number of trains passed the second line of interdiction throughout the summer. But after the bombing of the bridges of the Seine and the Loire began, the number of trains crossing the first line of interdiction fell to a mere trickle. (*Table 12*) This might seem to suggest that the Transportation Plan failed.[127] But it does not. The routes across the Loire, and also those of the Gap between the Seine and the Loire, were open more than they were closed. What prevented the Germans from exploiting the relatively ineffective attack of the Allied air forces against these bridges was the strafing of the fighter-bombers. And armed

123. Maj Gen Günther Blumentritt, "Normandy, 6 June–24 July, 1944," MS B-248, RG 338, 26.

124. Roland G. Ruppenthal, *Logistical Support of the Armies, May 1941–September 1944* [U.S. Army in World War II: The European Theater of Operations] (Washington, 1953), 571.

125. *Ibid.*, 143–45.

126. See, for example, Rostow, *Pre-Invasion Bombing Strategy*, 72–87.

127. AAF Eval Bd/ETO, "Effectiveness of Air Attack Against Rail Transportation in the Battle of France," Jun 1, 1945, 8.

Table 12. Trains Crossing the First Two Lines of Interdiction, March–August 1944

Week Ending	Number of Trains Crossing the:						
	First Line of Interdiction (Toward the Tactical Area)				Second Line of Interdiction (From the North and East)		
	Seine	Gap	Loire	Total	North	East	Total
Mar 31	213	441	344	998	—	—	—
Apr 7	243	482	391	1,116	721	417	1,138
Apr 14	208	477	310	995	619	406	1,025
Apr 21	141	469	312	922	633	385	1,018
Apr 28	134	392	275	801	528	284	812
May 5	155	275	319	749	461	252	713
May 12	86	303	357	746	451	267	718
May 19	64	398	346	788	381	293	674
May 26	50	343	236	629	386	243	629
Jun 2	8	256	202	466	256	225	481
Jun 9	—	66	135	201	199	240	439
Jun 16	—	4	14	18	175	270	445
Jun 23	—	—	22	22	145	251	396
Jun 30	—	—	29	29	117	108	225
Jul 7	—	—	68	68	176	140	316
Jul 14	—	7	27	34	191	190	381
Jul 21	—	9	15	24	173	136	309
Jul 28	—	9	30	39	189	203	392
Aug 4	1	17	33	51	215	168	383
Aug 11	—	12	—	12	145	78	223

SOURCE: Army Air Forces Evaluation Board in the European Theater of Operations, "The Effectiveness of Air Attack Against Rail Transportation in the Battle of France."

reconnaissance was as much a part of the Transportation Plan as it was of the rival design.

The critics of the Transportation Plan, moreover, have framed the issue too narrowly. The basic question was never the Transportation Plan versus the Oil Plan, or even the Transportation Plan versus the Oil Plan plus a French STRANGLE. It was rather the Transportation Plan versus the deception of FORTITUDE. For any program of bridge-bombing sufficient to disrupt German preparations in Normandy to the extent that Zuckerman's design did would have had to include the bridges of the Loire; and that, as the reaction to the experimental bombing of the Seine bridges on May 7 shows, might well have caused the Germans to abandon their confidence that the Pas de Calais was the Allied objective. The success of FORTITUDE was one of the truly indispensable conditions of Allied victory; even an equal allocation of resources between *AOKs* 7 and *15* might have spelled disaster for OVERLORD.

Section II

The Korean War

American Tactical Aviation After World War II

The position that interdiction occupied in the thinking of the American airmen at the end of World War II was paradoxical. On the one hand, interdiction stood on a pinnacle of accomplishment; on the other, many officers doubted that tactical aviation had much of a future. The paradox was concisely expressed in August 1945 by Maj. Gen. Lauris Norstad, one of the executors of Operation STRANGLE and then Assistant Chief of the Air Staff, Plans. The tactical air force, Norstad observed, had been "one of the greatest developments" of World War II, but he added that the atomic bomb might have made tactical forces "as old-fashioned as the Maginot line."[1]

Such doubts did not subvert established doctrine; neither interdiction nor any other kind of tactical operation was repudiated. A thoroughly revised Field Manual 31–35, *Air–Ground Operations*, published in August 1946, incorporated the lessons of World War II and proved a generally adequate guide in the Korean War.[2] Several factors nonetheless worked to reduce the size and capability of the tactical forces. One was that the U.S. Army Air Forces (which upon attaining independence from the Army in September 1947 became the U.S. Air Force) shrank dramatically under budgetary pressures in the postwar years. The U.S. Army Air Forces had planned for a postwar establishment of seventy groups; the U.S. Air Force wound up with forty-eight. Another major consideration was that, as Chiefs of Staff Carl A. Spaatz and Hoyt S. Vandenberg emphasized, the overriding responsibility of the postwar air service was to develop an intercontinental bomber force capable of delivering atomic weapons. The rather distant second responsibility was to prepare to defend the United States from such attack.[3] Tactical forces could only suffer in this climate. "If, at any time, it appears that expenditures for tactical aviation will jeopardize developments in strategic," one staff officer

---

1. Robert Frank Futrell, *Ideas, Concepts, Doctrine: A History of Basic Thinking in the United States Air Force, 1907–1964* (Maxwell AFB, 1971), 90.
2. Robert T. Finney, "The Development of Tactical Air Doctrine in the U.S. Air Force, 1917–1935" (Maxwell AFB, 1952), K110.7017-2, 45.
3. Futrell, *Ideas, Concepts, Doctrine*, 108–9, 125–26.

wrote in 1948, "the former will have to be sacrificed." The Director of Plans for the Tactical Air Command, Col. William M. Momyer, explained the strategic rationale for this position: The Tactical Air Command would enter combat only if the atomic offensive against the enemy failed, leaving the war to be decided as World War II had been. Momyer doubted an all-out atomic attack would fail to defeat the enemy. But if perchance it did, he estimated that conventional warfare on a large scale would begin no sooner than two years after the commencement of hostilities—time enough, presumably, to reconstitute the tactical forces.[4]

The effects of financial stringency on the tactical forces and the supremacy of the strategic mission were exacerbated by yet another development—the Air Force's conversion to jet-powered fighters and bombers. The new aircraft were considerably more expensive than their piston-engined predecessors. The flyaway costs of the P–47 and the P–51 in 1945 were, respectively, about $83,000 and $51,000. The approximate flyaway costs in 1949 of the F–80C and the F–84, the jet aircraft most widely used for interdiction in Korea, were $93,000 and $212,000.[5] This meant, given the budgetary constraints, that the jets would be fewer than the aircraft they replaced. When the Korean War began in June 1950, the U.S. Air Force possessed 957 F–80s and 323 F–84s. These 1,280 aircraft constituted the entire force of fighter-bombers on active service. (Several hundred F–51s, as the P–51 Mustang had been redesignated, still existed in storage.) In January 1946 the Army Air Forces had had on hand 1,235 P–38s, 4,322 P–47s, 4,616 P–51s, and 288 of the new P–80s, a total of more than 10,000 fighter-bombers. The decline of the tactical bomber force had been nearly as dramatic. In January 1946 the Army Air Forces had a total of 3,353 medium bombers (B–25s and B–26s) and 2,343 light bombers (A–20s, A–26s, and A–36s). In June 1950 the entire tactical bomber force consisted of 762 A–26s, redesignated the B–26 Invader after the original B–26 Marauder was phased out.[6]

The decline of the size of the tactical force was to have important consequences in Korea. At no time after the Chinese entered the war was the number of tactical aircraft available to the U.S. Air Force in Korea adequate for the coordinate responsibilities of air superiority, interdiction, and close air support. The numerical insufficiency of this force was not apparent as long as North Korea was the only enemy. The U.S. Air

4. *Ibid.*, 123.

5. Marcelle Size Knaack, *Encyclopedia of U.S. Air Force Aircraft and Missile Systems*, vol 1: *Post–World War II Fighters, 1945–1973* (Washington, 1978), 10, 31, 303, 305.

6. *Army Air Forces Statistical Digest: 1946* (Washington, 1947), 123; *United States Air Force Statistical Digest: January 1949–June 1950* (Washington, 1951), 179–89.

Force's effective attacks on North Korean communications during the first months of the Korean War were a kind of Indian summer for aerial interdiction. The onslaught recapitulated on a smaller scale the formula that had worked so well in Europe: relentless attacks on fragile lines of communication in an environment of unchallenged air supremacy. But when China entered the war, the effectiveness of interdiction declined precipitously. There were, to be sure, temporary successes when, as during the Chinese spring offensive of 1951, the enemy's consumption escalated sharply. More often, however, some combination of low force levels, action by the Chinese Air Force, effective antiaircraft defenses, low consumption, and flexible and redundant communications thwarted interdiction operations.

Chapter 8

---◆---

The Pusan Perimeter
August 3–September 23, 1950

The hasty dispatch of American divisions to South Korea after the North Korean invasion of June 1950 nearly led to one of the greatest military disasters in the history of the United States. The ill-prepared Americans and their South Korean allies were quickly pushed all the way back to the southern tip of the Korean peninsula, where they were besieged around the port city of Pusan. The evidence for the effect of American air power on North Korean operations is not extensive. But what evidence is available in the form of captured documents and interrogation reports suggests at the very least interdiction seriously hindered the reinforcement and resupply of the North Korean Army during the siege of Pusan. The conditions that permitted the U.S. Air Force to hamper North Korean operations resembled those which had facilitated operations against the Germans in the last half of World War II: The interdictor benefited from air supremacy, while the interdicted suffered from a dependence on vulnerable railroads and an inadequate stock of motor transport. The North Koreans' logistical plight was made worse by a level of consumption that, while slight compared to that of the Germans in the world war, was high in relation to their means.

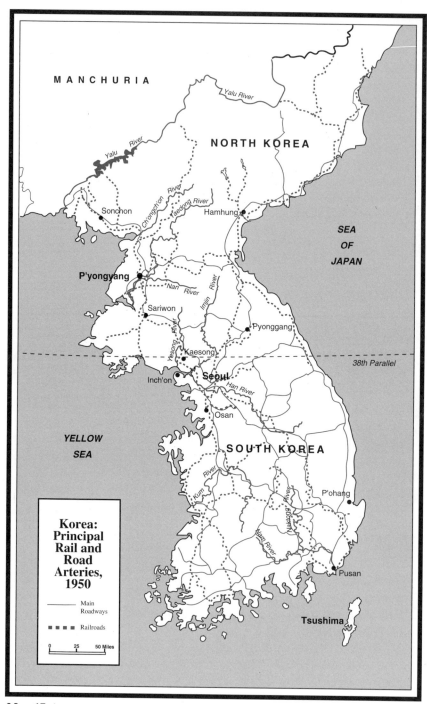

MANCHURIA

Yalu River

NORTH KOREA

Yalu River

Sonchon

Chongch'on River

Taedong River

Hamhung

SEA
OF
JAPAN

P'yongyang

Nan River

Imjin River

Sariwon

Pyonggang

Yesong River

Kaesong

38th Parallel

Inch'on

Seoul

Han River

Osan

YELLOW
SEA

SOUTH KOREA

River

Kum

River

Naktong

P'ohang

Nan River

Korea:
Principal
Rail and
Road
Arteries,
1950

Pusan

Main
Roadways

Railroads

Tsushima

0   25   50 Miles

Map 17.

The origins of the Korean War are ultimately to be found in Japan's victories over China (1894–1895) and Russia (1904–1905), which led to her annexation of the Hermit Kingdom in 1910. During the Second World War the Allies decreed that Korea should again be independent. In August 1945, American and Soviet forces jointly accepted the surrender of the Japanese in Korea. The two victorious powers soon after agreed upon the 38th Parallel as a temporary line of demarcation between their zones of occupation until they had decided how to fulfill their wartime pledge to the Koreans. After two years of fruitless negotiations with the Soviets, the United States referred the question to the United Nations. In 1947 the international organization created the United Nations Temporary Commission on Korea to supervise elections throughout the divided country. The USSR, however, declined to cooperate, and elections were held only in the American zone. They resulted in the establishment of the Republic of Korea (ROK), which the United Nations duly recognized. The first president was Syngman Rhee, an elderly nationalist leader, who assumed office in 1948 and established his government in Seoul, Korea's traditional capital.

The Soviets, meanwhile, had established a client state in the north, the Democratic People's Republic of Korea, which had its capital at P'yongyang. In 1948 the USSR announced the withdrawal of its forces from Korea, although Soviet advisers actually remained behind in large numbers to assist in the formation of a North Korean Army. The United States followed suit in 1949, leaving behind an advisory group of about 500 men to advise the fledgling South Korean Army. Throughout 1949 and 1950 there was a constant state of tension along the 38th Parallel, as each Korean government staged raids against the other. The North Koreans were more active, or at least more adept, at this activity, and a substantial guerrilla movement existed under their direction in the south.

Both governments claimed to be the only legitimate Korean government, and each threatened the use of force to achieve unification. One consequence of this was that the United States withheld armor, heavy artillery, and aircraft from the South Korean Army, for fear that Syngman Rhee would seek to make good his claims.

By the spring of 1950 the South Korean Army numbered 98,000 men organized into eight divisions and support units. Barely a year old, it was in no respect combat-ready, for it lacked not only heavy weapons but reserves. Quite different was the North Korean Army, a force of 135,000 organized into ten divisions, support units, and a tank brigade equipped with approximately 120 of the excellent Soviet T–34 tanks. About 25,000 North Korean soldiers were veterans of the Chinese civil war; a lesser number had fought with the Soviet Army in World War II. The North Koreans also had a small air force of less than 200 combat aircraft. All were obsolescent, propeller-driven aircraft of Soviet manufacture.[1]

It appears to have been the fixed purpose of the North Korean leader, Kim Il Sung, to conquer the south. Early in 1950 he persuaded the Soviet dictator, Joseph Stalin, to accede to his plan. Kim reportedly argued that he could overrun South Korea too quickly for the United States to intervene. Stalin, however, was sufficiently cautious to withdraw Soviet advisers from North Korean combat units. The invasion of the south began at first light on June 25, 1950. The thrust is usually described as a complete surprise. This, however, is not quite true. As the Central Intelligence Agency was still in its infancy, and in any event effectively banned from the area controlled by General of the Army Douglas MacArthur's Far East Command (FEC), the U.S. Air Force had organized an intelligence service of its own through its Office of Special Investigations (OSI). The 6006th Air Intelligence Squadron, commanded by Chief Warrant Officer John Nichols, controlled a network of agents that extended into North Korea. One of them provided advance warning of the impending attack, which Nichols passed up through channels. But the information was ignored, in all probability because of the many false war scares of the preceding two years.[2]

---

1. For the general diplomatic and military background, see Roy E. Appleman, *South to the Naktong, North to the Yalu (June–December 1950)* [U.S. Army in the Korean War] (Washington, 1961), 1–18; Joseph C. Goulden, *Korea: The Untold Story of the War* (New York, 1982), 3–41; and William Whitney Stueck, Jr., *The Road to Confrontation: American Policy Toward China and Korea, 1947–1950* (Chapel Hill, 1981), 1–175. For the South Korean Air Force, see Robert F. Futrell, *The United States Air Force in Korea: 1950–1953*, rev ed (Washington, 1983), 98.

2. See, for example, General Earle E. Partridge's foreword to Nichols's privately published memoir, *How Many Times Can I Die?* (Brooksville, Fla., 1982), 4–6. (Nichols later attained the rank of major.) See also intvw, Lt Col John Rey-

Jumping off from staging areas near Yongch'on, the North Korean Army crossed the 38th Parallel in two columns; their axes of advance converged on Seoul. The four South Korean divisions on the border were quickly swept aside. The South Korean capital, less than forty miles from the border, fell before the ROK's other divisions, which had been fighting guerrillas in the mountains of the southeast, could be brought north. On June 25 the Security Council of the United Nations, in response to an American initiative, called upon member states to help the South Koreans. Two days later, President Harry S. Truman announced that American air and naval forces would aid South Korea. All hopes that it would be unnecessary to commit the U.S. Army were dashed on June 28 when MacArthur visited Seoul and found the South Koreans in headlong retreat, too demoralized to resist even with American air support. On June 30 President Truman ordered him to commit American troops from the force of occupation in Japan. The U.S. Eighth Army, commanded by Lt. Gen. Walton F. Walker, was ill-prepared for this fateful step. It consisted of four understrength and poorly trained divisions, spoiled by an easeful occupation. Much of their basic equipment was missing; the rest was mostly war-weary.

The first division sent to Korea was the 24th Infantry Division, commanded by Maj. Gen. William F. Dean. Two of the remaining divisions, the 25th Infantry and the 1st Cavalry, were alerted for imminent departure. MacArthur had hoped that what he called an "arrogant display of strength" would overawe the North Koreans. This hope soon proved groundless. Because the FEC was short of transport, the 24th Division arrived in Korea piecemeal. Its orders were to fight a series of delaying actions in order to buy time for the organization of stronger resistance in the lower reaches of the Korean republic. Task Force Smith, an understrength infantry battalion with an attached artillery battery, met the advancing North Koreans at Osan on July 4; it resisted for seven hours until its ammunition was exhausted. This action showed that the 2.75-inch rocket launchers with which the troops were armed could not penetrate the armor of the North Korean T-34s. The credible performance of Task Force Smith was not equaled by other units of the 24th Division that met the North Koreans. With little or no support from their South Korean allies, they fled as soon as they had been flanked. With what remained of his division Dean attempted to organize the defense of Taejon. After a bitter fight of five days, the division began a disorderly exodus from the city on July 20. Dean was captured after having fought bravely in the

nolds, Maj Robert S. Bartanowicz, and Capt Phillip S. Meilinger, USAF Academy, with General Earle E. Partridge, Feb 16, 1977, K239.0512.1111, 62-65. For Kim's talks with Stalin, see Stueck, *Road to Confrontation,* 161.

streets as a common soldier. The 25th Infantry and 1st Cavalry Divisions had meanwhile disembarked in southeastern Korea.

The North Koreans were now advancing on a broad front. Their ultimate objective was Pusan, the only port in the as yet unconquered part of South Korea capable of sustaining the American expeditionary force. Their progress was somewhat delayed, however, by diversions to capture smaller ports on the western coast of Korea. The North Korean command had apparently decided that some supply by sea was necessary to augment what could be carried over the poorly developed roads and rail lines of the south. This was fortunate, as an all-out lunge for Pusan might well have succeeded and rapidly brought the war to a victorious conclusion for the invaders. The delay gave General Walker the opportunity to organize a perimeter around the all-important logistical base of Pusan. The Pusan Perimeter was a roughly rectangular area that measured about 100 miles north to south, and roughly 50 east to west. The Naktong River formed the western boundary, except for a small distance in the south where it turned eastward after meeting the river Nam. The strait of Tsushima formed the southern boundary, the Sea of Japan the eastern. Entry into the perimeter was impeded on the north by very formidable mountains that ran from the Naktong to P'ohang on the Sea of Japan. The bridges across the Naktong were blown on August 4.[3] (*Map 17*)

The Far East Air Forces (FEAF), under the command of Lt. Gen. George E. Stratemeyer, carried out its first offensive action on June 28 when twelve B-26s bombed the marshaling yards at Munsan, South Korea. FEAF comprised three numbered air forces: the Fifth, the Twentieth, and the Thirteenth. The last was responsible for the defense of the Philippines and played no direct role in Korea. The largest of the subordinate commands was the Fifth Air Force, later described by its commander, Lt. Gen. Earle E. Partridge, as a "small but highly professional tactical-type air force." It had two fighter-bomber wings and one interceptor wing (all with F-80C Shooting Stars), two all-weather fighter squadrons (F-82 Twin Mustangs), and an understrength light bombardment wing of B-26 Invaders. The primary mission of the Twentieth Air Force was the aerial defense of Okinawa and the Marianas. For this purpose it had one interceptor wing (F-80Cs) and one all-weather fighter squadron (F-82s). It also had one group of B-29 Superfortresses, which by 1950 were classified as medium bombers. The B-29s were ordered to Japan on June 27, where they were joined in early July by two groups of

---

3. For the best account of the fighting on the ground, see Appleman, *South to the Naktong, North to the Yalu.*

The effectiveness of the F-80, a formidable ground-attack aircraft, was limited in the summer of 1950 by the absence of serviceable airfields in Korea. The F-80s had to be based in Japan, which left them little fuel for operations when they arrived over the battlefield.

B–29s transferred to Japan from the Strategic Air Command in the United States. FEAF organized the three groups into the FEAF Bomber Command (Provisional), under the command of Maj. Gen. Emmett O'Donnell. Before this augmentation, FEAF had 365 F–80s, 32 F–82s, 26 B–26s, and 22 B–29s, as well as reconnaissance and transport aircraft. Although the Air Force already had in its inventory the F–84 Thunderjet, an aircraft specifically designed as a fighter-bomber, none was present in the Far East because the runways of FEAF's airfields were too short to accommodate it.[4]

While designed as a fighter, the F–80 ultimately proved a formidable ground-attack aircraft. Its high speed enabled it to take the enemy unawares while its freedom from propeller torque made its machineguns more accurate than those of piston-driven aircraft. It was also more resistant to ground fire.[5] Initially, however, serious obstacles prevented the effective employment of the Shooting Star as a fighter-bomber. None of the F–80s in Japan was outfitted with bomb racks, although they did

4. Intvw, Arthur K. Marmor, Office of Air Force History, with General Earle E. Partridge, Aug 1966, K239.0512–610, 3; Futrell, *U.S. Air Force in Korea*, 2–4, 59, 46–47.
5. United States Air Force Evaluation Group, "An Evaluation of the United States Air Force in the Korean War" (hereafter cited as Barcus Rpt), vol 3: "Operations and Tactics," Mar 12, 1951, K168.041–1, 25–26, 32–35.

have midwing posts for carrying up to sixteen five-inch high-velocity rockets. Bombs could be attached to the wing-tip shackles for the outrigger fuel tanks, but with its internal store of fuel alone the F–80 had a combat radius of only 100 miles. This was far too short for operations over Korea, as there were no airfields in that country capable of handling jets before the end of the fighting at Pusan. With standard wing-tip tanks and a load of rockets, the F–80 had a combat radius of about 225 miles. But this, too, was inadequate at the beginning of the war when targets were often 350 miles from FEAF's Japanese bases, and only marginally adequate during the battle for Pusan when the front was 180 miles distant. The standard tanks allowed little time for armed reconnaissance, a serious handicap for interdiction operations when FEAF lacked both adequate maps of South Korea and timely intelligence.[6]

A partial solution to the F–80's problems was found in the fabrication in Japan of oversize wing-tip tanks that extended the aircraft's combat radius to 350 miles. The new tanks, however, were in short supply through the Pusan battle, and were no answer to the F–80's lack of midwing bomb racks. The ground forces particularly regretted the jets' inability to carry napalm, which was effective against the formidable T–34s with which the enemy spearheaded his attack.[7] The Fifth Air Force's B–26s, while able to range over virtually all Korea, were also seriously handicapped in some respects. They, too, had to be based in Japan, far from the fighting and unresponsive to fast-breaking opportunities. Because of its high wing-loading, moreover, the B–26 was sluggish in maneuver and therefore poorly suited for low-level attacks in mountainous Korea.[8]

A partial solution to the shortcomings of the F–80 and the B–26 was found in thirty-six F–51 Mustangs taken from storage in Japan. In early July FEAF partially reequipped two fighter squadrons with the Mustangs and requested more from the United States. The F–51s were initially based at Taegu and P'ohang in South Korea. This allowed a rapid response to requests for close air support and reports of interdiction targets. The Mustangs also had the range to reach any target in South Korea and to carry out extended armed reconnaissance. They had, moreover, bomb racks on their wings and could therefore carry the prized na-

---

6. Futrell, *U.S. Air Force in Korea*, 59, 65, 67.
7. *Ibid.*, 95; Barcus Rpt, 3:25; Hist, 49th Fighter-Bomber Grp, Jun 25–Oct 31, 1950, K–GP–49–HI (FTR), 82–84. (Unit histories not otherwise specified are to be found at the Air Force Historical Research Agency, Maxwell Air Force Base.)
8. Barcus Rpt, 3:56.

palm. The aircraft carrier *Boxer* delivered an additional 145 Mustangs after a high-speed run across the Pacific. These aircraft were ready for action by July 27.[9]

American commanders planned from the first to use interdiction to break the momentum of the North Korean onslaught. MacArthur's initial orders to FEAF on June 27 called for attacks on the enemy's lines of communication. He placed special emphasis on the destruction of the bridges across the Han River at Seoul, which the South Koreans had left intact during their hasty retreat. Stratemeyer concurred, stating on July 8 that the isolation of the battlefield was, after close air support, FEAF's paramount objective since air superiority could be taken for granted.[10] Notwithstanding the limitations of its aircraft and the heavy demands of the Army for close air support, FEAF scored some significant early successes against the invaders.

These were chiefly due to the fact that the North Koreans, as though unaware of the deadly potential of air power, initially moved by day. On July 10, a flight of F–80s, released from a close-air support mission, found a North Korean column backed up bumper-to-bumper behind a destroyed bridge. A call for reinforcements went out and additional aircraft soon joined the hunt. The pilots claimed the destruction of 117 trucks, 38 tanks, and 7 half-tracks.[11] The North Koreans, however, quickly took such lessons to heart and began to travel almost entirely at night.[12] (*Table 13*)

Stratemeyer defined areas of operation for FEAF's interdiction campaign on July 13. He directed its Bomber Command to attack the enemy's communications from the Han River north to the Manchurian border, together with the industrial sites and storage areas that served his military. The Fifth Air Force was to harry North Korean supply lines in South Korea.[13] The impression of orderly and comprehensive interdiction that this directive conveys is misleading. FEAF was troubled, first, by constant diversions of aircraft to support the hard-pressed infantry. So desperate was the situation that MacArthur insisted that even the B–29s should be used for close support, though they were scarcely suited for the role. "Effectiveness of FEAF interdiction plan," Stratemeyer cabled

---

9. USAF Historical Division, *United States Air Force Operations in the Korean Conflict, 25 June–1 November 1950* (USAF Hist Study 71, Washington, 1955), 20; Barcus Rpt, 3:27.

10. *Ibid.*, 35; Futrell, *U.S. Air Force in Korea*, 24.

11. USAF Hist Div, *U.S. Air Force Operations in the Korean Conflict*, 25 Jun–1 Nov 1950, 40.

12. Appleman, *South to the Naktong, North to the Yalu*, 123, 256.

13. Mission Directive, FEAF, Jul 13, 1950, K720.3211.

Table 13. Number of Far East Air Forces Sorties, by Type, June–September 1950

Period	Sortie Type			
	Close Air	Interdiction	Strategic	Other
Jun 25–30	408	59	0	100
Jul 1–31	4,635	1,023	56	1,827
Aug 1–31	7,397	2,963	539	4,582
Sep 1–30	5,969	3,818	158	5,382

SOURCE: *The Employment of Strategic Bombers in a Tactical Role, 1941–1951* (USAF Hist Study 88, Maxwell AFB, 1954), 134.

to Headquarters, U.S. Air Force on July 24, "is hampered by close and general support requirements necessarily imposed by CINCFE [Commander in Chief, Far East]."[14]

FEC controlled targeting through the interservice General Headquarters (GHQ) Target Group, which had been established on July 14 to coordinate the aerial operations of the Air Force and the Navy with each other and with the requirements of the Army. The group was, however, dominated by the Army, and even the Navy's representative was not a flyer. The Army's idea of interdiction was to disrupt the enemy's lines of communication immediately behind the front. FEAF's Vice Commander for Operations, Maj. Gen. Otto P. Weyland, likened this to "trying to dam a stream at the bottom of a waterfall." The Target Analysis Group was also inadequately provided with staff, and its maps were even more obsolete than those of FEAF. Aircraft were often directed to targets that were of dubious value or even nonexistent.[15]

To remedy the deficiencies of the GHQ Target Group, Stratemeyer proposed on July 21 that there be created within MacArthur's headquarters a FEC Target Selection Committee composed of senior and appropriately experienced officers of the several services. This organization would decide whether targets proposed by the GHQ Target Group and FEAF's own target section should be attacked. MacArthur approved Stratemeyer's proposal on July 22, agreeing with the airman that the need for comprehensive and effective interdiction was more urgent than ever. Weyland represented the Air Force on the new committee, which first met on July 24. He convinced his colleagues, not without difficulty, that the B-29s were wasted on battlefield targets in all but the most ex-

14. USAF Hist Div, *U.S. Air Force Operations in the Korean Conflict*, 25 Jun–1 Nov 1950, 35.
15. Futrell, *U.S. Air Force in Korea*, 51–55, 128.

traordinary of circumstances. As a result, two groups of Superfortresses were assigned to full-time interdiction north of the 38th Parallel, while the third was temporarily retained for close support. On August 3, MacArthur, alarmed by reports of widespread North Korean movements by road and rail, called upon Stratemeyer to put "a line . . . across Korea, north of Seoul, to stop all communications moving south." To that end, MacArthur granted full control of the third group of B–29s to FEAF, which was now, in practice, almost entirely free to select its own targets, as the FEC Target Selection Committee tended to follow FEAF's recommendations rather than those of the GHQ Target Group, which was shortly disbanded.[16]

The Air Force, free from what it had regarded as uninformed meddling, dated effective interdiction in Korea from August 3, the day of its liberation from the GHQ Target Group. The directive of July 13 remained in effect under the new dispensation; except for now rare missions in direct support of the Eighth Army, Bomber Command operated over North Korea and the Fifth Air Force over the south, save for Seoul where the areas overlapped.[17] Fifth Air Force generally selected its own interdiction targets, while those of Bomber Command were in the first instance selected by the FEAF Target Committee, composed of representatives of the Deputy Chiefs of Staff for Operations and Intelligence, and then approved by the FEC Target Selection Committee. The FEAF Target Committee in short order drew up two interdiction plans for North Korea—one for railways, the other for roads.[18]

North Korea had only two ports of any consequence: Wonsan and Hamhung. Rail lines ran from both to P'yongyang. Between the North Korean capital and Pusan all major arteries, road and rail, were confined to a narrow corridor running through Kaesong on the 38th Parallel, to Seoul, and thence through Taegu to Pusan. The forbidding Taebaek Mountain range, which dominates the entire eastern half of the Korean peninsula except for a narrow strip along the eastern coast, dictated this concentration. The Han River constituted the principal barrier to travel north to south. All major rail and road routes converged at Seoul to cross the Han on three bridges. A more particular circumstance increased the importance of the Han. Most Korean rivers are fordable, but this was especially true in the summer of 1950; the summer monsoon had

---

16. *Ibid.*

17. See, for example, Barcus Rpt, vol 5: "Target Selection and Intelligence," 2.

18. FEAF Directorate of Intelligence, "Major Accomplishments During the Period 26 June 1950 to 25 October 1950," n.d., K720.601A; USAF Hist Div, *U.S. Air Force Operations in the Korean Conflict*, 25 Jun–1 Nov 1950, 37.

failed, and rainfall was but a quarter of normal. The defenders of Pusan noted with concern that even the Naktong, Korea's second greatest river, was fordable at points. The Han alone still ran deep.[19]

Bomber Command's initial targets were the marshaling yards at Wonsan, Hamhung, P'yongyang, and Seoul and the railway bridges near the latter three cities. The marshaling yards, their attractiveness as targets heightened by a large backlog of supplies that had collected because of the limited capacity of the railroads, had been obliterated by August 10. Two days later Bomber Command began to concentrate on a list of forty-four rail and road bridges, augmented by two groups of B–29s newly arrived from the United States. Progress was rapid, and after August 20 only two groups were needed for bridges; the other three were devoted to the bombardment of factories, arsenals, and storage areas. General O'Donnell reported on September 4 that his B–29s had destroyed all but seven of the designated bridges, and they were so damaged as to be unusable.[20]

This was an impressive accomplishment, especially as it had been the work of inexperienced crews forced to use unguided bombs.[21] The success, however, was not so unmitigated as the bald statistics suggest, for the North Koreans were never wholly deprived of their capacity to cross the crucial Han. Two of the three bridges had been destroyed by mid-July, but the third, the western railroad bridge, survived daily attacks and repeated hits by bombs as heavy as 4,000 pounds. The decking was often blown away, but the sturdy cantilever frame resisted destruction. The North Koreans diligently replaced the deck with wooden planks and used the bridge for vehicular traffic. The structure finally fell on August 20 after a strike by Navy fighter-bombers. But as long as the North Koreans occupied Seoul, they nightly deployed a pontoon bridge across the Han that, cunningly concealed by day, resisted FEAF's best efforts to destroy it. On one occasion night-flying B–26s, their run illuminated by flares dropped from a B–29, bored in only to find that the floating bridge was not in the anticipated place. Bomber Command also sowed the Han with bombs fitted with delayed-action fuzes. This may have slowed the nightly traffic across the Han, but certainly failed to halt it.[22]

---

19. Appleman, *South to the Naktong, North to the Yalu*, 269, 337–39.

20. USAF Hist Div, *U.S. Air Force Operations in the Korean Conflict*, 25 Jun–1 Nov 1950, 37; Futrell, *U.S. Air Force in Korea*, 129–30.

21. Attempts to employ radio-guided Razon bombs met with little success because the weapons had deteriorated in storage and the aiming equipment, designed for the B–17, could not be satisfactorily fitted to the B–29. FEAF, "FEAF Operations History," Aug 23, 1950, 1:14, K720.302A; USAF Hist Div, *U.S. Air Force Operations in the Korean Conflict*, 25 Jun–1 Nov 1950, 46.

22. Futrell, *U.S. Air Force in Korea*, 125, 130–31.

Between August 3 and September 23, the day the Eighth Army completed its breakout from the Pusan Perimeter, Bomber Command flew approximately 1,800 sorties against communications targets (bridges, marshaling yards, port facilities, tunnels, and storage areas) throughout North Korea and in South Korea around Seoul. No B-29s were lost to enemy action in this period. As this loss rate attests, North Korea's small and obsolescent air force was no threat to American aerial operations over any part of Korea. By early August, probably fewer than thirty of its aircraft were still operational, and at no time were the North Korean pilots aggressive in their attacks on the B-29s, which could fly without escort.[23]

The bombing of North Korea presented few problems of intelligence. FEAF had prepared target folders for many sites in the north before the war. The Japanese, moreover, had built almost all the factories and bridges that Bomber Command attacked. FEAF was therefore able to obtain much useful information about the targets either by contacting the firms that had built them and by seeking knowledgeable individuals through advertisements in the Japanese press.[24] Intelligence in the south, on the other hand, was a major problem, particularly before the battle-lines stabilized around Pusan. Because of the disorganization of the routed South Korean Army, and the piecemeal commitment of the American ground forces, Fifth Air Force often had no idea of where the enemy was to be found.

To compound the problems caused by the lack of battlefield intelligence, the Fifth Air Force had only a slight capacity for photographic reconnaissance and was seriously short of trained intelligence analysts. Its ability to carry out signals intelligence was also poor, and its efforts in that direction met with little success. Such information as FEAF had from communications intercepts was too highly classified to be disseminated to the Fifth Air Force. The reports of pilots who had spotted targets on their ways to and from their assigned objectives were sometimes useful. But the utility of the intelligence was seriously limited by the basing of most of the Fifth Air Force's aircraft in Japan, at such a remove that only rarely could they take advantage of fleeting opportunities. That it was possible to plan interdiction strikes at all in South Korea during the summer of 1950 was chiefly due to two circumstances. The first was the rudimentary state of the country's communications: The paucity of

---

23. *Ibid.*; FEAF, "FEAF Operations History," vol 1, Jun 25–Oct 31, 1950, K720.302A; Futrell, *U.S. Air Force in Korea*, 101.

24. FEAF Directorate Intel, "Major Accomplishments"; "Items to Be Brought to the Attention of Officers of the Directorate of Intelligence, USAF," attachment to *ibid.*; Futrell, *U.S. Air Force in Korea*, 130.

railroads and good roads meant that the North Koreans had little flexibility in their routing of supplies to the front. The second was that OSI's
network of Korean agents continued to report from behind enemy lines.
This, it appears, was the best source of intelligence for the interdiction
campaign.[25]

Information about the North Koreans' routes and schedules—the
kind of intelligence that agents can best supply—was particularly important because of the enemy's extensive resort to cover of darkness. This
was of course well known to the Fifth Air Force: North Korean convoys
and trains were simply not to be seen by day after the massacre of July
10, save for a period in late July when Partridge's command was so burdened by requests for close air support from the hard-pressed Eighth
Army that the percentage of sorties dedicated to interdiction fell well
short of his goal of 33 percent.[26] Once again, accordingly, the U.S. Air
Force had to confront its greatest operational limitation: its slight capacity to conduct tactical ground attack operations at night. There was even
less capability than there had been at the end of the world war, for there
were no longer any units trained as night intruders. Nor were there any
aircraft suited to the role. Most of the all-weather F–82s, of which there
were few, had to be retained for the aerial defense of Japan. The F–80s
were too fast to acquire targets at night. The F–51s were not handicapped in that respect, but their guns were so situated that their flashes
blinded the pilots. The role of night intruder thus fell by default to the
B–26, and fighters flew very few night interdiction sorties after August
12. But the B–26 was a most imperfect instrument. It had no radar altim-
eter, short-range navigation radar, or blind-bombing radar. These limitations, taken with its lack of maneuverability, made the aircraft hazardous
to fly through Korea's mountains and valleys by night.[27]

General Stratemeyer, alarmed by reports of extensive North Korean
movements by night, placed great emphasis on night interdiction. On August 8, he instructed General Partridge to achieve fifty intruder sorties
nightly. He also brought into the theater two British airmen, veterans of
intruder operations in Italy, to lecture to the B–26 squadrons. When the
enemy's convoys first began to move at night in early July, the suicidal
propensity of the North Koreans to travel with their lights on eased the
task of the intruders briefly. A few drubbings soon taught them that the

25. "Miscellaneous Substantiating Data Pertinent to Barcus Report Turned
In by Colonel Alvin Hebert," Statement of Lt Col O'Wighton D. Simpson, Assistant Deputy for Intelligence, Fifth Air Force, n.d., Barcus Rpt, vol 16; Hist,
49th Fighter-Bomber Grp, Jun 25–Oct 31, 1950.
26. Futrell, *U.S. Air Force in Korea*, 125.
27. *Ibid.*, 135; Barcus Rpt, "General Appendix: Recorded Interviews—General Edward J. Timberlake," Oct 22, 1950.

The B-26 Invader *(left)* was the mainstay of night intruder operations in Korea. A B-29 Superfortress *(below)* awaits the signal to depart on a night bombing mission.

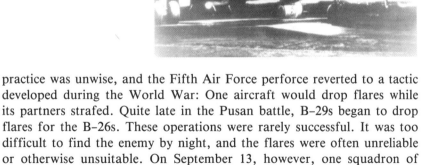

practice was unwise, and the Fifth Air Force perforce reverted to a tactic developed during the World War: One aircraft would drop flares while its partners strafed. Quite late in the Pusan battle, B-29s began to drop flares for the B-26s. These operations were rarely successful. It was too difficult to find the enemy by night, and the flares were often unreliable or otherwise unsuitable. On September 13, however, one squadron of B-26s did succeed in destroying three moving trains with the aid of flares dropped from a B-29.[28]

Between August 3 and September 23, the Fifth Air Force flew 21,979 sorties, of which 5,224, or 24 percent, were devoted to interdiction. Night intruder missions totaled 959, about 18 percent of all interdiction missions. This figure represents an average of 18.8 sorties a night, far short of Stratemeyer's goal of fifty. In this period the Fifth Air Force lost, on sorties of all kinds, forty-five F-51s, eight F-80s, three B-26s, and one F-82.[29] By September 12, FEAF was able to claim that it had, with help from the Navy, destroyed 140 bridges between Seoul and the front. It had also established and maintained forty-seven rail cuts—nine

---

28. Futrell, *U.S. Air Force in Korea*, 135; Barcus Rpt, "General Appendix: Recorded Interviews—General Edward J. Timberlake."
29. Ops Hist, FEAF, Aug 3–Sep 23, 1950.

on the main line between Seoul and Taejon, the remainder on secondary lines. In the immediate vicinity of Pusan an additional ninety-three bridges had been rendered unserviceable. FEAF also claimed the destruction of 280 locomotives and 1,314 railway cars. During the same period, all the United Nations forces, both ground and air, claimed the destruction of 875 motor vehicles of all types.[30]

The battle for Pusan entered its most critical phase on August 26 when the North Koreans crossed the Naktong at several points and drove deeply into the thinly defended perimeter. By September 10, however, the danger was past. Hard fighting, General Walker's skillful use of his small reserve, and intensive air support had stemmed the North Korean thrust. General MacArthur had meanwhile conceived and put into preparation a daring plan for a landing at Inch'on to recapture Seoul and sever the enemy's communications at a single stroke. A breakout from Pusan was to follow. The operation began on the morning of September 15 when U.S. marines descended on the island of Wolmi-do in Inch'on's harbor; that evening, joined by the Army's Seventh Infantry Division, they moved into the city. Surprise was total; there were barely 2,000 North Koreans to defend the place. The next day, the Communists' troubles grew still worse, for 180 miles to the south the Eighth Army began a counteroffensive that soon put the besiegers of Pusan to flight. The North Korean Army, caught between the hammer and the anvil, had crumbled even before Seoul fell to the force from Inch'on on September 26. Probably no more than 30,000 North Koreans regained the 38th Parallel. As many more were prisoners, the rest of the more than 100,000 men who had crossed the frontier on June 25 were dead.

That the North Koreans' campaign ended disastrously should not obscure its accomplishments. Their initial advantages were considerable, but so were the obstacles of terrain and American material superiority. As late as the first week in September, the vigor of the push across the Naktong impressed the Joint Chiefs of Staff.[31] The collapse of the Communists shortly afterward produced much information in the form of prisoners and documents. Fragmentary and largely anecdotal, it is by no means either as complete or as authoritative as the archival remains of the *Wehrmacht*. But it suffices to show that even before the crossing of the Naktong the North Korean Army was in parlous logistical straits. Its resupply had dwindled steadily since early July, if the surviving records of one division are typical. (*Table 14*)

---

30. Futrell, *U.S. Air Force in Korea*, 131; USAF Hist Div, *U.S. Air Force Operations in the Korean Conflict*, 25 June–1 Nov 1950, 45.
31. Appleman, *South to the Naktong, North to the Yalu*, 494.

Table 14. Average Supplies Received by a Representative North Korean Division, June–September 1950

Period	Type of Supply, in Tons			
	Food	Quartermaster	Petroleum, oil, and lubricants	Ordnance
Jun 25–Jul 15	18	10	12	166
Jul 16–Aug 15	9	5	7	30
Aug 16–Sep 20	2.5	—	2	17

SOURCE: *USAF Hist Div, U.S. Air Force Operations in the Korean Conflict, 25 June–1 Nov 1950*, 50.

The steady decline in the supply of arms, ammunition, and fuel throughout the campaign is particularly striking, for in early September the North Korean command, responding to the reduced capacity of its logistical system, had ordered that nothing else should be forwarded to the front. One consequence of this drastic decision was to aggravate an already severe shortage of food. The southern countryside, always poor and now drought stricken, did not reward foraging. At the beginning of the campaign, the daily ration of the North Korean soldier had been 800 grams of rice, dried fish, meat, and vegetables. By the period July 15–August 15 this had fallen to 600 grams a day, which consisted almost entirely of rice. In the last month of the fight for South Korea, the daily ration fell to 400 grams. "By August 21," the captured chief of staff of the North Korean *13th Infantry Division* later testified, "50 per cent of the personnel had lost the stamina necessary to fight in mountainous terrain."[32] A survey of North Korean prisoners revealed that the lack of food was the principal cause of the low morale that prevailed in the communist forces by early September. (*Table 15*)

As Table 14 suggests, the situation of the North Koreans was problematic even with respect to the favored logistical categories: ordnance, and petroleum, oil, and lubricants. Replacement of heavy weapons continued but, as had been the case with the German armies in Italy, the resupply of artillery ammunition was very difficult. The *13th Division*'s chief of staff stated, for example, that the unit had but 200–250 shells left on the day of his desertion (September 20), although small-arms ammunition was even then relatively plentiful.[33] One battalion of the *7th Infantry Division* was less fortunate. On September 14, according to a cap-

32. USAF Hist Div, *U.S. Air Force Operations in the Korean Conflict, 25 Jun–1 Nov 1950*, 49–50. See also Appleman, *South to the Naktong, North to the Yalu*, 310, 333, 342, 365, 393.
33. Interrogation Rpt, HQ Eighth U.S. Army, Korea (EUSAK), Senior Col Lee Hak Ku, Sep 21, 1950, K720.619-1.

Table 15. Reasons Given by Captured North Korean Soldiers for Their Low Morale

Reason Given	Number Responding	Percentage of Respondents
Shortage of food	176	21.4
Fear of aircraft	148	17.9
Lack of training	93	11.3
Lack of equipment	81	9.8
Insufficient rest	68	8.2
Forced induction	52	6.3
Casualties	51	6.2
No cause for fighting	40	4.9
Artillery	39	4.7
Desertions	28	3.3
Harsh officers	13	1.6
Lack of replacements	12	1.5
Inadequate clothing	10	1.2
All other causes	14	1.7
Total	825	100.0

SOURCE: *USAF Hist Div, U.S. Air Force Operations in the Korean Conflict*, 25 Jun–1 Nov 1950, 52.

tured status report, it consisted of 6 officers and 135 men, for whom there were only 82 individual weapons and 6 machineguns, for which there were only 300 rounds apiece. The supply of individual weapons was clearly a major problem: By mid-August only a third of the front's requisitions could be met.[34] Fuel, too, seems to have been short. The *13th Division*'s chief of staff reported that his unit had had only a "very small amount of gasoline remaining" at the time of his defection, while the motor officer of the 8th Infantry Division stated that by September 20 only 7 liters of gasoline remained for each of its 30 trucks, and there was no hope of resupply.[35]

While far from complete, the information about North Korean supply is at all points consistent and supports the conclusion that the Communist forces were fighting on a shoestring. It is doubtful that this can be attributed entirely to interdiction. The North Koreans planned for a short campaign against a weak foe; they got a war against a strong one. Neither were the North Koreans aided by the last-minute withdrawal of

---

34. Appleman, *South to the Naktong, North to the Yalu*, 393, 546. See also USAF Hist Div, *U.S. Air Force Operations in the Korean Conflict*, 25 Jun–1 Nov 1950, 52.

35. Lee Interrogation Rpt, Sep 21, 1950; USAF Hist Div, *U.S. Air Force Operations in the Korean Conflict*, 25 Jun–1 Nov 1950, 50.

Soviet advisers from their formations. Logistics is one of the most demanding aspects of military operations, and perhaps the least easily mastered by the army of a backward state. By the time of the Pusan battle, moreover, the North Koreans were at the very end of their supply lines. Until then, finally, they had benefited from Korea's geography: The only respectable roads and rail lines ran north to south along their axis of advance. But with the envelopment of Pusan, they had to depart somewhat from the narrow corridor through which good lines of communications could be established. Those North Korean divisions that tried to enter the perimeter from the north, for example, had to pass through some of the least hospitable terrain in the inhabited world.

It is nonetheless probable that interdiction contributed substantially to the North Koreans' logistical plight. Their problems bear close comparison with those of the German armies in Italy, although the Germans had the advantages of greater technical proficiency and access to a much better network of roads and rail lines. In both cases, the interdicted army, fighting without air cover, had little or no use of the railroads within the zone of interdiction and had to move supply convoys by night. The North Koreans, like the Germans, continued to run trains on segments of lines between destroyed bridges. In this they may have been more successful because Korea's railroads depended less on bridges than Italy's did; tunnels were the crucial engineering feature, and they afforded cover and concealment for trains by day. But destroyed bridges, damaged roadbeds, and the confinement of travel to hours of darkness imposed delays incompatible with the efficient conduct of military operations. One prisoner, for example, related that it had taken a month for his train to make the journey of 280 miles from P'yongyang to the front at Pusan.[36]

As in Italy, the diminished capacity of the railroads added burden on an inherently less efficient means of transport, the motor convoy. American aircraft, moreover, reduced the efficiency of the enemy's convoys still more by forcing them to operate at night. And while the night intruders may not have destroyed many vehicles, the threat they posed was sufficiently great that the trucks ran blacked out. Without lights it was difficult to travel more than twenty to thirty miles a night over the dirt roads of the south. It may not be coincidental that the precipitous decline in the capacity of the supply system began in July when the convoys had to seek the cover of darkness. This had been the case in Italy, where the roads were much better. In contrast to Italy, however, it is un-

---

36. USAF Hist Div, *U.S. Air Force Operations in the Korean Conflict*, 25 Jun–1 Nov 1950, 49–50. See also Appleman, *South to the Naktong, North to the Yalu*, 123, 256.

likely that the destruction of bridges greatly discommoded the North Koreans' vehicular traffic. There was little need for road bridges in the droughty Korea of 1950, and the Korean Communists were adept at the construction of underwater bridges from rocks and sandbags, a practice pioneered by their Soviet mentors in World War II.[37]

It appears that the North Koreans were reasonably well provided with trucks: American intelligence estimated the North Korean Army had slightly fewer than 3,000 when the war began. Given the industrial development of North Korea, it is likely that a considerable number of additional vehicles were obtained from the civilian economy.[38] And given FEAF's limited capacity for night interdiction and the skill with which the North Koreans hid their vehicles by day, it is unlikely that their losses were prohibitive. Resupply of Soviet-made trucks, moreover, continued throughout the fighting at Pusan, and into September prisoners continued to claim that the North Korean Army appeared to have many vehicles left.[39]

Taking the likelihood that the loss of trucks was not crippling with the considerable evidence of logistical distress afflicting the North Koreans during the siege of Pusan, it is probable that strategic interdiction worked in Korea during the summer of 1950 for the same reasons that it had worked earlier in Italy during Operation STRANGLE: Systematic attacks on the enemy's railroads reduced their capacity to such an extent that trucks had to substitute for trains. But because motor transport is so much less efficient than rail, it is exceedingly difficult to supply large armies engaged in heavy fighting with trucks when there is any great distance between the railheads and the front. Even the famous Red Ball Express with which the splendidly equipped American armies in France attempted to supply their advance toward Germany proved an inadequate substitute for railroads crippled by Allied bombing and German sabotage.[40] There was a further resemblance to STRANGLE in that American

---

37. Appleman, *South to the Naktong, North to the Yalu*, 301–2, 437.

38. Directorate of Intelligence, "A Report on the Effectiveness of the Interdiction Program Against North Korea," Sep 13, 1950, Records of Headquarters U.S. Air Force, RG 341, NARA.

39. *Ibid.* For the skill with which the North Koreans hid vehicles, see FEAF Ops Analysis Ofc 12, "Combat Area Interdiction with Fighter Bombers," Aug 2, 1950, K720.3101-12. For the resupply of vehicles, see USAF Hist Div, *U.S. Air Force Operations in the Korean Conflict*, 25 Jun-1 Nov 1950, 50. Prisoners claimed to have witnessed the destruction of about 800 trucks, most by aircraft. But this figure is impossible to evaluate without some knowledge of how many vehicles were drawn from the civilian economy.

40. Roland G. Ruppenthal, *Logistical Support of the Armies, September 1944-May 1945* [U.S. Army in World War II: The European Theater of Operations] (Washington, 1959), 571.

aircraft denied the North Koreans the use of roads by day, which greatly increased their demand for motor transport. The effect of heavy consumption under these circumstances was probably to hasten the onset of an already inevitable logistical constriction.

Chapter 9

Korean Interdiction
Campaigns of 1951

The intervention of the Chinese in the Korean War fundamentally altered the conditions under which the U.S. Air Force had to practice interdiction. The scale of the war expanded enormously and taxed the limited number of aircraft at the disposal of the post–World War II service. The Soviet Union, moreover, provided the Chinese with large numbers of modern jet fighters, antiaircraft guns, and trucks. Successive American interdiction campaigns foundered as the inevitable difficulties of attempting to interdict a sophisticated and determined foe who consumed little were compounded by an insufficient degree of air superiority and by losses that the Air Force's inadequate force levels could not sustain.

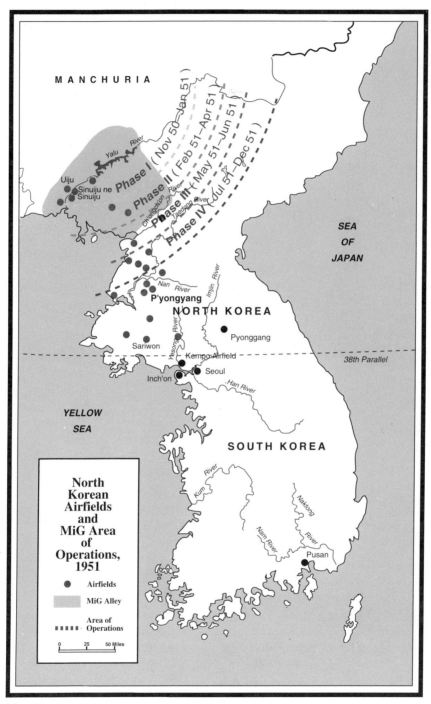

MANCHURIA

Yalu   River

Phase I (Nov 50 – Jan 51)

Phase II (Feb 51 – Apr 51)

Phase III (May 51 – Jun 51)

Phase IV (Jul 51 – Dec 51)

Uiju

Sinuiju ne
Sinuiju

Chongchon   River

Taedong   River

Nan   River

P'yongyang

Imjin   River

NORTH KOREA

SEA
OF
JAPAN

Sariwon

Yesong River

Pyonggang

Kempo Airfield

38th Parallel

Seoul

Inch'on

Han River

YELLOW
SEA

SOUTH KOREA

Kum   River

Nam River

Naktong   River

Pusan

North
Korean
Airfields
and
MiG Area
of
Operations,
1951

●   Airfields

    MiG Alley

▪▪▪▪▪   Area of
     Operations

0   25   50 Miles

Map 18.

Dramatic reversals of fortune marked the first year of the Korean War. The North Korean invasion of South Korea in June 1950 was initially successful. In little more than a month the Communists drove the defending South Korean and American forces to the southern extremity of the Korean peninsula. Throughout August they besieged Pusan, victory seemingly within their grasp. But in September General Douglas MacArthur's landing at Inch'on and a subsequent sally from Pusan precipitated the rapid collapse of the North Korean Army. The United Nations Command thereupon surged north, taking the Communist capital of P'yongyang on October 20. By late November, advance elements of both the American and the South Korean Armies had reached the Yalu River, which forms the border between Korea and China. Then the Chinese intervened in overwhelming force, and Seoul fell once more to the Communists. Logistical difficulties soon after caused the Chinese to lose momentum, and in late January 1951 the United Nations successfully counterattacked. There were desperate Chinese counteroffensives in April and May, but by June the United Nations Command had redeemed all South Korea and in places advanced into the North. But Washington had decided against a second attempt to conquer North Korea, and in June both sides dug in along the 38th Parallel.[1]

The Korean War thereafter somewhat resembled the stalled Italian campaign of early 1944. Once more an allied army in which Americans predominated faced a foe entrenched on a narrow peninsula, a foe whose lines of communication were vulnerable to aerial attack. The resemblance was not lost on the commander of the Fifth Air Force, Maj. Gen. Ed-

---

1. For the ground war in this period, see Bevin Alexander, *Korea: The First War We Lost* (New York, 1986), 228–425.

ward J. Timberlake.[2] He named the interdiction campaign that the Fifth Air Force planned for the summer of 1951 after the one undertaken by the Mediterranean Allied Air Forces in 1944: STRANGLE. But the Korean War differed from the Italian theater in three fundamental respects. First, the stalemate was, as far as the intentions of the United Nations were concerned, permanent. No Rome beckoned. Second, the enemy had in Manchuria a sanctuary adjacent to Korea. To keep the war limited, Washington had ordered that no part of China should be attacked. Across the Yalu, plainly visible to American airmen, were airfields, railroads, and logistical centers, all inviolable. Third, the U.S. Air Force failed to win air supremacy over North Korea; it had to settle for a continually disputed and incomplete air superiority. In Italy and France the *Luftwaffe* had had only a negligible effect on interdiction operations. But in Korea the Chinese Air Force figured importantly in a carefully conceived strategy that frustrated successive American interdiction campaigns.

Reduced to its essentials, the strategy of the Chinese was to blunt the American ability to attack their lines of communication while making the supply routes themselves more defensible. The former objective they accomplished through the deployment of antiaircraft artillery and the skillful use of the large force of jet fighters at their command; the latter they realized by camouflage, concealment, and the redundancy of their logistical system. While these measures are not unfamiliar to students of the Korean War, there has been little appreciation that all were aspects of a coherent strategy. It has been too readily assumed conditions were so hostile to the success of interdiction that the actions of the Communists were almost irrelevant.[3] It is of course true that the consumption of the Communist armies was low, the front quiet throughout much of 1951, and the advantages of the Manchurian sanctuary great. But none of this should distract attention from how the Chinese made the failure of interdiction more complete than it need have been. The role that the Chinese air force played in foiling interdiction has been particularly overlooked. Historians have been somewhat beguiled by the great success of

---

2. Timberlake had recently succeeded to the command of the Fifth Air Force when the previous commander, Lt Gen Earle E. Partridge, went to Tokyo to command the Far East Air Forces (FEAF) after the previous commander, Lt Gen George E. Stratemeyer, suffered a heart attack on May 20. Partridge's and Timberlake's appointments were temporary; both had already been selected for commands in the United States. Lt Gen Otto P. Weyland was named to head FEAF, and Maj Gen Frank P. Everest, to command the Fifth Air Force. Both Weyland and Everest assumed their duties about June 1, 1951.

3. See, for example, Gregory A. Carter, *Some Historical Notes on Air Interdiction in Korea* (The Rand Corp., P–3452, Santa Monica, 1966).

the American F–86 Sabre jets in their duels with the Chinese MiG–15s. With respect to interdiction, however, the American pilots won battles but lost a war.

By the spring of 1951 the Chinese understood the importance of air power, having felt it in their flesh. "If we had had strong air support," a Special Aviation Inspection Group of the Chinese General Staff lamented late in 1951, "we could have driven the enemy into the sea and the protracted defensive battles raging from 25 January to 22 April . . . should have been avoided." As early as February 1951, American intelligence officers learned that the Chinese were planning to introduce close–air support aircraft. A captured staff officer explained that each regiment of the *Fourth Field Army* had sent officers to Mukden to learn how to coordinate air strikes. In March there was reliable information that the Chinese had moved two regiments of Ilyushin Il–10s—the latest version of the famous Soviet Stormovik ground-attack aircraft of World War II—to Manchuria.[4]

The Il–10s were useless, however, as long as American fighters dominated the Korean sky. Early in 1951, as American intelligence subsequently learned, the commander of the Chinese Air Force, General Liu Ya-liu, devised a plan to wrest air superiority from the United Nations in order to introduce the Il–10s. In the Soviet-built MiG–15 the Chinese had an aircraft capable of mastering the F–80 and matching any other fighter the Americans might introduce. The Chinese prefaced their bid for air superiority by obtaining more MiGs from the USSR. In December 1950 the People's Republic had a force of 650 combat aircraft; six months later it had 1,050, of which 445 were MiG–15s. (The Fifth Air Force, by contrast, had only fifty of the F–86 Sabre jets, the only comparable American fighter.)[5]

Two limitations, one political and the other technical, dictated the rest of General Liu's plan. The Chinese government strenuously forbade

---

4. Far East Air Forces (hereafter FEAF), "Weekly Intelligence Roundup," No. 69 (Dec 22–28, 1951), K720.607A; General Headquarters, United Nations and Far East Commands (hereafter GHQ, UN/FECs), "Daily Summary of Intelligence," No. 3204 (Jun 18, 1951), K712.606; FEAF, "Command Reference Book," Apr 1, 1951, K720.197.

5. FEAF, "Weekly Intelligence Roundup," No. 40 (Jun 3–9, 1951); Fifth Air Force (hereafter 5AF), "Fifth Air Force Review," May 1951, K730.197. The memoirs of General Yang Dezhi, who commanded the Chinese *19th Army Group* in the Korean War, identified the commander of the Chinese Air Force as Liu Zhen. Yang Dezhi, *For Peace* (Translation FTD-[RS]T-1143-88 by the Foreign Technology Division of the Air Force Systems Command, 1989; original vol, Beijing, 1987), 110.

its commanders to use Manchurian airdromes for staging attacks on the United Nations Command, fearing retaliation against Chinese soil.[6] The second restriction was the limited combat radius of the MiG–15, for which there were as yet no drop-tanks. With a combat radius of only about 100 miles, the MiGs could barely fly south of the Ch'ongch'on River in northwestern North Korea. This limitation led a Chinese commission to conclude, somewhat prematurely, that the fighter was not suitable for use in Korea.[7] The Chinese could only seek air superiority by a steady march of their airdromes down the Korean peninsula. General Liu envisioned the establishment of air superiority in the region of North Korea closest to the Yalu. That done, bases could be established in the southern reaches of the newly established zone of air superiority, MiGs flown in, and the area of air superiority extended yet again. Once it had reached the 38th Parallel, the Chinese planned to garrison forward bases with Il–10s, and commence ground support operations.[8]

The Chinese plan never came close to success. During the spring of 1951, and again in the fall, the Communists made intensive efforts to build new airfields in North Korea and to recondition old ones. The first phase of this program saw a daring attempt to open an advance base as far south as Sariwon. There was also a clever effort to build a concealed airfield in downtown P'yongyang. Teams of workers razed buildings to turn 6,400 feet of street into runways. Far East Air Forces (FEAF) kept these and other projects under surveillance and destroyed them with Bomber Command's B–29s as they approached completion. In the fall the Chinese were more cautious. They confined their base building to the far north of Korea so that fighters based in Manchuria could cover the work. By November MiGs had been stationed in Uiju, just across the Yalu from Manchuria. (*Map 18*) This base and two others nearing completion had the potential to extend by nearly 100 miles the aerial no-man's-land that American airmen called MiG Alley. In this area the MiGs, by virtue of their numbers and the proximity of their Manchurian

---

6. FEAF, "Weekly Intelligence Roundup," No. 69. This apprehension was justified, for early in 1951 Washington had authorized such retaliation. Robert F. Futrell, *The United States Air Force in Korea, 1950–1953*, rev ed (Washington, 1983), 285–86. The United Nations Command therefore enjoyed a sanctuary in South Korea. The Chinese had throughout the war a force of Soviet-built Tu-2 bombers which had the range to attack much of South Korea, but chose not to exercise the option. In December 1951 the Fifth Air Force estimated that the force of Tu-2s numbered 180 and had the capacity to make night attacks on a number of major air bases in South Korea. Hist, 5AF, Jul 1–Dec 31, 1951, "Intelligence Annex: December 1951," vol 3, app 18, K730.01.
7. FEAF, "Weekly Intelligence Roundup," No. 69.
8. GHQ, UN/FECs, "Daily Summary of Intelligence," Nos. 3200, 3223 (Jun 14, Jul 7, 1951); FEAF, "Weekly Intelligence Roundup," No. 69.

bases, ranged freely, seriously interfering with American aerial operations of all kinds. But the new bases, like the old, were destroyed by the B-29s, though now the bombers, for fear of the MiGs, flew only at night.[9]

The scheme to extend a mutually supporting network of bases throughout North Korea failed because the Chinese lost the concurrent battle for air superiority. The MiGs had appeared in combat even before the first clash of American and Chinese armies; they claimed their first B-29 on November 10, 1950.[10] They overmatched the F-80 Shooting Stars, and the Air Force rushed a wing of the new F-86 Sabre jets to Korea, which began operations from Kimp'o airfield outside Seoul in mid-December. The two opposing jets had roughly comparable performance, the MiG having perhaps a slight advantage.[11] This was redressed, however, by the superior training and experience of the American airmen. In the spring of 1951, and then again in the fall, the Chinese accompanied their base building with bids for air superiority within MiG Alley. (*Table 16*) Each time they failed. Fighting at unfavorable odds, the Sabres destroyed thirteen MiGs for each of their number lost in action. (The overall loss ratio between the American and Chinese air forces was 1:9.)[12] These impressive successes, however, should not obscure the fact that even with their failure to win air superiority in MiG Alley, let alone over North Korea generally, the MiGs were able with increased numbers and the fitting of drop-tanks to extend their area of operations ever farther south throughout 1951. By fall, they were a major obstacle to Fifth Air Force's attempts to interdict Chinese supply lines.

FEAF implemented three plans in 1951 to interdict the communications of the Chinese and North Korean Armies: Interdiction Plan No. 4 (December 15, 1950–May 30, 1951), Operation STRANGLE (May 31–August 17, 1951), and the Rail Interdiction Program, which was launched on August 18, 1951.[13] The first of these operations was the most ambitious.

---

9. USAF Historical Division, *United States Air Force Operations in the Korean Conflict, 1 November 1950–30 June 1952* (USAF Hist Study 72, Washington, 1955), 127–31.

10. *Ibid.*, 21.

11. For an extended comparison of the performance characteristics of the MiG-15 and F-86, see *ibid.*, 116–18.

12. *Ibid.*, 107–10.

13. The Rail Interdiction Program was also initially known as STRANGLE. As it became clear that the operation was not living up to its name, FEAF began to refer to it circumspectly as the "Rail Interdiction Program." Futrell, *U.S. Air Force in Korea*, 441–42. The author has chosen to employ this latter name for the clarity of his discussion.

Base crewmen check an ice-bound F–86 Sabre jet before a day's operations.

It combined an effort to paralyze the entire rail system of North Korea with intensive armed reconnaissance. The destruction of the railroads was designed to leave the Chinese no recourse but motor transport to meet the demands of their front, which American intelligence put at 2,000 tons of supplies a day. As the round trip between Manchuria and the main line of resistance required about ten days by road, and each of the enemy's Soviet-made GAZ trucks could haul two tons, it followed that 10,000 vehicles would be required to prevent the logistical collapse of the front. The Americans at this time believed the Chinese and North Koreans to have only about 4,000 trucks.[14]

The destruction of the North Korean railroad system was an inherently difficult task. The Japanese had developed this portion of the peninsula as an industrial center during their long occupation. The railroads, accordingly, were more highly developed than those of the south. The east coast line had only a single track, which made it particularly vulner-

---

14. Futrell, *U.S. Air Force in Korea*, 317; GHQ, UN/FECs, "Command Situation Report," May 1951, K712.02.

Table 16. MiG–15 Aircraft Observed, Engaged, and Destroyed, by Date

Month	Number of MiG–15s				
	Observed	Engaged	Destroyed	Probably Destroyed	Damaged
Nov 1950	315	139	3	2	11
Dec 1950	361	260	8	2	6
Jan 1951	189	189	4	2	9
Feb 1951	102	86	0	0	0
Mar 1951	374	243	9	4	14
Apr 1951	531	413	14	4	40
May 1951	280	137	9	1	15
Jun 1951	389	309	14	1	34
Jul 1951	370	194	9	1	6
Aug 1951	309	197	4	0	3
Sep 1951	1,177	911	14	2	34
Oct 1951	2,573	2,166	32	8	50
Nov 1951	2,326	1,381	20	9	56
Dec 1951	3,997	1,849	27	5	34

SOURCE: USAF Hist Div, *U.S. Air Force Operations in the Korean Conflict, 1 Nov 1950–30 Jun 1952*, 109.

able to bombing. Long stretches of it, moreover, ran close to the shore and could be taken under fire by warships. But the central and western lines were extensively double tracked, and the latter was at no point close to the littoral. The major routes were also linked by a goodly number of transverse lines, which meant that limited destruction could be readily bypassed, albeit at the cost of circuitous routes. (See *Map 17*) If North Korea's railroads were to be paralyzed, they had to be approached as a single target system. FEAF's target committee therefore divided the country into eleven zones wherein it identified 172 targets: 45 railway bridges, 12 highway bridges, 13 tunnels, 39 marshaling yards, and 63 supply centers. The plan called on the B–29s of FEAF's Bomber Command to attack the zones in order of their priority. Zone A included the vital communications center of Sinuiju, where the main rail lines from Manchuria crossed the Yalu. Zone B encompassed Manp'ojin, where another major line entered Korea, while the north's most important rail hub, the capital city of P'yongyang, fell in Zone C.[15] (*Map 19*)

---

15. Futrell, *U.S. Air Force in Korea*, 317–18; FEAF, "Report on the Korean War," K720.04D, 2:94–97.

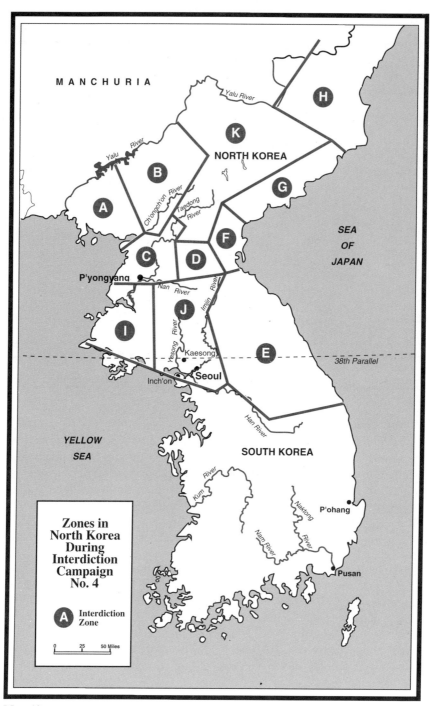

MANCHURIA

NORTH KOREA

Yalu River

H

K

B

A

Yalu River

Ch'ongch'on River

Taedong River

G

F

C

D

P'yongyang

Nan River

SEA
OF
JAPAN

I

J

Yesong River

Imjin River

Kaesong

E

Inch'on

Seoul

38th Parallel

Han River

YELLOW
SEA

SOUTH KOREA

Kum River

Nam River

Naktong River

P'ohang

Pusan

**Zones in
North Korea
During
Interdiction
Campaign
No. 4**

A Interdiction
Zone

0   25   50 Miles

Map 19.

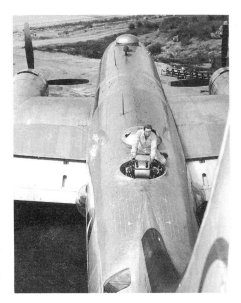

A crewman checks a remotely operated turret on this B-29 Superfortress before a mission over North Korea.

The strategy of attacking the zones sequentially soon proved flawed. The enemy was able to use the less efficient eastern coastal route while the higher priority western zones were under attack. This pattern of attack, moreover, eased his task of repair because he was able to concentrate the very considerable resources he had dedicated to reconstruction in the zone under attack. Whether or not FEAF's planners appreciated these limitations is not apparent. They had, in any event, no real alternative to the sequential approach if they were to attack North Korea's communications comprehensively. Most of the northern targets had to be assigned to Bomber Command, whether because of the ordnance they required, considerations of distance, or because the Fifth Air Force was so heavily occupied with armed reconnaissance and close air support. By December 1950, Bomber Command had been reduced to three groups of B-29s, two having been withdrawn because of the global commitments of the Strategic Air Command. This force, which at no time achieved its authorized strength of ninety-nine aircraft, was too small to attack the North Korean rail system in its entirety, to say nothing of other communications targets. In March the Navy agreed to assume responsibility for interdiction with the easternmost zones—F, G, and H—which ran from Wonsan north to the Siberian frontier.[16] But even with this help the B-29s were overextended.

---

16. Futrell, *U.S. Air Force in Korea*, 318. The Fifth Air Force was originally assigned bridges in Zone A, but it soon asked to be relieved of the responsibility

Bomber Command was responsible for forty-eight railway bridges. With its other commitments, it had a daily average of twenty-four sorties to devote to *all* of its interdiction targets. In the fall, when there had been little flak and no significant opposition from fighters, it had taken the B–29s an average of 13.3 sorties to destroy a bridge. At that rate, it would have taken Bomber Command about twenty-seven days to destroy just the railway bridges on its target list, even if it attacked no other type of target. The Communists, however, rarely took more than four days to repair a bridge, and often did the job much sooner. Worse, by 1951 the B–29s could no longer equal the accuracy of bombing they had achieved earlier in the war. After the MiG–15 appeared, they no longer had the luxury of repeated passes at difficult targets. The enemy's flak, more-over, had so improved that the medium bombers were forced to attack bridges from 21,000 feet. This they could do with only the greatest difficulty because the settings of their intervalometers—devices that timed the release of bombs—could not be altered appropriately. The combination of high altitudes and narrow targets also taxed the Norden bombsights of the B–29s. The altimeters fitted to the bombers, finally, were insufficiently accurate to allow optimum use of the sights. In the case of the important Yalu bridges there was an additional difficulty. The B–29s were forbidden to penetrate Chinese air space. In making their bomb runs, accordingly, they could not fly down the length of the bridges, but rather had to approach them from the sides, which presented the bombardiers with an almost impossibly narrow target.[17]

It was, however, not Bomber Command's numerical insufficiency, but enemy fighters that most severely limited its participation in Interdiction Plan No. 4. In November, heavy and effective flak had contributed to a decision to suspend attacks on the Yalu bridges, although the primary reason had been the thick ice that had formed on the river, making the bridges less necessary.[18] By late March, however, it had thawed, and the impending enemy offensive made the destruction of the bridges between China and Korea highly desirable. In a series of raids that began on March 29, Bomber Command destroyed the Korean terminals of the rail and road bridges at Sinuiju, as well as cantilever and pontoon bridges at Ch'ongsongjin; the B–29s also dropped several spans of the important Manp'ojin rail bridge and damaged the highway bridge at Uiju. But the bridges at Sinuiju, the main gateway into Korea, resisted

---

because the fighter-bombers proved ineffectual for reasons unspecified. *Ibid.*, 317.

17. USAF Hist Div, *U.S. Air Force Operations in the Korean Conflict, 1 Nov 1950–30 Jun 1952*, 23.

18. *Ibid.*, 24. Japanese engineers had explained to FEAF that the winter ice on the Yalu was so thick that they had been able to lay railroad track on it.

destruction. On the mission of March 30 to Ch'ongsongjin, the Chinese directed heavy and accurate flak against the Superfortresses. MiGs intercepted the mission of April 7 against Cho-ri, Uiju, and Sinuiju, downing one bomber. The climax of the campaign against the Yalu bridges came on April 12. Brig. Gen. James E. Briggs, who had led Bomber Command since January, sent all three groups of B–29s against the bridges at Sinuiju. The formation was attacked by as many as 100 MiGs, which for the first time intercepted the bombers long before they reached the target. The interceptors, determined to reach the B–29s at all costs, broke through the escorting F–84s and F–86s. They destroyed three bombers and damaged seven. General Stratemeyer, deeply disturbed at the losses, put Sinuiju off limits for Bomber Command. The Chinese, meanwhile, had set about constructing no less than *eight* bypass bridges to the main rail bridge there.[19]

In spite of the defeat at Sinuiju, Bomber Command had by mid-April rendered at least temporarily unserviceable forty-eight of the sixty bridges then on its target list. It had also closed twenty-seven of the thirty-nine marshaling yards assigned to it. But for all of this there had been a price. In less than a month Bomber Command had lost eight B–29s to MiGs and other operational causes, leaving it with only seventy-five operational aircraft on April 14. The Air Force's Chief of Staff, General Hoyt S. Vandenberg, acceding to urgent requests from Stratemeyer, promised to attempt to build Bomber Command up to its authorized strength of ninety-nine B–29s. But he warned Stratemeyer that the Air Force could not support Bomber Command at a sortie rate of greater than twelve per day. He also admonished FEAF's commander that "the use of bombers in flights of small numbers against many small targets is an expensive and arduous method of achieving small results." Stratemeyer now began to direct the B–29s primarily against marshaling yards and supply centers, suitable targets for the larger formations that Vandenberg wanted. But the drastic reduction of its sortie rate, the successful defense of Sinuiju, and the urgent necessity of defeating the first phase of the enemy's efforts to extend his airfields marked the effective end of Bomber Command's attempt at a comprehensive attack on North Korean communications. Interdiction was thereafter primarily the responsibility of FEAF's tactical component, Fifth Air Force.[20]

---

19. USAF Hist Div, *U.S. Air Force Operations in the Korean Conflict, 1 Nov 1950–30 Jun 1952*, 59–60; Futrell, *U.S. Air Force in Korea*, 321–22.

20. Futrell, *U.S. Air Force in Korea*, 323; USAF Hist Div, *U.S. Air Force Operations in the Korean Conflict, 1 Nov 1950–30 Jun 1952*, 84. The halving of Bomber Command's sortie rate was especially serious because of the failure of the radio-guided Tarzon bomb at about the same time. The Tarzon was essentially a larger version of the Razon which had been such a disappointment in the

During the first days of the Chinese intervention, American pilots had found the enemy's motor transport an easy target. But the Chinese learned quickly and after mid-December moved their convoys mostly at night. And they soon showed that they were, as General Partridge observed, "masters of camouflage." When not using them, the Chinese hid their trucks in ravines, woods, bunkers, or houses. Sometimes they disguised vehicles as haystacks or other common objects.[21] It was obvious that if Communist motor transport was to be effectively attacked, it had either to be rooted from its daytime hiding places or intercepted on its nightly moves. The former seemed the more realistic alternative in the spring of 1951. The B–26 Invader was FEAF's only night intruder, and it was poorly suited for the role. It lacked advanced instrumentation, and suffered from poor maneuverability and slow acceleration—serious drawbacks in mountainous Korea. FEAF, indeed, would ultimately conclude that the B–26 was "nearly completely inadequate to perform the night intruder mission and there is not too much that can be done to develop that airplane to perform in the proper night intruder role."[22] This was not so apparent early in 1951 as it was later. There were also too few B–26s. Production of the aircraft had stopped in 1945, and many of those that remained were needed in Europe. The Fifth Air Force never had more than 123 Invaders, of which, on an average day, only about 75 were operational.[23]

In February 1951 Fifth Air Force inaugurated a new plan to catch the enemy's elusive motor vehicles by day. It defined a zone of interdiction that extended back fifty miles from the front. The zone was divided into three regions, and to each was assigned a fighter wing—two from the Air Force and one from the Marine Corps. Relays of fighters, F–51

---

late summer of 1950. (See Chapter 8.) By late fall, the Razon had been made to work reasonably well, but four of these expensive weapons were required to destroy an average bridge. They had, moreover, been out of manufacture since 1945, and the stock was low. The Razon, accordingly, was phased out in favor of the Tarzon, a behemoth of 12,000 pounds. For several months the new weapon was in short supply, but trials were promising. But on March 29, 1951, a group commander and his crew were lost in an attempt to ditch their B–29 shortly after they had taken off with a Tarzon on board. This incident raised concerns about the weapon's safety, which a near tragedy on April 30 showed were justified. The Tarzon, it had developed, could not be safely jettisoned at low altitude because the bomb's tail assembly tore away on impact, arming the weapon and causing its immediate detonation. Use of the Tarzon was immediately suspended, and in August the program was discontinued without another guided bomb's being available. Futrell, *U.S. Air Force in Korea*, 320–23.

21. Futrell, *U.S. Air Force in Korea*, 262–63; Lt Gen Earle E. Partridge, "Master of Camouflage," *Air Intelligence Digest* 4 (Jul 1951):4–20.

22. USAF Hist Div, *U.S. Air Force Operations in the Korean Conflict, 1 Nov 1950–30 Jun 1952*, 86.

23. 5AF, "Fifth Air Force Reviews," Jan through Dec 1951.

Mustangs for the Air Force and F4U Corsairs for the Marines, patrolled each region; the wings, in turn, divided their regions into squadron sectors. This procedure allowed a pilot to become familiar with the territory assigned to his wing and therefore better able to detect dispersed and hidden trucks. "There is only one way to detect camouflaged vehicles," one group commander reported, "and that is by flying low and slow and thoroughly searching every foot of ground. Every building, hay stack, ravine, wooded area and side road must be checked and rechecked." To guide each day's search, Fifth Air Force's Joint Operations Center prepared each morning an overlay recording the locations of all vehicles sighted during the night.[24] Because the jets were too fast and used too much fuel to employ the search techniques of conventional aircraft, the Fifth Air Force in early March developed a method to allow their participation in the newly intensive armed reconnaissance. F–51s flew singly to areas where, on the strength of reports from the night intruders, it appeared likely that trucks were hidden. The Mustangs circled the area and directed previously dispatched flights of jets to whatever targets they found.[25]

Aircraft assigned to armed reconnaissance initially flew in flights of two. A leader searched for concealed vehicles from an altitude of 100 to 300 feet, while his wingman covered him from 1,000 feet—a tactic the Chinese came to call "planes searching the mountains." In response, the enemy nearly doubled his antiaircraft weaponry between April and July and inaugurated a "Capture the Flying Bandits Competition" among the antiaircraft units. Losses of F–51s and F–80s, the planes principally used for armed reconnaissance, peaked in the spring. (*Chart 10*) The Communists, moreover, had begun to rely less upon concealing and dispersing their vehicles than on concentrating them in stout bunkers, often cut into the sides of hills, which they defended with concentrations of automatic weapons. Truck hunters were forced to fly ever higher and faster and to devote most of their effort to protecting themselves. By late spring, flights of four were standard; one plane searched at 300 feet while its three companions scouted for flak at 3,000 feet.[26] In March, Fifth Air

---

24. Futrell, *U.S. Air Force in Korea*, 332–34; Hist, 5AF, Jan 1–Jun 30, 1951, 2:172–76.

25. Futrell, *U.S. Air Force in Korea*, 332–33.

26. *Ibid.*, 333–34; Yang, *For Peace*, 108. General Yang records, "In order to counter the enemy's war of strangulation, our young troops of the anti-aircraft units thought up many ideas. For example, one idea was to hide anti-aircraft units near bridges, train stations, and traffic hubs. When the enemy reconnaissance planes arrived, we would pretend that we did not know and would wait for a large group of planes to come. Then we would fire on them with many guns all at once, and the enemy would be caught unprepared." Further, "In order greatly to weaken the enemy's air strength, we selected some advantageous terrain to

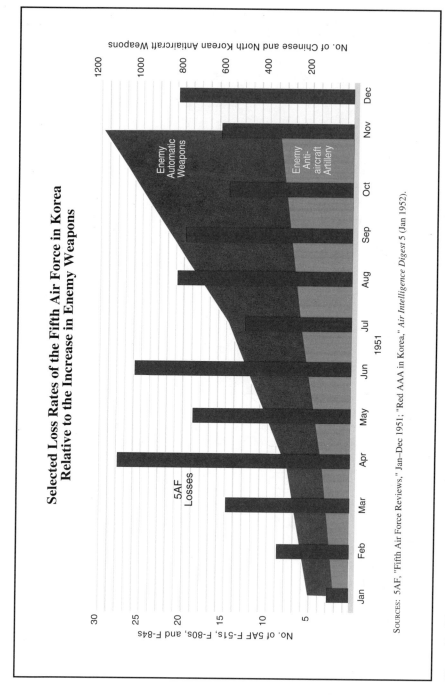

Chart 10. These selected loss rates of the Fifth Air Force illustrate the growing effectiveness of the Communist antiaircraft weaponry, although some of the Fifth Air Force's aircraft were lost to fighters and to small arms.

Force claimed to have destroyed 2,261 vehicles; in April, 2,336. But in May the claim fell to 1,245, and in June, to 827.[27]

The Chinese offensives of April and May 1951 plainly showed that the effects of interdiction had been less than desired. Much evidence, to be sure, pointed to logistical constriction caused by interdiction at a time of greatly increased consumption as an important reason for the failure of the offensive. In particular, intercepted communications revealed that the conveyance of food had suffered with the need to rush ammunition to the front. But the fact remained that the Chinese had amassed enough supplies to hurl six armies (eighteen divisions) against the United Nations Command.[28] This was reason enough to reassess the interdiction program, for which General Stratemeyer had made the Fifth Air Force primarily responsible.[29] An equally compelling reason was that the losses

---

make come counterfeit cargo trucks, and we hid our anti-aircraft artillery in this advantageous terrain. . . . During the first phase after the Volunteer Army entered Korea, at the end of the year in 1950, we had only one anti-aircraft artillery regiment. By the end of July 1951, this had developed into four divisions, three regiments, and five independent battalions." Yang, *For Peace*, 109.

27. Futrell, *U.S. Air Force in Korea*, 334–36. General Hong Xuezhi, deputy commander of the Chinese forces in Korea, later wrote that in the early stages of the war American aircraft and artillery destroyed 42.8 percent of Chinese trucks. Jonathan D. Pollack, "The Korean War and Sino-American Relations" (unpublished paper, author's collection, 1989), 35.

28. 5AF, "Fifth Air Force Reviews," Apr, May, Jun 1951; GHQ, UN/FECs, "Command Situation Reports," Apr, May 1951. The quartermaster of the Chinese Fourth Field Army reported, "Currently the food situation at the front is so serious that we cannot issue food, and the soldiers are becoming very tired of the war. If food supplies cannot be given to use immediately, we shall be facing difficult and serious conditions. . . ." On May 10 the chief of staff of the Fourth Field Army named the shortage of food among the major reasons for the failure of the offensive. GHQ, UN/FEC, "Daily Summary of Intelligence," No. 3204. In his memoirs, Marshal Peng Dehuai, commander of the Chinese forces in Korea, seems to accord the problem of food some weight as a cause of the offensive's failure. General Yang provides some details in his memoirs: "Since our army had engaged in continuous combat, the provisions and ammunition which we carried with us would soon be exhausted, and for a short while rear support could not provide us with material assistance. Since continuing the attack was already difficult, we made our minds up to halt the attack." General Yang attributes the problems of supply to interdiction: "At the time, our most pressing problem was the serious difficulty in providing ammunition and supplies as a result of the extremely poor transportation conditions created by enemy bombing." He confirms that the food had to be sacrificed to ammunition as a logistical priority. Peng Dehuai, *Memoirs of a Chinese Marshal: The Autobiographical Notes of Peng Dehuai*, translated by Zheng Longpu (Beijing, 1984), 480–81; Yang, *For Peace*, 83–84.

29. As noted earlier, the restrictions on Bomber Command's sortie rate, together with the guidance he had received from Vandenberg, led Stratemeyer to limit operations chiefly to marshaling yards and supply centers. Sometime in April or May, he made Fifth Air Force responsible for rail and road interdiction. Futrell, *U.S. Air Force in Korea, 323.*

during the program of intensive armed reconnaissance had exceeded the rate at which aircraft could be replaced. In January 1951, Fifth Air Force lost nineteen aircraft of the types used for interdiction (B–26s, F–51s, F–80s, and F–84s) to operational causes; in April the loss climbed to forty-four.[30]

Toward the end of May, General Timberlake launched Operation STRANGLE. It appears that this flamboyant (if unoriginal) name was chosen to impress the ground commanders, who after the major Chinese offensive were perhaps less than convinced of the efficacy of the interdiction to which the Air Force had devoted so much effort.[31] The purpose of STRANGLE was to ease the advance of the Eighth Army to the 38th Parallel and, over the longer term, to prevent the Chinese from resupplying sufficiently to permit their returning to the offensive.[32] STRANGLE's interdiction zone was slightly deeper than that of the preceding operation: It ran from the enemy's railheads, which tended to be along the 39th Parallel, south to the front, a distance of about seventy rather than fifty miles. Planners again divided the zone into three sectors, although the Fifth Air Force now patrolled only one, the others having been assigned to the 1st Marine Air Wing and the Navy's Task Force 77. STRANGLE deemphasized armed reconnaissance. The focus was now not on vehicles, increasingly well protected in their flak-guarded complexes of bunkers, but on roads. All bridges in the zone of interdiction were attacked as a matter of course, but STRANGLE's distinctive tactic was the cratering of roads and their mining by delayed-action bombs. Historically, these had not been among the more effective techniques for disrupting motor transport because of the ease with which vehicles could avoid such obstacles. But summer was the rainy season in Korea, and as virtually all roads ran along paddy dikes for some portion of their length, the tactic seemed promising. In general, the jet fighter-bombers (F–80s or the increasingly common F–84s) dealt with the bridges, while the roads fell to the F–51s. B–26s dropped cluster bombs around craters to delay repairs. The weapons broke apart in the air, dispensing butterfly-

---

30. USAF Hist Div, *U.S. Air Force Operations in the Korean Conflict, 1 Nov 1950–30 Jun 1952*, 156; 5AF, "Fifth Air Force Review," May 1951. It is not possible to tell from the statistics how many aircraft were lost on interdiction missions and how many while performing close air support. The Navy's losses also rose in the same period, from seven in January to twenty-three in May. Richard P. Hallion, *The Naval Air War in Korea* (Baltimore, 1986), 89.

31. Hist, 5AF, Jul 1–Dec 31, 1951, "Notes on Use of the Term 'Operation STRANGLE'," n.d., K730.01, vol 3, app 2.

32. Hist, 5AF, Jul 1–Dec 31, 1951, 1:13.

shaped bomblets that fluttered to the earth, where they lay until contact with man or vehicle set them off.[33]

A second squadron of B–26s began night operations in June, quite possibly in part because the United Nations Command had the month before raised by 50 percent its estimate of the trucks available to the Chinese.[34] The night intruders continued to face major obstacles to their effectiveness. In addition to the inadequacies of the B–26, there was no means but the unaided human eye for detecting convoys. The illumination of targets proved scarcely less vexatious. The previous fall's efforts to use B–29s to drop flares for the Invaders had not worked well: The only flare available for use with the Superfortresses had a failure rate of more than 50 percent.[35] In January Fifth Air Force had begun to use C–47 cargo planes to drop reliable parachute flares obtained from the Navy. The new technique had worked very well, so well that the ground forces had appropriated most of the sorties of the flare-dropping C–47s to support their own operations. A further limitation was that the C–47s could be flown no more than twenty or thirty miles north of the battleline because of their vulnerability to flak and the enemy's few night fighters. (About April the Fifth Air Force concluded that the Chinese had begun to make limited use of a Soviet version of the Messerschmitt Me 262, as a night interceptor.[36]) Now the C–47s were unable to provide illumination for many intruder missions in the zone of interdiction, let alone for those penetrating nearly to the Yalu. On deeper missions, therefore, B–26s had to provide their own illumination, a practice employed with varying degrees of success since the early days of the war. In February, underwing flares were fitted experimentally to the Invaders. The attempt seems not to have been successful, for in July both wings of B–26s modified a number of aircraft to carry flares in their bomb bays. In a common method of attack, a flare-carrying B–26 accompanied a strafer. Upon detecting a convoy, the latter would block its path with an incendiary bomb; the illuminating aircraft would then prepare the target for strafing by dropping its flares in a line parallel to the road. Single intruders employed a tactic more difficult to accomplish successfully:

---

33. *Ibid*, 12–13; Futrell, *U.S. Air Force in Korea*, 324.

34. Futrell, *U.S. Air Force in Korea*, 330. The estimate of vehicles available to the Chinese was increased from 4,200 to 5,000, and then to 6,000. GHQ, UN/FECs, "Command Situation Report," May 1951.

35. USAF Hist Div, *U.S. Air Force Operations in the Korean Conflict, 1 Nov 1950–30 Jun 1952*, 165.

36. Hist, 5AF, Jul 1–Dec 31, 1951, 1:257–59, 261–62. The impression that a Soviet version of the Me 262 was operating against allied forces in Korea was almost certainly false. Two early Soviet experimental aircraft—the Sukhoi Su–9 and the Su–11—did closely resemble the Me 262, but neither went into production.

An F–84 Thunderjet *(left)* lifts off the runway at an airbase in Korea. Two crewmen *(right)* in the bomb bay of a B–26 Invader fuze photo-flash bombs used to illuminate enemy convoys at night.

They dropped their flares and then descended to make figure-eight passes on the target.[37]

Whatever the method, the use of flares to hunt enemy trucking was of limited utility and very dangerous. The least degree of fog or haziness diffused the glow of the flares and blinded the crews. If the flares were dropped too high, or if the aircraft descended below them, the danger from antiaircraft fire increased markedly.[38] Amid the rugged hills of eastern Korea, the intruders could make their firing runs on convoys from altitudes no lower than 5,000 to 6,000 feet. In the west, where the terrain was less forbidding, the passes were made at 1,500 to 2,000 feet. The common opinion within the Fifth Air Force was that even the lower altitude was too high for effective gunnery.[39]

The Communists soon adopted countermeasures. The North Koreans had the responsibility for maintaining the supply routes. They assigned twelve engineer regiments to the task, each of which had three battalions of 550 men. They stationed repair crews strategically along the main supply routes; often as little as three kilometers separated them. Local civilians, additionally, were impressed as needed. The crews usually managed

---

37. USAF Hist Div, *U.S. Air Force Operations in the Korean Conflict, 1 Nov 1950–30 Jun 1952*, 166–67.
38. *Ibid.*, 167.
39. Futrell, *U.S. Air Force in Korea*, 329.

to fill craters in a matter of a few hours; they cleared butterfly bombs by the simple expedients of detonating them with rifle fire or dragging a rope across the stretch of road affected.[40] American aircraft saw a steadily increasing number of vehicles on North Korea's roads. In early July the G-2 Section of the United Nations Command estimated that the enemy was stockpiling supplies at the rate of 800 tons a day, which promised to give him very shortly an unprecedented degree of logistical preparedness. Fears of a renewed Chinese offensive were acute by September.[41] It was "increasingly apparent," the Fifth Air Force's historian noted, "that the intensive aerial effort against the Communists' highway main supply routes was not proving too successful." The only evidence of success, in fact, was the mounting claims of the night intruders. In June the two wings of night flying B-26s claimed 554 vehicles destroyed (out of a total of 827 for the entire Fifth Air Force); the next month the supposed total was 711.[42]

The evidence that STRANGLE had failed led the Eighth Army and Fifth Air Force to undertake a joint reappraisal of the Chinese Army's logistical system. The study was not published until September, but information collected for it from captured documents, the interrogation of prisoners, and various other intelligence sources influenced the planning for the operation that succeeded STRANGLE: the Rail Interdiction Program.[43] There emerged from the data a picture of a system of supply which, while primitive in some respects, was on the whole effective. The enemy's requirements were minimal. South of Sariwon the Chinese had about 600,000 men in sixty divisions. Each division required about forty tons of supplies a day to sustain itself under prevailing conditions. (This estimate was raised to fifty to sixty tons later in the year.) An American infantry division, slightly less than twice the size of its Chinese counterpart, needed 500 tons daily. A high degree of redundancy characterized the entire Chinese logistical system, both in its general organization and in such details as the practice of routinely building several bypasses for even undestroyed bridges.

The Chinese observed the so-called delivery forward principle used by the Soviets in World War II, whereby supplies flowed through a hier-

---

40. 5AF, "Intelligence Summary," Dec 28, 1951, K730.604.

41. GHQ, UN/FECs, "Command Situation Reports," May, Jun, Jul 1951; GHQ, UN/FECs, "Daily Summaries of Intelligence," Nos. 3221, 3236 (Jul 5, 20, 1950); Hist, 5AF, Jul 1–Dec 31, 1951, "TWX Concerning Possibility of Another Communist Offensive, September 1951," vol 3, app 8.

42. Hist, 5AF, Jul 1–Dec 31, 1951, "TWX Concerning Possibility of Another Communist Offensive," 1:28; 5AF, "Fifth Air Force Reviews," Jun, Jul 1951.

43. Hist, 5AF, Jul 1–Dec 31, 1951, 1:28–29.

archically organized chain of logistical units, each of which was responsible for supplying the next lower unit. There were six logistical commands, each commanded by a general officer, to support the front in Korea. Below the logistical commands, a system of fours governed: Each logistical command had up to four main depots, each of which served up to four subdepots. Each subdepot in turn controlled up to four divisional supply points. This organization was inherently redundant because the Chinese tactical system was triangular: Each army had three divisions; each division, three regiments; and so on. Each subdepot supported an army, with the result that there were four divisional supply points for every three divisions. The extra supply point provided a margin of safety to compensate for losses or to provide for divisions in transit, without prejudicing the supply of those in place. There was a further margin in that each supply point could support 13,000 men for ten days, while each division had only 10,000 men.

Each logistical command controlled a supply base and a transportation section of four motor-transport regiments (each with 120 GAZ trucks), a porter battalion, and an aircraft spotter unit of 1,200 men. These soldiers deployed nightly along the supply routes at intervals of several thousand feet to scout for damage and to provide warning of the night intruders by firing their weapons. The main depots controlled two motor-transport companies, each with sixty-five trucks. Responsibility for the movements of supplies forward of the divisional supply points fell to the divisions themselves. Lacking organic motor transport, they had to rely on porters and oxcarts to convey their requirements to the front. Artillery and mortar ammunition, which the logistical commands conveyed all the way to the front, were the only exceptions.

The joint study concluded that the enemy's logistical system, while impressive, had its weaknesses. Command and control were hampered by poor communications and a certain rigidity, and "a fatal lack of coordination between the field and logistical commands" was often apparent during offensives. The "main weakness," however, stemmed "from the use of old and often insufficient vehicles and rolling stock."[44] These conclusions, following on STRANGLE's failure to destroy the enemy's road net and Bomber Command's reduced effort against northern bridges, suggested to the Fifth Air Force's planners that they might profitably attack the railroads with their fighter-bombers. The destruction of bridges alone would not suffice; the Navy had done an effective job of destroying bridges along the eastern coast, only to observe the enemy shuttling

---

44. 5AF, "Intelligence Summary," Dec 28, 1951; GHQ, UN/FECs, "Daily Summary of Intelligence," No. 3249 (Aug 2, 1951).

trains between the downed spans. An experiment that had been conducted in late July suggested what might be done. For several weeks one wing of the Fifth Air Force had applied STRANGLE's technique of cratering roads to rail lines. The latter, being narrower, were more difficult targets. But they were also harder to repair and, most important, none of the aircraft that attacked the railroads had been lost to flak, perhaps because so much of it was covering the main supply routes.[45]

The premise of the Rail Interdiction Program was that if railroad traffic throughout North Korea could be reduced to naught, the Chinese would be unable to supply their front with motor transport alone. The plan was explained to General Vandenberg in considerable detail when he visited Korea in mid-November. According to American estimates, the sixty divisions south of Sariwon required about 2,400 tons of supplies daily. Upon the assumption that the round trip between the forward units and Antung, the logistical center in Manchuria from which the Chinese armies were supplied, took five days, the enemy needed 6,000 trucks to maintain his forces in the battle area, if each GAZ truck carried an average of two tons. Ordnance officers of Eighth Army supplied estimates, based on their own experience, of the probable life-span of these vehicles. They indicated that the attrition rate for 6,000 vehicles under Korean conditions, exclusive of combat losses, was 120 per day. The Fifth Air Force believed itself capable of destroying at least 150 trucks a day. It therefore seemed "conservative" to conclude that the enemy would then lose 250 trucks daily, or 7,500 monthly. "We don't feel," Fifth Air Force's briefer told Vandenberg, "that the Chinese can support a requirement of 7,500 trucks a month and don't feel that the Soviets would feed them that many."[46]

The Rail Interdiction Program, as an estimate of August 14, 1951, explained, called for fighter-bombers to attack rail lines throughout North Korea. The Fifth Air Force estimated that using only its own aircraft it could destroy the entire system in six to eight months. But to reduce the period to ninety days, the Air Force called on the Navy to assume responsibility for interdicting the lateral line between Samdong-ni and Kowon, and the east coast line from Hungnam through Wonsan to P'yonggang. The plan also designated five bridge complexes as targets. Bomber Command, however, would assume responsibility for the destruction of only four—those at P'yongyang, Sonchon, Sunch'on, and Sinanju. It declined to attack the bridges at Huich'on because of their proximity to Manchuria—and the bases of the MiGs. The Eighth Army, for

45. Futrell, *U.S. Air Force in Korea*, 439.
46. "As Told to General Vandenberg: The Story of 'Operation Strangle'," *Air Intelligence Digest* 5 (Jan 1952):4–10.

its part, agreed to limit its requests for close air support to ninety-six sorties a day in order to free aircraft for interdiction. The Fifth Air Force set about its task confidently. The estimate of August 14 stated that the objective was to render the enemy incapable of "opposing the U.S. Eighth Army effectively," should the United Nations resume the offensive. In November, one of Vandenberg's briefers ventured the prediction that interdiction alone would compel the enemy to retire from the 38th Parallel to a line "generally from P'yongyang through Kowon. . . ."[47] This was a much more ambitious purpose than those of the previous interdiction campaigns, the object of which had simply been to prevent the enemy from taking the offensive. The reasons for this assurance are not readily apparent, given that the two previous interdiction plans had undeniably failed. Part of the confidence was perhaps due to the fact that by the time the Rail Interdiction Plan began on August 19, the Fifth Air Force had finally succeeded in moving all its fighter-bomber wings to Korean bases from Japan.[48]

The initiation of the Rail Interdiction Plan caught the Chinese by surprise and initially unprepared to deal with a systematic assault on their rail system, different from earlier onslaughts. The night intruders reported that they had never before seen so many vehicles, many lighted, as convoys struggled to redress the diminished capacity of the railroads. A record number of vehicles for the war, 4,000, was counted on the night of August 26.[49] While the Navy harried the east coast line between Hamhung and P'yonggang, the Fifth Air Force fought to close the western coastal line between Sonchon and Sariwon. If these two stretches could be kept inoperable, crucial transverse lines in the vicinity of P'yongyang would be useless. Each fighter wing was assigned a specific section of the line, fifteen to thirty miles in length. The attacks coincided with Sabre sweeps designed to draw the MiGs away from the fighter-bombers. Wing commanders enjoyed considerable latitude in planning their raids. Most used "group gaggles" of thirty-two to sixty-four aircraft, which broke away in small flights to bomb tracks with either 1,000-pound bombs or, more commonly, two 500-pound bombs. The attackers employed both glide-bombing and dive-bombing. The former, which entailed a long approach parallel to the ground, was favored for its accuracy. But where flak was heavy, dive-bombing was necessary to reduce a plane's exposure to it. Comparing pilots' claims against evidence from photographic reconnaissance, the Fifth Air Force's Operations Analysis Office found that claims exceeded confirmed cuts by 220

---

47. *Ibid.*; Futrell, *U.S. Air Force in Korea*, 339–40.
48. 5AF, "Fifth Air Force Review," Aug 1951.
49. FEAF, "Weekly Intelligence Roundup," No. 52 (Aug 26–Sep 1, 1951).

percent. But nearly 13 percent of all bombs dropped severed track in the early stages of the Rail Interdiction Program, and nearly a quarter of all sorties resulted in cuts. During World War II, IX Tactical Air Command had managed to cut tracks only once for each eight or nine sorties.[50] Following the bombing, the gaggles of fighter-bombers broke up into flights for armed reconnaissance. This practice, however, was markedly less effective than it had been formerly, for the enemy's flak now forced the searching element to fly at about 3,000 feet.[51]

Throughout the Rail Interdiction Program, the night intruders, flying an average of about sixty sorties nightly, claimed the lion's share of vehicles. One wing of B–26s, based at Kunsan, was responsible for roads in western North Korea, while the other, flying from Pusan, covered the roads in the other half of the country. It became increasingly common to dispatch the Invaders singly so that all the major routes could be covered at least once during the night. This became increasingly feasible during the Rail Interdiction Program. The intruders turned increasingly from strafing to bombing, and bombardiers in the glass-nosed B–26Cs believed that they could dispense with the illumination that an accompanying aircraft would otherwise have had to provide. The B–26s carried proximity-fuzed 500- and 260-pound fragmentation bombs. A common load was four of the former and fourteen of the latter.[52]

It appears that the chief reason for the increased resort to bombing was that most of the B–26s sent to Korea as replacements were Model Cs rather than the "hard-nose" Model Bs. The latter, with guns rather than glazing in the nose, had been specifically designed as strafers, and for that reason sent first to Korea. Whatever the reason for it, the change soon seemed vindicated by the claims of the night intruders. In July, they had claimed to have destroyed 750 vehicles and to have damaged 1,550. In August the figures shot up to 1,935 and 3,633, respectively. On the night of August 24 alone the B–26s claimed to have destroyed or damaged nearly 800 vehicles. These numbers invited skepticism. The Fifth Air Force, accordingly, ruled in September that a vehicle must be seen to burn or to explode before it could be claimed as a kill. But in October the intruders went on to claim the destruction of 6,761 trucks. Claims for November and December were, respectively, 4,571 and 4,290.[53]

---

50. Futrell, *U.S. Air Force in Korea*, 442; 5AF Operations Analysis Office, "Validity of Pilots' Claims During Operation STRANGLE," Sep 24, 1951, K730.8101–9.

51. USAF Hist Div, *U.S. Air Force Operations in the Korean Conflict, 1 Nov 1950–30 Jun 1952*, 150.

52. *Ibid.*; Futrell, *U.S. Air Force in Korea*, 454–56.

53. USAF Hist Div, *U.S. Air Force Operations in the Korean Conflict, 1 Nov 1950–30 Jun 1952*, 170.

The claims of the night intruders were almost always unverifiable because pilots rarely had anything like an exact idea of where they had executed an attack, and the Fifth Air Force, perennially short of reconnaissance aircraft, could not afford random searches for destroyed vehicles. The claims of the fighter-bombers, on the other hand, were comparatively easy to assess with photography. If exaggerated, they were nonetheless impressive. From Sinuiju south, the western coastal line was double tracked. By cannibalizing one line to repair the other, the enemy was at first able to keep the route open until repeated attacks had devastated long stretches of roadbed. During the first month of the Rail Interdiction Program, 70 percent of the coastal line between Sinuiju and Sinanju was reduced to a single track; for the stretch between Sinanju and P'yongyang the figure was 90 percent, and from P'yongyang to Sariwon it was 40 percent.[54]

During the second month of the campaign, the interdictors began to destroy trackage faster than the enemy, who had exploited most of his opportunities for easy repairs, could replace it. The western coastal line was abandoned between P'yongyang and Sariwon after October 2. The segment Sinanju to Sukch'on went out of service about October 25, and only through the greatest exertions could the Communists keep open the stretch between Sinuiju and P'yongyang. The same was true of the central line from Huich'on through Sunch'on to Yangdok. By mid-November the interdictors had pulled still farther ahead: All the direct routes from Manchuria to the enemy's major railheads at Yangdok and Samdung had been severed. They could still be reached, but only circuitously, by using the western coast route to Sinanju, taking the lateral line to Kunu-ri, and then traveling south through Sunch'on. It was also possible to travel down the central route from Kanggye to Kunu-ri, and thence through Sunch'on to the railheads. Both routes were uncertain, however, as Bomber Command was intermittently able to put the bridge at Sunch'on out of service. Notwithstanding their primary mission of defeating the second phase of the enemy's push to extend his airfields, the B–29s also managed to reduce the serviceability of the bridges at P'yongyang, Sinanju, and Sonchon. As the Navy had succeeded in keeping the eastern coastal line between Kilchu and Wonsan closed, the severing of the single short segment of line between Kunu-ri and Sunch'on would stop all through traffic between Manchuria and the central Korean railheads.[55]

In mid-November victory seemed within the Fifth Air Force's grasp. It was then that General Vandenberg heard the prediction that the Chi-

---

54. *Ibid.*, 149.
55. *Ibid.*, 149–50.

nese and North Koreans would be forced to retire from the 38th Parallel. But scarcely had these confident words been uttered, the enemy's countermeasures began to turn the tide of battle. There had been hints of this as early as September. Throughout the Rail Interdiction Program the Communists continued the increase of antiaircraft weaponry begun earlier in the year. The number of automatic weapons, very effective against low-flying fighter-bombers, grew particularly rapidly. (See *Chart 10*) Losses mounted quickly, soon surpassing once again the rate at which aircraft could be replaced; repair crews were first overworked and then swamped as they struggled to return damaged aircraft to service. In August, the Fifth Air Force lost 30 craft; another 24 were damaged. In September, 33 were lost and 233 damaged; in October, the figures were 33 and 239, and in November, 24 and 255.[56] By October the fighter-bombers were being forced to expend 20 percent of their effort in largely unsuccessful efforts to suppress flak.[57] They were also forced, moreover, to use dive-bombing almost to the exclusion of glide-bombing in order to reduce the danger from the enemy's spreading flak, with the result that the effectiveness of their bombing decreased accordingly. By December, only 7 percent of their bombs were cutting tracks.[58]

The halving of the fighter-bombers' accuracy was serious. But there was worse: Fewer aircraft were finding the opportunity to bomb the railroads. The introduction of drop-tanks steadily expanded the MiGs' area of operations. October found them as far south as P'yongyang. (See *Map 18*) A "train" of sixty to eighty Chinese jets would fly into Korea at an altitude of 35,000 feet. As the force flew down the center of the peninsula, sections peeled off to battle the patrolling Sabres, while the main body continued south. Over P'yongyang it would converge with another train of about equal size that had flown down the western coast. The resulting formation, often containing a hundred or more aircraft, then dropped to an altitude of 15,000 feet to search for fighter-bombers working the railroads. So great was the number of MiGs that the F-86s could no longer effectively screen the F-80s and F-84s. As early as September, MiGs had forced the fighter-bombers to confine their operations

---

56. *Ibid.*, 150–51, 156; Futrell, *U.S. Air Force in Korea*, 446.

57. USAF Hist Div, *U.S. Air Force Operations in the Korean Conflict, 1 Nov 1950–30 Jun 1952*, 150–51. The lead flights of fighter-bombers were equipped with proximity-fuzed bombs to suppress flak. The enemy gunners, however, learned to take cover until these aircraft were past. The flak-suppression flights were then put in the rear of the formation. The new practice, while it may have caught more of the enemy's gunners, did little to ease the way for the pilots who had to bomb the tracks.

58. USAF Hist Div, *U.S. Air Force Operations in the Korean Conflict, 1 Nov 1950–30 Jun 1952*, 151; Futrell, *U.S. Air Force in Korea*, 446.

to the area south of the Ch'ongch'on River. The MiGs had the initiative by November; they regularly "bounced" the fighter-bombers north of P'yongyang. Losses were few, but the American jets often had to jettison their bombs to escape from their tormentors.[59]

The effect of the MiGs on the operations of Bomber Command was also drastic. The threat that the Soviet-built aircraft posed to the aging medium bombers had been evident since the spring when Bomber Command had been forced to curtail its operations in MiG Alley. The fullness of the danger, however, was not apparent until late October. On October 22, nine B–29s, having just bombed an airfield under construction at Taechon, were jumped by three MiGs after forty others had drawn away twenty-four escorting F–84s. One Superfortress went down. The next day, in a carefully planned interception, fifty MiGs attacked eight B–29s on their way to bomb the airfield at Namsi-dong. Recklessly disregarding fifty-five escorting F–84s, they broke upon the bombers, sending three to earth and seriously damaging the rest. On October 24 eight B–29s, escorted by ten F–84s and sixteen British Meteors, were intercepted by between forty and seventy MiGs. Once again the relatively low-performance escorts could not fend off the attackers, and a Superfortress went down in Wonsan harbor. In Washington a gloomy Vandenberg exclaimed, "Almost overnight, Communist China has become one of the major air powers of the world."[60] Thereafter the B–29s operated only at night. This conferred, for the time being, immunity from the MiGs, and with the use of a system of radar navigation known as Shoran, the medium bombers were able to attack bridges successfully. But by denying the daytime sky to Bomber Command, its sortie rate was so cut that it could pursue its first priority, the neutralization of the enemy's advance airfields, only at the expense of the Rail Interdiction Program.[61]

---

59. 5AF Deputy for Intelligence, Estimates Director, "The Growth of MiG Alley," Dec 1951, in Hist, FEAF, Jul 1–Dec 31, 1951, K720.01, vol 3, app 27; Futrell, *U.S. Air Force in Korea*, 404–05, 413–14.

60. Hist, FEAF Bomber Command, Jul 1–Dec 31, 1951, K713.07-20, 31–34; Futrell, *U.S. Air Force in Korea*, 410–12. Information recently released in the Soviet Union suggests that many of the MiGs were flown by Soviet pilots. Steven J. Zalaga, "The Russians in MiG Alley," *Air Force Magazine*, Feb 1991, 74–77.

61. Futrell, *U.S. Air Force in Korea*, 446. The decision to suspend daytime operations was made at a commanders' conference held on Oct 28, 1951. Hist, FEAF Bomber Command, Jul 1–Dec 31, 1951, 34. Shoran was not a bombing radar, as understood today; it was a navigation radar. An aircraft under its guidance transmitted signals to beacons of known position, which amplified and returned the signal to the airplane. Measurement of the time required for each signal to return established a fix of the aircraft's location precise enough to attack even small targets. USAF Hist Div, *U.S. Air Force Operations in the Korean Conflict, 1 Nov 1950–30 Jun 1952*, 179.

Even as the sortie rate of Bomber Command dwindled, and the fighter-bombers became less able to cut trackage, the Communists grew steadily more proficient in their repair work. Korean agents of the U.S. Air Force's Office of Special Investigation, active in North Korea throughout the war, observed the work firsthand. Maintenance of the railroads was entrusted to the North Korean Railroad Bureau, which controlled three repair brigades, each of which comprised 7,500 men. These numbers are by themselves misleading, for the men of the repair brigades served as cadre for laborers, who were impressed as needed. Small units of cadre patrolled sections of track about four miles in length along the major lines. By day they walked the tracks to check for damage and to recruit labor for the work of repair, which began in late afternoon. Experienced foremen directed the work and effected the actual repair of rails and ties. The North Koreans stored repair materials at intervals along the railroads and by all bridges. They relied heavily upon prefabricated wooden sections to repair bridges and to build the inevitably alternate bypasses. Tools were crude, but manpower was plentiful. The Fifth Air Force observed ruefully that the enemy always repaired roadbeds within two to six hours, and needed no more than two to four days to replace even the largest bridges.[62] The Communists were aided by the bitter cold of the Korean winter. As the ground froze deeper, bombs frequently bounced back into the air before exploding, and the craters of successful strikes were shallower than before.[63]

By December the defense had triumphed. In that month confirmed cuts numbered 2,400, down from November's 4,100. The 8th Fighter Group, one of the Fifth Air Force's best units, tried repeatedly to sever the crucial segment between Kunu-ri and Sunch'on, but the Communists

---

62. Hist, 5AF, Jul 1–Dec 31, 1951, "Methods of Railroad Maintenance in North Korea," Dec 31, 1951, vol 3, app 16; 5AF, "Intelligence Summaries," Dec 28, 1951, Feb 2, 1952. The Chinese appear to have used deception extensively to protect their bridges. In one instance, photographic reconnaissance revealed that they were using a crane to remove sections of a rail bridge by day in order to simulate bomb damage. This practice seems to have been widely employed to protect road bridges: "... We would prepare boards, each of which was the appropriate size for a hole in the bridge left by a bomb. ... When the trucks arrived, we would fix up the bridge with the boards. When the trucks left, we would pull the boards off. The enemy planes would see that it was still a wrecked bridge and would not bomb it again. They [the engineers] constructed some bridges which could be taken apart and put back together again. When our trucks came, we would put them together. When the enemy planes came, we would take them apart. At night, they would be put together, and, during the day, they would be taken apart." 5AF, "Intelligence Summary," Nov 25, 1951; Yang, *For Peace,* 113.
63. USAF Hist Div, *U.S. Air Force Operations in the Korean Conflict, 1 Nov 1950–30 Jun 1952,* 151; Hist, 5AF, Jul 1–Dec 31, 1951, 1:73–74.

filled the craters faster than the F-80s could blast them out. And while doing that, they built a whole bypass line for the much attacked P'yong-yang–Sinanju segment and began another for the stretch, Sunch'on–Kunu-ri. The Sunch'on bridges were kept in service, and the B-29s could not keep the crossings at Sinanju unserviceable for more than two days at a time. Bypass bridges were also constructed at P'yongyang, Sinanju, and Sonchon faster than earlier structures could be destroyed.⁶⁴ The Rail Interdiction Program continued through February 1952, but the Fifth Air Force conceded defeat on December 28, 1951: "The enemy's highly developed repair and construction capability of both bridges and rail lines has broken our railroad blockade of P'yongyang and has won for him the use of all key rail arteries."⁶⁵

FEAF's strenuous efforts to interdict Chinese lines of communication were not without effect. Captured Chinese soldiers told their interrogators how, for fear of aircraft, they had marched furtively from Manchuria by night and hid like hunted animals by day. Most had experienced an attack on their marching camps; many told of fellow replacements who exhibited signs of combat fatigue before reaching the front.⁶⁶ A considerable diversion of resources was required to keep the system operational. Men who might have fought, worked behind the lines and consumed part of what would otherwise have gone to the front.⁶⁷ Interdiction, moreover, certainly limited the capacity of the enemy's supply system by confining travel to hours of darkness and interfering with schedules. American intelligence, which routinely broke the enemy's codes, reported that the messages of Chinese commanders frequently complained of serious shortages.⁶⁸ The Chinese were chronically short of artillery ammunition, usually a reliable indication of disrupted communications.⁶⁹ The extent to which interdiction was responsible for shortages of various commodities at the front is uncertain, but its contribution was probably considerable, especially during the enemy's offensives of April and May.

---

64. Hist, 5AF, Jul 1–Dec 31, 1951, 1:73–74.
65. 5AF, "Intelligence Summary," Dec 28, 1951.
66. Memo, 5AF Operations Analysis Office, "Abridgement of Memorandum No. 43, Physical and Psychological Effects of Interdiction Air Attacks as Determined from POW Interrogations," May 21, 1951, K720.3101-43.
67. An intercepted Chinese communication of May 11 ordered the mobilization of 400,000 workers (one suspects a mistranslation or a typographical error) to work, building trenches and bunkers on the supply route from Sinuiju to the front. GHQ, UN/FECs, "Daily Summary of Intelligence," No. 3204 (Jun 18, 1951).
68. See note 28.
69. Walter G. Hermes, *Truce Tent and Fighting Front* [U.S. Army in the Korean War] (Washington, 1966), 174–75.

It is nonetheless clear, however, that FEAF failed to achieve not only its maximal objective—the enemy's retirement from the 38th Parallel—but also the lesser goal of rendering the Communists incapable of offensive action. After a careful collation of intelligence information, the G–2 Section of the United Nations Command judged on September 2, 1951, that the Chinese had developed, since their offensive of the spring, "a potent capability for offensive action." A week later the enemy was credited with having "achieved a logistical basis considerably in excess of any he had enjoyed at the launching of any past offensive."[70] That there was no offensive was in all probability due to the fact that China, like the United States, had achieved her minimal political objective: She had preserved North Korea, as the Americans had South Korea.[71]

Effective interdiction in Korea was difficult for at least four reasons. First, the enemy's consumption was inherently low; there was also little heavy fighting after the first half of 1951. Second, the enemy had a large supply of labor to devote to the task of keeping his communications open. Third, FEAF had too few aircraft for the tasks given to it. Bomber Command was not nearly large enough to attack the enemy's communications comprehensively within a period sufficiently short to overwhelm efforts at repair. The force of fighter-bombers in particular was too small, and its replacements too few, to bear the loss of even twenty to thirty aircraft a month. Most of the machines that FEAF employed were out of production (B–29s, B–26s, F–51s, and F–80s), and the Korean War occurred when the global commitments of the U.S. Air Force, particularly the demands of the recently formed North Atlantic Treaty Organization, had strained its resources to the limit. Fourth, but by no means least, the Air Force lacked in Korea, as it had lacked in World War II, the technological capacity for effective interdiction at night. The B–26 was completely inadequate, and the impressive claims of the night intruders were, in a word, inflated. In 1952 Maj. Gen. Glenn O. Barcus took command of Fifth Air Force and, deeply skeptical of the intruders' claims, arranged an experiment. The two wings of B–26s assigned to night interdiction provided crews chosen for their expertise; *in broad daylight* they attacked with bombs and machineguns derelict trucks

---

70. GHQ, UN/FECs, "Daily Summaries of Intelligence," Nos. 3280, 3288 (Sep 2, 10, 1951).

71. Later in the fall, the United Nations Command concluded from a study of the enemy's dispositions that he was able to attack but had chosen not to do so. GHQ, UN/FECs, "Daily Summary of Intelligence," No. 3350 (Nov 11, 1951).

on a target range. The results were unambiguous: "The current night intruder program is not effective in destroying enemy vehicles because of [an] inability to hit the targets."[72]

These factors perhaps made the frustration of interdiction inevitable. One Navy report concluded in December 1951 that "it is probably impossible to achieve complete interdiction of a country only partially industrialized [and] possessing mass manpower except by physical occupation."[73] What is most interesting, however, is the strategy that the Chinese used to increase the margin of their success. While benefiting from the low consumption of the Chinese armies and an abundance of labor, the strategy depended upon neither and could have been applied in quite different circumstances. The Chinese first limited FEAF's access to their air space while steadily making their communications more defensible. The process began with the battle for the Yalu bridges. First flak, and then the MiGs, put crucial bridge complexes beyond reach of the B-29s. Then, during the fall of 1951 the MiGs halved the striking power of Bomber Command by denying it the daytime sky over North Korea. All the while the Communists steadily increased their antiaircraft artillery, particularly the automatic weapons so deadly to fighter-bombers. Flak ended the intensive aerial reconnaissance of Interdiction Plan No. 4, and made the postholing of roads during STRANGLE prohibitively expensive; by the end of the Rail Interdiction Program it had nearly halved the accuracy of the fighter-bombers' attacks, even as the great MiG "trains," sweeping southward from P'yongyang, reduced the number of sorties during which bombs could be directed at trackage. The success of the Chinese Air Force has been unduly obscured by the famous 13:1 ratio that the F-86s enjoyed against the MiGs. The Sabres may have won all the aerial duels, but they were too few to occupy more than a fraction of the enemy's fighter force; the remainder pressed on to harass the interdicting fighter-bombers.

While thus reducing FEAF's striking power, the Chinese decreased the vulnerability of their communications by camouflage that grew ever more expert, together with the maximum dispersion of resources. Trucks,

---

72. USAF Hist Div, *U.S. Air Force Operations in the Korean Conflict, 1 Nov 1950–30 Jun 1952,* 174–75. Even under these ideal conditions only 5 percent of the bombs fell within 75 feet of the aiming point, and it was found that trucks not laden with explosive or incendiary cargos were rarely damaged by bombs that exploded more than 50 feet away. All in all, 1.8 trucks were destroyed for every 100 bombs dropped. The gunnery of the B-26s was no better: From a range of 2,000 feet, hits on a 10-foot by 10-foot target amounted to no more than 1 or 2 percent of all rounds expended. *Ibid.*
73. Hallion, *Naval Air War in Korea,* 96.

for example, traveled in convoys of as few as five, even singly.[74] The principle of redundancy was observed throughout the enemy's logistical system—in the superfluity of the divisional supply points, the great number of bypass bridges, and even in the creation of supplementary rail lines. Even with all these precautions, FEAF continued to cut roads and rail lines and to put bridge complexes out of service. But the logistical constriction that resulted from these blows was minimized by the amazing ability of the Chinese and the North Koreans to repair the damaged facilities.

---

74. 5AF, "Intelligence Summaries," Oct 3, 10, 1951.

Section III

The War in Southeast Asia

Massive Retaliation and the
Unheeded Lessons of Korea

American efforts to interdict Chinese communications in Korea were only intermittently effective during 1951. The chief reasons for the general lack of success (as discussed in Chapter 9) were the low consumption of the Chinese armies, the privileged sanctuary of the Chinese Air Force in Manchuria, the U.S. Air Force's small number of tactical aircraft, and the effectiveness of Chinese antiaircraft defenses. The same problems hobbled Operation SATURATE in 1952. SATURATE was an attempt to cut Chinese communications by directing around-the-clock attacks against short segments of rail lines. There were some initial successes, but the Fifth Air Force again found that its force of fighter-bombers was too small to permit the simultaneous interdiction of a sufficient number of rail lines to obtain the desired effect. Once the Chinese began to concentrate their flak along the main lines, the Fifth Air Force's losses quickly became unsustainable.[1]

There were many criticisms of the Air Force's interdiction programs, both in the press and by the leaders of other services. General Lemuel C. Shepherd, commandant of the Marine Corps, pronounced the Korean STRANGLE a "fizzle." The Air Force defended its efforts by claiming that the Chinese had at least been prevented from amassing sufficient supplies to mount a general offensive.[2] But since the Chinese, having realized their minimum goal of preserving North Korea, had no compelling motive to launch a major offensive, the claim remained unproven. Some evidence cast doubt upon it. In July 1951, for example, the Chinese expended only 8,000 mortar and artillery rounds. In May 1952, they fired 102,000 rounds at the forces of the United Nations. Nor was the Air Force's case for interdiction strengthened when it deemphasized the practice in the spring of 1952 in favor of the Air Pressure Campaign, an es-

---

1. Robert F. Futrell, *The United States Air Force in Korea, 1950–1953* (Washington, 1983), 451–53.
2. *Ibid.*, 471; Robert Frank Futrell, *Ideas, Concepts, Doctrine: A History of Basic Thinking in the United States Air Force, 1907–1964* (Maxwell AFB, 1971), 180.

sentially political strategy designed to bring the Communists to a truce by inflicting an intolerable level of damage on the economic infrastructure of North Korea.[3]

Two of the reasons for the disappointing outcome of interdiction operations in Korea—the low consumption of the Chinese armies on a stalemated front and the sanctuary of the Chinese Air Force in Manchuria—were peculiar to an unusual war. But the small numbers of American fighter-bombers, which had made the losses to Chinese antiaircraft fire so serious, reflected an intrinsic weakness of the U.S. Air Force. American airmen appear to have understood perfectly well what the problem had been. "Nothing is so bad in air campaigns as not to have enough force to do a job correctly," observed Lt. Gen. Otto P. Weyland, who commanded the Far Eastern Air Forces after June 1951. Yet no significant improvement in the position of tactical aviation followed Korea.

The tactical forces continued to languish because of the continuing primacy of strategic aviation. One reason for this was that the Air Force was led largely by men who had commanded bombers and witnessed firsthand the successes of strategic bombing in World War II. But the most pressing reason for the allocation of resources to the strategic forces was the need to deter the Soviet Union. The United States had dismantled its conventional forces faster and to a greater extent than the Soviet Union had after the war. The strategic forces had to redress the balance, and to do so at a time of severe budgetary constraints. The leadership of the Air Force had agreed in 1948 that its highest priority should be the rapid development of the Strategic Air Command. The emergence of a somewhat creditable Soviet strategic force shortly after the end of the Korean War reinforced the existing priorities. So, too, did the Eisenhower administration's attempts to economize by emphasizing a cost-effective "massive retaliation" over conventional deterrence.[4]

The importance accorded to the Strategic Air Command led to what one historian has called the "denigration of tactical air forces and air mobility forces."[5] The increased reliance on nuclear weapons inevitably shaped both the doctrine and the equipment of the Tactical Air Command. In 1953, Project VISTA, a study conducted for the Air Force by

---

3. Futrell, *U.S. Air Force in Korea*, 471, 475–504.
4. David Alan Rosenberg, "The Origins of Overkill: Nuclear Weapons and American Strategy, 1945–1960," *International Security* 7 (Spring, 1983):19, 28–44.
5. Robert F. Futrell, "The Influence of the Air Power Concept on Air Force Planning, 1945–1962," in Lt Col Harry R. Borowski, ed., *Military Planning in the Twentieth Century: Proceedings of the Eleventh Military History Symposium, 10–12 October 1984* (Washington, 1986), 266.

the California Institute of Technology, concluded that "the tactical employment of our atomic resources" held "outstanding promise" for defending Western Europe. Both the Air Force and President Eisenhower accepted this line of reasoning.[6] The tactical forces came increasingly to resemble a theater-level imitation of the Strategic Air Command. Maj. Gen. Edward J. Timberlake, commander of Tactical Air Command's Ninth Air Force, declared in 1956 that in response to an "overt act by an aggressor nation," tactical forces in the theater would "launch an atomic punch aimed . . . at turning the enemy military machine into a relatively innocuous group of men by depriving it of the means of waging war."[7] Small wonder that airmen joked that Tactical Air Command had been "SACumcized."

If tactical forces were to be used to deliver nuclear weapons, it followed that they, unlike their predecessors of the world war, would not need large numbers of aircraft. The new emphasis on atomic weapons, the budgetary constraints, and the calculation that the threat of massive retaliation would deter the Communists from starting local wars as well as a general conflict kept the tactical forces quite small. The number of tactical fighter-bombers remained approximately constant through the 1950s. On the last day of 1953 the Air Force had a total of 5,881 fighters, of which 1,966 were jet-propelled fighter-bombers (1,693 F–84s and 273 F–80s). On June 30, 1960, the Air Force had 5,032 fighters, of which 2,102 were jet fighter-bombers (204 F–80s, 94 F–84s, 1,524 F–100s, 193 F–104s, and 87 F–105s). The situation was not greatly different on June 20, 1965, just as ROLLING THUNDER, the first phase of the bombing of North Vietnam, was about to begin. The total number of fighters was down to 3,792, of which 2,281 were fighter-bombers (402 F–4s, 27 F–5s, 950 F–100s, 222 F–104s, and 680 F–105s). But of this number, only 1,082 (the F–4s and the F–105s) were at all suitable for use over North Vietnam. By June 30, 1972, shortly after the second phase of the bombing of North Vietnam—LINEBACKER I—had begun, total fighter strength was down to 2,575 aircraft, of which 2,024 were fighter-bombers (1,427 F–4s, 19 F–5s, 115 F–100s, 18 F–104s, 110 F–105s, and 335 F–111s). By this time, only the F–4s and the F–111s were suitable for strike operations over North Vietnam, and the F–111 was not yet present in the theater.[8]

---

6. Rosenberg, "Origins of Overkill," 20, 34.

7. Mark Clodfelter, *The Limits of Air Power: The American Bombing of North Vietnam* (New York, 1989), 30–31.

8. *United States Air Force Statistical Digests: Fiscal Years 1954, 1960, 1965, and 1972* (Washington, 1954–72), 109, 75, 81, and 165, respectively. It should be borne in mind that the numbers given for tactical aircraft are merely aggregates. At all times, considerable numbers of them were detailed for special purposes and were unavailable for interdiction missions. Virtually all of the F–105s still in

The nuclear emphasis changed the design of tactical aircraft in ways that made them quite unsuited to carry out interdiction missions with conventional ordnance. The F–105 Thunderchief, which entered service in 1958 and flew 75 percent of all the sorties against North Vietnam in ROLLING THUNDER (1965–1968), exemplified the trend. Having been designed as a tactical nuclear bomber, it was unmaneuverable and vulnerable to antiaircraft fire. About 43 percent of all the F–105s built were shot down during ROLLING THUNDER. The Thunderchief was withdrawn from combat before the bombing of North Vietnam resumed in 1972. The F–4 Phantom, the fighter-bomber principally employed during the renewed offensive, had been designed as a high-altitude interceptor. It, too, was little suited for conventional interdiction, as its cockpit afforded poor visibility and its engines belched black smoke that gave the enemy early warning of its approach. Like the F–105, the F–4 was vulnerable to ground fire; neither aircraft had the self-sealing gas tanks that had been standard in World War II.[9]

In sum, the strategic emphasis of the 1950s put the U.S. Air Force in the position of having to wage interdiction in Vietnam with relatively small numbers of aircraft poorly suited for the role. This boded ill for operations in Southeast Asia, for the technology of antiaircraft defense had not stood still: The 1950s saw the introduction of the antiaircraft missile, a weapon that was to put serious constraints on American operations over North Vietnam and Laos.

---

service in 1972, for example, had been refitted to serve as WILD WEASELs, the function of which was to ferret out and destroy antiaircraft weapons.

9. Pacific Air Forces, Activity Input to Proj Corona Harvest, *In-Country and Out-Country Strike Operations in Southeast Asia, 1 January 1965–31 December 1969*, vol 2: *Hardware: Strike Aircraft* (S) (HQ PACAF, Nov 1970), 32–107.

Chapter 10

———◆—————

Operation COMMANDO HUNT VII
Southern Laos
1971–1972

Laos was the principal corridor for the supplies and reinforcements that the government of North Vietnam sent to its forces fighting in South Vietnam. After the end of American air attacks on North Vietnam in 1968, Laos became the focus for the efforts of the U.S. Air Force to staunch this flow. The tempo of logistical operations was largely determined by the alternating dry and rainy seasons. The relative impassability of the Laotian roads during the rainy season required the North Vietnamese to accomplish most of their resupply during the dry season. American efforts at interdiction, accordingly, were most intensive during the dry seasons. COMMANDO HUNT VII was the last and most interesting of the dry season interdiction campaigns. Measured in terms of sorties, it was slightly smaller than the preceding dry season campaign, COMMANDO HUNT V. But COMMANDO HUNT VII represented the technological culmination of Laotian interdiction operations. It was also interrupted by the North Vietnamese Easter Offensive of 1972, an event that provided a gauge of effectiveness more objective than any available for earlier operations. COMMANDO HUNT VII also saw a major improvement in North Vietnamese antiaircraft defenses in Laos, which made it a more compelling test than its predecessors of the limits of interdiction.

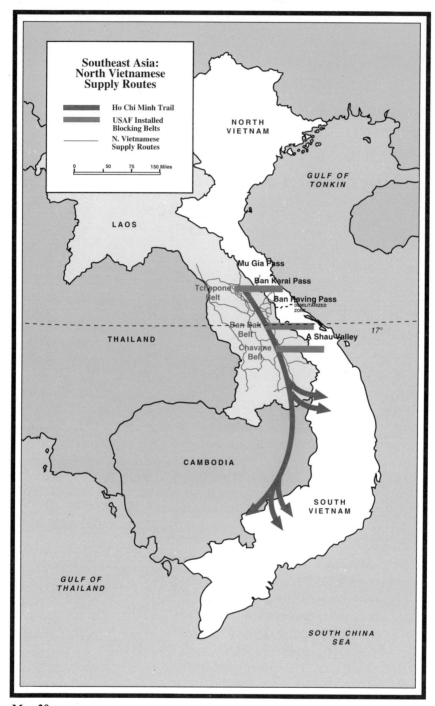

Southeast Asia:
North Vietnamese
Supply Routes

- Ho Chi Minh Trail
- USAF Installed Blocking Belts
- N. Vietnamese Supply Routes

0   50   75   150 Miles

NORTH VIETNAM

GULF OF TONKIN

LAOS

Mu Gia Pass

Ban Karai Pass

Tchepone Belt

Ban Raving Pass

DEMILITARIZED ZONE

THAILAND

Ban Bak Belt

A Shau Valley

17°

Chavane Belt

CAMBODIA

SOUTH VIETNAM

GULF OF THAILAND

SOUTH CHINA SEA

Map 20.

In 1945, Vietnamese nationalists led by the veteran Communist Ho Chi Minh began an insurrection against France. The Geneva Accords of 1954 marked the end of the first phase of their struggle. The victory of the Communists was less than total, for the Geneva agreement divided Vietnam in two at latitude 17° north. The north fell to Ho, who promptly organized the People's Republic of Vietnam. But the south, which became the Republic of Vietnam, came under the control of conservative elements associated with the defeated French and, increasingly, with the United States. The agreement of 1954 stipulated that elections should be held in 1956 to unite the country. It was soon clear, however, that neither the South Vietnamese authorities nor their foreign backers were disposed to permit a national referendum. In October 1957, South Vietnamese Communists, acting on orders from the north, organized thirty-seven companies of guerrillas to begin an insurrection. Two years later, the North Vietnamese created the 559th Transportation Group to provide for the logistical support of the southern rebels. One of its missions was improvement of the infiltration routes used earlier against the French. This was the origin of the famed Ho Chi Minh Trail.

At the time, the routes to the south were no more than a web of jungle trails that the aboriginal inhabitants of southeastern Laos and northeastern Cambodia had used since time immemorial. Improvements were not quickly made. In 1964, the Central Committee of the North Vietnamese Communist Party sent Col. Bui Tin and a team of military specialists south to monitor the progress of the rebellion. For five weeks the party toiled on foot along narrow foot paths over mountains and through steamy rain forests. Colonel Bui, a hardened veteran, later described the journey as "extremely arduous." He returned to Hanoi to report that there was little hope that the insurrectionists could, at their cur-

rent level of support from the north, prevail against the Republic of
Vietnam, which was by this time the object of lavish American subsidies.
His report confirmed a decision already made in his absence: that North
Vietnamese regulars should be committed to the war in the south. With
this resolution, improvement of the trail became an urgent necessity. A
great engineering effort, led by Col. Dong Si Nguyen, began in 1964. Engineering battalions with earth-moving equipment set to work, constructing every manner of facility to support the passage south of thousands of
soldiers and the supplies to sustain them.[1]

The terrain through which the construction battalions inched their
way south was varied but almost uniformly hostile to the passage of
man. The Laotian Panhandle, which the Americans called STEEL TIGER,
is dominated by uplands, largely plains and plateaus but also mountains
taller than 5,000 feet. The mountains are steep; much of the remaining
terrain is karst, eroded limestone formed into cliffs and ridges, sinks and
caves. The Annamite Mountains form a natural barrier between Vietnam
and Laos. They channel movement from North Vietnam to Laos through
three passes: Ban Karai, in lower North Vietnam; Mu Gia in the northern Panhandle; and Ban Raving, just east and slightly north of what was
in 1971 the Demilitarized Zone (DMZ) between the two Vietnams. Nature similarly dictates the exits from Laos to South Vietnam. Immediately below the DMZ, where the Annamite Mountains are cut by the Xe
Pon River, rolling plateaus afford travelers from the north ready access
to northern South Vietnam. Farther south, below intervening mountains,
a pass leads into the A Shau Valley of northwestern South Vietnam.
Much farther to the south, a third pass exists near the junction of the
Vietnamese, Laotian, and Cambodian borders. (*Map 20*)

Climate was also a determinant of military operations in southern
Laos. The region knows two major seasons: the rainy and the dry. The
former lasts from mid-May to mid-September, the latter begins about
mid-October. Between the two are transitional periods of six to eight
weeks. Annual rainfall varies from as little as 50 inches to more than
200. Even at the height of the rainy season the variation in precipitation
is considerable; monthly averages range from 8 to 50 inches.

The vegetation of the Panhandle is determined primarily by altitude.
From the river valleys to elevations of about 800 feet, bamboo thickets
and heavy undergrowth predominate. Passage off-trail is usually impossible without hacking. Higher, to an altitude of about 2,500 feet, are tropi-
cal rain forests. Trees are very tall and form layered canopies that shield
the ground from aerial observation. Scattered undergrowths of bamboo,

---

1. Stanley Karnow, *Vietnam: A History* (New York, 1983), 237, 330–34.

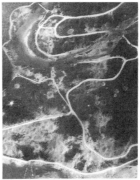

Indicative of the karst topography that differentiates Laos from Vietnam is the view *(left)* seen in the STEEL TIGER area. This is the region of Laos through which the Ho Chi Minh Trail passed. An example of the extensive network of well-tended and redundant roads in Laos is seen in the photograph *(right)* taken in the Mu Gia Pass. *Left photo, personal collection of Lt. Col. Vance Mitchell, USAF Ret.*

air plants, and banana palms make for difficult passage. From 2,500 to 4,000 feet, the canopy is broken; there are extensive grasslands with scattered thickets of bamboo. The monsoon forest begins at about 4,000 feet. Pines, scrub oak, and rhododendron form a broken canopy; the forest floor is relatively clean.

By 1971, the 559th Transportation Group had become the 559th Military Region, and the Ho Chi Minh Trail had grown from a fragile net of jungle footpaths into more than 2,700 miles of well-tended motor roads. Southern Laos was subdivided into fifteen military districts, or "Binh Trams." The commander of each semiautonomous Binh Tram was responsible for all functions within its borders. He controlled transportation, engineer, antiaircraft, and liaison battalions as well as support elements. The task of moving supplies through the Binh Tram fell primarily to the transportation battalions. The primary duty of the engineer battalions was to build and repair roads, although they also moved supplies when required. The liaison battalions handled the infiltration of personnel through the Binh Tram along trails separate from the roads used for the transport of supplies. The support elements were responsible for food, shelter, medical services, and other staff functions.[2]

---

2. Directorate of Intelligence, Task Force Alpha, "North Vietnamese Army Logistic System in STEEL TIGER," n.d. [late 1972], K744.0721–15, 6–9; Hist, U.S. Military Assistance Command, Vietnam (MACV), Jan 1972–Mar 1973 (hereafter MACV Hist), vol 1, annex A, 43–44.

The cellular North Vietnamese logistical system somewhat resembled that developed by the Chinese Communists during the Korean War. In both cases, the purpose of decentralization was to obtain a degree of redundancy sufficient to minimize the effects of interdiction. Southern Laos was not simply a conduit between the two Vietnams. The region was "saturated" (to use a term favored by American intelligence) with a very large number of widely dispersed storage areas. This principle of operation was costly in that it required that the logistical system contain large quantities of supplies regardless of demand. But it was safe and supremely flexible. Even extensive bombing was unlikely to destroy many of the stores, and obstructed routes could be circumvented with less likelihood of time-consuming detours and relocations.[3]

American intelligence was able to trace how the process of saturation proceeded during the last dry-season interdiction campaign of the war in Southeast Asia—COMMANDO HUNT VII. In early November 1971, as the roads dried, the North Vietnamese began to fill the supply dumps in northern STEEL TIGER near the points of entry from their homeland. By January, their trucks had begun to move supplies into central STEEL TIGER, which the Americans designated the "core route structure." By early February, the process of saturation had reached the entrances into South Vietnam and Cambodia. North Vietnamese forces in South Vietnam and Cambodia had meanwhile been sustained by the supplies that remained in Laos from the previous dry season. Task Force Alpha, the intelligence organization created to monitor North Vietnamese activity in STEEL TIGER, estimated in August 1971 that this residue amounted to approximately 20,000 tons.[4]

The logistical strategy of the North Vietnamese depended on the extensive network of roads in Laos, which they indefatigably extended each dry season. In 1966, the Ho Chi Minh Trail consisted of 820 miles of fair-weather roads. By the fall of 1971, 2,710 miles of roads were known to American intelligence, which acknowledged that there were routes of which it knew nothing. During COMMANDO HUNT VII, the Americans plotted the construction of an additional 310 miles, which figure did not include many small additions, such as cutoffs and bypasses.[5]

Parallel routes, connected by innumerable spurs and bypasses, ran north to south through STEEL TIGER. The constant bombing of the roads indirectly contributed to the system's redundancy. Serious damage was

---

3. MACV Hist, 35–36.

4. *Ibid.*, 37; EOTR, Col D.L. Evans, Dir/Intel, Task Force Alpha, Jul 6, 1972, 1005110, 11.

5. Directorate of Intelligence, Task Force Alpha, "North Vietnamese Army Logistic System in STEEL TIGER," 38; Hist, Seventh Air Force, "COMMANDO HUNT VII" (S), Jun 1972 (hereafter 7AF Hist, "CH VII"), K740.04–14, 20.

This strike photo *(left)* catches the destruction of a Communist truck park. A post-strike reconnaissance photo *(right)* shows damage to another truck park after it had been bombed and strafed by fighter-bombers.

circumvented by the construction of local bypasses which proliferated enormously over the years. The roads ran through every sort of terrain; some were sheltered by the dense canopy of the rain forest, others meandered through the karst. Still others were boldly laid through grassy savannahs. The original roads were usually built along rivers and in valleys, following paths of least resistance. With experience and better equipment, however, the North Vietnamese increasingly laid their routes on higher ground less liable to flooding. There, too, it was possible to use to better advantage the shelter of the rain forest. The roads were narrow, 12 to 15 feet across. A few were asphaltic, but most were naturally surfaced, graveled or corduroyed with logs or bamboo where drainage was poor. The system could not sustain heavy traffic during the rainy season but was rarely wholly impassable. Truck parks, repair facilities, storage areas, and camps were situated at the ends of access roads, 600 to 1,000 feet from the major roads, near sources of water when possible. The North Vietnamese usually parked their trucks by twos and threes in revetments camouflaged with branches and leaves.[6]

---

6. Directorate of Intelligence, Task Force Alpha, "North Vietnamese Army Logistic System in STEEL TIGER," 11–14; 7AF Hist, "CH VII," 89.

The operation, maintenance, and expansion of the logistical system in STEEL TIGER required a heavy commitment of manpower. During COMMANDO HUNT VII, American intelligence put the enemy force at 96,000, an increase of 35,000 from the previous year. To judge from the speed with which roads were built and repaired, a considerable portion of this number must have been committed to construction. Apart from a few bulldozers, little earth-moving machinery was available. The engineer battalions scattered throughout STEEL TIGER worked for the most part with simple hand tools. It appears that Laotian villagers were sometimes drafted for brief periods to assist with the more arduous tasks. However crude the means, the system was effective. Roads cratered by bombs during the night were quite often repaired by dawn.[7]

That many of the roads of Laos were unusable for much of the rainy reason was the most serious constraint on the capacity of the Communists' logistical system. In partial compensation, they developed several of Laos's rivers into an alternative means of transport. The same rains that made the roads impassable swelled the rivers, creating powerful currents that could bear containers of supplies swiftly over considerable distances. Two rivers in particular, the Kong and the Banghiang, were used for this purpose. Tributaries of the latter flowed across the DMZ from North Vietnam into STEEL TIGER. The river itself ran southwest past major supply depots near Tchepone and Muong Phine before running into the Mekong. The Kong River and its tributaries flowed through southern Laos into Cambodia. Where necessary, the North Vietnamese dammed the rivers to ensure sufficient depth. The flow of supplies downstream was channeled by driving bamboo poles into the riverbed so that they formed curtains aligned with the flow of the water. At intervals of several miles there were transshipment points where supplies were retrieved by booms or nets for storage or further conveyance by trucks or porters.[8]

By 1972, there existed a supplement to both roads and waterways: pipelines. Their northern terminus was Vinh, a city in the panhandle of North Vietnam where tankers from the USSR and other Communist states docked. From Vinh three pipelines ran into Laos through the Mu Gia Pass to serve truck parks and other facilities around Ban Phanop. A fourth ran through Ban Raving Pass to a distribution point near Tchepone. From there lines extended to the Lao Bao Pass and the A Shau Valley, both major entrances into South Vietnam. The pipes, im-

7. Directorate of Intelligence, Task Force Alpha, "North Vietnamese Army Logistic System in STEEL TIGER," 12–13; 7AF Hist, "CH VII," 20.
8. Bernard C. Nalty, "Interdiction in Southern Laos, 1968–1972" (S) (Manuscript, Office of Air Force History), 223–26, 231–32.

ported from the Soviet Union, were constructed of plastic but were joined by metal couplings. Pumps, also from the USSR, drove motor oil, gasoline, diesel fuel, and kerosene through the lines. The pumps, small and portable, were spaced about every half mile on level ground, but sometimes much closer in hilly terrain. Different kinds of petroleum products could be sent along the same line: Water mixed with detergent separated the shipments and prevented contamination.[9]

Until President Lyndon B. Johnson declared a halt to the bombing of North Vietnam on November 1, 1968, the efforts of the U.S. Air Force to prevent the North Vietnamese from resupplying their forces in the south had been primarily directed against North Vietnam itself. The end to the bombing in the north perforce shifted the focus of interdiction to Laos. The change was marked by the beginning of the COMMANDO HUNT series of interdiction campaigns on November 15, 1968. Successive dry-season campaigns were assigned odd numbers (COMMANDO HUNTs I, III, V, and VII), while the campaigns of the rainy seasons bore even numbers (COMMANDO HUNTs II, IV, and VI). Interdiction was most intensive during the dry season, for it was then the North Vietnamese bent every effort to resupply their forces in the south. The trucks that plied the roads during the dry season were in any case the most lucrative and vulnerable targets in STEEL TIGER. The road system itself was too redundant and easily repaired to be a good target. The deposits of supplies hidden throughout southern Laos were much bombed but were too numerous and too well hidden to be the focus of the COMMANDO HUNT campaigns.

It might be thought that the system of waterways would have been vulnerable to aerial attack. This, however, was not the case. Barrels and plastic bags filled with supplies barely broached the surface as they floated along, and were exceedingly difficult to detect from the air. The dams and channeling walls were not particularly difficult to discover, but they were hard to hit and easy to repair. Bombs could only scatter the loosely piled stones of the dams, which the enemy had merely to recollect to effect his repairs. The channeling walls, no more than bamboo poles hammered into the river beds, were even easier to fix. The destruction of these structures occasionally caused containers to go aground in shallow waters where they could be attacked with cluster bombs. But such successes were not frequent, for not only were the channeling walls easily repaired, but the enemy kept watchers along the river banks to divert the floating supplies to shore before they reached the damaged sections of the system. Mines fitted with magnetic-influence fuzes dropped

---

9. *Ibid.*, 234–39, 244–48.

into the waterways proved ineffectual. As they had been designed for use against steel-hulled ships, only a dense agglomeration of metal containers sufficed to detonate them. The North Vietnamese, moreover, soon learned to sweep the mines by wrapping chains around logs.[10]

The North Vietnamese sought the shelter of night to protect their supply vehicles. This drove the Americans to develop specialized systems for tracking and destroying trucks in the dark. Foremost among these were the fixed-wing gunships which, fitted with a technically advanced array of sensors, substantially overcame the inability to operate at night that had so limited the effectiveness of earlier interdiction campaigns. The gunships had originally been developed for close air support in South Vietnam but were soon drafted for service in Laos. In 1971, two types were in use: the AC–130 and the AC–119K.

The most effective of the gunships was the Lockheed AC–130 Spectre. This aircraft, equipped with four turboprop engines, had been developed from the C–130 Hercules transport. By 1971, two models were in use, the AC–130A and the AC–130E. Their primary armament was two 40-mm cannon backed by a pair of 20-mm cannon. A few were outfitted with a 105-mm cannon that replaced one of the 40-mm cannon. There were various configurations of sensors, but three were standard: infrared detectors to pick up the heat of engines and exhausts, low-light television, and ignition detectors to register the electrical emanations of operating internal combustion engines (BLACK CROW).[11]

The AC–119 Stinger derived from the Fairchild C–119 Flying Boxcar, which had seen service in the Korean War. The principal reason for converting C–119s into gunships was the reluctance of the Tactical Air Command to part with additional C–130s. The final version, the AC–119K Stinger, had two pod-mounted jet engines to help the two internal combustion engines originally fitted to bear the weight of added armament. Stingers carried four 7.62-mm "miniguns"—latter-day Gatling guns—and two 20-mm cannon. Their basic sensors were light-intensifying "starlight scopes" and infrared detectors.[12] The AC–119 was appreciably less effective than the AC–130. It had a limited range and could not linger long on-station; and its low operating altitude of 6,500 feet, a function of the comparatively short range of the 20-mm cannon, meant that it could not operate in regions heavily defended by antiair-

---

10. *Ibid.*, 228–30.
11. Jack S. Ballard, *Development and Employment of Fixed-Wing Gunships, 1962–1972* [U.S. Air Force in Southeast Asia] (Washington, 1982), 77–175; Nalty, "Interdiction in Southern Laos," 75.
12. Ballard, *Development and Employment of Fixed-Wing Gunships*, 176–220.

Gunships of Vietnam. The armament fitted to this AC–130 (*upper left*) included twin 40-mm cannon and two miniguns. Also visible just above the nosewheel is the BLACK CROW. The AC–130A aircraft, shown firing its 40-mm guns (*lower left*), was the leading Communist truck killer. Its on-board equipment was augmented by ground sensors to find targets. The AC–119K (*upper right*) is shown carrying an infrared night observation device (the spherical dome above the nose wheel). The openings just forward of the propeller warning line are emergency smoke evacuation doors. The final photo (*lower right*) shows an AC–119K in flight.

craft weapons, as the more important parts of the North Vietnamese logistical network were. Its 20-mm guns, finally, were much less capable of damaging trucks than the 40-mm weapons of the AC–130s.[13]

The two other principal strike aircraft used during COMMANDO HUNT operations, the F–4 Phantom fighter-bomber and the B–57 Canberra light bomber, were even less effective than the AC–119 as truck

13. EOTR, Maj Gen Alton B. Slay, DCS/Ops, Aug 1, 1971–Aug 14, 1972, K740.131.

hunters. Maj. Gen. Alton B. Slay, the Seventh Air Force's Deputy Chief of Staff for Operations during COMMANDO HUNT VII, described the former as "ineffective" and the latter as a "disaster."[14] The F–4 was handicapped by its lack of terrain-avoidance radar and of any of the sensors that made the AC–130 so effective.[15] The Phantom was not particularly maneuverable, and its large turning radius was a serious handicap in mountainous Laos. Its fuel capacity was limited; operating at ranges 200 miles and more from base, it could loiter on-station only briefly in Laos.[16]

In lightly defended areas, the Phantoms sometimes operated at night with C–130s outfitted for dropping flares. North Vietnamese antiaircraft defenses ruled out this technique over most of Laos because it required the C–130 to fly slowly at only 6,000 to 8,000 feet. The F–4s employed three methods of night operation in STEEL TIGER. The first, NIGHT OWL, was a tactic of armed reconnaissance. Aircraft using it generally operated in flights of two; larger formations proved unwieldy and hazardous. One ship dropped flares for the other in one of two patterns. In the first, it released sixteen to twenty flares in two rows parallel to the suspected location of a road and about one to two nautical miles distant. The second was more complex: The pilot of the lead aircraft flew down the road, beginning to drop pairs of flares about one to two miles short of where trucks were believed to be. After each drop he turned 15°–20° in alternating directions while maintaining a ground speed of 420 knots. If the location of the road was known, and the course correctly calculated, intermittent patches of road would be illuminated. The following strike aircraft then tried to detect targets in the fleeting pools of light.[17]

A pilot's chances of destroying trucks using the tactics of NIGHT OWL were slight. The Phantoms, as noted, were not well equipped for detecting targets on their own; and even when they had been alerted to the presence of vehicles by other aircraft, and the flares were correctly placed, their high speed made it exceedingly difficult for pilots to find their quarry within the short-lived patches of light. The dropping of flares, moreover, gave the enemy an opportunity to pull off the road before the strike aircraft arrived. The hunting of the elusive prey was fur-

14. *Ibid.*

15. Pacific Air Forces (hereafter PACAF) Activity Input to Proj Corona Harvest, *In-Country and Out-Country Strike Operations in Southeast Asia, 1 January 1965–31 December 1969*, vol 2: *Hardware: Strike Aircraft* (S) (HQ PACAF, 1970), 103.

16. Maj Victor B. Anthony, *Tactics and Techniques of Night Operations, 1961–1970* (S) [U.S. Air Force in Southeast Asia] (Washington, 1973), 133.

17. *Ibid.*, 134–42.

The OV–10 Bronco *(right)* equipped with PAVE NAIL to direct laser-guided bombs often teamed with the faster F–4 Phantoms *(above)*. Slow flying Broncos spotted enemy trucks and illuminated them with their lasers for the F–4s to attack.

ther hindered by a network of telephone-linked spotters throughout STEEL TIGER that provided advance warning of the thunderous approach of the jets.[18]

Because of these difficulties, the Phantoms frequently worked with the small, propeller-driven observation aircraft used in Laos by forward air controllers, chiefly Cessna O–2As and North American OV–10 Broncos. While these aircraft had no sensors more sophisticated than light-intensification devices (starlight scopes), they had the advantage of stealth. A favorite practice was to switch off the engines of these light aircraft and glide for considerable distances. Pilots marked targets by means of flares, white phosphorus rockets, and so-called marker logs— flares that burned on the ground for long periods. By 1971, some of the OV–10s were outfitted as PAVE NAILs, which carried a laser designator to guide laser-guided bombs to the illuminated targets.[19] Laser-guided bombs were conventional bombs, generally 2,000 pounders, each fitted with a sensor and computer-controlled canard surfaces that enabled it to home on reflected laser light. The Phantoms also used several kinds of "area munitions," which dispersed bomblets over areas about the size of a football field. The favorite device was the Mk–35/36 Funny Bomb,

---

18. Directorate of Intelligence, Task Force Alpha, "North Vietnamese Army Logistic System in STEEL TIGER," 10–11.

19. *Ibid.*, 75–81, 92–96; 7AF Hist, "CH VII," 240–41.

which dispensed incendiary bomblets that ignited on impact. Cluster bomb unit (CBU)–24 antipersonnel bombs scattered steel pellets over an area of equal size, but they were less effective because only fire could assure the destruction of a truck with its cargo. Conventional napalm bombs were deadly but covered an area only about a quarter as great as that covered by the Funny Bombs.[20]

As General Slay observed of the hunter-killer teams of observation aircraft and F–4s, "the problem again was in finding the trucks."[21] In much of Laos, it was hard enough to find trucks by day on tree-shrouded roads. It was no easier at night using the starlight scope, which afforded views of the ground that were quite bright but indistinct and lacking in contrast. Observation aircraft, moreover, were driven to steadily higher altitudes by the enemy's increasingly effective antiaircraft fire. A system known as COMMANDO BOLT, inaugurated in 1969, seemed in principle a promising solution to the problem of locating the enemy's trucks. The chief features of COMMANDO BOLT were arrays of sensors (IGLOO WHITE) implanted along Laos's roads to detect the passage of vehicles, and Phantoms fitted with Loran D, a precise radio navigation system used as a bombing aid. An associated computer gave the pilot a readout of his position and directions to his target. The F–4s so equipped served to guide others while information from the sensors established the presence of targets, their speed, and the direction of their travel. This information was radioed to the pathfinder aircraft, which then led its flight to what was calculated to be the current location of the targets. "I don't think that anyone can prove that we killed a single truck with the COMMANDO BOLT operation," General Slay commented on this obviously far from exact system of targeting. "We harassed the enemy and dropped a lot of bombs . . . but in-so-far as truck killing capability is concerned, the COMMANDO BOLT operation was poor."[22]

Also promising in theory but disappointing in practice were the specially equipped B–57s known as TROPIC MOON IIIs. The Martin B–57 was developed in 1953 from the British Canberra light bomber. Its age notwithstanding, the aircraft was in many respects well suited for interdiction. Long a mainstay of the interdiction program in Laos, it had a strong airframe capable of withstanding the maneuvers necessary for tactical operations. It carried up to 9,000 pounds of bombs, internally and on wing stations. The long tailpipes of its wing-mounted engines reduced noise and the jet plume at night. Its broad wings enabled it to maneuver

---

20. Anthony, *Tactics and Techniques of Night Operations*, 79–80, 127. Laser bombs are discussed at some length in Chapter 11.

21. Slay EOTR, 34.

22. *Ibid.*; Anthony, *Tactics and Techniques of Night Operations*, 144–45.

like a far slower aircraft, although they did block downward vision. In 1967, the TROPIC MOON II program tried to mate the B–57B with some of the new sensors then coming into service, especially low-light television. TROPIC MOON II aircraft first saw combat in 1967, but proved ineffective.[23]

Introduced to Southeast Asia in October 1970, the TROPIC MOON III B–57G aircraft were fitted with low-light television, infrared sensors, forward-looking Doppler-shift radar, and an advanced digital computer. The radar was the chief sensor. Tested in the United States, it had shown itself capable of detecting jeep-sized targets at eight miles. B–57s equipped with this device were designed to operate at 2,000–3,000 feet and at airspeeds of 200–300 knots. Since the sensors were forward-looking, the aircraft had to follow roads as it searched for trucks. Upon discovering a target, the pilot aligned the aircraft for attack and selected his weapon. At the proper point, the computer released the bombs, generally the much-favored Mk–36s. Soon after its appearance in combat, however, the B–57G showed itself to be the "disaster" that General Slay had described. Since the system had been designed, the North Vietnamese had greatly strengthened their antiaircraft defenses. The B–57G, forced by its forward-looking radar to fly along the roads where the enemy had deployed his guns, simply could not survive at its designed operating altitude. At 6,000 to 8,000 feet the B–57G, protected by advanced ceramic armor and foam-filled fuel cells, was reasonably safe, but the capability of its sensors was seriously downgraded and its guns were much less effective. Normally, the aircraft was upon a target before the sensors detected it. The crew was then obliged to make a second pass, which gave the intended prey a chance to drive off the road to safety.[24]

The main source of intelligence about North Vietnamese logistical operations in Southern Laos was the IGLOO WHITE electronic surveillance system. Operated by Task Force Alpha in Thailand, it had three basic components: the sensors themselves, the relaying aircraft, and the Infiltration Surveillance Center. Task Force Alpha also planned and directed the sensor strings' implantation, the locations of which were determined by intelligence requirements and technical considerations. Among the latter were terrain (which in rugged Laos could mask transmissions), the nature of the jungle canopy (practically impenetrable in places), soil conditions (the sensors had to sink into the ground), and the orbits of the relay aircraft (which were potentially subject to enemy interference).[25]

---

23. Anthony, *Tactics and Techniques of Night Operations*, 125, 127–28.
24. *Ibid.*, 129–32; Slay EOTR, 33.
25. Directorate of Intelligence, Task Force Alpha, "North Vietnamese Army Logistic System in STEEL TIGER," 46–47.

While earlier models of the B–57 had proved valuable as daytime attackers, the sensor-laden B–57G (shown here) was a severe disappointment as a night interdictor.

Four types of sensors were used in the IGLOO WHITE system: ADSID III (air delivered seismic intrusion detector), ACOUSID III (acoustic seismic intrusion detector), COMMIKE III (commandable microphone), and EDET III (engine detector). The names of the devices are pretty much self-explanatory: ADSID III was sensitive to vibrations transmitted through the ground, and ACOUSID III to seismic vibrations and air-transmitted sounds. COMMIKE III was a sensitive microphone that could be turned on and off at will, while EDET III, like BLACK CROW, picked up electromagnetic emanations from ignition. All were ruggedly constructed cylinders, slightly more than a yard long and 3 to 5 inches in diameter. They were fitted with flanges to prevent their sinking too deeply into the soil; their antennas were made to resemble plants. All contained low-power radios for transmitting to the relay aircraft. ADSID III and ACOUSID III were the constituent parts of the sensor strings laid along major supply routes for COMMANDO HUNT VII.[26]

The 25th Tactical Fighter Squadron based at Udorn, Thailand, began to implant the sensor strings for COMMANDO HUNT VII on September 8, 1971. F–4s fitted with Loran D carried underwing dispensers for the sensors. They flew at 500 to 2,000 feet and 550 knots, protected by their speed from antiaircraft artillery. Explosive cartridges, triggered by a sophisticated intervalometer that permitted proper spacing regardless of airspeed, ejected the sensors from the dispensers. Because a knowledge of the exact location of individual sensors was necessary for a correct interpretation of their transmissions, a camera aboard the Phantom photographed each sensor as it fell away. By comparing the resulting photo-

---

26. *Ibid.*, 47–50.

graphs with large-scale photograpic maps of the region where the sensors were dropped, the exact location of the aircraft at the moment of release could be determined. Ballistics tables for the sensors were then used to calculate the point of impact. Sensors had to be within 100 meters of the road for monitoring to be effective.[27]

Aircraft flying in three orbits over Laos relayed the signals from the sensors to the Infiltration Surveillance Center, where computers processed the data. Computer programs allowed sounds of interest to the center (trucks and bulldozers, for example) to be distinguished from those of no interest (such as thunder or animals). From the pattern of sensor activations, the direction and speed of traffic could be calculated, together with the number of vehicles in a convoy. Information so obtained was used in real time to direct attacks on the enemy's traffic, when it seemed sufficiently heavy to warrant the effort. Data from the sensors were stored so that traffic patterns and trends in logistical activity could be calculated.[28]

The sensors developed for the war in Southeast Asia represented an effort to solve the problem that darkness had posed for previous interdiction operations. Another novelty, the blocking belt, addressed another limitation upon the effectiveness of interdiction: True choke points are quite rare in road systems, which tend to be heavily redundant. A resourceful enemy, moreover, will design his logistical system in such a way that potential choke points are circumvented. Blocking belts were in essence movable choke points, emplaced on major arteries where they could not be readily bypassed.

Each belt comprised two to six blocking points. At each point, the road was cut with laser-guided bombs. The area about it was then heavily seeded from the air with two types of mines: antipersonnel and antimatériel. The former were sowed first. When the road had been cut, F–4s dropped CBU–14 gravel mines. Dispersed from canisters, gravel mines were about the size and shape of teabags. Each contained enough explosive to incapacitate anyone unfortunate enough to step on it. After the gravel mines had been dispersed, another flight of Phantoms dropped a second kind of antipersonnel mine, the CBU–24 wide-area antipersonnel mine. The CBU–24, also dispersed from canisters, was a small fragmentation munition about 2⅜ inches in diameter. Upon striking the ground, it ejected trip wires, 25 feet in length. Last laid were Mk–36 Destructor mines, which were dropped by the Navy's A–7 attack aircraft. The Mk–36 was a 500-pound bomb fitted with a magnetic-influence fuze.

---

27. *Ibid.*, 50–51.
28. *Ibid.*, 54–57.

The gravel and the wide-area antipersonnel mines served, in theory, to make it harder for the enemy to repair the cuts and to clear the Mk–36 Destructors. Once emplaced, the belt was kept under surveillance so that attempts at removing it could be foiled and attacks could be directed against traffic backed up behind it.[29]

Such were the weapons for COMMANDO HUNT VII, the last dry-season interdiction campaign in Laos. The operation's planners were the beneficiaries of much experience, but they were also somewhat handicapped by reduced force levels mandated by the Nixon administration's policy of "Vietnamizing" the war. For COMMANDO HUNT VII, the Department of Defense had allocated 10,000 fighter-bomber sorties monthly, and 700 gunship sorties. These limits represented, respectively, a reduction of 4,000 and 300 sorties monthly from the levels of the previous dry-season campaign, COMMANDO HUNT V. The operation had three phases, keyed to the weather and the enemy's technique of logistical saturation.[30]

Phase I, or entry interdiction, was to begin with ARC LIGHT strikes by B–52s of the Strategic Air Command upon the passes through which the convoys of the North Vietnamese entered Laos. Sensors were to be implanted in the bombed areas to warn of attempts at repair. When such efforts were detected, fighter-bombers would attack the earth-moving equipment with laser-guided bombs. As the roads began to dry and become repairable, the preponderance of ARC LIGHT B–52 strikes was to be directed against the southern passes of Ban Raving and the western DMZ to force traffic through the northern passes of Mu Gia and Ban Karai. This was designed to force upon the North Vietnamese longer and less efficient routes, more vulnerable to attack.[31]

Phase II was to begin when the enemy's supplies reached the core route structure in central STEEL TIGER. Aircraft would then sow blocking belts across supply routes, particularly where the terrain forced roads to merge or run close to one another. The purpose of the new obstacles was again to force the North Vietnamese to use inefficient and circuitous routes; secondarily, they might also create lucrative targets in the forms of traffic jams and backlogged supplies. With the passage of traffic into central STEEL TIGER, gunships, withheld from the vicinity of the passes because of the dangers posed by the enemy's fighters and missiles, were

---

29. 7AF Hist, "CH VII," 45–47; PACAF Activity Input to Proj Corona Harvest, *In-Country and Out-Country Strike Operations in Southeast Asia, 1 January 1965–31 December 1969*, vol 2: *Hardware: Munitions* (S) (HQ PACAF, 1970), 122, 124–25.

30. 7AF Hist, "CH VII," 14.

31. *Ibid.*, 15.

B–52s, integral to the execution of COMMANDO HUNT VII, conducted ARC LIGHT bombing strikes against mountain passes along the trails from Laos into South Vietnam. Here, a Stratofortress armed with 500-pound bombs leaves U Tapao Air Base on a mission to interdict supplies and interrupt North Vietnamese repair efforts on the supply routes.

to become active, as would the forward air controllers who directed the strikes of the fighter-bombers. In general, the latter were expected to concentrate more on stationary targets such as truck parks and storage areas than upon moving traffic. The approach of the enemy's program of saturation to South Vietnam would trigger Phase III, exit interdiction. During this phase, the gunships and fighter-bombers would remain active, while the B–52s would begin to bomb the passes into South Vietnam, particularly where the terrain was sufficiently open to limit the effectiveness of blocking belts.[32]

In keeping with the well-established principle of centralized control of air power, overall responsibility for the direction of COMMANDO HUNT VII resided in the Tactical Air Control Center of the Seventh Air Force. For the first time since COMMANDO HUNT I, however, Task Force Alpha was given an operational role in an effort to make air strikes more responsive to the intelligence developed by the specialists who monitored the sensors and collated the information so derived with that from other sources. In its new role, Task Force Alpha was equipped to convert grid coordinates into data usable in the Loran navigation systems used by the AC–130s and by selected F–4s.[33]

COMMANDO HUNT VII began on November 1, 1971. Phase I, entrance interdiction, was dominated by the B–52s, which struck the passes into STEEL TIGER. Each pass fell within an interdiction area. These were in turn subdivided into boxes, ranging in size from one kilometer by one kilometer to one kilometer by three, which corresponded to the possible bomb patterns of a cell of three B–52s. The Mu Gia entry interdiction area, which contained the boxes designated Alpha, measured approxi-

---

32. *Ibid.*, 15–16.
33. *Ibid.*, 17, 22–23.

mately thirteen by eighteen nautical miles. The Ban Karai entry interdiction area, which contained the Bravo boxes, was fourteen nautical miles square. The Ban Raving and western DMZ areas, which contained the Charlie and Delta boxes, measured, respectively, twenty by twenty-one and five by twelve nautical miles. During the three weeks of Phase I, the principal task of the tactical aircraft was to cut roads. During the twenty-two days of the entrance phase of COMMANDO HUNT VII, the B–52s and tactical aircraft together dropped 14,400 instantaneously fuzed Mk–82 500-pound bombs, 17,100 Mk–117 750-pound bombs, and small quantities of specialized ordnance, principally Mk–84 2,000-pound laser-guided bombs, Mk–36 magnetic-influence mines, and CBU–24 antipersonnel mines.[34]

The results of the entrance phase of COMMANDO HUNT VII are difficult to assess. The Seventh Air Force claimed only that enemy traffic had been slowed some of the time in some places. At the beginning of Phase I, roads in the Mu Gia entry interdiction area were in bad shape from the bombing during the rainy season. They were drying rapidly, however, and, beginning November 4, the North Vietnamese made a major effort at repair. The Mu Gia was important because among its karst formations were the caves that the North Vietnamese used to shelter their supplies in northern STEEL TIGER. From November 3 through 10, the Mu Gia was the entry area most used. Heavy bombing between November 10 and 17 reduced traffic by half, although the roads were reported in good condition throughout. Except for the southern portion of the interdiction area, the roads were generally in good to excellent condition. The North Vietnamese were observed engaged in the more-or-less continuous shuttling of supplies between storage areas as they proceeded with their program of logistical "saturation."[35]

At the beginning of COMMANDO HUNT VII, the Ban Karai Pass was still flooded. Many roads were impassable, and fords on the Nam Ta Le River could not be used. While waiting for better conditions, the North Vietnamese worked to improve those roads that were usable. Reconnaissance flights observed that several routes were being extensively graveled. For the first nine days of November, B–52s and tactical aircraft worked with some success to keep these roads closed. But on November 9, the B–52s were withdrawn from operations around the Ban Karai Pass because of the suspected presence of surface-to-air missiles (SAMs). Tactical aircraft alone were unable to keep the roads closed—only the extensive cratering produced by the B–52s sufficed for that. Traffic surged

---

34. *Ibid.*, 23–27.
35. *Ibid.*, 30–33.

after the fords on the Nam Ta Le became passable on November 14. The B–52s resumed operations on November 20, after a reevaluation of the intelligence that had suggested the presence of missiles. Flights were suspended later the same day, however, after a lone MiG fired a missile at a B–52. The big bombers returned to Ban Karai on November 21 for the last two days of Phase I.[36]

There were comparatively few signs of movement in the Ban Raving Pass, even on the better roads. It accounted, accordingly, for only 3 percent of the tactical strikes and a fifth of the ARC LIGHT effort. The heaviest traffic into STEEL TIGER passed through the western DMZ. From November 6 through 20, the enemy steadily increased his activity, undeterred by fully 40 percent of the B–52s' total effort. At least one major route through the western DMZ was always open.[37]

From the bald statements in contemporary documents it is quite clear that the prodigious expenditure of ordnance during the entry phase of COMMANDO HUNT VII slowed the enemy's traffic only slightly. Aerial photographs of the passes suggest why so much effort seems to have had little effect. After years of heavy bombing, the landscape of the passes, stripped of vegetation and pockmarked by craters, was lunar. This probably made it easier for the North Vietnamese to keep the passes open. The pattern of the bombs dropped by a cell of B–52s was so adjusted that they were distributed evenly through a box. Relatively few bombs would, on average, strike the narrow roads. Where they did, temporary bypasses could be readily constructed in treeless areas where the soil, tilled by thousands of bombs, had become easier to work. Craters in the road could be filled with the spoil from adjacent craters. The greatest obstacle the North Vietnamese faced was the seasonal rains that turned all to mud. This condition the bombing made worse—during the rainy season. But thereafter the soil dried more quickly than it would have otherwise, for little vegetation survived to slow runoff and evaporation.

Phase II of COMMANDO HUNT VII began on November 23. The southward diffusion of supplies into the core route structure had proceeded to such an extent that it had become appropriate to activate the blocking belts. The first belt was seeded on November 23 near Tchepone, a major logistical center. Successive belts were activated as the enemy's logistical saturation approached the exit areas into South Vietnam. On December 24, the first belt was emplaced in the region of Ban Bak. The last belt was activated near Chavane on February 15. The beginning of Phase II did not end the attacks of the B–52s upon the entry areas. As

---

36. *Ibid.*, 33–34.
37. *Ibid.*, 34–35.

planned, the emphasis of the attacks shifted to Ban Karai and the western DMZ in an effort to impose longer routes upon the North Vietnamese. By early December, however, the enemy had shifted some of his antiaircraft missiles to cover the passes of Ban Karai and Mu Gia. The B–52s were withdrawn from operations over the former on December 7 and from the latter on December 11. Neither pass was attacked again for the duration of COMMANDO HUNT VII, save for two attacks on the Ban Karai, on March 9 and 10, 1972. By January, moreover, the North Vietnamese had so pressed their road building in the Ban Karai Pass that the B–52s, which were in great demand, could not have kept pace with it, even had they been free to attack. "Enemy movement," the Seventh Air Force concluded, "continued at a moderate to heavy level in the Ban Karai area throughout the campaign."[38]

With the surge of supplies into central STEEL TIGER, the problems facing the interdictors multiplied. These may be conveniently divided into three categories: intelligence, equipment, and North Vietnamese countermeasures. Southern Laos, as noted earlier, was an entangled webwork of roads and trails. The effectiveness of interdiction critically depended on an understanding of this system, which American intelligence had only partially unraveled. Task Force Alpha's director of intelligence remarked that "a great deal" of the new construction that occurred during COMMANDO HUNT VII went unobserved because of the dense jungle canopy. The North Vietnamese had developed an entire route structure in western Laos that was "almost uncharted" and "nearly devoid of sensor coverage since no one knows where the roads really are or how many of them there are." Just how important a factor the unknown roads were became evident during the North Vietnamese's Easter Offensive that began on March 30, 1972. Several hundred enemy tanks appeared in southern South Vietnam, having traversed the length of STEEL TIGER undetected by the sensors, save for a few random instances that resolved themselves into no discernable pattern.[39]

The problems of intelligence were compounded by a decision to change the composition of the sensor strings. As originally designed, the sensor field for COMMANDO HUNT VII was to consist of 160 strings arrayed to monitor approximately thirty-three target areas.[40] Each string, as in the past, was to consist of eight sensors: five ADSIDs and three

---

38. *Ibid.*, 39–40, 44.
39. Evans EOTR, 44, 59; Slay EOTR, 26.
40. By the beginning of the operation, only 99 effective strings had been implanted. By the end of January, there were 175. The average number of strings in operation was 153, a substantial increase from COMMANDO HUNT V's average of 101. 7AF Hist, "CH VII," 66–67.

ACOUSIDs. But before the sensors were seeded, the Seventh Air Force directed Task Force Alpha to reduce the sensors in each string to five: three ADSIDs and two ACOUSIDs. This was a seemingly logical response to the enemy's expanded route structure: Fewer sensors per string meant that more strings could be implanted. While it was recognized that there would be a loss of accuracy, the need for broader coverage seemed too urgent to deny.[41]

Serious problems soon developed. The sensors had a fairly short lifespan, which varied from 60 to 160 days with normal use. As the implantation of the strings had begun on September 8, 1971, the sensors were starting to need replacing just about the time that COMMANDO HUNT VII began. A program called ISLAND TREE, designed to detect infiltrating soldiers, had begun in the interim and competed with COMMANDO HUNT VII for both sensors and for reseeding sorties. To compound the problem, the Seventh Air Force continued to demand more strings for the latter operation. By November, Task Force Alpha was seeding and reseeding strings at a rate, nine a day, incompatible with high standards of accuracy. The number of strings became a burden on Task Force Alpha's computers. Previous to COMMANDO HUNT VII, moreover, sensor strings were reseeded as soon as a degradation of their reliability was detected, even if all sensors were still transmitting. This could no longer be done with the computer system working close to its absolute capacity, as defective but still transmitting sensors competed for computer time with their replacements. The result was that the information transmitted to the strike forces was neither as complete nor as accurate as it could have been.[42]

Various countermeasures of the North Vietnamese occasionally further limited the effectiveness of the sensors. They had learned that an aircraft dropping sensors dived differently from one engaged in bombing. They sometimes knew, therefore, the general location of sensor strings and might undertake comprehensive searches to neutralize those located in critical locations. The records of COMMANDO HUNT VII, however, do not suggest that any significant number of sensors was so neutralized. The North Vietnamese also attempted to defeat airborne sensors. Having read of BLACK CROW in American aeronautical publications, they began to wrap their ignition systems with aluminum foil to suppress electromagnetic emanations. This technique apparently was successful in reducing BLACK CROW's effectiveness. Upon learning of the American use of in-

---

41. Directorate of Intelligence, Task Force Alpha, "North Vietnamese Army Logistic System in STEEL TIGER," 65–66.

42. *Ibid.*, 66–67; Slay EOTR, 23–24.

frared sensors, they employed mats of banana leaves and bamboo to shield the hot spots of vehicles. No evidence exists to suggest how successful this technique was.[43]

The limitations on American intelligence meant that much of the enemy's activity in STEEL TIGER passed unnoticed. But intelligence was not the only problem. The Seventh Air force experienced serious difficulties in attempting to curtail even the traffic that it did observe. One of its most serious problems was the limited effectiveness of the blocking belts. Since the enemy's route structure was not fully understood, the probability existed that he could bypass the belts. The munitions used in the barriers, moreover, had not been changed since the late 1960s, and the North Vietnamese were therefore experienced in dealing with them. "We found," recalled Brig. Gen. Richard Cross, the Seventh Air Force's Assistant Deputy Chief of Staff for Operations, "that the enemy was quite adept at clearing road blocks regardless of the type of ordnance used to create them."[44]

The North Vietnamese usually began their efforts to breach the blocking belts by casting rocks tied to cords into the mined area. These, drawn back, engaged the trip wires of the wide-area antipersonnel mines. As they worked their way into the belt, the sappers could clear the pressure-sensitive gravel mines by simply picking them up. This phase of the operation was helped by the tendency of the gravel mines to fail rapidly in the damp Laotian climate. Once a path through the antipersonnel mines had been cleared, it was relatively easy for demolition crews to defuse magnetic-influence Mk–36 mines. Where the North Vietnamese were able to marshal their resources, they could clear a blocking point in fewer than twelve hours.[45]

A further limitation on the effectiveness of the belts was that they were quite difficult to establish properly. Four waves of aircraft from two services had with the greatest precision to seed the area selected for the belt. Any discrepancy in the patterns of dispersion for the munitions would compromise the belt. Upon occasion, for example, the Mk–36 mines were dropped beyond the protection of the antipersonnel mines. Sometimes there were problems of coordination between waves of aircraft. On November 23, for example, the first attempt to establish a

---

43. Robert Shaplen, *Bitter Victory* (New York, 1985), 160; Michael Horrocks, "The Air Force in Southeast Asia: The Sensor War, 1966–1971" (Manuscript, Office of Air Force History), 17–19.
44. EOTR, Brig Gen Richard G. Cross, Jr., Jan 22, 1973, K740.131, 2.
45. 7AF Hist, "CH VII," 47, 133; PACAF Activity Input to Proj Corona Harvest, *In-Country and Out-Country Strike Operations in Southeast Asia*, vol 2: *Hardware: Munitions*, 130; Slay EOTR, 28–29.

blocking belt in the core route structure came to nought when the road-cutting high-explosive bombs were dropped *last* and detonated the mines previously implanted.[46]

COMMANDO HUNT VII saw the establishment of three major blocking belts in Laos. (See *Map 20*) The Tchepone Belt consisted of six separate blocking points put in place between November 23 and January 22. The second belt was installed fifty miles to the south at Ban Bak. It consisted of two blocking points, established on December 24 and 26. The third and last belt was put in near Chavane. It comprised two blocking points, one established on February 15, the other on March 2. The Chavane Belt proved to be something of a mistake in that enemy traffic in the area was very light, an example of the intelligence problems that made operations in Laos so difficult. The Chavane Belt was quickly abandoned to permit a concentration of resources on the entrance routes into South Vietnam.[47]

During the lifetime of the Tchepone Belt—November 29, 1971, to February 2, 1972—fighter-bombers dropped twenty-four "munitions packages" to maintain it against destructive climatic conditions and North Vietnamese engineers.[48] These were supplemented by thirty-four "sweetening packages"—munitions packages without the road-cutting high-explosive bombs. Fighter-bombers and gunships flew a total of 125 protective sorties in response to signals from sensors in the vicinity of the blocking points that indicated the enemy was trying to breach the mine fields or that traffic was backing up behind them. These resulted in claims for the destruction of eight trucks and one bulldozer.

The accompanying table shows what could reasonably be expected of a well-laid and heavily defended blocking belt. (*Table 17*) Of the five points seeded with mines for appreciable periods, three were blocked much of the time. But one of the remaining two—Point 427 on Route 92C—never closed, because the North Vietnamese concentrated their resources there and swept the mines about as fast as they were sown. The breach at Point 427 meant that the North Vietnamese could at all times pass through the Tchepone Belt, albeit at the cost of detours.[49]

The history of the Ban Bak blocking belt was similar. Twelve munitions and seven sweetening packages were required to establish and maintain its two blocking points. There were also twenty-six protective sorties,

---

46. Slay EOTR, 28–29; 7AF Hist, "CH VII," 118.
47. 7AF Hist, "CH VII," 48–49, 122–127.
48. A munitions package was the collection of road-cutting high-explosive bombs, wide-area antipersonnel mines, gravel antipersonnel mines, and Mk–36 antimatériel mines used to establish a blocking point.
49. 7AF Hist, "CH VII," 121.

Table 17. Tchepone and Ban Bak Blocking Belts: Effectiveness as a Percentage of Days Closed

Blocking Point	Dates of Belt		Number of Days of Belt	Number of Days Closed	Percent Effective
	From	To			
		Tchepone Belt			
258	Nov 23, 1971	Feb 1, 1972	71	41	58
427	Nov 26, 1971	"	68	0	0
412	Nov 27, 1971	"	20	15	75
510	Dec 6, 1971	"	57	23	40
420	Nov 24, 1971	"	70	54	77
529	Jan 22, 1972	"	11	3	27
		Ban Bak Belt			
414	Dec 24, 1971	Feb 1, 1972	40	10	25
244	Dec 26, 1972	Feb 2, 1972	8	1	12.5

SOURCE: 7AF Hist, "CH VII," 121, 124.

for which the destruction of three trucks and two bulldozers was claimed. As Table 17 shows, the North Vietnamese were able to keep both points breached most of the time.[50] To keep these results in perspective, it must be remembered that the Tchepone and Ban Bak blocking belts covered only what American intelligence believed to be the more important roads in the core route structure. Other known routes were not blocked for want of resources, and there were of course the roads that were never identified, particularly in western Laos.

A total of eighteen AC–130 and sixteen AC–119 fixed-wing gunships were employed in COMMANDO HUNT VII. These aircraft were, for the reasons described earlier, the most effective truck-hunters. At the height of the campaign, in late January and early February, the AC–130s claimed an average of 8.3 trucks destroyed or damaged per sortie; the AC–119s, 3.3. The B–57s claimed two, and fighter-bombers only 0.29. The Seventh Air Force claimed a total of 10,609 trucks—4,727 destroyed and 5,882 damaged. Of these, the AC–130s claimed 7,335, the AC–119s 940, the B–57s 461, and the fighter-bombers 1,873. The accuracy of these claims (discussed below) is open to question. They may, however, be taken as an indication of the relative effectiveness of the strike aircraft used in Laos. To a considerable extent, accordingly, the history of truck

50. *Ibid.*, 124.

Aircraft, by Service	Month					Total Sorties
	Nov 1971	Dec 1971	Jan 1972	Feb 1972	Mar 1972	
USAF						
F–4	624	650	789	936	1,210	4,209
AC–130	133	312	292	304	325	1,366
AC–119	32	116	127	82	83	440
B–57	56	88	113	79	66	402
USN						
A–4	0	0	0	218	207	425
A–6	33	56	77	56	93	315
A–7	88	149	260	257	298	1,052
F–4	44	43	114	129	162	492
Total	1,010	1,414	1,772	2,061	2,444	8,701

Table 18. Number of Antitruck Sorties, by Aircraft Type: COMMANDO HUNT VII

SOURCE: 7 AF Hist, "CH VII," 75.

hunting in COMMANDO HUNT VII is the story of the gunships, though fighter-bombers flew more sorties.[51] (*Table 18*)

At the beginning of COMMANDO HUNT VII, the North Vietnamese, by American estimates, had about 3,000 trucks in STEEL TIGER. Their activity, as monitored by sensors, did not rise until mid-November from the levels recorded in the wet season. There was a surge in early December, which slightly subsided at midmonth, and immediately resurged, to peak in mid-January. As the end of the dry season drew near in April, traffic subsided to about the level of late December. (*Chart 11*) As in previous campaigns, the enemy moved mostly by night. The trend, however, was toward greater daytime travel: About one-third of all sensors readings fell between the hours of 0600 and 1800, though most of this traffic occurred in the two hours before sunset.[52]

The change was due to the realization by the North Vietnamese that the delicate sensors of the AC–130s, which they had come to fear, were blinded by the heat and light of day. At dusk, moreover, it was difficult to detect targets visually. As General Slay recalled, "we never did get a handle on the early movers at dusk and the late movers at dawn." The North Vietnamese, as an additional response to the AC–130s, had to a greater extent than ever before begun to cut their roads through triple-canopy jungle. They also resorted to elaborate camouflage: transplanted

51. *Ibid.*, 80–82.
52. *Ibid.*, 67.

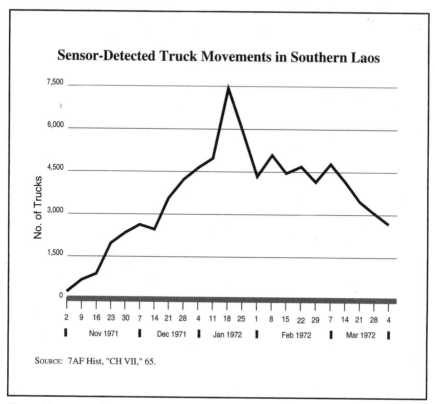

Sensor-Detected Truck Movements in Southern Laos

SOURCE: 7AF Hist, "CH VII," 65.

Chart 11.

trees created canopies where there had been none, and vines were strung to shield roads from aerial view. Along the stretches so concealed, trucks moved by day with impunity. "All through the day," General Slay wrote, Task Force Alpha would, with its ground-based sensors, "monitor truck movements on segments of those roads where there was very dense triple canopy. We could never find the trucks."[53]

Attacks on what Seventh Air Force called "logistical area targets" were an integral part of Phase II. Logistical area target was a catch-all term for truck parks and storage areas for various classes of supplies. The former were found at the end of access roads that communicated with major routes. The storage areas for ammunition, gasoline, and other goods were less elaborate. Supplies were often hidden in camouflaged bomb craters, caves, or underground bunkers. The enemy's skill

---

53. Slay EOTR; Shaplen, *Bitter Victory*, 58–59.

at camouflage made these difficult targets. Information about their location was developed from sensor data, photographic reconnaissance, communications intercepts, and agent reports. Traffic patterns, in particular, were closely studied in an attempt to locate storage areas. Gunships, B–57s, fighter-bombers, and B–52s all attacked suspected sites. During COMMANDO HUNT VII, there were 10,626 sorties against suspected storage areas in Laos and Cambodia.[54]

The success of these strikes was gauged by the presence of fires or secondary explosions. Such effects were observed more often than not to follow strikes in STEEL TIGER. The high point for claims came in January when an average of 0.94 fires or secondary explosions were identified per sortie. The low point, 0.42, fell in November when the logistical saturation of STEEL TIGER had scarcely begun. The overall average for the campaign was 0.73.[55]

The enemy's growing array of antiaircraft weapons proved a more serious impediment to COMMANDO HUNT VII than to any previous campaign. Its exact size seems to have been the subject of a dispute between Task Force Alpha and the Seventh Air Force. The position of the latter organization was that the enemy began the dry-season campaign with 345 guns, ranging in size from 23 to 57 mm, and that the number rose during the campaign to 554, which figure was said to include six 85-mm weapons and one 100-mm. Task Force Alpha, however, argued that the North Vietnamese had 600–700 guns by the end of COMMANDO HUNT V and that the number rose to 1,500 during COMMANDO HUNT VII. How the guns were apportioned by type was also disputed. The Seventh Air Force asserted that 23- and 37-mm weapons predominated and that there were no more than 72 57-mm guns by the end of the latter dry season campaign. Task Force Alpha, on the other hand, maintained that the 57-mm guns were much more plentiful. Both sides agreed that the North Vietnamese increased the effectiveness of their weapons during COMMANDO HUNT VII by introducing high-velocity magnum ammunition.[56] The records of the Pacific Air Forces show that a total of eighteen aircraft were lost over southern Laos to either definite or suspected ground fire during COMMANDO HUNT VII. Among them was an AC–130, brought down by a 57-mm gun on March 30.[57]

The number of SAMs in STEEL TIGER also increased during COMMANDO HUNT VII. By the close of COMMANDO HUNT V, there had been

---

54. 7AF Hist, "CH VII," 89–91.
55. *Ibid.*, 91–93.
56. Evans EOTR, 47–48; 7AF Hist, COMMANDO HUNT VII," 227–29.
57. There were, as follows, 9 F–4s, 5 OV–10s, 1 A–4 (Navy), 1 A–7 (Navy), 1 AC–130, and 1 A–1. PACAF, "Summaries: Air Operations Southeast Asia," Nov 1971 through Mar 1972, K717.306–1.

eight missile battalions in and around northern STEEL TIGER and southern North Vietnam. During the dry season of 1971-1972, the number rose to about twenty-five. During COMMANDO HUNT V there had been 49 firings; there were 153 during COMMANDO HUNT VII. SAMs were first reported on November 9 in the Ban Karai Pass, from which, as noted earlier, the B-52s were withdrawn on December 7. On December 12, the Mu Ghia Pass was designated an area of threat after an F-105 was destroyed by a missile launched from its environs. The B-52s ceased operations there also. In both places, the area of threat extended twenty-four miles into Laos—the range of the Soviet-made SAM-2. By January 13, missiles had been based near Tchepone in STEEL TIGER, the most important part of the core route structure. The AC-130s were withdrawn from central STEEL TIGER until an intensive series of strikes by fighter-bombers, which lasted from January 11 to 15, had reduced the threat. The AC-130s returned to the region for another 2½ months. But on March 29, an AC-130 and its crew of fourteen were destroyed by a SAM-2 missile ten nautical miles northwest of Tchepone. The AC-130s were then withdrawn from most of the core route structure. That another three AC-130s and as many AC-119s had been damaged by antiaircraft fire in March contributed to this decision.[58]

The effect of the North Vietnamese air defenses upon COMMANDO HUNT VII was considerable. First, they forced the B-52s to stop bombing two of the major routes into Laos. Then, as supplies moved south into the core route structure, the antiaircraft artillery and missiles restricted the ability of American aircraft to intercept them. The gunships, as noted, were much the most effective weapon for hunting trucks; yet the AC-119s, nearly half the force of gunships, could not venture into the heart of the enemy's logistical network for fear of its defenses. By the end of the campaign, even the more capable AC-130s had been driven out, although this was so late as to make no practical difference. Another effect of the growing problem with the North Vietnamese defenses was the diversion of sorties from truck hunting to attacking antiaircraft guns and missiles. A total of 4,066 sorties was devoted to suppressing antiaircraft fire, a figure nearly equal to the 4,209 sorties that fighter-bombers flew against trucks. An additional but apparently unrecorded number of sorties was devoted to attacking the missiles installed near Tchepone.[59]

A serious potential threat to COMMANDO HUNT VII existed in the form of MiG-17 interceptors deployed to two new airfields in southern

---

58. 7AF Hist, "CH VII," 38, 40, 140-141, 231. During COMMANDO HUNT VII the overall loss rate per 1,000 sorties was 0.30 aircraft throughout the theater. No specific figure, it appears, was calculated for STEEL TIGER.

59. *Ibid.*, 139. Col D.L. Evans, Task Force Alpha's director of intelligence,

North Vietnam, Khe Phat and Ha Tinh. The former was constructed about fifteen nautical miles east of the Mu Gia Pass, the latter about forty nautical miles north of it. The pilots of the MiG–17s were known to have been trained to attack slow-moving aircraft like the fixed-wing gunships used in interdiction. During COMMANDO HUNT V, MiGs had overflown Laos on only six occasions; more than seventy-five incursions occurred during COMMANDO HUNT VII. Enemy flyers were not aggressive and mostly confined their flights to Northern Laos. Their only attempt to interfere with ARC LIGHT came on November 20 when a MiG fired an air-to-air missile at a B-52 near the Mu Gia Pass. The projectile missed its target. During thirteen encounters between MiGs and American fighters, five MiGs were destroyed for the loss of one Phantom.[60]

A small number of trucks, quite probably carrying supplies that had been stored in Laos during the rainy season, entered South Vietnam in November. The first strikes on some of the seven exit areas that American intelligence had designated to cover the known routes into the Republic of Vietnam began that month, continued sporadically during December, and became heavier as the enemy's program of logistical "saturation" approached the borders of South Vietnam. These attacks were primarily confined to cutting roads and bombing fords or whatever other features were designated as interdiction points. The implantation of blocking belts began in February, when sensors began to indicate traffic heavy enough to justify the effort. Less information is available on the effectiveness of these belts than of those of the core route structure.

Available data suggest, however, that there, too, the North Vietnamese could force a belt whenever they chose to concentrate their resources. The belt in Exit Area 966, for example, was established on February 3 and had been breached within two days. Additional mines were implanted on February 6, 10, and 17. Yet Exit Area 966 was counted closed for only seven of the belt's operational life of fifty-eight days, and 162 trucks entered South Vietnam through it in February alone. The effectiveness of the belts was in any event somewhat beside the point. The Seventh Air Force lacked the resources to block all the known routes into South Vietnam; it could not, in fact, devote an adequate number of sorties to defending the blocking points that it had established.[61]

COMMANDO HUNT VII was abruptly terminated on March 31, 1972, when the North Vietnamese began a major offensive against South Vietnam. The resources of the U.S. Air Force in Southeast Asia were insufficient, even with considerable augmentation, to continue interdiction in

---

put the number of diverted sorties at more than 6,000. Evans EOTR, 61.
60. Evans EOTR, 48; 7AF Hist, "CH VII," 21–22, 51, 141–42.
61. 7AF Hist, "CH VII," 51–58, 132, 133.

Laos while seeking to blunt the enemy's bold thrust in South Vietnam itself.

Officially, COMMANDO HUNT VII was hailed a success. Seventh Air Force's report on the operation claimed that 4,727 trucks had been destroyed and 5,882 damaged. It concluded that of 30,947 tons of supplies that had entered STEEL TIGER, only 5,024, or 16 percent, reached South Vietnam or Cambodia.[62] Yet there was a good deal of skepticism about the effectiveness of the operation. General Slay, who had directed it, devoted much of his end of tour report to discussing the factors that accounted "for the failure of the interdiction effort to produce a higher degree of success." His deputy, Brig. Gen. Richard G. Cross, stated flatly in his end of tour report that "this interdiction effort failed to prevent the enemy from positioning sufficient supplies to initiate an all-out offensive against South Vietnam."[63]

In the absence of North Vietnamese records, the results of COMMANDO HUNT VII are difficult to assess. General Cross touched on one of the principal reasons for doubts about the operation's effectiveness—the so-called Easter Offensive of the North Vietnamese that brought COMMANDO HUNT VII to an early end. But as this was the first general offensive since that of Tet, 1968, the possibility remains that COMMANDO HUNT VII did succeed in crimping the enemy's logistical system and that the supplies used in the Easter Offensive had been carefully husbanded and stored in Laos over a period of four years. This argument entails a paradox, however, for the preceding dry-season interdiction campaigns had been hailed as successes on the strength of the same indices upon which any claims for the success of COMMANDO HUNT VII must be based. The Seventh Air Force's operations plan for the latter operation, OPLAN 715, stated, for example, that COMMANDO HUNT V had reduced the enemy's "throughput of supplies to about one third of the previous dry season": "His present logistic posture indicates that the enemy will be seriously limited in the size and duration of his tactical initiatives in the near future."[64]

The conundrum, in other words, is this: The same kind of statistical indices that "proved" the success of COMMANDO HUNT V also "proved" the success of COMMANDO HUNT VII. But if the latter operation succeeded, there could have been no Easter Offensive unless COMMANDO HUNT V had failed. The question inevitably arises, then, how valid were

---

62. 7AF Hist, "CH VII," 61, 82.
63. Slay EOTR; Cross EOTR.
64. Quoted in Evans EOTR, 13.

the statistics? The major indices were the claims for trucks destroyed and damaged, and the calculated throughput of the North Vietnamese logistical system.

The criteria for claiming trucks destroyed or damaged were the same during COMMANDO HUNTs V and VII.[65] In the earlier operation, which lasted from October 10, 1970, through April 30, 1971, the Seventh Air Force claimed a total of 11,009 North Vietnamese trucks destroyed and 8,208 damaged, considerably more than COMMANDO HUNT VII's claims of 4,727 destroyed and 5,882 damaged.[66] The claims for trucks damaged can be quickly dismissed as meaningless. The criteria for claiming a truck as damaged were undemanding: It sufficed that the truck should have been hit by gunfire and then observed not to move. But since the drivers abandoned their vehicles when attacked and did not return to them until the attackers left, many trucks that were merely holed but otherwise undamaged must have been included in the list of claims. Tests conducted in the United States, moreover, showed that trucks are surprisingly hard to destroy if they do not burn. It is quite likely that many of the vehicles actually hit by gunfire did not have to be taken out of service for long, if at all. The North Vietnamese maintained extensive repair facilities in Laos to deal with such damage.[67]

The validity of the claims for trucks destroyed depended in the first instance on the accuracy of reports supplied by aircrews. They cannot be assessed at this remove. It must be said, however, that the criteria for claiming trucks as destroyed—that they be seen to burn or explode—were much more stringent than for claiming them as damaged. There remain two other ways of putting the claims for trucks destroyed into perspective. They can be compared against North Vietnam's imports of trucks, which presumably bore some relation to operational losses, and also

---

65. The criteria for claiming trucks varied with the aircraft employed: For the **AC-130s** and **AC-119s**, a truck was counted as *destroyed* if it exploded or suffered a sustained fire. It was held to have been *damaged* if it received a direct hit from the aircraft's guns and was not seen to move again. For the **B-57s** and **fighter-bombers**, a truck was counted as *destroyed* if it was no longer visible after a direct hit from a bomb, observed to burn, reduced to wreckage, or "rendered unusable and irreparable after a strike." A truck was counted as *damaged* if it was missing parts after having been hit, "stopped and obviously unable to continue after the strike," or overturned. 7AF Hist,"CH VII" (S), 80. *Cf.* Hist, Seventh Air Force, "COMMANDO HUNT V" (S), May 1971, K740.422-2, 56.

66. 7AF Hist, "CH V," May 1971, 57.

67. For the repair facilities, see Directorate of Intelligence, Task Force Alpha, "North Vietnamese Army Logistic System in STEEL TIGER," 14–16. A variety of tests that the Air Force conducted during the war showed how hard it was to destroy trucks that could not be made to burn. See, for example, Nalty, "Interdiction in Southern Laos," 250–51.

against North Vietnam's inventory of trucks on hand. As *Chart 12* suggests, there is a rough correspondence between the number of trucks the North Vietnamese imported from their allies and the number of those the Air Force claimed to have destroyed in Laos. This does not prove the validity of the claims; but there is at least not the kind of gross discrepancy that would discredit them prima facie.

It is, accordingly, not unreasonable to take the claims for trucks destroyed as a basis for discussion. Even if the U.S. Air Force destroyed 4,727 trucks during COMMANDO HUNT VII, such losses were probably insufficient to disrupt the logistical operations of the North Vietnamese for extended periods, if at all. The following table shows the Seventh Air Force's estimate of trucks available to North Vietnam at (presumably) the beginning of COMMANDO HUNT VII. (*Table 19*) It will be noted that the number of trucks estimated to be in STEEL TIGER was 2,000–3,000. This figure (assuming its correctness) must have been close to that needed for the functioning of the supply system. The trucks and drivers assigned to a Binh Tram worked only within that Binh Tram; supplies were shuttled from one Binh Tram to the next.[68] This served the purpose of redundancy and assured that drivers would be familiar with the roads of their Binh Trams—an important consideration, given the hazards of driving at night. The only additional trucks (other than replacements) needed to make the system work were those that carried the supplies through the passes of the Annamite Mountains to leave their cargos with the northwestern Binh Trams. These vehicles would only be a small fraction of those based in STEEL TIGER, if they were based in STEEL TIGER at all. The other significant figure comes from photographic reconnaissance, which showed that the North Vietnamese had about 9,850 trucks in storage. Even if it be assumed that the 3,000 initially in STEEL TIGER were destroyed twice over (which was not claimed), the North Vietnamese would still have been able to replace the trucks destroyed with those in reserve at the beginning of the dry season, to say nothing of those subsequently received from the Soviet Union and other Communist countries.

The remaining statistical index was the estimate of throughput, that is, the percentage of supplies entering southern Laos that reached the Republic of Vietnam and Cambodia. The accuracy of this estimate depended, in the first instance, on the ability of the sensors in northern STEEL TIGER to determine the number of trucks arriving from North Vietnam. That figure was multiplied by three tons at the beginning of the dry season, and by four tons once the road had fully dried. (Four tons was the maximum burden of the North Vietnamese trucks under good

---

68. Evans EOTR, 30.

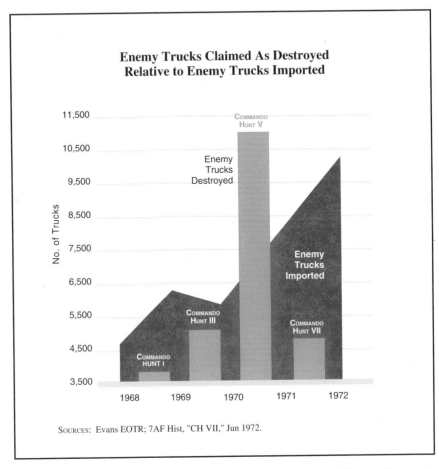

**Enemy Trucks Claimed As Destroyed
Relative to Enemy Trucks Imported**

No. of Trucks

11,500
10,500
9,500
8,500
7,500
6,500
5,500
4,500
3,500

COMMANDO HUNT V

Enemy Trucks Destroyed

Enemy Trucks Imported

COMMANDO HUNT III

COMMANDO HUNT I

COMMANDO HUNT VII

1968   1969   1970   1971   1972

Sources: Evans EOTR; 7AF Hist, "CH VII," Jun 1972.

Chart 12. The data presented for trucks imported into North Vietnam is by calendar year; that for trucks destroyed is by dry season. Evans does not state the source of his information on the importation into North Vietnam of trucks from the Soviet bloc, but he seems confident of its accuracy. He derived his estimate of imports in 1972 from the information that the North Vietnamese had ordered 5,617 trucks from the USSR for 1972, and from the assumption that other members of the Soviet bloc would increase their contributions proportionately. Evans EOTR.

conditions.) The result was the logistical input into STEEL TIGER. From the input was subtracted the tonnage of supplies presumed destroyed when trucks were destroyed or damaged, as determined by formulas which, somewhat simplified, resulted in the following adjustments: For each southbound truck destroyed under way, 3 tons were subtracted from the input figure, and 1.5 tons if the truck was parked. For each

361

Table 19. Distribution of North Vietnam's Trucks

Area	Number of Trucks
Vietnam	
Truck park storage	9,850
Hanoi-Haiphong	4,400
North Vietnamese Panhandle	1,500–2,000
Other provinces	
Laos	
STEEL TIGER	2,000–3,000
Northern Laos	100–200
Cambodia	250–350

SOURCE: 7 AF Hist, "CH VII," 226.

southbound damaged truck, 1 ton was subtracted from the input if the truck was moving, 0.5 ton if it was stopped. If the direction of travel of a stopped truck could not be determined, the subtraction from the input was divided by two. Further subtractions from the input accounted for effects of raids on storage areas. For each fire observed, 0.2 ton was subtracted, for each explosion 0.5 ton. What remained of the input value after these subtractions was the throughput.[69]

This method was the subject of considerable controversy. The Central Intelligence Agency denounced what it called a "numbers game," contending that the Seventh Air Force's calculations were flatly refuted by its "highly reliable sources"—agents within the enemy's ranks. These sources reported that the Communist forces in South Vietnam were only occasionally inconvenienced by interdiction.[70] However that may be, the throughput calculations are open to some rather obvious objections quite apart from the arbitrary assumptions upon which they were based. First, they depended on a reliable estimate of the input, which was derived from the sensor strings. Since the North Vietnamese were able, as the Easter Offensive showed, to send several hundred tanks through STEEL TIGER to Military Regions III and IV in South Vietnam, almost entirely undetected by the sensors, the input estimates must be regarded as suspect.[71]

No inconsiderable portion of the subtraction from the input value, moreover, resulted from the supplies presumed destroyed when trucks were damaged. This part of the subtraction must be regarded as doubly

---

69. *Ibid.*, 16.
70. Nalty, "Interdiction in Southern Laos," 148.
71. Slay EOTR, 26.

suspect: first, because of the problems, reviewed above, that attend the entire question of the claims for trucks damaged, and second, because of a characteristically simple but effective technique used by the North Vietnamese. The cargos of southbound trucks were frequently covered with several layers of rice-filled sacks. This was an effective means of protecting the cargo from gunfire, unless the truck burned, in which case it would not have been counted as damaged.

No final resolution of the throughput controversy is likely without the cooperation of the Vietnamese. There are enough doubts about the data from which the throughput figures were calculated, however, that it seems unwise to let claims based on them outweigh the undeniable fact that the North Vietnamese were able, on March 31, 1972, to begin a general offensive that would have soon destroyed the Republic of Vietnam, but for the massive reintroduction of American air power into Southeast Asia. The greatest single advantage of the Communists in resisting interdiction, other than their low logistical requirements, was that they were usually free to give battle or to decline it at will.[72] Nothing in either the political or the military realm forced them to undertake what was their greatest effort to date in March 1972. Had they been considerably discommoded by COMMANDO HUNT VII, it is not likely that they would have done so.

The conclusion suggested by the fact of the Easter Offensive—that COMMANDO HUNT VII failed to have the intended effect upon the enemy's logistical system—is further buttressed by a systematic analysis of the campaign itself. At every stage, the operation was hobbled by failures fully recognized and admitted by participants, including General Slay, who directed it. These began in December when, with the dry season barely begun, the enemy's antiaircraft missiles drove the B-52s from two of the major passes leading into southern Laos. Even before December, there had been no notable success in closing these avenues. Thereafter, the North Vietnamese had virtually unimpeded access to STEEL TIGER.

Once through the mountains, the enemy's trucks descended into a sea of trees. There they moved on a net of roads imperfectly understood by American intelligence, supplemented by waterways and pipelines nearly invulnerable to attack. The blocking belts tended to slow the

---

72. The requirements of the Communist forces in South Vietnam were the subject of much controversy. All estimates agreed that they were low. In 1970 Seventh Air Force stated that the enemy's requirements as of 1968 had been only 340 tons a day for both the Viet Cong and North Vietnamese Regulars. Seventh Air Force, "Southeast Asia Air Interdiction Handbook," April 1970, K740.1455-3, 1.

progress of the trucks only intermittently, whether in the core route structure or on the borders of South Vietnam. The only aircraft able to hunt vehicles by night with consistent effectiveness were the slow-moving and vulnerable fixed-wing gunships, the AC–119s and the AC–130s. The enemy's antiaircraft defenses kept the former from an important part of his logistical system; the latter were driven from the core route structure temporarily in January and permanently in March. The North Vietnamese defenses also frustrated the B–57Gs, promising weapons but for the vulnerability to ground fire inherent in their mode of operation. Because of the growing threat to the vital fixed-wing gunships, it is questionable whether a COMMANDO HUNT IX would have been possible, had the U.S. Air Force been present in the dry season of 1972–1973 to wage it.

Chapter 11

———◆◆◆———

The Easter Offensive
March 30–September 16, 1972

On March 30, 1972, three divisions and several independent brigades of the North Vietnamese Army, powerfully equipped with tanks and artillery, crossed the border between North and South Vietnam to open a major offensive against the Republic of South Vietnam. Other divisions struck from Laos shortly afterward. President Richard M. Nixon responded by ordering the mining of Haiphong, North Vietnam's major port, and the recommencement of major aerial operations against the Communist state. The primary military purpose of the renewed campaign was to interdict the flow of supplies from China through North Vietnam to the fronts in South Vietnam. FREEDOM TRAIN and LINEBACKER I, as the two phases of this effort were called, graphically illustrate the difficulties inherent in attempting to interdict the communications of an enemy possessed of a competent air force, heavy antiaircraft defenses, and abundant motor transport.

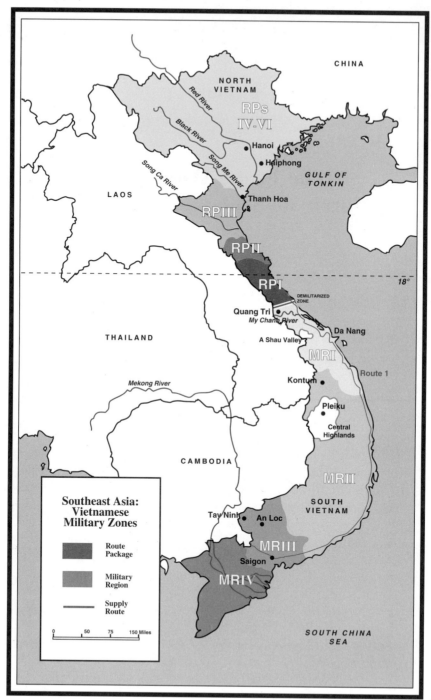

Map 21.

In mid-1971 the government of North Vietnam decided upon a general offensive in South Vietnam. The date ultimately set for the operation was March 30, 1972, Maundy Thursday. Though what came to be called the Easter Offensive represented their greatest military effort to that point, the aims of the North Vietnamese appear to have been largely political—to erode even further the flagging support of the American public for the war in Southeast Asia and to influence the forthcoming presidential election.[1] Their invasion would present President Richard M. Nixon with unpalatable alternatives. If the American leader was to prevent the collapse of the Republic of Vietnam, he would have to intensify the air war, as American divisions had been almost entirely withdrawn from the war zone. That, however, could only exacerbate the already serious political divisions in the United States. The North Vietnamese could reasonably expect, therefore, that when their negotiators returned to Paris, the site of desultory negotiations since 1968, they would find the position of their American counterparts weakened by renewed manifestations of disaffection at home.[2]

The offensive promised other gains. The efforts of the South Vietnamese government to strengthen its control of the countryside had made considerable strides since 1969. One objective of the Easter Offensive was to erase them. President Nixon's diplomatic approaches to the Soviet Union and the People's Republic of China, moreover, had caused the North Vietnamese to fear that their allies might desert them to pursue their own accommodations with the United States. A hard-fought dem-

---

1. Truong Nhu Trang, *A Vietcong Memoir: An Inside Account of the Vietnam War and Its Aftermath* (New York, 1985), 200-1, 210-11.
2. *Ibid.*, 211-13.

onstration of the strength of the Communist cause in Vietnam would make it harder for the Soviets and Chinese to disregard North Vietnam's interests.[3]

Contrary to much public speculation at the time, the Communist offensive did not entirely surprise American intelligence. As early as April 1971, the Central Intelligence Agency (CIA) had argued that the approach of an election year made it probable that the North Vietnamese would do something to convince the American public that there was no "light at the end of the tunnel." The CIA's prescience was blinkered, however. In what was to be a recurrent error, it asserted that the North Vietnamese were incapable of a reprise of 1968's Tet Offensive.[4] This estimate was not altered by the detection of extensive logistical preparations on the part of the Communists throughout the fall of 1971 nor by the understanding that COMMANDO HUNT VII, frustrated by reduced force levels and countermeasures, had not greatly impaired the enemy's buildup in either Laos or Cambodia. In January 1972, the CIA stated emphatically that Hanoi could not during what remained of the dry season in South Vietnam "launch a nationwide military offensive on anything approaching the scale of Tet 1968," whether with its own forces or with what remained of its South Vietnamese allies, the Viet Cong. This view was widely shared. Testifying before Congress in February 1972, Secretary of Defense Melvin Laird dismissed an offensive of that size as "not a serious possibility." Even after the attack proved *larger* than that of 1968, the Army's chief of staff, General William Westmoreland, opined that the drive would falter "in a matter of days" because "the staying power of the enemy is not great."[5] As it happened, the heaviest fighting of the war raged through the summer.

Theretofore, American reconnaissance had usually been able to detect large forces on the march, and always the movement of armor. In 1971–1972, however, the North Vietnamese succeeded in driving hundreds of tanks undetected through Laos.[6] There were random sightings of armored vehicles, but they were too few to form coherent patterns. This stealthy deployment, together with the persistent perception that the enemy's logistical system was less efficient than it was, deflected American intelligence analysts from a correct understanding of Communist plans.[7]

---

3. *Ibid.*, 200–2.
4. General Bruce Palmer, Jr., "U.S. Intelligence and Vietnam," *Studies in Intelligence* 28 (special issue, Spring 1984):91.
5. *Ibid.*, 91; Stanley Karnow, *Vietnam: A History* (New York, 1983), 640.
6. For a discussion of the problems that faced American intelligence in its efforts to keep abreast of North Vietnamese actions in Laos, see Chapter 10.
7. Capt Charles A. Nicholson, *The USAF Response to the Spring 1972 NVN*

About the turn of the year, two, possibly three, new North Vietnamese divisions were located in Kontum and Pleiku provinces of Military Region (MR) II. (*Map 21*) This discovery focused attention on the Central Highlands, a plausible locale for a new offensive. The sway of the South Vietnamese government was shaky in this sparsely populated region, and the two divisions charged with its defense were weak. Reconnaissance had shown that the adjacent region of the Laotian panhandle, where the enemy had made particular efforts to expand his network of roads, was the scene of intensive logistical preparations. An unusual number of tanks, finally, had been observed in and around MR II. But there, as elsewhere, the sightings were too few to permit an adequate appreciation of the scale of the impending offensive.[8]

There were also some indications of an impending offensive in MR I, particularly in the northernmost of South Vietnam's provinces, Quang Tri. In western Quang Tri, the Communists had improved the roads from Laos. Reconnaissance flights, moreover, had occasionally seen tanks in MR I, as well as in the adjacent regions of Laos and North Vietnam.[9] But there was even less appreciation of the danger that the enemy's preparations posed in this quarter than in MR II. The signs of imminent initiatives were much clearer in and around MR II. Intelligence officers, moreover, were quite certain that the North Vietnamese would not strike across the demilitarized zone (DMZ) between the two Vietnams, for fear that so blatant an act would lead to the renewed heavy bombing of their homeland, a policy suspended, save for occasional forays, since the spring of 1968.[10] As the Communists were believed incapable of attacking in two regions at once for logistical reasons, it was presumed that they would begin their offensive in MR II, with the fighting to spread to MR I only after the passage of some weeks. This line of reasoning clearly shows the tenacity with which the Americans and their South Vietnamese allies clung to their belief that the border between North Vietnam and South Vietnam would remain inviolate. For an attack across the frontier would so relieve the pressure on the tortuous sup

---

Offensive: Situation and Redeployment (Project CHECO, 7AF DOAC, 1972), 21; Capt Peter A.W. Liebchen, *Kontum: Battle for the Central Highlands, 30 March–10 June 1972* (Project CHECO, 7AF DOAC, 1972), 1–6.

8. Liebchen, *Kontum*, 1, 3–5; Nicholson, *USAF Response to the Spring 1972 NVN Offensive*, 18. For a summary of the intelligence information available early in 1972, see PACAF/Corona Harvest, *USAF Operations in Defense of South Vietnam, 1 July 1971–30 June 1972* (S) (HQ PACAF, 1972), 53–56.

9. Capt David Mann, *The 1972 Invasion of Military Region I: Fall of Quang Tri and Defense of Hue* (Project CHECO, 7AF CDC, 1973), 4–5; Nicholson, *USAF Response to the Spring 1972 NVN Offensive*, 20–21.

10. Palmer, "U.S. Intelligence and Vietnam," 93.

ply lines through Laos as to make simultaneous attacks in MR I and MR II feasible upon any reasonable estimate of the enemy's logistical capacity.[11]

MR III was in south-central South Vietnam, which the North Vietnamese could reach only from the southern extremities of the Ho Chi Minh Trail in Cambodia.[12] It therefore seemed to the allies scarcely likely to be the scene of a major effort by a foe whose logistical capabilities were limited. Moreover, evidence of a recent vintage supported this presumption. About the turn of the year, the South Vietnamese had mounted several incursions into Cambodia from MR III. They failed to find any evidence at all of the supply caches that were to be expected if an offensive impended. Shortly after the South Vietnamese withdrew from Cambodia, elements of two North Vietnamese divisions were detected, infiltrating into Tay Ninh Province. They appeared, however, insufficiently numerous to require a revision of the estimate that any action in MR III would be a sideshow to the more serious thrust in II.[13]

Once the enemy's preparations were evident, most intelligence analysts favored Tet (mid-February) or President Nixon's visit to China (late February) as the most probable times for the long-expected offensive. Once February had come and gone, summer became the favored date, for the American presidential campaign would then be under way. But preparations for the offensive had so long been in evidence, and the move itself so long predicted, that the attack of March 30 was less than a complete surprise. The weight and scope of the thrust, however, were different matters.[14]

For meteorological if not for political reasons, late March was the optimum time for the North Vietnamese to act. The months of April and May mark a gradual change from the northeast to the southeast monsoon. The former brings clouds that blanket nearly all of Vietnam, though little rain. The latter, on the other hand, has many clear days but also much rain, particularly in Laos. The Easter Offensive began fairly late in the northeast monsoon, which did not fail until early May. This afforded the North Vietnamese two advantages: nearly five months of dry roads in Laos—vital to the supply of their forces in MRs II and III—

---

11. Nicholson, *USAF Response to the Spring 1972 NVN Offensive*, 18.

12. After the overthrow of the Cambodian ruler Prince Sihanouk in March 1970, the North Vietnamese were no longer able to use Cambodian ports for resupply.

13. Nicholson, *USAF Response to the Spring 1972 Offensive*, 18–19; Maj Paul T. Ringenbach and Capt Peter J. Melly, *The Battle for An Loc, 5 April–26 June 1972* (Project CHECO, 7AF CDC, 1973), xiii.

14. Palmer, "U.S. Intelligence and Vietnam," 92; Nicholson, *USAF Response to the Spring 1972 NVN Offensive*, 11–14, 17–20.

and a month of low ceilings to shield the opening phase of their attack from tactical aircraft. This latter advantage was particularly important in MR I, where ceilings of 500 feet prevailed throughout April.[15] In MRs II and III, camouflaged roads effectively concealed the Communists' movements, but in MR I, their major axis of advance lay across the coastal plain, an open area of grassy savannas.

It was, then, contrary to all American calculations that the North Vietnamese opened their drive in MR I. Two divisions and a number of independent regiments, supported by heavy artillery and several hundred tanks, crossed the DMZ into Quang Tri Province on March 30. A third division crossed into Quang Tri from Laos. In all, the invaders of MR I numbered somewhat more than 50,000. The next day, 160 miles south of the DMZ in the Central Highlands of MR II, another North Vietnamese force of about 28,000 began a drive in Kontum Province. On April 4, a third front opened in Binh Long Province of MR III, 375 miles from the DMZ and but 60 miles from Saigon. Here the invaders numbered about 31,000. The North Vietnamese and the Viet Cong together fielded about 200,000 men.[16]

The success of the Communists was at first overwhelming. Shielded from tactical aircraft by low-lying clouds, they advanced on Quang Tri City, which was abandoned by its defenders on May 1. A disorderly retreat toward Hue ensued. The South Vietnamese President, Nguyen Van Thieu, appointed an effective new commander in MR I. This officer, General Ngo Quang Truong, formed a defensive line on the southern bank of the My Chanh River, where he awaited the enemy. In MR II the South Vietnamese were better prepared, but as surely routed. Dak To and many smaller outposts in the Central Highlands quickly fell. Kontum City came under siege on May 14. In MR III the North Vietnamese destroyed a South Vietnamese division in the first several days of their attack and quickly took the district capital of Loc Ninh; by April 13 they had closely invested the provincial capital of An Loc, which had to be supplied by air.[17]

The strength of American forces in South Vietnam had fallen steadily as a consequence of the policy of "Vietnamization" inaugurated in 1969. From a high of about 500,000, American strength was scheduled to decline to 69,000 on May 1, 1972. The U.S. Air Force was no exception. By early 1972, it had handed four major bases over to the Republic of Vietnam, and its overall tactical strike force in South Vietnam and

---

15. Hist, Seventh Air Force, Jul 1, 1971–Jun 30, 1972, 270, 278.
16. Nicholson, *USAF Response to the Spring 1972 NVN Offensive*, 22.
17. Mann, *1972 Invasion of Military Region I*, 13–52; Liebchen, *Kontum*, 28–44; Ringenbach and Melly, *Battle for An Loc*, 1–16.

Thailand had declined from a high of about 535 aircraft to approximately 375. Most of those that remained were used for interdiction in Laos, while the fledgling South Vietnamese Air Force provided close air support for the South Vietnamese Army, with its small force of obsolescent aircraft.[18] The scale of the Easter Offensive required that all allied aircraft be devoted to the battle in South Vietnam. For this alone, to say nothing of continuing interdiction in Laos, the forces in Southeast Asia were insufficient.

It had long been obvious that air and naval units would have to carry the battle in the event of a major North Vietnamese initiative. In early November 1971, Headquarters, Pacific Air Forces (PACAF), had developed Operations Plan C–101, COMMANDO FLASH, to augment the Seventh Air Force. Pursuant to this plan, six F–4 Phantoms, with crews and support personnel, arrived in December in South Vietnam from Clark Air Base in the Philippines. In early February, amid gathering signs of trouble, the rest of the squadron (twelve aircraft) from which the first reinforcements had been drawn deployed to bases in South Vietnam and Thailand.[19]

In February 1972, PACAF developed a second plan for the augmentation of the Seventh Air Force by the Fifth. Operations Plan C–103, COMMANDO FLY, provided for a squadron of eighteen F–4s to be deployed from Korea to Clark Air Base for deployment to Southeast Asia. Admiral John S. McCain, Jr., Commander in Chief, Pacific Command (CINCPAC), ordered the execution of COMMANDO FLY on April 1; by April 3, eight F–4s from Kunsan Air Base in South Korea had been deployed to Ubon Royal Thai Air Force Base in Thailand and to Da Nang Air Base in South Vietnam.[20] Before the Easter Offensive was many hours old it was evident that Seventh Air Force would require reinforcements from the continental United States. Another plan, CONSTANT GUARD, provided for this contingency.[21]

Strike aircraft redeployed under CONSTANT GUARD in three phases, all going to Thailand.[22] CONSTANT GUARD I sent thirty-six F–4s from Seymour Johnson Air Force Base, North Carolina, to Ubon, and four EB–66s, equipped for electronic warfare, from Shaw Air Force Base, South Carolina, to Korat Royal Thai Air Force Base. Also dispatched to

---

18. The strike aircraft of the South Vietnamese air force were primarily propeller-driven A–1 Skyraiders and T–37 jet trainers modified to carry bombs, which so configured were called A–37s.

19. Nicholson, *USAF Response to the Spring 1972 NVN Offensive*, 24–26.

20. *Ibid.*, 29–37.

21. *Ibid.*, 38.

22. There was also a CONSTANT GUARD IV. It, however, was designed to augment the capability for tactical airlift in Southeast Asia.

Korat from Seymour Johnson were twelve F–105s. These aging fighter-bombers had been reequipped to suppress antiaircraft missile batteries by directing antiradiation missiles against the radars. All these actions had been completed by April 16.[23] CONSTANT GUARD II sent two squadrons of F–4s, each with eighteen aircraft, to Udorn Royal Thai Air Force Base. Both units came from Florida, one from Eglin Air Force Base, the other from Homestead. This redeployment had been completed by May 2. CONSTANT GUARD III necessitated the reopening of Takhli Royal Thai Air Force Base in Thailand, which had been closed in 1970, to receive a wing of seventy-two F–4s from Holloman Air Force Base, New Mexico. The redeployment was completed on May 13.[24]

Beginning in February, a series of operations named BULLET SHOT began to augment the force of strategic bombers in Southeast Asia. Under BULLET SHOT I, thirty B–52s deployed to Andersen Air Force Base, Guam. BULLET SHOTS II–V sent 126 B–52s to Southeast Asia between April 4 and June 4. This brought to slightly more than 200 the number of B–52s committed to Southeast Asia. All these aircraft were based at Andersen in Guam or U-Tapao Royal Thai Navy Airfield in Thailand. Before the end of June, the number of supporting KC–135 tanker aircraft in the theater had risen from 30 to 114.[25] Between April 1 and May 24 the number of strike aircraft that the U.S. Air Force had available for operations in Southeast Asia rose from 375 to 625; by the end of July, it was nearly 900.[26]

Both the Marine Corps and the Navy also redeployed substantial numbers of aircraft to Southeast Asia during the Easter Offensive. On March 30 the Marines had no aircraft in the theater, but on April 5 the Joint Chiefs of Staff (JCS) sent two squadrons of F–4s (twenty-eight aircraft) to Da Nang. Another squadron of twelve F–4s followed at mid-month. Two squadrons of A–4s went to Bien Hoa Air Base in South Vietnam at about the same time. Two aircraft carriers, *Hancock* and *Coral Sea*, had been on station off Vietnam at the beginning of the Easter Offensive. During the first week of April they were joined by *Kitty Hawk* and *Constellation*. *Midway* arrived on April 30, followed by *Oriskany* (27 June) and *America* (3 July), which relieved *Constellation*. Each carrier had sixty strike aircraft.[27] All told, the number of American strike

---

23. Hist, PACAF, Jul 1, 1971–Jun 30, 1972, 1:116.

24. Nicholson, *USAF Response to the Spring 1972 NVN Offensive*, 45–47.

25. PACAF Hist, Jul 1, 1971–Jun 30, 1972, 1:121–22.

26. 7AF Hist, Jul 1, 1971–Jun 30, 1972, 273–77; Nicholson, *USAF Response to the Spring 1972 NVN Offensive*, 38, 67.

27. Nicholson, *USAF Response to the Spring 1972 Offensive*, 123–24.

A KC–135 refuels a bomb-loaded F–4E Phantom over Southeast Asia.

aircraft in Southeast Asia rose during the three and a half months after March 30 from about 495 to approximately 1,380.

Upon hearing of the invasion, President Nixon inclined to a vigorous counter response: "I cannot emphasize too strongly," he wrote to Secretary of State Henry M. Kissinger, "that I have determined that we should go for broke. . . . I intend to stop at nothing to bring the enemy to his knees." He had soon resolved not only to resume the systematic bombing of North Vietnam but to take a step from which his predecessor had shrunk—the mining of North Vietnam's harbors.[28]

On April 4, 1972, the JCS informed CINCPAC that "a new set of rules" would soon apply to the conflict in Southeast Asia and solicited "recommendations to make maximum impact upon the enemy through imaginative application of new initiatives." After consultation with subordinate units, CINCPAC forwarded a consolidated list of proposals to the chairman of the JCS. These included the mining of North Vietnam's harbors, an extensive use of naval gunfire against coastal targets, both north and south of the DMZ, and aggressive actions to cripple the enemy's air force. Both messages breathed relief that the new bombing campaign against North Vietnam would be free of some of the restric-

28. Richard M. Nixon, *RN: The Memoirs of Richard Nixon* (New York, 1978), 606.

tions that had hobbled its predecessor, ROLLING THUNDER.[29] The military objectives of the renewed campaign, however, were the same as those of the earlier operation: to restrict the flow of supplies to North Vietnam from its allies, to destroy stores of military equipment in North Vietnam, and to restrict the movement of supplies from North to South Vietnam.[30]

On May 9 President Nixon appeared on American television to announce that American naval aircraft had begun to mine North Vietnam's harbors and coastal waters at 0900 Saigon time and that the mines would be activated at 1800 hours on May 11. Five ships left Haiphong harbor before the deadline; thirty-one remained to unload their cargos and were trapped. From the day the mines came alive through September, no vessels are known to have entered or to have left North Vietnam's ports. To a limited extent, cargos were taken to shore by lighters from ships anchored beyond the twelve-mile limit. This, however, was a slow and burdensome procedure; it could take as long as a month to unload a freighter of 6,000 tons. Patrolling naval aircraft limited the activity to hours of darkness, and the liberal distribution of mines made it hazardous. The Commander of Seventh Air Force, General John W. Vogt, Jr., stated that Operation POCKET MONEY, as the mining was called, had been "almost a hundred percent" successful in preventing the resupply of North Vietnam by sea."[31]

Renewed air strikes against North Vietnam were first authorized on April 2. On that date, the JCS directed CINCPAC to attack antiaircraft surface-to-air missiles (SAMs), artillery, and logistical targets no farther north than twenty-five nautical miles from the DMZ. But as the JCS began to appreciate the full extent of the catastrophe that had befallen the South Vietnamese in MR I, which the face-saving reports of South Vietnamese commanders had initially obscured, the attacks reached deeper into North Vietnam. On April 3, the JCS authorized strikes as far north as 17°35' (53 nautical miles north of the DMZ). On April 5 the limit was extended to 18° (60 nautical miles north of the DMZ). On that date, too, the operation was given the name FREEDOM TRAIN. The area subject to

---

29. Melvin F. Porter, LINEBACKER: *Overview of the First 120 Days* (Project CHECO, 7AF DOA, 1973), 14–15.

30. Lt Gen George J. Eade, "Air Power Halts an Invasion," *Air Force Magazine*, Sep 1972, 66.

31. Porter, LINEBACKER, 16–17. The Chairman of the Joint Chiefs of Staff, Admiral Thomas H. Moorer, USN, told a congressional committee on Jan 9, 1973, that no vessel had yet been observed either to enter or to leave Haiphong. Hearings before the Subcommittee on the Department of Defense of the Committee on Appropriations, House of Representatives, *Bombing of North Vietnam*, 93d Cong, 1st sess (Washington, 1973), 2.

attack continued to expand until the inauguration of FREEDOM TRAIN's successor, LINEBACKER I, on May 10. On April 8 the JCS extended the northern border of the target area to 19° (138 nautical miles from the DMZ). On April 25 it went to 20° (218 nautical miles), and several days later, to 20°25′ (231 nautical miles). The last adjustment made all of the North Vietnamese "panhandle" subject to American air strikes.[32]

Responsibility for the execution of FREEDOM TRAIN fell to the tactical aircraft of the Seventh Air Force, the naval aircraft of Carrier Task Force 77 (CTF–77), and, to a lesser extent, to the B–52s of the Strategic Air Command. The objective of the operation, as set forth in the Seventh Air Force's operations order of April 5, was "to achieve maximum damage to NVN [North Vietnam's] SAM sites, GCI [ground-controlled intercept] (radar) sites, AAA [antiaircraft artillery], long range artillery, tanks, troops and logistical targets below 18 degrees North"—the northern limit of the target area effective on that date. The North Vietnamese had moved many of their SAMs as far south as the DMZ to provide for the air defense of their forces in MR I. The Seventh Air Force's initial mission was to destroy them. Thereafter, its task was to engage artillery and antiaircraft guns while flying armed reconnaissance along lines of communication leading into South Vietnam. To preclude interference with naval operations, the Seventh Air Force's area of operations was generally confined to the DMZ and the area immediately north of it. CTF–77 was responsible for the rest of the target area to its northern limit.[33]

When the area subject to armed reconnaissance was pushed northward to 19° on April 8, the Seventh Air Force became responsible for Route Package (RP) I, a region that extended from the DMZ north to a line just near the 18th Parallel. (See *Map 21*) CTF–77 thereupon began to operate in RP II and that portion of RP III lying south of the 19th Parallel. The Navy's interdiction plan protected three phases. Phase I would entail the attacks on transshipment points and storage areas—fleeting targets, the destruction of which might have an effect on the battle to the south. During Phase II the focus would shift to the enemy's lines of communication—primary targets designated were engineering features associated with highways, railroads, and waterways. Phase III, to be initiated concurrently with Phase II upon completion of Phase I, would see concentrated armed reconnaissance against targets of opportunity found along lines of communication.[34] In practice, however, neither

32. PACAF/Corona Harvest, *USAF Air Operations Against North Vietnam 1 July 1971–30 June 1972* (S) (HQ PACAF, 1973), 52–60, 1007439.
33. *Ibid.*, 60.
34. *Ibid.*, 61.

the Navy nor the Air Force had at first much opportunity for armed reconnaissance, as there was little sign of motor transport on North Vietnam's highways during the first month of the Easter Offensive. As late as June 1, PACAF's "North Vietnamese Current Assessment" noted that the enemy has "shown no signs of response to the interdiction by massive use of trucks; therefore it is estimated that only a small amount of material is entering NVN via the highway system."[35]

During FREEDOM TRAIN (April 6–May 9), the Seventh Air Force and the Navy flew approximately 2,500 attack sorties against North Vietnam; B–52s were responsible for an additional 89. Nearly all were confined to the North Vietnamese panhandle. Before the mining of North Vietnam's harbors in early May, most supplies reached the embattled nation by sea. On April 16, American aircraft, including eighteen B–52s, struck at storage areas, rail yards, and transshipment points in and around the port of Haiphong and the nearby capital city of Hanoi. This marked the first time that B–52s were employed north of the panhandle.[36]

North Vietnamese resistance was from the first heavy. It quickly grew more skillful, though it did not complicate the execution of FREEDOM TRAIN as much as it would that of LINEBACKER I. During April, May, and June, 52 American aircraft were lost over North Vietnam, 7 of them to causes unknown. Of the remaining 45, 17 were lost to SAMs, 11

35. PACAF, "North Vietnamese Current Assessment," Jun 1, 1972, in Corona Harvest Document Collection, "U.S. Air Force Operations in Defense of RVN," Vol 7, K717.03-219, 6. Walter W. Rostow, economist and sometime adviser to presidents, recalled that he had learned from Alexander M. Haig, White House Chief of Staff, that the Chinese had for three weeks after the mining of Haiphong refused to ship supplies to North Vietnam and barred transshipment of Soviet supplies three months: "This was just to let the North Vietnamese know who lived on their border." This report, probably based on the failure to spot much traffic on North Vietnam's roads during May, is probably not true. The tenor of intelligence reports during the summer of 1972 was that both the Chinese and the Soviets stepped up their support for North Vietnam. By the end of June, moreover, the North Vietnamese were receiving oil and gasoline through a newly built pipeline from China (of which more below). The Soviet Union was the ultimate source for this fuel. Similarly, the North Vietnamese heavily expended Soviet-made antiaircraft missiles and artillery ammunition for their Soviet-made guns throughout the summer of 1972. Mark Clodfelter, *The Limits of Air Power: The American Bombing of North Vietnam* (New York, 1989), 167; Hist, MACV, Jan 1972–Mar 1973, annex A, 2.

36. The following were struck once during FREEDOM TRAIN: airfields at Bai Thuong, Dong Hoi, Haiphong, Cat Bi, Kien An, Quan Lang, and Vinh; the naval base and shipyard at Haiphong; railroad yards at Vinh; storage areas and barracks at Haiphong, Hanoi, and Trung Nghia; transshipment points at Ben Thuy, Ham Rong, and Quang Te; and four warehouse areas at Haiphong and one at Thanh Hoa. PACAF/Corona Harvest, *USAF Air Operations Against North Vietnam*, 65.

to antiaircraft fire, 3 to small-arms fire, and 14 to MiGs.[37] The North Vietnamese fired SAMs at an unprecedented rate: 777 in April, 429 in May, and 366 in June. The expenditure was coupled with newly sophisticated tactics which for the first time made missiles a greater danger than antiaircraft fire. The North Vietnamese had learned to employ several techniques to reduce the effectiveness of American antiradiation missiles: One was to employ optical guidance systems, which, as they used no radars, offered no targets to the sensors of the American antiradiation missiles. Another effective tactic was to turn on radars so briefly that only with difficulty could antiradiation missiles acquire their targets. Particularly dangerous were ripple firings (sometimes called the high-low technique) of firing two missiles at an aircraft—the first high, the second low. The first SAM caused the aircraft to take violent evasive action. The resulting loss of speed and maneuvering potential rendered it vulnerable to the following missile.[38]

All the American services flew 27,745 tactical sorties (both attack and support) over North Vietnam during April, May, and June 1972. (Table 20) The loss of 52 aircraft represented a loss rate of slightly less than 2 per 1,000 sorties.[39] That the losses were held to acceptable levels in the face of a determined defense was largely due to the extensive use of countermeasures. Chaff, dropped from dispensers fitted to F-4s, was used to foil the enemy's radars in particularly dangerous areas.[40] It was always used when B-52s ventured over North Vietnam. No aircraft was lost while flying in a chaff corridor. The B-52s were outfitted with equipment to jam radars, and none was lost to enemy action. Pods containing such equipment were also fitted to F-4s. EB-66s, especially equipped for electronic warfare, were not often used over North Vietnam because they were slow and vulnerable to MiGs.[41]

Another measure for coping with SAMs was Iron Hand, the codename for the operations of the F-105 Wild Weasels and their radar-

37. Air Ops Summaries, PACAF, Southeast Asia, Apr, May, Jun 1972, K717.3063. One of the losses attributed to SAMs was regarded as probable rather than as certain.

38. PACAF/Corona Harvest, USAF Air Operations Against North Vietnam, 121–24. The "ripple-firing" technique had apparently been devised for the North Vietnamese by the Soviets after the examination of radar homing and warning equipment from downed American aircraft.

39. Air Ops Summaries, PACAF, Southeast Asia, Apr, May, Jun 1972.

40. Chaff, lightweight strips of metal foil or fiberglass cut to various lengths, was packed in small bundles and dispensed in flight so that, as the packages broke open, clouds of reflective materials formed, thus interfering with enemy radars.

41. PACAF/Corona Harvest, USAF Air Operations Against North Vietnam, 126–28.

Table 20. Number of Tactical Sorties, by Service, Over North Vietnam, April–June 1972

Month	Attack Sorties				Support Sorties				Grand Total
	USAF	USN	USMC	Total	USAF	USN	USMC	Total	
Apr	628	1,250	7	1,885	570	2,274	3	2,847	4,732
May	1,919	3,920	23	5,862	1,348	3,682	0	5,030	10,892
Jun	2,125	4,151	34	6,310	2,044	3,766	1	5,811	12,121
									27,745

SOURCE: Air Ops Summaries, PACAF, Southeast Asia, Jun 1972.

homing missiles. The threat of IRON HAND at first compelled the North Vietnamese to use as sparingly as possible the radars that guided their SAMs, with a resultant effect upon accuracy. The use of IRON HAND decreased markedly after mid-May, however, as the threat of MiGs grew, for the Seventh Air Force was simply too small to be able to escort adequately both bomb-laden Phantoms and the WILD WEASELs. A tactic related to IRON HAND was HUNTER/KILLER. A HUNTER/KILLER formation consisted of a single F–105 WILD WEASEL and a flight of F–4s. The WILD WEASEL searched for SAM sites with its radar-detection equipment. When it found a site, the Phantoms attacked with high-explosive or cluster bombs. This technique was used mostly in the southern route packages, where the North Vietnamese found it difficult to resupply their batteries with SAMs, and where their antiaircraft defenses were less formidable than they were around Hanoi and in the northern route packages.[42]

North Vietnam possessed more than 4,000 antiaircraft guns, which ranged in caliber from 23 to 100 mm. About half of this array was concentrated around Hanoi and Haiphong. These weapons were less effective than those used during ROLLING THUNDER because of the advent of laser-guided bombs, which were dropped from a much higher, and therefore safer, altitude than that used for unguided munitions.[43]

The 200 jet fighters of the North Vietnamese Air Force, however, posed a potentially formidable threat to FREEDOM TRAIN. A third of these aircraft were advanced MiG–21s. The balance consisted mainly of obsolescent MiG–17s and MiG–19s. During FREEDOM TRAIN the North Vietnamese used their air force more conservatively than they had during ROLLING THUNDER, reacting strongly only to attacks near Hanoi and

---

42. *Ibid.*, 129–30.
43. *Ibid.*, 131.

Haiphong. Only one American aircraft was lost to the MiGs during FREEDOM TRAIN, while nine North Vietnamese aircraft were downed. This changed during LINEBACKER I, however, once the North Vietnamese revived and perfected tactics they had developed during ROLLING THUNDER. Ground controllers directed MiG-21s onto the tails of American formations entering North Vietnamese airspace, heavy with fuel and bombs. The Communist jets made supersonic passes from the rear, firing air-to-air missiles as they closed with the American planes. In maneuvering to avoid the missiles, American aircraft lost speed, which made them vulnerable to the attacks of lower performance MiG-19s, which, fitted for the first time with missiles, trailed the MiG-21s at a lower altitude. These tactics were inherently hard to counter, and the situation was made worse by the poor American radar coverage of North Vietnam, which provided pilots with little or no warning of impending attacks. In May, the MiGs downed fourteen American jets while losing twenty-one of their own. In June, however, they downed seven American aircraft while losing only five. In July, both sides were about even: Five American aircraft were lost as were six North Vietnamese.[44]

The answer to this unsatisfactory state of affairs was TEABALL, a weapons control center in Thailand established to coordinate the data arriving from all airborne radars stationed over Laos and the Gulf of Tonkin that covered North Vietnam's airspace. Once a minute, each provided TEABALL with the locations of all aircraft detected over North Vietnam. TEABALL collated this information and used it to issue warnings to endangered American aircraft. The system was inaugurated on August 1, 1972, and immediately had a positive effect on the fortunes of the American fighters. Between August 1 and October 15, they downed nineteen MiGs while losing only five of their own.[45]

FREEDOM TRAIN's attacks on railyards and storage areas did not discernibly affect the ability of the North Vietnamese to prosecute their offensive in the Republic of Vietnam. Far to the south in MR III, for example, the North Vietnamese began the siege of An Loc in early April by firing an average of 1,300 rounds of artillery a day, a rate maintained or exceeded into May. A barrage of 7,000 shells, heavy even by American standards, preceded an effort to storm the town on May 11. In the period May 11–15, expenditure averaged 5,500 rounds a day. Throughout South Vietnam, moreover, the Communists initiated nearly half again as

---

44. *Ibid.*, 132–36; Air Ops Summaries, PACAF, Southeast Asia, Apr, May, Jun 1972.

45. Seventh Air Force, "History of LINEBACKER I Operations, 10 May 1972–23 October 1972," n.d., 1006559, 51–52.

many actions in May as in April.[46] The continuing peril to South Vietnam led President Nixon to decide to mine North Vietnam's waters and to launch LINEBACKER, the greatly intensified bombing of the north.

Pursuant to the President's orders, the JCS ordered CINCPAC on May 9, 1972, to undertake an expanded campaign against North Vietnam's transportation network. The entire country was now subject to attack, save for a narrow buffer zone along the Chinese border, twenty-five to thirty nautical miles wide. South of that, the only restriction was that attacks should result in minimal civilian casualties and cause no damage to the ships trapped in North Vietnam's ports. Railroads and roads acquired a new emphasis as targets, as their importance was presumed to have grown with the successful mining of Haiphong. CINC-PAC apportioned areas of responsibility as follows: the Marine Corps was primarily responsible for RP I; the Navy for RPs II, III, and VIB; and the Air Force for the especially critical RPs V and VIA, adjacent to China. (See *Map 21*) These were areas of primary responsibility only; the Air Force, for example, was active in RP I throughout LINEBACKER I.[47]

PACAF's interdiction plan, forwarded to the Seventh Air Force on May 12, observed that while North Vietnam's ports had been closed, "land lines of communication remain relatively intact." The principal objective of LINEBACKER was to attack these routes "to isolate Hanoi as a key logistics center; destroy stored logistic material and logistic concentrations which result from disruption of the flow; and, finally, to destroy command and control targets in the Hanoi area in order to confuse and disrupt the NVN defensive posture." PACAF ordered that guided munitions be used to the greatest extent possible.[48]

The directive outlined four phases for LINEBACKER: During Phase I the railroad bridges in and around Hanoi were to be destroyed together with those on the northeast railway line from China. Phase II's targets were all primary storage areas and marshaling yards, and Phase III's, the storage and transshipment points established to cope with the damage inflicted during Phases I and II. All targets were to be attacked as often as necessary to deny their use to the North Vietnamese. The targets of Phase IV comprised sites directly associated with the enemy's defenses: command-and-control centers, airfields, and antiaircraft batteries, along

---

46. Ringenbach and Melly, *Battle for An Loc*, 40–42; Air Ops Summaries, PACAF, Southeast Asia, May 1972; MACV Hist, Jan 1972–Mar 1973, annex A, 54.

47. PACAF/Corona Harvest, *USAF Air Operations Against North Vietnam*, 89.

48. *Ibid.*, 89–90.

with the facilities that supported them. These were to be engaged whenever necessary to execute Phases I through III.[49]

The Seventh Air Force's role in LINEBACKER did not detract from its concurrent responsibilities in RP I, the DMZ, and the adjacent areas of Laos. Although systematic attacks on parts of this target system had begun with the better flying weather that set in about May 1, no directive was published until May 21. This plan, too, had four phases. During Phase I, all-important bridges, ferries, and fords in MR I were to be destroyed. Upon completion of Phase I, the bridges, ferries, and fords of RP I were to come under attack, while the B-52s flew thirty sorties a day against storage areas in RP I. During Phase III, a choke point was to be established around Dong Hoi in RP I. To that end, all bridges on Routes 101 and 1A were to be destroyed, together with boats on adjacent waterways, transshipment points, and repair facilities. Phase IV, which was never implemented because of demands elsewhere, was to see heavy strikes on storage areas and lines of communication in Laos.[50]

LINEBACKER was subject to constant modification. Citing the Defense Intelligence Agency (DIA) to the effect that trains and trucks could deliver twice the volume of supplies that had previously passed through Haiphong, CINCPAC slightly reordered the campaign's priorities on May 24. They became (1) northeast and northwest rail lines from China; (2) rail and road links between China and the Hanoi-Haiphong area, and thence south to the DMZ; (3) storage areas for oil and gasoline; (4) power stations; and (5) rolling stock and storage areas other than those for gasoline. Another partial reordering of priorities came in mid-June, after CINCPAC had reviewed progress to date. In descending order, the priority of targets became (1) the northeastern and northwestern rail lines and any forces deployed to clear the minefields at Haiphong; (2) the rail and road links that linked Hanoi and Haiphong to China and the DMZ, as well as inland waterways, which were showing signs of new importance; (3) storage areas for oil and gasoline; (4) the surviving power stations; (5) rail and road targets other than those stipulated in *(2)*; and (6) North Vietnam's industry.[51]

Planners of LINEBACKER I regarded the northern route packages as more important than the southern ones. "I consider RP V and VI (and to some extent IV) to be the most vital segment of NVN, from the point of view of enemy capability to sustain his long range combat potential," Admiral McCain signaled on June 24. These regions contained most of North Vietnam's railway lines, repair facilities, and marshaling yards.

---

49. *Ibid.*, 90–91.
50. *Ibid.*, 91–92.
51. *Ibid.*, 94–95.

There, too, were the major storage and transshipment points of Kep, Hanoi, Haiphong, Nam Dinh, and Thanh Hoa, where supplies that had arrived from China by rail or (before the mining of Haiphong) from the USSR by sea were loaded onto trucks and watercraft, for movement south. (Further movement by rail was impossible on a regular basis because the southern route packages had only a single, vulnerable rail line, so close in places to the shore that it could be blocked by naval gunfire.) In southern North Vietnam, moreover, few obstacles to travel north to south existed, whereas in the north several great rivers, notably the Red and the Black, intervened.[52] There was, however, little correspondence between the apportionment of air effort and the relative importance of the route packages. In May, RP I claimed 86.6 percent of the Seventh Air Force's attack sorties, and RPs V and VIA but 0.7 and 5.2 percent, respectively. Little changed throughout the summer. The Navy and the Marine Corps devoted even less to the northern route packages, in keeping with the allocation of responsibilities among the services. (*Table 21*)

Circumstances compelled the apparently irrational apportionment of sorties. Even with the Air Force's great buildup for the Easter Offensive, the number of aircraft was limited, relative to need. Support for the battle in the south, urgently required during the summer, was necessarily at the expense of LINEBACKER. As Table 21 shows, in September, when the fighting in South Vietnam was essentially over, the weight of effort directed against RPs V and VIA increased greatly. Operations in the northern route packages were gravely further handicapped by the presence of North Vietnam's heaviest antiaircraft defenses. Strike aircraft had to be heavily escorted for protection against MiGs, SAMs, and antiaircraft artillery. Typically, half or more of the aircraft in a formation were dedicated to these protective functions. From the first days of FREEDOM TRAIN, the ratio of support to strike aircraft on missions to Hanoi and Haiphong was *4:1*.[53] By May, the same was true throughout RPs V and VIA, for the North Vietnamese quickly strengthened their defenses there once LINEBACKER threatened their communications with China. The limited number of sorties in the northern route packages was to a certain extent offset by the consideration that they had first claim on the limited

---

52. *Ibid.*, 95; General William W. Momyer, *Air Power in Three Wars* (Washington, 1985), 174–75, 183–96.

53. The strike element typically consisted of eight to twelve bomb-laden F–4s escorted by four to eight more F–4s assigned as escorts (MiG combat air patrols) and four IRON HAND F–105s and several EB–66s to jam enemy radars. In a heavily defended area, an additional eight to twelve F–4s would be assigned to drop chaff. This in turn increased the number of aircraft required for the MiG patrols and IRON HAND. All these aircraft had to be supported by tankers. Seventh Air Force, "History of LINEBACKER I Operations, 12–14.

Table 21. Number of Attack Sorties (and Percent Distribution),* by Route Package and Service, April–September 1972

Month	Route Package							Total†
	I	II	III	IV	V	VIA	VIB	
			Seventh Air Force					
Apr	511 (81.4)	4 (0.6)	6 (1.0)	59 (9.4)	2 (0.3)	34 (5.4)	12 (1.9)	628 (100.0)
May	2,205 (86.6)	19 (0.7)	8 (0.3)	86 (3.4)	19 (0.7)	132 (5.2)	78 (3.1)	2,547 (100.0)
Jun	3,939 (84.3)	32 (0.7)	29 (0.6)	92 (2.0)	92 (2.0)	231 (4.9)	257 (5.5)	4,672 (100.0)
Jul	1,973 (85.4)	44 (1.9)	12 (0.5)	17 (0.7)	8 (0.4)	127 (5.5)	129 (5.6)	2,310 (100.0)
Aug	1,844 (87.3)	7 (0.3)	10 (0.5)	8 (0.4)	56 (2.7)	115 (5.4)	72 (3.4)	2,112 (100.0)
Sep	1,098 (47.8)	2 (0.1)	3 (0.1)	8 (0.4)	421 (18.3)	551 (24.0)	214 (9.3)	2,297 (100.0)
			Navy and Marine Corps					
Apr	440 (35.0)	409 (32.5)	132 (10.5)	138 (11.0)	2 (0.2)	0 (0.0)	136 (10.8)	1,257 (100.0)
May	1,037 (19.9)	1,521 (29.3)	1,122 (21.6)	782 (15.0)	2 (0.0)	50 (1.0)	684 (13.2)	5,198 (100.0)
Jun	1,261 (13.5)	3,055 (32.7)	2,257 (24.1)	1,303 (14.0)	2 (0.0)	72 (0.8)	1,396 (14.9)	9,346 (100.0)
Jul	246 (5.9)	1,391 (33.2)	841 (20.0)	616 (14.7)	0 (0.0)	68 (1.6)	1,031 (24.6)	4,193 (100.0)
Aug	417 (8.7)	2,201 (46.0)	1,131 (23.7)	504 (10.5)	0 (0.0)	5 (0.1)	526 (11.0)	4,784 (100.0)
Sep	426 (10.7)	1,312 (32.9)	1,027 (25.8)	544 (13.7)	5 (0.1)	20 (0.5)	648 (16.3)	3,982 (100.0)

*Exclusive of B–52s.
†Totals include the Gulf of Tonkin.
SOURCES: Air Ops Summaries, PACAF, Southeast Asia, Apr, May, Jun, Jul, Aug, Sep 1972.

supply of guided bombs. But the inability to devote many strike sorties to the most valuable and vulnerable segments of the enemy's lines of communication while the battle raged in the south was a serious limitation on the effectiveness of LINEBACKER I.[54]

Another factor controlling the apportionment of sorties was that neither the Air Force nor the Navy was well equipped for night operations. Until the Air Force reintroduced the F–111 in September, it had in Southeast Asia no tactical aircraft other than fixed-wing gunships specifically designed for night operations, and they dared not venture over North Vietnam. Throughout the Easter Offensive the Air Force used flare-dropping F–4s in MR I and RP I to interrupt North Vietnamese movements and resupply. The practice became more common as the Communists began to move increasingly by night, and by summer about a third of all tactical strike sorties were at night. But the Phantom was seriously handicapped in this role by its lack of terrain-avoidance radar and sensors for acquiring targets in the dark. To be used most effectively at night, the Phantom needed specially fitted C–130s (LAMPLIGHTERs) to drop flares.[55] But these aircraft could not survive over northern MR I, to say nothing of RP I. In the A–6 the Navy had an aircraft with some capacity for night operations, but the demands of daytime operations permitted an average of only four A–6 sorties nightly in the spring.[56]

While generally freer of restrictions than ROLLING THUNDER, LINE-BACKER was nonetheless subject to strict guidelines. In addition to the buffer zone along the Sino-Vietnamese border, two circular areas twenty miles in diameter centered on Hanoi and Haiphong were designated controlled areas. No strikes in any of these areas were permitted without the approval of the JCS. Dams, dikes, civilian watercraft, population centers, and shipping (other than North Vietnamese) were never to be attacked under any circumstances. These restrictions, particularly the one on attacks within the buffer zone, were more significant than they might at first appear. Except for the period between May 21 and June 5 when President Nixon was visiting Moscow, the JCS readily approved many targets in the vicinities of Hanoi and Haiphong. It did so only gingerly

---

54. Memo, General William W. Momyer to General Richard H. Ellis, subj: Corona Harvest ("USAF Operations Against North Vietnam, 1 July 1971–30 June 1972"), Apr 4, 1975, 1024374; PACAF/Corona Harvest, *USAF Air Operations Against North Vietnam*, 120.

55. See Chapter 10 for a description of night operations and a discussion of the Phantom's unsuitability for them. For details of the night operations in MR I during the Easter Offensive, see Msg, General John W. Vogt to PACAF, May 3, 1972, subj: Daily Wrap-Up, Papers of General John W. Vogt (hereafter Vogt Papers), Center for Air Force History.

56. Center for Naval Analysis, "Preliminary Summary of LINEBACKER," Feb 14, 1973, 1010888, 35–36.

along the Chinese border. None was approved until May 16, when four critical bridges and tunnels were validated, and then only for a period of four days. Between May 20 and June 2, strikes within the buffer zone along the Chinese border were allowed for only one day. On June 2, the JCS signaled its approval for attacks on all rail lines, bridges, and tunnels in the buffer zone to within ten nautical miles of the Chinese border. On June 11, however, the JCS rescinded CINCPAC's authority to attack within the buffer zone. Air strikes north of 20°25' were canceled on June 13 because of diplomatic considerations and were not resumed until June 18. These restrictions hampered LINEBACKER to a certain extent in that some of the best choke points in North Vietnam lay within the rugged terrain of the buffer zone. Some of these desirable targets were never attacked. Others were destroyed but then repaired and returned to use when restrictions put them off limits.[57]

LINEBACKER's attacks on North Vietnam's railways were nonetheless highly successful. This was largely due to the laser-guided bomb, a conventional bomb (usually a Mk–84 general-purpose 2,000 pounder) to which a laser-seeking head, a small computer, a special tail assembly, and canard control surfaces had been fitted.[58] The seeker was gimbal-mounted on the nose of the bomb. Once the weapon had been released from the aircraft and had begun to fall toward the target, a ring-tailed fin aligned the laser-seeking head with the flight path. A laser-projector aboard one of the attacking aircraft had meanwhile begun to illuminate the target. Once the seeker detected the energy of the laser being reradiated from any point within its 240° field of view, the bomb's computer began to control the canard control fins to direct the missile to the target.[59]

To a lesser extent, an electro-optically guided bomb called the Walleye also saw use during LINEBACKER I. Unlike the laser-guided bomb, which had to be guided all the way to the target, Walleye was a launch-and-leave glide-bomb with a slant range of 40,000 feet. It was guided by a television camera and a computer. The computer directed the bomb to the target by reducing the telemetric data to patterns, which were then matched to a pattern of the target stored in its circuits. The system was rather rudimentary and could only identify high-contrast targets. It was, moreover, easily diverted by camouflage, clouds, or smoke. Neither

---

57. PACAF/Corona Harvest, *USAF Operations Against North Vietnam*, 98–103.

58. About 90 percent of the laser-guided bombs used in Southeast Asia were Mk–84s. Air Ops Rpt 74/4, 7AF Tactical Analysis Div, "An Analysis of Laser Guided Bombs in SEA," Jun 28, 1973, K740.041–4, 2.

59. *Ibid.*, 3.

could it be used at night. The laser-guided bomb suffered from none of these limitations and was on balance more accurate. It was also less expensive and easier to maintain. The decisive drawback of Walleye, however, was that it had to be released at about 6,000 feet, with the carrying aircraft recovering from its dive at 4,500 feet. This, as General Vogt observed in another connection, was "much too low for operations in Route Packages 5 and 6. . . ." The laser-guided bombs, by contrast, were released at 10,000 to 14,000 feet.[60]

The great superiority of the laser-guided bomb over conventional ordnance was dramatically evidenced early in LINEBACKER I by the destruction of the Thanh Hoa bridge across the Song Me River. This span, 56 feet wide and 540 feet long, was of steel construction and set upon a massive concrete pier. Its military importance derived from the fact that it was a key link on both Route 1 and the rail line to the North Vietnamese panhandle. (See *Map 21*) Attacked unsuccessfully throughout ROLLING THUNDER, it was famous among American pilots as the bridge that "would never go down." During the first attack on April 3, 1965, for example, 79 F-105s dropped 638 750-pound bombs and fired 298 rockets, and yet it remained in service. Five aircraft were lost in the attempt. On May 13, 1972, by contrast, four flights of F-4s (16 aircraft) armed with 15 guided Mk-84s, 9 guided Mk-118s (3,000 pound demolition bombs), and 48 unguided Mk-82 bombs totally wrecked the bridge. The Seventh Air Force calculated that to have inflicted comparable damage, no less than 2,400 unguided bombs would have been required.[61]

Once Haiphong had been mined, the railroads from China were the most efficient means of resupply available to the North Vietnamese. In the first two weeks of LINEBACKER I, F-4s equipped with laser-guided bombs destroyed ten bridges on the northwestern rail line from China and four more on the northeastern line. Other bridges were destroyed throughout North Vietnam. On May 26 intelligence analysts concluded that service on both lines had been seriously disrupted. A week of bad weather and few strikes ensued. By June 1 a number of bridges on a bypass route of the northeastern line had been repaired, and indications were that service had been restored to within thirty miles of Hanoi. On June 2, however, a break in the weather permitted the destruction of a bridge on the bypass line. Other bridges were destroyed in the next several days, and the northeastern line was again closed to all but short-distance shuttle traffic between downed bridges.[62]

---

60. *Ibid.*, 6; Porter, LINEBACKER, 19–21; Msg, Vogt to PACAF, Jul 24, 1972, subj: Daily Wrap-Up, Vogt Papers.
61. Porter, LINEBACKER, 22–25.
62. PACAF/Corona Harvest, *USAF Air Operations Against North Vietnam*, 103–4.

An F-4 Phantom *(upper right)* releases a Mk-84 laser-guided bomb. The arrival of these 2,000-pound precision munitions in the theater late in the war allowed pilots to strike pinpoint targets such as the Thanh Hoa bridge *(lower left)*, which was successfully destroyed on May 13, 1972. This structure had suffered previous bombings, but until the arrival of laser-guided weapons, it had always defied destruction.

The northwestern line remained wholly interdicted throughout June. The northeastern line, somewhat protected by weather and the beneficiary of intensive repair efforts, was open for part of the time. But the rebuilding of the bridges generally failed to keep pace with their destruction. "As fast as they would build them," General Vogt remarked without much exaggeration, "we would knock them out again."[63] Except for brief respites granted by bad weather, this remained the case through the summer.

LINEBACKER was less successful in coping with the enemy's other means of communication. North Vietnam possessed an abundance of inland waterways. Those in the Red River Delta in the northern part of the country became particularly important once air strikes had brought rail travel to a near standstill. On June 30 the JCS called the waterways "the most difficult system to attack by use of TACAIR [aircraft sorties other than those flown by B–52s and strategic airlift]. . . ." The Seventh Air Force employed three methods of attack: armed reconnaissance to detect and destroy vessels on the waterways, the sowing of Mk–36 mines in the channels, and attacks on places where supplies were transshipped to or from vessels. In the southern route packages, where the waterways were

---

63. *Ibid.*, 105; Porter, *LINEBACKER*, 25. Laser-guided bombs were also used to cut trackage and to destroy cars halted on sidings. These were quite minor features, however, of the campaign against North Vietnam's railways. Porter, *LINEBACKER*, 28.

often close to the coast, these techniques were supplemented by naval gunfire.[64]

Any discernable effect on waterborne traffic is attributable to armed reconnaissance and naval gunfire alone. In the lower route packages, the threat of air attacks and shelling forced the Communists to use rivers and canals only at night. In the north, however, waterways remained heavily used by day as well. Strike sorties in the northern route packages were too few to pose any deterrent. Mines had little effect. The only mine that the F–4 could deliver, the Mk–36, was detonated by magnetic influence, and nearly all the small craft that plied the waterways were constructed of wood. The hope that the system would prove vulnerable at transshipment points proved chimerical; all that was required to load and unload the vessels was a firm bank and a few planks.[65]

Before the mining of Haiphong, about 90 percent of North Vietnam's supply of gasoline and other petroleum products came from the Soviet Union by sea. Pipelines constructed in 1968 ran from Haiphong to various points in the DMZ and Laos. The lines, only four inches in diameter, were exceedingly difficult to attack from the air. Automatic shut-offs prevented serious losses of fuel when the pipes were severed. The lines were heavily patrolled, moreover, and breaks were soon discovered and repaired by means of rubber hoses. Pumping stations, spaced at an average distance of a kilometer (much closer in difficult terrain) were easier to find, and their destruction disrupted service longer than severed lines did. The Vietnamese accordingly went to considerable lengths to camouflage them with fast-growing vegetation: Pumps themselves were wheeled to facilitate replacement. Facilities for storage and distribution were the most vulnerable parts of the system, but by 1972 they had been widely dispersed. North Vietnam's system of pipelines, in short, was virtually immune to serious disruption.[66]

The mining of Haiphong ended the supply of petroleum products to North Vietnam by tanker while the first days of LINEBACKER took a toll of the primary storage areas around the port. PACAF estimated that about 10 percent of North Vietnam's supply of petroleum products had been destroyed by the end of May, and another 5 percent consumed. A

---

64. PACAF/Corona Harvest, *USAF Air Operations Against North Vietnam*, 111–13.

65. *Ibid.*; Pacific Air Forces (hereafter PACAF) Activity Input to Corona Harvest, *In-Country and Out-Country Strike Operations in Southeast Asia, 1 January 1965–31 December 1969*, vol 2: *Hardware: Munitions* (S) (HQ PACAF, 1970), 122.

66. Melvin F. Porter, *Interdiction of Waterways and POL Pipelines, SEA* (Project CHECO, 7AF DOA, HQ PACAF, Dec 11, 1970), 14–23; PACAF/Corona Harvest, *USAF Air Operations Against North Vietnam*, 113–14.

U.S. aircraft struck oil and gasoline supplies in Hanoi and along routes south.

crisis clearly impended, and by early June there were signs that the North Vietnamese had begun to build a pipeline to China. On June 14 PACAF outlined a program to stop the construction. It featured the destruction of pumping stations and the use of antipersonnel mines to inhibit repairs. The effort failed for the reason that attacks on pipelines almost always fail: The target was too difficult to detect, too hard to hit, and too easy to repair. Construction of bypass lines in parallel, moreover, had made this particular pipeline redundant. The new system was operational by early July. The "completion of the pipeline from China," PACAF noted in a study of LINEBACKER, was "a serious setback" to the effort to deplete North Vietnam's reserves of petroleum products.[67]

---

67. PACAF/Corona Harvest, *USAF Air Operations Against North Vietnam*, 116–17.

Also serious was the failure to diminish traffic on North Vietnam's highways. Long experience in Laos had shown that the North Vietnamese were adept at maintaining their roads in the face of even the heaviest air attacks. And in RPs V and VI, the roads were much more highly developed than they were in Laos, and the air defenses much stronger. There was of course no possibility of using the vulnerable fixed-wing gunships, which had proved effective in Laos. But there had to be an attempt to stop traffic on the northern roads, for it was clear from the DIA's estimates and other information that motor vehicles could in substantial measure replace the ships that no longer reached Haiphong.

For most of May there was little evidence that motor transport was being used to counter the effects of the mining. But by early June it was clear, as CINCPAC observed, that "large numbers of trucks are moving through NVN, particularly between the PRC [People's Republic of China] and Hanoi/Haiphong." By late May, the Seventh Air Force and the Navy had jointly developed a plan to disrupt traffic on the roads between Hanoi and China. It entailed destruction of bridges, attacks on truck parks, and armed reconnaissance. Several problems were immediately apparent. "This is a very high risk area," General Vogt noted on May 26, and "the support packages required for operations rules [sic] out armed recce [reconnaissance] in the usual sense." In other words, the number of aircraft required for defense against MiGs, missiles, and antiaircraft guns too severely limited the number of strike sorties, the usual problem in the northern route packages.[68] There was, in fact, no armed reconnaissance as such in the northern route packages. Rather, the regular strike sorties searched for vehicles as they flew out of North Vietnam, after having attacked their primary targets. Little was accomplished. In May and June the Air Force and the Navy claimed the destruction of 489 vehicles in RP I, but of only 38 in RPs V and VIA.[69]

The Navy devoted a considerable number of sorties to armed reconnaissance in RPs II and III and, in lesser measure, in RPs IV and VI. But the Navy, like the Air Force, had little ability to attack vehicles at night, when the enemy's convoys moved. Forcing the North Vietnamese

---

68. A later assessment noted that Linebacker had shown, as had earlier experience in Southeast Asia, that road networks were "extremely difficult to effectively interdict by virtue of their simplicity, redundancy, and maintainability. Achieving a desired degree of interdiction for such target systems may require a level of effort which is unobtainable in view of the availability of air resources and the priority of other tasks to be accomplished." PACAF/Corona Harvest, *The USAF in Southeast Asia, 1970–1973: Lessons Learned and Recommendations: A Compendium* (S) (HQ PACAF, 1975), 82, 1009474.
69. PACAF/Corona Harvest, *USAF Air Operations Against North Vietnam*, 107–8; Msg, Vogt to PACAF, May 26, 1972, subj: Daily Wrap-Up, Vogt Papers; Air Ops Summaries, PACAF, Southeast Asia, May, Jun 1972.

to confine their traffic to hours of darkness doubtless reduced the volume of supplies, but the number of trucks available to them was apparently too great for the effect to have been substantial. CINCPAC concluded on June 28 that "based on truck sightings, tonnages involved in shipments from China to NVN could easily equate to the amounts received via NVN ports prior to U.S. mining operations."[70] The CIA's earlier estimate that at least 85 percent of North Vietnam's needs could be supplied overland in the event of a blockade was thus more or less substantiated.[71]

Conditions in South Vietnam were more conducive than those in the North to effective interdiction. There were no MiGs, shorter flight times permitted higher sortie rates, and the threat from SAMs and antiaircraft fire was less. Most sorties were therefore strike sorties, and the fixed-wing gunships could operate. A significant exception, however, existed in MR I. By February, the North Vietnamese had established at least twelve missile batteries just north of the DMZ. The threat they posed was demonstrated on March 23 when an AC–130 gunship was downed in Laos just west of the DMZ. Mobile batteries of SAMs and antiaircraft artillery accompanied the invasion force, putting most of MR I off limits to the lumbering gunships.[72] Near the DMZ, the volume of antiaircraft fire was deemed about equal to that encountered over Hanoi earlier in the war.[73]

One basic fact, however, militated against the effectiveness of interdiction in South Vietnam: COMMANDO HUNT VII's earlier failure to halt the flow of supplies that the enemy had directed into the Republic of Vietnam and the adjacent areas of Laos in preparation for the Easter Offensive. The result was that intelligence reviewed by DIA early in May indicated that the North Vietnamese had on hand supplies to support their current level of activity for at least another two or three months.[74]

---

70. PACAF/Corona Harvest, *USAF Air Operations Against North Vietnam*, 109.

71. Palmer, "U.S. Intelligence and Vietnam," 97–98. In fact, the CIA's position was that most combat matériel (weapons, ammunition, etc.) had *always* been shipped overland.

72. Mann, *1972 Invasion of Military Region I*, 11, 13.

73. Maj A.J.C. Lavalle, ed., *Airpower and the 1972 Invasion* [USAF Southeast Asia Monograph Series] (Washington, 1985), 34.

74. A possible indication of the favorable logistical position of the North Vietnamese is that they did not avail themselves of the drastic curtailment of American air strikes in Laos after the start of the Easter Offensive to bring additional supplies down the Ho Chi Minh Trail. Because of the heavy commitment of air power in South Vietnam, the Air Force's tactical strike sorties in Laos fell during April by 75 percent from March's level—from 6,261 to 1,565. The sorties of the B-52s fell off even more sharply—from 617 to 68. The trend continued into May, when tactical strike sorties numbered only 740, a mere 39 by B-52s. In May, the southwest monsoon brought rains that intermittently flooded parts of

PACAF's own intelligence officers accepted this estimate, adding the gloss on June 1 that LINEBACKER could therefore not be "expected to have an immediate and widespread impact" on the battle.[75]

Because of the prepositioned supplies, it is improbable that interdiction had much effect on the fighting in MRs II and III. The battles at Kontum and An Loc had both ended by early June, before the enemy's stores were likely to have been exhausted. In MR II, Kontum came under close siege on May 12. The fighting was so desperate at times that B–52s bombed within 1,000 meters of South Vietnamese positions. The North Vietnamese, locked in combat with Kontum's defenders, made an excellent target for the bombers. In April and May the B–52s flew 1,682 sorties in MR II, most of which were devoted to punishing the North Vietnamese, first as they advanced on Kontum, then as they lay about it. Pressure on the city eased rapidly after the failure of an all-out assault on May 25. The enemy had definitely begun to withdraw from the city by June 6. The siege of An Loc began on April 12 and peaked on May 11 when an attempt to storm the town was repelled. There, too, the besieged benefited from extraordinarily heavy air support, which included a total of 727 sorties by the B–52s.[76] The North Vietnamese had withdrawn from the immediate vicinity of An Loc by May 19, and in mid-June the South Vietnamese government official declared the siege ended.[77]

What little information is available about the logistical position of the North Vietnamese in MRs II and III suggests that supply had little to do with their failure to take An Loc. The senior American advisor in MR III reported on May 19 that "all available information indicates enemy decimated units have withdrawn from the immediate vicinity of An Loc, a result of the heavy losses inflicted by TACAIR and B–52 strikes." PACAF offered an identical analysis.[78] But even after the North Vietnamese had failed in their maximum effort at An Loc, General Vogt worried about their apparent ability to resupply themselves. On May 16 he noted their "heavy expenditure" of artillery ammunition and fretted

---

the Ho Chi Minh Trail. But in April, when Laos was still dry, sensors indicated that traffic had not surged. In fact, estimates in April decreased slightly for supplies sent through the Laotian panhandle. Air Ops Summaries, PACAF, Southeast Asia, Mar, Apr, May 1972.

75. PACAF, "North Vietnamese Current Assessment," Jun 1, 1972.

76. No figures are available for tactical air sorties in MRs II and III because the Air Force's statistics on in-country operations at this phase of the war were not broken down by military region.

77. Air Ops Summaries, PACAF, Southeast Asia, Apr, May 1972; Hist, SAC, Jul 1, 1971–Jun 30, 1972, 461–467; Msg, Maj Gen James F. Hollingsworth to General Creighton W. Abrams, Jr., May 19, 1972, Vogt Papers.

78. Msg, Hollingsworth to Abrams, May 19, 1972; Air Ops Summaries, PACAF, Southeast Asia, Apr, May 1972.

over the inability of the Seventh Air Force to discover routes by which it was delivered. As late as early June, the Communists were still pouring 300 rounds a day into An Loc. This was, to be sure, a considerable reduction from May's rate. But whether the lower expenditure was due to logistical problems or simply to the abandonment of plans to take An Loc is not known.[79] Less information exists about the supply situation of the North Vietnamese at Kontum. It is perhaps significant, however, that PACAF's intelligence analysts made no claims for effective interdiction. In April, in fact, they noted that the enemy had "with some success" replaced his heavy losses. Through the summer PACAF cited no logistical limitation on the North Vietnamese in MR III, other than those which ensued from the monsoon's flooding of the roads in Laos.[80]

In contrast to the relatively brief although exceedingly violent fighting in MRs II and III, the struggle in MR I lasted through the summer. For the first month of the Easter Offensive, the monsoon shrouded the North Vietnamese advance and allowed only a relatively small number of strikes by South Vietnamese low-performance tactical aircraft (A-1s and A-37s) able to operate under the low ceilings of about 500 feet. The B-52s also directed 554 sorties to MR I during April, mostly against suspected concentrations of troops. The effect of these on the North Vietnamese cannot be determined, as both the weather and the rapid retreat of the South Vietnamese precluded investigation. Around May 1, however, the weather cleared, and there began intensive interdiction of the enemy's lines of communication. The effort was aided by many generally successful strikes on missile batteries throughout the zone of interdiction, although at first the North Vietnamese fired as many as twenty-four SAMs daily from sites scattered throughout MR I. On April 8, a near-miss seriously damaged a B-52. The shoulder-fired SAM-7, recently introduced into the war, also posed a threat to aircraft operating over northern MR I. On June 18, just southwest of Hue, a SAM-7 destroyed the first AC-130 to be lost in the Republic of Vietnam. The threat of SAMs thereafter kept the gunships out of most of MR I.[81]

---

79. Msg, Vogt to PACAF, May 16, 1972, subj: Daily Wrap-Up, Vogt Papers; PACAF/Corona Harvest, *USAF Operations in Defense of South Vietnam*, 100. On May 17 Vogt informed PACAF once more of his concern "about the amount of supplies reaching An Loc to support the enemy ground offensive." Msg, Vogt to PACAF, May 17, 1972, Subj: Daily Wrap-Up, Vogt Papers.

80. Air Ops Summaries, PACAF, Southeast Asia, Apr, May, Jun, Jul, Aug 1972.

81. *Ibid.*; Mann, *1972 Invasion of Military Region I*, 29; Lavalle, ed., *Airpower and the 1972 Spring Invasion*, 44; PACAF/Corona Harvest, *USAF Operations in Defense of South Vietnam*, 159-60, 278, 282. During April there were only four or five days of good flying weather. *Ibid.*, 110 fig. 17.

A Vietnamese Air Force pilot and his advisor look over a target map *(right)*. **An A-37, a low-performance Vietnamese Air Force tactical aircraft, flies a combat mission over South Vietnam** *(below)*.

May saw B–52s return to MR I 825 times. Most of these sorties were directed against troop concentrations although some were attacks on suspected supply points in the A Shau Valley. With clear weather, the tactical aircraft of the Seventh Air Force began a comprehensive attack on North Vietnamese communications in MR I. General Vogt reported on May 9 that he had ordered the destruction of "every bridge, ferry, and ford" between the My Chanh River and the DMZ, along the enemy's axis of advance. Forty-five bridges were destroyed in three days. Vogt claimed on May 14 that as of the preceding day "all bridges, fords, and ferries behind enemy lines have been struck, destroyed, or rendered impassable." Forward air controllers in F–4s—"Fast FACs"—ranged over enemy-held territory, calling in strikes on tanks and motor transport. At night, flare-dropping Phantoms patrolled the main roads. The daytime attacks, at least, took a heavy toll of trucks and tanks. The Phantoms attacked armored vehicles with both laser-guided and conventional bombs, the former proving about twice as effective as the latter.[82] In one particularly important action, F–4s caught twenty-three PT–76 light tanks as they tried to outflank the South Vietnamese positions on the My

---

82. Of attacks using laser-guided bombs on tanks, 33 percent resulted in damage to, or the destruction of, the target; only 17 percent of those using conventional bombs attained comparable results. PACAF/Corona Harvest, *USAF in Southeast Asia: Lessons Learned and Recommendations*, 4.

B–52s *(above)* **heavily attacked areas of suspected enemy concentration in the A Shau Valley** *(right)* **in the spring of 1972.**

Chanh line by traveling down a beach. In short order, the jets destroyed eleven and forced the others to withdraw. Between April 1 and August 15, 1972, interdiction and close air support accounted for about 285 tanks in MR I alone.[83]

As the front had stabilized by June, most of that month's 1,503 B–52 sorties in MR I were against suspected logistical targets in order to forestall an expected drive on Hue. Attacks on such targets each month in MR I ranged from 1,500 to 1,600 through September. By the end of that month, B–52 sorties in MR I totaled 8,072. The B–52s had returned to North Vietnam in July to bomb in RP I. There they flew 337 sorties that month, 560 in August, and 411 in September. Their targets were predominantly logistical: depots, truck parks, and storage areas for oil and gasoline.[84] As the Air Force's statistical summaries for tactical operations in South Vietnam are not given by military region for the last years of the war, it is uncertain how many sorties the fighter-bombers flew in MR I in the period July through September. The Air Force and the Navy together flew 6,004 attack sorties in RP I during those months.

83. Msgs, Vogt to PACAF, May 9, 15, 1972, subj: Daily Wrap-Up, Vogt Papers; Mann, *1972 Invasion of Military Region I*, 58–59; 7AF Hist, Jul 1, 1971–Jun 30, 1972, 281–86.

84. Air Ops Summaries, PACAF, Southeast Asia, Jul, Aug, Sep 1972; SAC Hist, Jul 1, 1971–Jun 30, 1972, 1:212.

Because the North Vietnamese increasingly relied on the cover of darkness, an effort to increase the percentage of night sorties had begun in June. Through the summer, approximately a third of all tactical sorties in RP I were at night. The effort was not notably successful in destroying trucks. From July through September both services claimed destruction of only 546 vehicles in RP I; virtually no claims appear for the other route packages. Half that many had been claimed in May alone before the North Vietnamese began to move their convoys almost entirely at night.[85]

The Communist offensive faltered in May and failed in June. In MR I, the North Vietnamese, supported by tanks and artillery, pressed their attacks on the My Chanh line. They forced the river at several points, but bitter resistance by the South Vietnamese infantry and hundreds of tactical air strikes pushed them back. The last North Vietnamese effort to break the My Chanh line failed May 25. On June 8, the South Vietnamese began a series of limited counterattacks which soon developed into a general counteroffensive. The North Vietnamese remained on the defensive through the summer. The South Vietnamese retook Quang Tri on September 16, but much of MR I remained permanently in Communist hands.

The heavy destruction of tanks moving toward the My Chanh line was undoubtedly most useful to the South Vietnamese defenders. Whether interdiction had any other serious effect on North Vietnamese operations in MR I is difficult to assess. The delay of three weeks between the fall of Quang Tri and the attack on the My Chanh line gave the South Vietnamese commander, Lt. Gen. Ngo Quang Truong, an invaluable respite. It is possible that the B-52s' constant pounding of the enemy's lines of communication contributed to the delay, but the proposition cannot be proved. Fragmentary intelligence information indicated that because of the heavy losses the North Vietnamese had incurred in taking Quang Tri, they were in no position to advance on Hue once the provincial capital had fallen. Given the generally feckless quality of the South Vietnamese's resistance to this point, it is quite likely that the B-52s were responsible for many of the casualties. But most of the bombers' strikes in MR I during the first two months of the Easter Offensive were in the nature of close air support rather than interdiction. It also seems that the North Vietnamese successfully carried out a major resupply operation before moving against the My Chanh line.[86]

---

85. Air Ops Summaries, PACAF, Southeast Asia, May, Jul, Aug, Sep 1972. The comparison is particularly telling when it is recalled that the great surge in motor transport did not begin until June.
86. Msgs, Maj Gen Frederic J. Kroesen to General Abrams, May 16, 18, 24,

While far from conclusive, the available evidence suggests that the North Vietnamese were not greatly plagued by logistical problems once they went over to the defensive in July. The South Vietnamese reached Quang Tri in July, but the Communists were not driven from the city's citadel until September 16. The North Vietnamese defended Quang Tri with six divisions, one of which, the 312th, had moved from Laos in the face of concerted attacks by the Seventh Air Force. The South Vietnamese attacked with only three divisions, but they probably had a numerical advantage because the North Vietnamese divisions were understrength. The Communists' strategy emphasized the use of artillery fire to compensate for the deficiency of infantry.[87] This approach is unlikely to have been adopted by an army experiencing, or expected to experience, severe logistical problems.

The enemy's ability to supply his artillery worried General Vogt even before the South Vietnamese offensive. Of particular concern was the Soviet-made 130-mm gun that had a range (27 kilometers) and a rate of fire nearly twice that of the 155-mm gun that the United States had supplied to South Vietnam. As Seventh Air Force was experimenting with various techniques to detect and suppress these formidable weapons, General Vogt somewhat sporadically kept track of the enemy's expenditure of 130-mm ammunition in MR I throughout the summer. His reports indicate the daily expenditure increased from 200 to 300 rounds a day in June to more than 1,000 in August. In MR I as a whole, the North Vietnamese appear to have been expending artillery ammunition in August at a daily rate exceeding of 3,000 rounds.[88] Inasmuch as an army's expenditure of artillery ammunition is a sensitive indicator of its logistical position, it is not likely that the North Vietnamese in MR I were subject to effective interdiction.[89]

In contrast to the Second World War, and even to Korea, information about the effects of interdiction during the Easter Offensive of 1972

25, subj: Daily Commander's Evaluation, Vogt Papers.

87. Msg, Brig Gen Harry H. Hifstand to General Abrams, Jun 27, 1972, subj: Daily Commander's Evaluation, Vogt Papers; Msg, Maj Gen Howard H. Cooksey to General Abrams, Jun 29, 1972, subj: Daily Commander's Evaluation, Vogt Papers; Lt Gen Ngo Quang Truong, *The Easter Offensive of 1972* [Indochina Monographs] (Washington, 1980), 67; MACV Hist, Jan 1972–Mar 1973, annex A, 53.

88. Msgs, Vogt to PACAF, Jun 1 to Aug 21, 1972, subj: Daily Wrap-Up, Vogt Papers; MACV Hist, Jan 1972–Mar 1973, 74, 79. General Truong notes in his memoirs that through the battle for Quang Tri his troops were plagued by "the enemy's ferocious artillery fire which averaged thousands of rounds daily . . . ." Truong, *Easter Offensive*, 69.

89. See, for example, Chapters 4, 5, 6, and 8.

is lacking. The following conclusions, accordingly, are offered only tentatively, and with the recognition that future disclosures by the Socialist Republic of Vietnam may alter them.

It is probable that the question of whether interdiction operations in North Vietnam affected the offensive phase of Communist operations in South Vietnam is almost beside the point. American intelligence believed that the North Vietnamese had prepositioned enough supplies in Laos and southern North Vietnam to sustain their operations through the summer; the Easter Offensive had faltered by late June. It seems unlikely that FREEDOM TRAIN and LINEBACKER so impeded the transit of supplies through North Vietnam as to have imperiled Communist resupply in South Vietnam once the prepositioned supplies had been consumed. The North Vietnamese probably had trucks in numbers sufficient to counteract the mining of Haiphong.[90] The enemy's antiaircraft defenses ruled out effective armed reconnaissance in the northern route packages: Exorbitant numbers of aircraft had to be used for escort, and all sorties had to be flown at altitudes too high, and speeds too great, for effective truck hunting. In RP I it was possible to suppress the defenses sufficiently for the Phantoms to conduct armed reconnaissance both day and night. But defenses were sufficiently strong to deny the airspace over RP I and MR I to the only aircraft able to hunt trucks effectively by night—the fixed-wing gunships.

Two other forms of transport resistant to interdiction—inland water transport and pipelines—supplemented the enemy's motor vehicles. North Vietnam's air defenses sheltered both, much as they sheltered motor transport. Not only did the United States lack mines suitable for use against the wooden craft that plied North Vietnam's waterways, it never found an effective way to attack pipelines, inherently hard to hit and easy to replace. It is difficult to see how FREEDOM TRAIN and LINEBACKER could have significantly slowed the flow of supplies through North Viet-

---

90. This conclusion rests on the estimates of the CIA and the DIA, cited in the text above. See also Chapter 10, Chart 12. Testifying before Congress in January 1973, the Chairman of the Joint Chiefs of Staff, Admiral Thomas H. Moorer, USN, described the number of trucks at the disposal of the North Vietnamese as "tremendous." In his testimony, Admiral Moorer claimed the closing of Haiphong harbor and the cutting of rail lines had reduced North Vietnam's imports to 30,000 tons a month. This figure is implausibly low. American intelligence put the number of trucks in North Vietnam at about 14,000 (see Chapter 10, Table 19). Accepting the admiral's statement that each of these trucks carried an average of four tons, and assuming that each truck could each month complete only one trip from the railheads on the Chinese border (an absurdly low figure), one would still have imports of about 56,000 tons a month. Hearings before the Subcommittee on the Department of Defense of the Committee on Appropriations, House of Representatives, *Bombing of North Vietnam*, 93d Cong, 1st sess (Washington, 1973), 8, 43.

nam unless the attacking force had been much larger, better able to suppress defenses, and able to operate by night as effectively as by day.[91]

Much harder to assess is the effect of interdiction undertaken within South Vietnam. It is probable that the early failure of COMMANDO HUNT VII and the relatively short duration of the fighting in MRs II and III make the question of interdiction's effectiveness moot with respect to the battles at An Loc and Kontum. The North Vietnamese appear to have had in South Vietnam and adjacent areas of Laos supplies sufficient to see them through their defeats, which were the accomplishments of the South Vietnamese infantry, tactical close air support, and the B–52s.[92] In MR I, where fighting raged until fall, the North Vietnamese had the advantage of relatively short supply lines, protected by much the same complex of factors that had worked to thwart FREEDOM TRAIN and LINE-BACKER. American air power took a heavy toll of North Vietnamese manpower and tanks in MR I. It is possible that these losses slowed the North Vietnamese drive and gave the South Vietnamese a chance to rally along the My Chanh River. But against these somewhat conjectural observations must be set another: that the heavy reliance of the North Vietnamese on artillery through the summer of 1972 does not suggest that their lines of communication were effectively interdicted.

---

91. For a different view of the vulnerability of North Vietnam's overland communications, see Clodfelter, *Limits of Air Power*, 173.

92. This was the position of the CIA, which cited the well-supplied offensives in MRs II and III as proof of its early contention that interdiction had failed in Laos. Palmer, "U.S. Intelligence and Vietnam," 98–99.

Conclusion

An Analytical Overview of American Interdiction
Operations, 1942–1972

The American experience with interdiction during the three decades that followed the spectacularly successful inaugural venture of the Army Air Forces in Tunisia suggests three general conclusions about the nature and evolution of interdiction operations in that period: (1) That of the eight conditions favoring interdiction described in the introduction—*intelligence, air superiority, sustained pressure, identifiability, concentration, channelization, high consumption,* and *logistical constriction*—three (*intelligence, air superiority,* and *identifiability*) have been necessary for effective attacks upon an enemy's communications, while the remaining five conditions have been contributory in the sense that they have not uniformly characterized successful interdiction operations; (2) that the three ways in which interdiction has degraded communications—*attrition, blockage,* and *the creation of systemic inefficiencies*—each has tended to be effective through only a specific range of conditions; and (3) that interdiction was on balance much less efficacious in Korea and Southeast Asia than it had been in Europe during World War II. There are several reasons for the reduced effectiveness of interdiction in the later wars. American tactical aircraft were usually too few in number and, in Southeast Asia, at least, were hampered by having been designed for missions quite different from interdiction. The Chinese and the North Vietnamese, moreover, were not so vulnerable to interdiction as the Germans had been. The consumption of their armies was less, and their motor transport was more plentiful. Communist antiaircraft defenses were a greater deterrent to low-flying aircraft than were those of the Germans, and their air forces were more dangerous than the *Luftwaffe* was by the time of the great Allied interdiction campaigns of 1944.

Necessary and Contributory Conditions for Interdiction

Wherever they have significantly influenced the course of the ground battle, interdictors have enjoyed *air superiority* in the form of virtually unimpeded access to the enemy's air space and adequate *intelligence* about his logistical system. The targets of the campaign have been readily *identifiable*. The Italian STRANGLE reduced German resupply because the Allies could enter German airspace at will to destroy bridges and strafe convoys with only trifling losses. Conversely, German antiaircraft fire denied the air space over the Strait of Messina to the Northwest African Tactical Air Force and made possible the virtually unhindered evacuation of German divisions from Sicily. There is no better demonstration of the value of *intelligence* to an interdiction campaign than in North Africa. The Allies had virtually complete information about the movements of the enemy's shipping and the schedules of his air transport service. They planned their interdiction campaign around this information, which was clearly one of the most important determinants of its success. But the inability of American intelligence to discover large segments of the enemy's road net in southern Laos was an important reason for the failure of COMMANDO HUNT VII. The importance of *identifiability* is too obvious to require elaboration—if targets cannot be detected, they cannot be engaged. Nothing has so consistently thwarted interdictors as the difficulties of conducting aerial operations at night. Truly effective night interdiction of vehicular traffic was impossible before the war in Southeast Asia and the introduction of the fixed-wing gunships with their advanced sensors. But even then the capacity of the U.S. Air Force for nocturnal interdiction was seriously limited by the vulnerability of these large and slow-moving aircraft.

Of the contributory conditions for successful interdiction—*concentration, channelization,* a *high rate of consumption, logistical constriction,* and *sustained pressure*—the latter has the best claim to being necessary. Indeed, in strategic interdiction campaigns—prolonged aerial "sieges" of enemy fronts—sustained pressure *has* been necessary to prevent the repair or replacement of engineering features and transport. Interdiction, to borrow a phrase from economics, tends to work "on the margin"—that is, except in the rarest of circumstances, it will stop only a small percentage of the troops or supplies that pass into the zone of interdiction. If the enemy's logistical system has any surplus capacity, failure to maintain sustained pressure will probably allow him to meet his requirements. But in tactical interdiction, where the concern is with the short term, the destruction of a single bridge at the right moment may be all that is required to bring about the desired result.

Concentration and *channelization* are both unambiguously contributory conditions. The fewer the vehicles and depots of a supply system, the easier they may be engaged. The task of Allied aviators during the Tunisian Campaign was made easier because of the apportionment of the Axis' supplies among a limited number of ships. Conversely, truck-based logistical systems in Korea and Southeast Asia were difficult to interdict in part because supplies were spread in small portions among a large number of vehicles. But where lines of communication are channelized, dispersion is of no advantage to the interdicted side. Large numbers of locomotives or railway cars are of little use when bridges are down and marshaling yards unusable.

Channelization simplifies an interdictor's work but is not necessary for the accomplishment of his mission if the enemy's conveyances are few or otherwise vulnerable. That the Axis' ships were confined to channels in the minefields of the Strait of Sicily was not nearly so important as the fewness of their numbers. Even had their courses not been so restricted, the information from ULTRA about their schedules and destinations would have prevented the Axis from gaining significantly from having some choice of routes.

Probably no condition had been more often described as necessary to the success of an interdiction campaign than *high consumption*. Many writers have attached undue importance to this factor because they have paid insufficient attention to *logistical constriction*. If an enemy's lines of communication are constricted, his rate of consumption is of comparatively little importance. In the spring of 1944, the consumption of the German armies on the Gustav Line and at Anzio was minimal during the lull that prevailed between the failed Allied attacks of March 1944 and the successful offensive of May, DIADEM. But STRANGLE reduced the Germans' resupply because their logistical system became seriously constricted once the Allied air forces had driven back *Heeresgruppe C*'s railheads, thereby increasing the burden on its already inadequate motor transport. During DIADEM, conversely, German consumption was high but there was little logistical constriction because the Allies attacked a narrow sector of the Gustav Line, which allowed the Germans to concentrate their transport in support of the few divisions engaged. But despite its importance, *logistical constriction* cannot be considered necessary for successful interdiction, for even the least constricted lines of communication may be interdicted if they are otherwise vulnerable.

Only a small fraction of the capacity of the French and Italian rail systems would have sufficed the Germans for resupply and the movement of reserves. But the Allies, by exploiting in one fashion or another the channelization characteristic of all railroads, were able to disrupt rail service whenever they chose to devote sufficient resources to the task.

It is possible to envision successful interdiction where only three necessary conditions were present. But it appears that in practice interdiction has exerted a marked influence on the ground battle only when at least one of the contributory conditions came into play.

The Three Basic Tactics of Interdiction

The Introduction briefly described the three fundamental ways in which aerial attack has degraded communications where the conditions for interdiction have been present in fruitful combinations. A closer examination of these tactics—*attrition, blockage,* and the creation of *systemic inefficiencies*—suggests that each has been practicable only under specific conditions.

Attrition has best served tactical interdiction because it is brief and focused. As noted above, it has rarely been possible to destroy more than a small portion of the vehicles at an enemy's command. But in the thick of battle even small losses can be grievous. The loss of one hundred trucks from an establishment of thousands is of scant account when the losses are incurred in different locations over a period of days. But if the hundred vehicles destroyed represent half of those available to meet a tactical emergency, their loss can be decisive. It has, moreover, been easiest to destroy vehicles on the battlefield when a crisis has compelled an enemy to throw caution to the wind. The march of the *Hermann Göring Panzer Parachute Division* to Valmontone affords an example of this, and the desperate effort of the *Panzer Lehr Division* to reach the Allied beachhead on the first day of OVERLORD another.

Because the effects of interdiction tend to be marginal, attrition has decided strategic interdiction campaigns only when the enemy was unusually handicapped in some way. During the Tunisian Campaign, for example, the Axis suffered because ships are particularly vulnerable to superior air power in that they cannot hide on the face of the sea, are employed in relatively small numbers, and are difficult to replace. Conversely, the limits of attrition in strategic interdiction have been most evident when the interdictors tried to disrupt an enemy's communications primarily through the destruction of a large number of easily replaced motor vehicles. One reasons for the failure of COMMANDO HUNT VII was that the supply of vehicles available to the North Vietnamese was, relative to the American ability to destroy them, inexhaustible.

Blockage: The conditions for the success of blockage have been even more stringent than for attrition. In tactical interdiction the judicious destruction of engineering features (bridges, tunnels, viaducts, etc.) can produce significant advantages even if the targets remain out of service for only a few hours. The approach march of the *21st Panzer Division*, the only German division to attack the Allied lodgment in Normandy on D-day, was slowed by several hours because all but one of the bridges across the river Orne had been destroyed. The entire division had to file across the remaining span. The resulting delay would have been insignificant in a strategic interdiction campaign; it was perhaps of some consequence in its tactical context.

In strategic interdiction, however, blockage has been effective only when the foe was heavily dependent upon railroads, the most channelized of all means of communication. During the Italian campaign, for example, the Allies were periodically able to paralyze rail traffic because the railroads of southern Italy depended upon a small number of marshaling yards, while the mountains of north-central Italy restricted the number of main lines and made them heavily dependent upon engineering features. Even so, it is doubtful that STRANGLE would have had the effect that it did if German antiaircraft defenses had not been so weak and the *Luftwaffe* conspicuous by its absence. The failure of three successive interdiction campaigns in Korea during 1951 shows how effective opposition in the air and strong antiaircraft defenses can render the constant attention required to keep bridges and railroads out of operation prohibitively expensive to the attacker during strategic interdiction.

Attempts to block the movement of motor transport in strategic campaigns have been almost uniformly unsuccessful. Road nets are inherently redundant, and it is a rare roadblock that cannot be circumvented without considerable disadvantage when time is not pressing. The failure of the Allies to stop German convoys making for the beachhead at Salerno by bombing roads and bridges is an illustration of this point; the dismal record of blocking belts in Laos is another.

Systemic Inefficiencies: Neither blockage nor attrition has been often successful in strategic interdiction because their length gives enemies the opportunity to resort to alternative routes and means of conveyance. The creation of systemic inefficiencies, accordingly, has been much more a method of strategic interdiction than of tactical. This usual procedure has been to use the threat of attrition and some degree of blockage to force upon the enemy circuitous routes, inconvenient scheduling, and reliance upon a less vulnerable but also less efficient means of transport. The Italian STRANGLE of 1944 remains the best excellent example of this. By relentlessly destroying the engineering features upon which the railroads of central Italy depended, the Allies forced the Germans to use railheads far from the front. Even so, the Germans would have had enough trucks to substitute for the railroads if their convoys had been able to operate around the clock. The Allied air forces, however, forced them to seek the cover of darkness. The requirement to move at night so increased the Germans' need for transport space that their supply of trucks ceased to be adequate. They were barely able to cover current consumption only because the front was unusually quiet during STRANGLE.

The Decreased Effectiveness of Interdiction After World War II

After years of comparative neglect, interdiction became the subject of a considerable body of writing, much of it sponsored by the U.S. Air Force, in the late 1960s. The decision not to invade North Vietnam perforce made interdiction a cardinal element of American strategy during the war in Southeast Asia. The interest of the military in interdiction remained after the withdrawal from Vietnam—sustained first by the realization that it had been shown that the balance of terror, while sufficient to keep the peace in Europe, had little power to dampen conflicts elsewhere, and then by the realization that threats of a reflexive nuclear response to a Soviet invasion were ceasing to be credible once the USSR had gained nuclear parity with the United States. Any nonnuclear strategy for the defense of Western Europe had to place considerable emphasis on interdiction, for if the already formidable Group of Soviet Forces in eastern Germany could have been quickly reinforced from the USSR once it had thrust into West Germany, NATO's chances of containing the attack would have been slight.

Those who turned their attention to how interdiction might be used to offset the Soviet advantage in conventional forces understandably tended to look most closely at the experience of World War II.[1] Korea and Vietnam seemed of little relevance. The consumption of supplies by the armies interdicted in the Asian wars was low, while a hypothetical European war would have entailed terrific consumption. Such a war, moreover, would have been characterized by sweeping maneuvers, while in Korea the front was static after the spring of 1951. The guerrilla warfare in Vietnam bore even less resemblance to what could be plausibly expected of a war on the continent.

---

1. Much the larger part of the historical research about interdiction sponsored by the Air Force, for example, has dealt with that war. Readily accessible examples include F.M. Sallagar's study of the Italian STRANGLE (discussed in Chapter 5) and the voluminous chronicles of interdiction campaigns throughout the European and Mediterranean theaters that Col Trevor N. Dupuy's Historical Research and Evaluation Organization assembled (cited in Chapters 5, 6, and 7). Another extensive series of reports is called SABRE MEASURES, prepared by the Air Force's Assistant Chief of Staff, Studies and Analysis, around 1970. All appear to have dealt with World War II. (One of them, *The Uncertainty of Predicting Results of an Interdiction Campaign*, is cited in Chapter 5.)

The strikingly different levels of consumption between interdicted armies in these wars, together with the general understanding that interdiction was at times successful in World War II but rarely so in Korea or Vietnam, encouraged the belief that consumption was the critical difference that spelled victory for interdiction in Europe but defeat in Asia.[2] The importance of consumption should not be underestimated, but the almost exclusive reliance on it to explain the differing outcomes of interdiction campaigns has obscured other fundamental differences between the earlier war and the later ones that affected the outcomes of interdiction operations as much or more.

The German Army, its close identification with the *Blitzkrieg* notwithstanding, was not heavily mechanized. German industry, even when augmented by the resources of occupied Europe, was simply not capable of motorizing the *Wehrmacht* on anything like the scale of the American and British armies. The *Panzer* divisions were few, a cutting edge behind which the mass of infantry divisions trudged on foot, just as they had in 1914. The trucks available to a German field army barely sufficed for short hauls between advance railheads and the army depots. The German supply system therefore depended heavily upon railroads which, fixed and channelized, were comparatively easy to disrupt. Neither the Chinese nor the North Vietnamese were so heavily dependent upon railroads nor, relative to their requirements, so poorly provided with trucks as the Germans.

Against the brittle German logistical system the Allies directed tactical aircraft in numbers which, by later standards, were extraordinary. At times during the first days of OVERLORD the number of tactical aircraft over the battlefields of Normandy undoubtedly exceeded the entire inventory of tactical aircraft with which the U.S. Air Force began the Korean War in 1950. In 1972, when LINEBACKER I started, the Air Force's inventory of tactical aircraft was barely more than a third of the force that had been marshaled for OVERLORD alone.[3] The jet-propelled aircraft used in Korea and Southeast Asia greatly exceeded in performance those used in World War II. But superior performance could not wholly offset comparatively small numbers. In Korea the Fifth Air Force had to curtail interdiction operations because the quite modest rates of attrition inflicted by the Chinese antiaircraft defenses considerably exceeded the rate

---

2. See, for example, Gregory A. Carter, *Some Historical Notes on Air Interdiction in Korea* (The Rand Corp., RP-3452, Santa Monica, 1966).

3. As noted in Chapter 7, on June 6, 1944, the Allies disposed 1,545 light and medium bombers and 5,409 fighters. Virtually all of these aircraft were suited for interdiction missions such as bombing and strafing. The U.S. Air Force began the Korean War with 1,280 tactical aircraft and had about 2,475 when LINEBACKER I began.

at which its losses could be replaced. The heavy commitment of tactical aircraft to LINEBACKER I required that interdiction cease entirely in Laos because the Seventh Air Force, even when heavily reinforced, was not large enough to continue operations against the Ho Chi Minh Trail while attacking North Vietnam.

The number of tactical aircraft with which the United States had to fight in Korea and Southeast Asia was small by comparison with World War II. This largely explains the third major difference between interdiction operations in those conflicts and those of the earlier struggle: the reduced margin of America air superiority, broadly conceived as the ability to overcome both the enemy's air force and his antiaircraft defenses. In Italy and France the Allies had the time to cripple the *Luftwaffe*'s daytime fighter force before they began interdiction. Having won air superiority, the Allies were able to devote most of their fighters to armed reconnaissance. In Korea, on the other hand, the Chinese had an active air force. While less effective than the U.S. Air Force, it was nonetheless able by the end of 1951 to disrupt the efforts to cut rail lines and to down the Yalu bridges. The American F–86 Sabres were too few to engage more than a part of China's large force of MiG–15s; their many victories were impressive but largely irrelevant as far as interdiction was concerned. The North Vietnamese air force was small but sufficiently aggressive to compel the Seventh Air Force to devote a disproportionate number of aircraft to escort missions. At times the strike force constituted only a third of attacking formations.

The Germans were unable to redress the weakness of the *Luftwaffe* by protecting their lines of communication with antiaircraft weapons. But in Korea, antiaircraft fire alone had sufficed to foil the Fifth Air Force's efforts at armed reconnaissance and line-cutting. Antiaircraft guns and missiles prevented the U.S. Seventh Air Force from conducting armed reconnaissance in the northern route packages of North Vietnam, and were yet another reason for the unfavorable ratio of escort to strike aircraft. In Korea and Southeast Asia it was not so much the absolute effectiveness of the defenses that told—both the Chinese and the North Vietnamese were on the whole *less* successful in bringing down aircraft than the Germans had been—as it was the shrunken size of American tactical aviation which could not absorb even quite modest rates of attrition.

Precision-guided munitions made it much easier to destroy bridges and other engineering features in Vietnam than had been the case in the earlier wars. But this new capability could not compensate for what had been lost: the ability to carry out extensive armed reconnaissance. A logistical system wholly dependent upon railroads can be crippled through the destruction of engineering features where the terrain dictates the widespread use of bridges and viaducts. But when it is possible to substitute trucks for railroads, even the widespread destruction of engineering features may gain the interdictor little for his pains. Road networks are normally redundant, and true choke points usually few and easily circumvented. Makeshift bridges for motor vehicles, moreover, are easily concealed. The destruction of virtually every known major bridge in North Vietnam had no discernable effect on the convoys that clogged the country's roads every night—and, in the northern route packages, by day as well. The Italian STRANGLE, which destroyed most of the bridges in a region where engineering features were unusually important to road travel, would not have curtailed German resupply except for the work of the strafing fighter-bombers that swept the roads of traffic by day. Even then the success of STRANGLE was critically dependent upon the meagerness of the Germans' motor transport. Had the Germans had just twice as many trucks as they actually had—still an establishment of motor vehicles much smaller than that of the Allies—STRANGLE would have presented few problems for them. As it was almost entirely unable to carry out armed reconnaissance north of the southern panhandle of North Vietnam, the Seventh Air Force never had much chance of seriously retarding the stream of supplies that flowed from China to the fronts in South Vietnam.

Select Bibliography

Manuscript Collections

Library of Congress, Washington, D.C.
Papers of Ira C. Eaker.
Papers of Carl A. Spaatz.
Papers of Hoyt S. Vandenberg.

National Archives and Records Administration, Washington, D.C.
Record Group 242: National Archives Collection of Seized Records.
    Records of the Headquarters, German Armed Forces High Command.
    Records of the Headquarters, Germany Army High Command.
    Records of German Field Commands: Army Groups.
    Records of German Field Commands: Armies.
    Records of German Field Commands: Corps.
Record Group 338: National Archives Collection of Commissioned Records.
    Foreign Military Studies Series, U.S. Army, Europe.
Record Group 341: Records of Headquarters United States Air Force.

Air Force Historical Research Agency, Maxwell Air Force Base, Alabama
General Records of the United States Air Force.

Books

Alexander, Bevin. *Korea: The First War We Lost*. New York: Hippocrene Books, 1986.

Appleman, Roy E. *South to the Naktong, North to the Yalu (June–November 1950)*. United States Army in the Korean War. Washington, D.C.: Office of the Chief of Military History, United States Army, 1961.

Bennett, Ralph. *ULTRA in the West: The Normandy Campaign, 1944–1945*. New York: Chas. Scribner's Sons, 1980.

Bidwell, Shelford, and Dominick Graham. *Firepower: British Army Weapons and Theories of War, 1904–1945*. London: Allen & Unwin, 1982.

Blumenson, Martin. *Salerno to Cassino*. United States Army in World War II: The Mediterranean Theater of Operations. Washington, D.C.: Office of the Chief of Military History, United States Army, 1969.

Bragadin, Commander Marc' Antonio. *The Italian Navy in World War II*. Translated by Gale Hoffman. Annapolis, Md.: Naval Institute Press, 1957.

British Air Ministry. *The Rise and Fall of the German Air Force (1933–1945).* London: His Majesty's Stationery Office, 1948.

Christienne, Charles, and Pierre Lissarrgue. *A History of French Military Aviation.* Translated by Francis Kianka. Washington, D.C.: Smithonian Institution Press, 1986.

Clark, General Mark W. *Calculated Risk.* New York: Harper & Bros., 1950.

Clodfelter, Mark. *The Limits of Air Power: The American Bombing of North Vietnam.* New York: Free Press, 1989.

Craven, Wesely F., and James L. Cate, eds. *The Army Air Forces in World War II.* 7 vols. Chicago: University of Chicago Press, 1948–1958.

Cross, Robin. *The Bombers: The Illustrated Story of Offensive Strategy and Tactics in the Twentieth Century.* New York: Macmillan, 1987.

D'Este, Carlo. *Bitter Victory: The Battle for Sicily, 1943.* New York: E.P. Dutton, 1988.

Dupuy, Colonel T.N. *Numbers, Prediction, and War: Using History to Evaluate Combat Factors and Predict the Outcome of Battles.* Indianapolis: Bobbs-Merrill Co., 1979.

Eisenhower, Dwight D. *Crusade in Europe.* Garden City: Doubleday & Co., 1948.

Fisher, Ernest F. *Cassino to the Alps.* United States Army in World War II: The Mediterranean Theater of Operations. Washington, D.C.: Office of the Chief of Military History, United States Army, 1977.

Futrell, Robert F. *Ideas, Concepts, Doctrine: A History of Basic Thinking in the United States Air Force.* United States Air Force Historical Study 139. Maxwell Air Force Base, Ala.: Aerospace Studies Institute, Air Univeristy, 1971.

———. *The United States Air Force in Korea.* Rev. ed. Washington, D.C.: Office of Air Force History, 1983.

Garland, Albert N., and Howard McGaw Smyth, with Martin Blumenson. *Sicily and the Surrender of Italy.* United States Army in World War II: The Mediterranean Theater of Operations. Washington, D.C.: Office of the Chief of Military History, United States Army, 1965.

Goulden, Joseph C. *Korea: The Untold Story of the War.* New York: Times Books, 1982.

Hallion, Richard P. *The Naval Air War in Korea.* Baltimore: Nautical & Aviation Publishing Co. of America, 1986.

———. *Strike from the Sky: The History of Battlefield Air Attack, 1911–1945.* Washington, D.C.: Smithsonian Institution Press, 1989.

Harrison, Gordon A. *Cross-Channel Attack.* United States Army in World War II: The European Theater of Operations. Washington, D.C.: Office of the Chief of Military History, United States Army, 1951.

Hastings, Max. OVERLORD: *D-Day and the Battle for Normandy.* New York: Simon & Schuster, 1984.

Hermes, Walter G. *Truce Tent to Fighting Front.* United States Army in Korea. Washington: Office of the Chief of Military History, United States Army, 1966.

Hinsley, F.H. *et al. British Intelligence in the Second World War.* 5 vols. London: Her Majesty's Stationery Office, 1979–.

Hoeppner, Ernst Wilhelm von. *Germany's War in the Air*. Translated by J. Hawley Larned. Leipzig: K.F. Koehler, 1921. Typescript in the Army War College Library.

Horne, Alistair. *To Lose a Battle: France, 1940*. Boston: Little, Brown & Co., 1969.

Howe, George F. *Northwest Africa: Seizing the Initiative in the West*. United States Army in World War II: The Mediterranean Theater of Operations. Washington, D.C.: Office of the Chief of Military History, United States Army, 1957.

Hurley, Alfred F. *Billy Mitchell: Crusader for Air Power*. New York: Franklin Watts, 1964.

Jackson, W.F.G. *The Battle for Italy*. New York: Harper & Row, 1967.

Karnow, Stanley. *Vietnam: A History*. New York: Viking Press, 1983.

Kesselring, Albert. *Kesselring: A Soldier's Record*. New York: William Morrow & Co., 1954.

Liddell Hart, B.H. *History of the Second World War*. New York: G.P. Putnam's Sons, 1971.

Matloff, Maurice, and Edwin M. Snell. *Strategic Planning for Coalition Warfare*. United States Army in World War II: The War Department. Washington, D.C.: Office of the Chief of Military History, United States Army, 1957.

Momyer, General William W. *Air Power in Three Wars*. Washington, D.C.: Department of Defense, 1978.

Morison, Samuel Eliot. *History of United States Naval Operations in World War II*. 15 vols. Boston: Little, Brown & Co., 1947–1962.

Murray, Williamson. *Strategy for Defeat: The Luftwaffe, 1933–1945*. Maxwell Air Force Base, Ala.: Air University Press, 1983.

Nicholson, Nigel. *Alex: The Life of Field Marshal Earl Alexander of Tunis*. New York: Atheneum, 1973.

Overy, R.J. *The Air War, 1939–1945*. New York: Stein & Day, 1981.

Pack, S.W.C. *Operation "HUSKY": The Allied Invasion of Sicily*. New York: Hippocrene Books, 1977.

Peng Dehuai. *Memoirs of a Chinese Marshal: The Autobiographical Notes of Peng Dehuai*. Translated by Zheng Longpu. Beijing: Foreign Languages Press, 1984.

Raleigh, Walter, and H.A. Jones. *The War in the Air*. 6 vols. Oxford: Oxford University Press, 1922–1937.

Richards, Denis, and Hilary St. George Saunders. *Royal Air Force, 1939–1945*. 3 vols. London: Her Majestry's Stationery Office, 1953–1954.

Rommel, Erwin. *The Rommel Papers*. Edited by B.H. Liddell Hart and translated by Paul Findlay. New York: Harcourt, Brace, 1953.

Roskill, Capt. S.W. *The War at Sea, 1939–1945*. 3 vols. London: Her Majesty's Stationery Office, 1954–1962.

Rostow, W.W. *Pre-Invasion Bombing Strategy: General Eisenhower's Decision of March 25, 1944*. Austin, Tex.: University of Texas Press, 1981.

Ruge, Friedrich. *Rommel in Normandy: Reminiscences by Friedrich Ruge*. San Raphael, Calif.: Presidio Press, 1979.

Ruppenthal, Roland G. *Logistical Support of the Armies.* United States Army in World War II: The European Theater of Operations. Washington, D.C.: Office of the Chief of Military History, United States Army, 1953.

Salewski, Michael. *Die deutsche Seekriegsleitung, 1935–1945.* 2 vols. Munich: Bernard & Graefe, 1975.

Saundby, Air Marshal Sir Robert. *Air Bombardment: The Story of Its Development.* New York: Harper & Bros., 1961.

Senger und Etterlin, Frido von. *Neither Fear Nor Hope.* New York: 1964.

Shaplen, Robert. *Bitter Victory.* New York: Harper & Row, 1985.

Slessor, Sir John. *The Central Blue: The Autobiography of Sir John Slessor, Marshal of the RAF.* New York: Praeger, 1957.

Stueck, William Whitney, Jr. *The Road to Confrontation: American Policy Toward China and Korea, 1947–1950.* Chapel Hill: University of North Carolina Press, 1981.

Tedder, Lord Arthur W. *Air Power in War.* Wesport, Connecticut: Greenwood Press, 1974.

——— . *With Prejudice: The War Memoirs of Marshal of the Royal Air Force Tedder.* Boston: Little, Brown & Co., 1966.

Truong Nhu Trang. *A Vietcong Memoir: An Inside Account of the Vietnam War and Its Aftermath.* New York: Harcourt, Brace, Jovanovich, 1985.

Truscott, Lucian K., Jr. *Command Missions—A Personal Story.* New York: E.P. Dutton, 1954.

Van Creveld, Martin. *Supplying War: Logistics from Wallenstein to Patton.* London: Cambridge University Press, 1977.

Vaughn-Thomas, Wynford. *Anzio.* New York: Rinehard & Winston, 1961.

Warner, Oliver. *Admiral of the Fleet: Cunningham of Hyndhope.* Athens, Ohio: Ohio University Press, 1967.

Westphal, Siegfried. *Erinnerungen.* Mainz: Hase & Koehler, 1975.

Wilmot, Chester. *The Struggle for Europe.* London: Collins, 1953.

Yang Dezhi. For Peace. Translation FTD–[RS]T–1143–88 by the Foreign Technology Division of the Air Force Systems Command, 1989. Original volume, Beijing, 1987.

Zuckerman, Solly. *From Apes to Warlords.* New York: Harper & Row, 1978.

Studies and Reports

Air Historical Branch of the British Air Ministry. "R.A.F. Narrative (First Draft): The Italian Campaign." 2 vols. London, n.d.

——— . "R.A.F. Narrative (First Draft): The Liberation of North West Europe." 5 vols. London, n.d.

——— . "R.A.F. Narrative (First Draft): The Middle East Campaigns." 10 vols. London, n.d.

——— . "R.A.F. Narrative (First Draft): The North African Campaign." London, n.d.

——— . "R.A.F. Narrative (First Draft): The RAF in Maritime War." 8 vols. London, n.d.

Anthony, Maj. Victor B., USAF. *Tactics and Techniques of Night Operations, 1961–1970* (S). The Air Force in Southeast Asia. Washington: Office of Air Force History, 1973.

Ballard, Lt. Col. Jack S., USAF. *Development and Employment of Fixed-Wing Gunships, 1961–1971*. Washington: Office of Air Force History, 1974.

Carter, Gregory A. "Some Historical Notes on Air Interdiction in Korea." Rand Report P–3452. Santa Monica, Calif.: Rand, 1966.

Deichmann, Paul. *German Air Force Operations in Support of the Army*. Edited by Littleton B. Atkinson, Noel F. Parrish, and Albert F. Simpson. USAF Historical Monograph No. 163. Maxwell Air Force Base, Ala.: Air University Research Studies Institute, 1962.

Dews, Edmund. "A Note on Tactical vs. Strategic Air Interdiction." Rand Memorandum RM–6239–PR. Santa Monica, Calif.: Rand, 1970.

FEAF Report on the Korean War. 2 vols. Tokyo: Headquarters, Far East Air Forces, 1954.

Felmy, General Hellmuth. "The German Air Force in the Mediterranean Theater of War." Unpublished manuscript, 1955.

Finney, Robert T. "The Development of Tactical Air Doctrine in the U.S. Air Service, 1917–1951." Maunscript, Office of Air Force History.

Historical Evaluation and Research Organization. *Tactical Air Interdiction by U.S. Army Air Forces in World War II: Allied Air Interdiction in Support of OVERLORD*. Dunn Loring, Va., 1971.

—————. *Tactical Air Interdiction by U.S. Army Air Forces in World War II: France*. Dunn Loring, Va., n.d.

—————. *Tactical Air Interdiction by U.S. Army Air Forces in World War II: Italy*. Dunn Loring, Va., n.d.

Horrocks, Michael. "The Air Force in Southeast Asia: The Sensor War, 1966–1971." Manuscript: Office of Air Force History.

Nalty, Bernard C. "Interdiction in Southern Laos, 1968–1972." Manuscript: Office of Air Force History.

Sallagar, F.M. *Operation "STRANGLE" (Italy, Spring 1944): A Case Study of Tactical Air Interdiction*. Rand Monograph R–851–PR. Santa Monica, Calif.: Rand, 1972.

United States Air Force, Assistant Chief of Staff, Studies and Analysis. *The Uncertainty of Predicting Results of an Interdiction Campaign*. Washington, 1969.

United States Air Force. Historical Division. *United States Air Force Operations in the Korean Conflict, 25 June–1 November 1950*. U.S.A.F. Historical Study No. 71. Washington, D.C.: United States Air Force Historical Division Liaison Office, 1955.

—————. *United States Air Force Operations in the Korean Conflict, 1 November 1950–30 June 1952*. U.S.A.F. Historical Study No. 72. Washington, D.C.: United States Air Force Historical Division Liaison Office, 1955.

Articles and Essays

Futrell, Robert F. "The Influence of the Air Power Concept on Air Force Planning, 1945–1962." In Lt. Col. Harry R. Borowski, ed., *Military Planning in the Twentieth Century: Proceedings of the Eleventh Military History Symposium, 10–12 October 1984*. Washington, D.C.: Office of Air Force History, 1986.

Lytton, Henry D. "Bombing Policy in the Rome and Pre-Normandy Invasion Aerial Campaigns of World War II: Bridge-Bombing Strategy Indicated —and Railyard-Bombing Strategy Invalidated," *Military Affairs* 47 (April 1983):53–58.

Palmer, General Bruce, Jr. "U.S. Intelligence and Vietnam." *Studies in Intelligence* 28 (special issue, spring, 1984).

Rosenberg, David Alan. "The Origins of Overkill: Nuclear Weapons and American Strategy, 1945–1960." *International Security* 7 (spring, 1983):19, 28–44.

Index

of Chinese Air Force, 305
COMMANDO BOLT system, 340
in DIADEM, 193, 201, 208, 209
failure destroying trucks, Vietnam, 397
importance of target identifiability, 402
ineffective technology, Korean War,
    317–18
Korea, 305–7
at Pusan, 278–79
Rail Interdiction Program, Korea,
    311–13
in Southeast Asia, 385, 385 n. 55
STEEL TIGER, 338–41
STRANGLE (Italy), 405
technological advances used in Southeast
    Asia, 336–37
NIGHT OWL, armed reconnaissance, 338–39
Nixon, Richard M., 385
    and Easter Offensive, 367, 370, 374
    intensifies bombing of north, 381
    mining of Haiphong harbor, 375
    "Vietnamization," 344, 371
Normandy beaches, France. See OVERLORD
Norstad, Lauris, 146, 147 n. 18, 150 n. 25,
    155, 261
North Africa
    bombing of ports, 41
    as theater of Anglo-German war, 15–16
North Atlantic Treaty Organization
    (NATO), 317, 406
North Korean Army
    average supplies received, 280–82
    collapse of, 289
    compared to German Army in Italy, 283
    food shortages, 281–82
    formation, 267–68
    low morale of, 282
    and motor transport, 284–85
    at Seoul, 280
Northwest African Air Forces, 32, 72 n.
    58
    and bombing of Italian rail centers, 144
    bombing missions Aug 17–Sep 30,
        1943, 93
    Desert Air Force, 86
    planning for invasion of Italy, 86
    raids on German buildup in Sicily,
        59–60
    Strategic Air Force, 51, 69, 71, 72,
        86–87, 105, 115, 122
    strength of, for invasion of Sicily, 58
    Tactical Air Force, 68–74, 77, 86, 115,
        121–22, 402
    united under MAAF, 115
Nuclear weapons
    atomic bomb, 261
    effect on Tactical Air Command, 324

interdiction as part of nonnuclear
    strategy for defense of Western
    Europe, 406

O'Donnell, Emmett, 271, 276
Office of Strategic Services (OSS)
    air attacks on bridges and marshaling
        yards, STRANGLE, 149–50
    on effectiveness of STRANGLE, 183–84,
        191–92
    Enemy Objectives Unit (EOU), 227–30
    German logistical requirements,
        STRANGLE, 155
Oil Plan, 228–31, 228 n. 40, 232 n. 52,
    254, 256–57
Okinawa, 270
OMAHA beach, 215, 244
OPLAN 715, 358
Oran, Algeria, 23, 28
Orne River, France, 245, 405
Osan, Korea, 269
OVERLORD, 83–84, 86 n. 4, 95, 112, 115,
    211–57
    aircraft involved, sorties and number,
        243–45, 247
    air plan for tactical operations, 232
    air superiority, 247, 256–57
    Allied air forces supporting, 220
    assault forces, 215
    attrition and, 404
    D-day counterattack, 245–46
    planning for, 213–15
    preinvasion bombing effectiveness,
        236–42
    Rommel's planned defense, 217–18
    shortages of fuel and ammunition,
        252–54
    slowness of German buildup, 251–52
    strafing, importance of, 256
    tactical aircraft inventory, 407–8
    tactical interdiction plan, 242
    Transportation Plan controversy, 221–23,
        225–32
    Transportation Plan implementation,
        232–36, 256–57

Pacific Air Forces, 355
Pacific Air Forces, Headquarters (PACAF)
    on effectiveness of interdiction, 393
    interdiction plan of, 381
    on North Vietnamese response to
        interdiction, 377
    Operations Plan C–101, COMMANDO
        FLASH, 372
    Operations Plan PC–103, COMMANDO
        FLY, 372
    and petroleum products supply to

*U.S. G.P.O.:1993-281-440:40008